AS IF

As If

*Modern Enchantment and the Literary
Prehistory of Virtual Reality*

Michael Saler

OXFORD
UNIVERSITY PRESS

OXFORD
UNIVERSITY PRESS

Oxford University Press, Inc., publishes works that further
Oxford University's objective of excellence
in research, scholarship, and education.

Oxford   New York
Auckland   Cape Town   Dar es Salaam   Hong Kong   Karachi
Kuala Lumpur   Madrid   Melbourne   Mexico City   Nairobi
New Delhi   Shanghai   Taipei   Toronto

With offices in
Argentina   Austria   Brazil   Chile   Czech Republic   France   Greece
Guatemala   Hungary   Italy   Japan   Poland   Portugal   Singapore
South Korea   Switzerland   Thailand   Turkey   Ukraine   Vietnam

Published by Oxford University Press, Inc.
198 Madison Avenue, New York, New York 10016

www.oup.com

Library of Congress Cataloging-in-Publication Data
Saler, Michael T., 1960–
As if : modern enchantment and the literary prehistory of
virtual reality / Michael Saler.
        p.   cm.
Includes bibliographical references and index.
ISBN 978-0-19-534316-8 (cloth : acid-free paper)—ISBN 978-0-19-534317-5
(pbk. : acid-free paper) 1. Fantastic, The, in literature. 2. Virtual reality in literature.
3. Marvelous, The, in literature. 4. Imaginary societies in literature. I. Title.
        PN56.F34S17   2011
        823′.08760908—dc22   2011010276

1 3 5 7 9 8 6 4 2

Printed in the United States of America
on acid-free paper

For
Chun Li
(The Real One)

TABLE OF CONTENTS

ACKNOWLEDGMENTS

I have spent many years not writing this book; somehow there was always just one more fantasy novel requiring "research." Over this long span of time numerous people have helped me and I'm happy to materialize the virtual appreciation for them that has been running through my head and heart: Douglas A. Anderson, Mike Ashley, David Biale, Matt Blessing, Kristin Bluemel, Matt Bowers, Will Chan, Deborah Cohen, Michael Collins, George Connell, Tom Crook, Patrick Curry, John Davies, Michael D. C. Drout, Lindsay Duguid, Matthew Feldman, Richard Gilmore, Martin Jay, Roger Johnson, S. T. Joshi, Kyu Kim, Charles Kinbote, Cathy Kudlick, Norma Landau, Joshua Landy, Jon Lellenberg, Erin Li, Peter Mandler, Ted Margadant, China Miéville, Samuel Moyn, Philip Nord, Kathy Olmsted, Heather Owen, Susan Pederson, Donald Pollock, Judith Priestman, Eric Rauchway, Benson, Joyce, and Bethel Saler, Peter Stansky, Steve Stockdale, Kathy Stuart, Maiken Umbach, Helen Vaughan, Robin Walz, Louis Warren, and Benjamin and Mary Louise Wright.

This history of imaginary worlds had its genesis during a year in residence at the Stanford Humanities Center, sister site to Shangri La, and I'm appreciative of its generous support. I benefited from being able to discuss my ideas at meetings hosted by the New York Consortium for Intellectual and Cultural History; Concordia College; the North American Conference on British Studies; and Oxford Brookes. Individuals at other institutions were also of inestimable help: Minny M. Oralia, at the University of Muri, patiently answered my queries about the works of the philosopher de Selby; and Christopher Blayre, at the University of Cosmopoli, set me straight on *foraminifera*. At the University of California, Davis, Assistant Dean Steven Roth helped me secure funds for publication costs.

Earlier versions of several of this book's chapters have appeared in journals and collections, although the material published here has been substantially revised and expanded. I am grateful to the editors and publishers of the following for giving me the opportunity to work out my arguments: the *American Historical Review*; *The Historical Journal*; *Philosophy and*

Literature; The Space Between; and *Vernacular Modernism: Heimat, Globalization, and the Built Environment,* edited by Maiken Umbach and Bernd Hüppauf (Stanford University Press, 2005).

At Oxford University Press, editors Shannon McLachlan and Brendan O'Neill shepherded this book from virtuality to tangibility, and production manager Rick Stinson ensured that it looks as nice as it does. I hope *As If* is judged by its cover, for artist George O'Connor captured the sense of wonder I struggled to put into words. (He is the author of the enchanting series "The Olympians," whose virtual abode resides at www.olympiansrule.com.)

Thanks are also due to the following for kindly granting me permission to reproduce copyrighted material: The Heritage Bookshop; Lail M. Finlay; Arthur M. Dula and The Robert A. & Virginia Heinlein Prize Trust; Norfolk Museums & Archaeology Service; and the Sherlock Holmes Society of London.

New Wye, Appalachia
Cedarn, Utana
Davis, California
July 2011

AS IF

INTRODUCTION

A map of the real world is no less imaginary than a map of an imaginary world.
—Alberto Blanco

FROM IMAGINARY TO VIRTUAL WORLDS

The modern West has been called "disenchanted," but that is a half-truth. It can equally be deemed an enchanted place, in which imaginary worlds and fictional characters have replaced the sacred groves and tutelary deities of the premodern world. Many spend protracted periods of time "inhabiting" their imaginations, residing in virtual worlds populated by characters drawn from the media. As a writer for the *New York Times* observed, "today there are hundreds of thousands, perhaps millions of people whose grasp of the history, politics and mythological traditions of entirely imaginary places could surely qualify them for an advanced degree."[1]

Such escapist behavior is usually ascribed to fantasy fans, who have been the most visible adherents of imaginary worlds. (Soap opera fans and romance readers tend to be less noticeable in public than people who wear Spock ears or Hobbit feet.)[2] They are often derided—sometimes affectionately, sometimes not—as geeks for wasting their youth playing Dungeons & Dragons and demeaning their adulthood by parsing sentences written in the Klingon or Elvish language. Poor, deluded creatures, they should "get a life," as William Shatner famously scolded *Star Trek* fans on an episode of *Saturday Night Live.* But the habits of this minority have arguably become those of the majority in the West: we are all geeks now.[3] Fantasy, a capacious category that subsumes subgenres such as science fiction and the supernatural, has blossomed from a niche interest to become one of the most popular and lucrative fields in contemporary entertainment.[4]

Even those who would never consider themselves as acolytes of Harry Potter or Luke Skywalker sojourn in imaginary worlds today, perhaps more than they realize. Practices that once seemed the exclusive, and rather odd, preserve of fantasy fans have now entered the mainstream.[5] References to geographies of the imagination have become commonplace: water-cooler conversations are as likely to be about the boss in *Mad Men* as one's own employer; everyday metaphors and similes are often rooted in the imaginary soil of nonexistent places. There are public commemorations of fictional worlds and characters (*Ulysses* readers have their Bloomsday) and physical analogues to unreal settings (Proust connoisseurs can stroll through his fictional town of Combray, courtesy of the real town of Illiers incorporating itself as Illiers-Combray in 1972). Online web pages and discussion groups are dedicated to innumerable fictional creations, from Jane Austen to Austin Powers.

Contemporary reference books juxtapose the fictional and the real in a manner that departs from earlier practice. For example, the nineteenth-century British *Dictionary of National Biography* included several "legendary" characters that were often mistaken as real, in order to set the record straight. But the *Oxford Dictionary of National Biography* (2004) boldly acknowledged that fictional characters have become integral to lived experience by including "a small but significant selection of articles on imaginary or at best shadowy subjects with an iconic status in the nation's political or cultural life," such as Springheel Jack, Robin Hood, and John Bull.[6] (Those preferring their reference works straight can turn to *The Dictionary of Imaginary Places, Imaginary People: An Encyclopedia,* and *An Atlas of Fantasy,* among many others.)[7] Denizens of fantasy worlds have also become tangible presences in ordinary life. The gritty, mean streets of New York and San Francisco commemorate ethereal characters of never-never land, from the statue of Ralph Kramden in front of the New York Port Authority's bus terminal, to a plaque at the juncture of Burritt Alley and Stockton Street in San Francisco that reads, "On approximately this spot Miles Archer, partner of Sam Spade, was done in by Brigid O'Shaughnessy."[8] A nine-foot-tall statue of Dick Tracy in Naperville, Illinois joins one of Superman in the same state, adding to the panoply of cartoon icons so honored across the country: Charlie Brown and Snoopy in Santa Rosa, California; Willy and Joe in Santa Fe, New Mexico; Andy Gump in Lake Geneva, Wisconsin.[9]

It's not simply the profusion of fictions in modern life that is noteworthy, but that rational adults devote sustained attention to them, often communally. Such persistent and communal habitation transforms an imagined world, which fiction has always provided, into a virtual world, a more recent phenomenon. The Internet has facilitated this by playing host to virtual worlds, from Massively Multiplayer Online Role-Playing Games (MMOR-PGs) set in fantastic environs (Everquest, World of Warcraft), to more free-form settings in which users can create their own environments and set their own goals (Second Life).[10] Virtual worlds are growing in popularity worldwide and undoubtedly will become an even greater part of everyday life in the future.[11]

Fantasy fans were pioneers here as well. Computer games and online virtual worlds were preceded by pencil-and-paper role-playing games such as Dungeons & Dragons in the 1970s, which itself was beholden to the surge of interest in fantasy novels, comics, and films during the 1960s. That decade was notable for the emergence of impassioned fan communities that immersed themselves in the imaginary worlds of J. R. R. Tolkien's *The Lord of the Rings*, Robert E. Howard's Conan the Barbarian, the Marvel Comics' Universe and the DC "Multiverse," and television shows such as *Doctor Who* and *Star Trek*.[12] At that time, fantasy became widely diffused through the media and attained a greater measure of critical respectability alongside its broader visibility.

The origins of organized fantasy fandom had deeper roots, however, extending back to the late 1920s and 1930s. It is tempting to locate the pre-history of contemporary virtual worlds to this fertile period, when fantasy readers inhabited imaginary worlds communally and persistently via the letters pages of popular fiction magazines and fanzines, as well as via clubs and conventions. These were the infrastructural means that enabled readers to collectively imagine and occupy virtual realities before that term came into popular use in the 1980s to describe more high-tech versions.[13] Writing in 1943 about pulp magazines "devoted to super-realistic 'wonder'—to the weird, the horrendous, the pseudo-scientific," Robert Allerton Parker was fascinated by the unusual imagined communities generated through magazines' letters pages:

> Successful communication may be likened to an electric current. Writer and reader, in such a communal experience, are lifted out of their individual isolation and fused into a single, all-enveloping identity. The I is transfigured by We. The reader-response published by the editors of the pulps, if authentic, is adequate testimony to this communal participation.[14]

Parker observed that fans "trade their cherished fantasies with each other," resulting in a synergistic meeting of minds that elaborated imaginary worlds, virtual realities of the imagination shared by participatory reading communities.[15]

Parker was prescient, but contemporary virtual worlds—defined here as acknowledged imaginary spaces that are communally inhabited for prolonged periods of time by rational individuals—began even earlier. Imaginary worlds of fiction first became virtual worlds, persistently available and collectively envisaged, in late nineteenth-century Europe and America, commencing with the first "virtual reality" character in fiction, Sherlock Holmes.[16]

There were, of course, earlier vogues for explicitly fictional characters since at least the eighteenth century. ("Mythological" and "legendary" characters have a more ambiguous ontological status; we are concerned with those figures unambiguously marked at the outset as "fictional.")[17] Yet the enthusiasm for Holmes during the fin-de-siècle, and the ways this was expressed, represented a distinct departure for fiction at that point. From the late eighteenth through the mid-nineteenth centuries, cultural constraints inhibited the transformation of fictional worlds into virtual worlds. During this period, the middle classes tended to view the imagination with ambivalence; overindulgence in fantasy eventuated in the squalid fate of *Madame Bovary* (1857), rather than the joyous liberation found within "The Secret Life of Walter Mitty" (1939).

As we shall see, during the second half of the nineteenth century the middle classes became gradually less wary of exercising their imagination, because of intertwined social, economic, and cultural reasons. By the late nineteenth century, they experienced fewer cultural prohibitions against pretending that imaginary worlds were real, and their creators irrelevant, if not fictional themselves. The assertion in the 1930s by a Sherlock Holmes fan club, the Baker Street Irregulars, that Arthur Conan Doyle was merely John Watson's literary agent is one such instance that will be explored. (Many at the time were amused, with the exception of Conan Doyle's heirs, who sued.)

The efflorescence of imaginary worlds at the turn of the century was beholden to the increased legitimacy accorded to the imagination at this time. But a greater tolerance for imaginative play doesn't fully explain why adult readers initially transformed fantastic, rather than realist, literary worlds into virtual worlds. Why were the marvelous geographies of Arthur Conan Doyle, H. P. Lovecraft, and J. R. R. Tolkien among the first to be collectively inhabited and obsessively elaborated by readers, rather than the equally cohesive worlds of contemporary realist writers like Émile Zola, Thomas Hardy, or Anthony Powell?[18]

This book will argue that the vogue for fantastic imaginary worlds from the fin-de-siècle through the twentieth century is best explained in terms of a larger cultural project of the West: that of re-enchanting an allegedly disenchanted world. Fantastic virtual worlds of the imagination emerged at the turn of the century not to replicate the everyday, as was the case for realist fiction, but to complement it—to secure the marvels that a disenchanted modernity seemed to undermine, while remaining true to the tenets intellectuals ascribed to modernity at the time, such as rationality and secularism.[19] Fantasy, cast in a rigorously logical mode replete with "objective" details, was one solution to the crisis of modern disenchantment. The widely felt need of the period for forms of wonder and spirituality that accorded with reason and science helps us to understand why fantastic yet rational imaginary worlds proliferated at the turn of the century and after.[20]

This specifically modern form of enchantment is ubiquitous now. By returning to the literary prehistory of virtual reality in the late nineteenth century, and following its developments through the twentieth, we can identify useful lessons for how to negotiate our increasingly virtual condition today. For example, imaginary worlds and their virtual manifestations have often been criticized as escapist, distracting us from the pressing problems of the real world; they also have been disparaged as dangerous sirens, seducing us from engaging in meaningful relations with others or appreciating our finite, corporeal existence.[21] These critiques can contain elements of truth, depending on the situation being analyzed, but we shall see that imaginary worlds can also attune their inhabitants to be more responsive to others, to the natural world, and to human finitude. On the one hand, imaginary worlds are autonomous from the real world, avowedly fictional spaces that provide an escape from a disenchanted modernity into self-subsistent realms of wonder. On the other hand, these worlds are inextricable from ordinary life and interpersonal engagements. They usually foreground critical reason even in their most outré imaginings. In their virtual instantiations, they provide safe and playful arenas for their inhabitants to reflect on the status of the real and to discuss prospects for effecting concrete personal and social changes. They challenge their inhabitants to see the real world as being, to some degree, an imaginary construct amenable to revision. As a result of collectively inhabiting and elaborating virtual worlds, many become more adept at accepting difference, contingency, and pluralism: at envisioning life not in essentialist, "just so" terms but rather in provisional, "as if" perspectives.

At this point in the argument, however, abstract concepts like "modernity," "enchantment," and "disenchantment" require more elaboration. They need to be placed in a historical context to give them heft, because they provided the foundation for modern imaginary worlds and their virtual manifestations. Following this brief consideration of the relevant historiography of "modernity and [dis]enchantment," I will outline how literary imaginary worlds were unexpectedly transformed into virtual worlds beginning at the fin-de-siècle.

MODERNITY, DISENCHANTMENT, AND
"DISENCHANTED ENCHANTMENT"

Modernity is one of the most ambiguous words in the historian's lexicon. The term is often used as if there were a common understanding of its meaning, whereas scholars continue to define it in different and sometimes contrasting ways. (One likened the term to a "multisided room of mirrors.")[22] In broad outline, modernity has come to signify a mixture of political, social, intellectual, economic, technological, and psychological factors, several of which can be traced to earlier centuries and other cultures, which merged synergistically in the West between the sixteenth and nineteenth centuries. These factors include (but are not exhausted by) the emergence of the autonomous and rational subject; the differentiation of cultural spheres; the rise of liberal and democratic states; the turn to psychologism and self-reflexivity; and the prevalence of secularism, nationalism, capitalism, industrialism, urbanism, consumerism, and scientism. These processes developed at different times, at different tempos, in different parts of the world, and often in ambiguous and contradictory ways. Scholars of the "postsecular," for example, have shown that secularism's unfolding in the West was intertwined with religious traditions and spiritual commitments, which continued to coexist within a broader secular ambit.[23] Others have discussed the range of "alternative modernities" that arose to challenge dominant paradigms of modernity.[24] There is one characteristic of modernity, however, emphasized fairly consistently by Western intellectuals since the eighteenth century: modernity is "disenchanted."[25]

Max Weber famously discussed the "disenchantment of the world" in a 1917 lecture, by which he meant the loss of the overarching meanings, animistic connections, magical orientations, and spiritual explanations that had characterized the traditional world, as a result of the ongoing "modern" processes of rationalization, secularization, and bureaucratization.[26] Ordinary existence threatened to become an arid and soulless "iron cage."[27] Weber's memorable phrases encapsulated a long-standing critique—begun by the romantics during the late eighteenth century and elaborated by "cultural pessimists" through the nineteenth and twentieth centuries—of the Enlightenment emphasis on reason and science at the expense of other ways of apprehending and being in the world.[28] Enchantment was associated not only with transcendent meaning and purpose, but also with wonder and surprise; those were the qualities that modernity, with its emphasis on inviolable natural laws, threatened to extirpate. By the late nineteenth century, the positivistic approach of scientific naturalism, which eschewed nonmechanistic accounts of existence, had become so widespread that Weber's account resonated with his contemporaries: "the increasing rationalization and intellectualization . . . means that principally there are no mysterious incalculable forces that come into play, but rather that one can, in principle, master all things by calculation. This means that the world is disenchanted."[29] Thus, whatever else modernity might be, in the particular discourse of "modernity and disenchantment" it was equated with a narrow, instrumental rationality and a hollow, expanding secularism permeating the West since at least the seventeenth century.

Perhaps proving that you can never get too much of a bad thing, the discourse of disenchantment continued to be dominant among Western intellectuals in the twentieth century, in two closely related modes that we can distinguish for heuristic purposes as the "binary" and the "dialectical." The binary discourse, which has been the most prevalent, defined enchantment as the residual, subordinate "other" to modernity's rational, secular, and progressive tenets. This marked a departure from the way enchantment had been used discursively from at least the Middle Ages, when it signified both "delight" in wonders, and the possibility of being "deluded" by them.[30] It could continue to have these ambivalent meanings in everyday speech, but as a result of the scientific revolution of the seventeenth century and the championing of the Enlightenment in the eighteenth, enchantment tended to be defined by elites in a more limited fashion, as a form of duplicity associated with the "superstitions" of organized religion and the dogmatic authority of monarchical rule. Reason would free individuals from being enthralled by such enchantments; science would affirm that the "wonders" and "marvels" of the past centuries, when examined empirically and without reliance on revelation, would be explicable in terms of uniform natural laws.

Enchantments did not disappear entirely within the binary model, but were marginalized in various ways as residual phenomena both subordinate to, and explicable by, modernity's rational and secular tenets. Elites increasingly relegated wonders to the ghetto of popular culture in the seventeenth and eighteenth centuries, and to the new mass culture that had emerged by the late nineteenth century.[31] In addition, enchantments became associated with the cognitive outlooks of groups traditionally seen as inferior by Western elites: "primitives," children, women, and the lower classes.[32] Rational adults could partake of enchantments through the cautious exercise of their imagination, but despite the protestations of romantics the imagination continued to be defined as secondary to reason, and a potentially dangerous instigator of desire, throughout much of the nineteenth century.[33]

Those who sought alternatives to the discourse of modern disenchantment were often tagged by their critics as reactionary antimodernists engaged in a futile struggle to recapture The World We Have Lost.[34] While the nineteenth century witnessed a range of responses to the discourse of disenchantment, until recently these have been depicted by scholars as an emotive rejection of the scientific and secular trends of modernity, a "revolt against positivism" in historian H. Stuart Hughes's well-known phrase.[35] The revolt was characterized by a fascination with spiritualism and the occult; a vogue for non-Western religions and art; and a turn to Aestheticism, neopaganism, and celebrations of the irrational will. Many participants in these movements seemed to accept the binary distinction between modernity and enchantment no less than their critics, as did their successors in the counterculture movements of the twentieth century.[36] This discourse was a performative one, advancing a climate antipathetic to wonder, imagination, and fantasy. Many intellectuals during the fin-de-siècle and after simply assumed that enchanted states of mind, and the enchantments of mass culture more generally, precluded reflexivity and rational critique.[37]

Closely related to the binary opposition between modernity and enchantment is the "dialectical" approach. Whereas the binary approach represents contemporary turns to the irrational and spiritual as atavistic reactions to the rational and secular tenets of modernity, the dialectical approach posits modernity itself as inherently irrational, a mythic construct no less enchanted than the myths it sought to overcome. In the binary approach, the disenchantment of modernity is often viewed ambivalently: Weber, for example, acknowledged the benefits entailed by rational procedures and bureaucratic organizations, even as he perceived the impoverishments of human experience that accompanied them. In the dialectical approach, however, there is far less ambivalence: modernity is exposed as dangerously oppressive and inhumane, a condition exacerbated by the hypocritical identification of modernity with reason, progress, and freedom. In the binary approach, modernity is inherently disenchanted, a situation viewed with regret as well as hope; in the dialectical approach, modernity is explicitly enchanted, in the negative sense, its universal promises exposed as self-interested ideologies, false consciousness, bad faith.

The dialectical approach is implicit in the thought of Karl Marx, whose writings on modernity abound with images of enchantment—specters, vampires, fetishes—linking the modern world with the religious world it supposedly had surmounted.[38] Weber's thought could be interpreted as straddling the binary and dialectic approaches, as could that of Sigmund Freud in such later works as *Civilization and Its Discontents* (1930), which warns that the repressive cultural forces of modernity, together with its advances in science and technology, could eventuate in humanity's self-destruction.[39]

It is thus not surprising that the most influential articulation of the dialectical approach was made by two philosophers who brought together the various insights of Marx, Weber, and Freud in a single, coruscating work.

Max Horkheimer and Theodor Adorno's *Dialectic of Enlightenment* (1947) indicts Western modernity as a globalizing enchantment whose reliance on instrumental reason abolishes individuality, distorts human nature, and re-presses autonomy. Modernity becomes a self-legitimizing force that trumps its own capacity for self-criticism: "For the scientific temper, any deviation of thought from the business of manipulating the actual . . . is no less sense-less and self-destructive than it would be for the magician to step outside the magic circle drawn for his incantation; and in both cases violation of the taboo caries a heavy price for the offender. The mastery of nature draws the circle in which the critique of pure reason holds thought spellbound."[40]

Horkheimer and Adorno's dialectical approach, like that of the binary approach, also condemns mass culture as a dangerous vector of delusion rather than delight, although their model defines nearly all forms of culture as complicit with the "totalitarian" logic of Enlightenment, "high" as well as "low." The two gesture toward a saving remnant of "genuine" artistic expres-sions that remain inassimilable to reductive reason and its attendant logic of capitalist commoditization, but on the whole the rational and secular claims of modernity stand condemned as the ultimate expressions of a beguiling enchantment: "The more completely the machinery of thought subjugates existence, the more blindly it is satisfied with reproducing it. Enlightenment thereby regresses to the mythology it has never been able to escape."[41]

The binary and dialectical approaches to the problem of modern en-chantment continue to influence scholarship, but in recent years there has been a concerted attempt to rethink the discourse from a vantage point that rejects the either/or logic of both of these slants. This is because the con-cept of modernity has come under renewed scrutiny in the past two decades by postmodern and postcolonial scholarship, with corresponding effects on the discourse of modernity and enchantment. The postmodern critique of binary oppositions has led to a rethinking of modernity that moves away from many of the categorical distinctions that had been so prominent in earlier discussions. Interrogations of the concept have been particularly fruitful in postcolonial studies: scholars argued that the binary approach was more ideological than real, a useful conceptual tool for Western colo-nial purposes that obscured the tensions and contradictions in the modern world. The seemingly universal distinctions championed by the Western "metropole" between modernity and tradition, or secularism and super-stition, often do not hold up when viewed from the "periphery" of non-Western cultures negotiating processes of modernization in complex ways.[42] Similarly, historians of science, religion, and mass culture explored how interdependent these phenomena have been, further eroding the sim-pler oppositions between science and religion, religion and rationality, ra-tionality and mass culture.[43]

Thus the binary and dialectical approaches are in the process of being replaced by the recognition that modernity is characterized by fruitful tensions between seemingly irreconcilable forces and ideas. Modernity is defined less by binaries arranged in an implicit hierarchy, or by the dialectical transformation of one term into its opposite, than by unresolved contradictions and oppositions: modernity is Janus-faced. This is reflected in new similes and metaphors that scholars use to capture the complexities of modernity made messy. Lynda Nead suggests that "modernity . . . can be imagined as pleated or crumpled time, drawing together past, present, and future into constant and unexpected relations," and Dipesh Chakrabarty characterizes modernity's "problem of entangled times" with the equally evocative image of a "timeknot."[44]

As a result of this reconceptualization, the long-accepted discourses of modernity and enchantment have been also reconceived. Scholars had criticized various aspects of the binary and dialectical formulations, but not until recently has the discourse as a whole been subject to searching critique. In 2001, James Cook expressed surprise that his fellow historians had not examined the ubiquity of magic and magicians in nineteenth-century America, and he suggested they had ignored this rich vein of cultural history because they had been mesmerized by the prevailing discourses: "It's almost as if academic historians have taken Max Weber's classic theory about the 'disenchantment of the world' as a guide for assessing the social significance of the magician during the nineteenth and twentieth centuries."[45] Alex Owen echoed this sentiment when she observed in 2004 that "[historians] have been slow to take up the challenge of modern enchantment."[46]

Scholars in recent years have demonstrated that science evoked wonder as well as disillusion; technology was considered to be marvelous as well as threatening.[47] Movements that were once defined as opposing modernity, such as the occult, magic, and heterodox spiritualities, are now seen as expressing it in particular ways.[48] Just as William James, in taking the measure of his own fin-de-siècle, insisted that there were *Varieties of Religious Experience* (1902), we too can insist that there are varieties of modern enchantment.[49]

We shall see that modern enchantment often depends upon its opposite, modern disenchantment. A specifically modern enchantment can be defined as one that enchants and disenchants simultaneously: a disenchanted enchantment. There were intellectuals in the late nineteenth century who recognized this and offered a nuanced understanding of enchantment as a state in which one could be "delighted" without being "deluded." Friedrich Nietzsche, for example, relentlessly punctured enchanting illusions—but he also recognized that such enchantments were necessary for human flourishing.[50] (As a child, he constructed an elaborate imaginary world focusing on "King Squirrel I"; as an adult, he put aside fantasies about the squirrel dynasty for those about the Aryan nobility.)[51] Nietzsche maintained that "invented world[s]" were not only necessary for human life, but in fact were fundamental constituents of it: "Indeed I am convinced that *the most erroneous assumptions are precisely the most indispensable for us,* that without granting the validity of the logical *fiction,* without measuring reality by the invented world of the unconditioned, the self-identical, man could not live; and that a negation of this fiction . . . is equivalent to a negation of life itself."[52] Nietzsche's solution was to embrace illusions without relinquishing an awareness of their contingent status as human creations: to promote a disenchanted form of enchantment. Many of those who followed Nietzsche's trajectory advanced related ideas about the importance of provisional fictions for a pluralistic, nonessentialized world.[53]

This self-conscious strategy of embracing illusions while acknowledging their artificial status, of turning to the "as if," has become integral to modern enchantment and is the focus of this book. We shall see that modernity remains enchanted in a disenchanted way, rendering the imagination compatible with reason, the spiritual with secular trends.[54] In its ideal form, such a self-reflexive form of enchantment delights without deluding. This book will also redress some of the recent pessimistic readings of mass culture (including Internet culture). They have usefully highlighted its pitfalls, from the incivility of public discourse to the dissipation of sustained attention, but have not always acknowledged corresponding social and intellectual benefits.[55] We will examine selected imaginary and/or virtual worlds from the late nineteenth and twentieth centuries, drawn primarily from British and American examples, to assess the potentials and perils of modernity's disenchanted enchantments.[56]

THE IRONIC IMAGINATION, ANIMISTIC REASON, AND PUBLIC SPHERES OF THE IMAGINATION

Self-reflexivity is not limited to the particular form of modern enchantment we will explore, but is a characteristic of modernity as a whole.[57] To be modern is, in part, to exercise a "double consciousness" and to embrace complementarities, to be capable of living simultaneously in multiple worlds without experiencing cognitive dissonance.[58] This is a cultural development. Cognitive psychologists have found that humans are able to engage in representations about representations—"metarepresentations," or a double consciousness—from a young age, suggesting an innate aptitude.[59] But the extent to which this ability is practiced also depends on cultural standards, as we shall see. The modern period is one in which the self-aware exercise of this double consciousness became widespread. According to the philosopher Charles Taylor, the salient feature of modernity

> is not that it has fostered materialism, or enabled people to recover a spiritual outlook
> beyond materialism . . . though it has done both these things. But the most important
> fact about it . . . is that it has opened a space in which people can wander between and
> around all these options without having to land clearly and definitively in any one.[60]

Modernist art often represents this perspectival attitude. Literary modernism since the mid-nineteenth century has employed irony to convey multiple meanings simultaneously, just as cubist and futurist paintings captured multiple perspectives of time and space within a single canvas.[61]

Similarly, in the late nineteenth century, adult readers seeking enchantment began to inhabit the imaginary worlds of fantastic fiction for extended periods of time without losing sight of the real world. They played with multiple identities and multiple realities, in the process training themselves to question essentialist outlooks and appreciate the contingent nature of narratives. These readers had recourse to what I call the *ironic imagination,* a form of double consciousness that became widely practiced during the nineteenth century and attained its cultural centrality in the twentieth. The ironic imagination enabled individuals to embrace alternative worlds and to experience alternative truths. The American critic Edward Wagenknecht observed this in 1946, as he tried to capture what was distinctive about contemporary works of fantasy literature. He found that many of these books were "devoured by adults with the same readiness by which they were consumed by children," and that they were concerned with imaginary worlds radically different from our own. These works "assume[d] the existence of another world, another set of beings, another scale of values besides those that we know—as in the writings of the late H. P. Lovecraft."[62] Such fantastic environs began to proliferate at the fin-de-siècle, frequently challenging normative understandings of the world. Readers were encouraged to visit these resources of enchantment repeatedly, often in the company of others. As a result, the ironic imagination became second nature, and secondary lives became the means to engage in thought experiments about one's primary life.

Many of these imaginary worlds stemmed from an innovative genre of literature, the "New Romance," which developed in Anglo-American literature during the fin-de-siècle as a direct response to the discourse of disenchantment. In the illustrated pages of the New Romance, readers found the wonders and marvels that realist literature and scientific naturalism disavowed. Yet the New Romance did not disdain modern science and rationality, in contrast to Aestheticism, which was the New Romance's contemporary rival in the creation of autonomous worlds of the imagination. Instead, works of the New Romance frequently adopted the rhetorical modes of fact-based science, by including footnotes, maps, photographs, glossaries, and appendices. These were "spectacular texts," combining the tropes of fantasy with those of objectivity.[63] The New Romance of the late nineteenth century became the wellspring for the subsequent marketing genres of science fiction, detective fiction, and fantasy fiction that appeared in the twentieth century.[64]

Contemporary critics who used the term New Romance perceived that the diverse works within this classification shared certain family resemblances. These included the combination of realism and romanticism, the creation of logically cohesive worlds intended to reconcile reason and enchantment, and a measure of self-reflexive irony about their truth claims. Robert Louis Stevenson's *Treasure Island*, H. Rider Haggard's *She*, and Bram Stoker's *Dracula* were clearly disparate works, yet all were understood to be New Romance. Detective stories of the period were also cast within the framework of modern enchantment; the seemingly realist investigations of contemporary crimes were often greeted as fantastic tales inspiring wonder. In her 1899 essay for *The Bookman* titled "The Renaissance of Wonder," Katherine Pearson Woods discussed Sherlock Holmes and other literary detectives in terms of how they combined the marvelous with the rational:

> That the Detective Novel should be classed as the child of Wonder . . . can surprise no one for longer than a moment. True, it involves no element of the mystical . . . but it is certainly included under the definition which we ventured . . . to offer of the supernatural, as that which cannot be immediately accounted for by any known natural law.[65]

Similarly, G. K. Chesterton portrayed detective fiction as modern fairy tales, noting in 1901 how "the investigator crosses London with something of the loneliness and liberty of a prince in a tale of elfland."[66]

Even after specific genre labels were established in the twentieth century for marketing purposes, critics acknowledged how permeable these makeshift categories were: underlying all of them was a similar amalgam of wonder and reason. In 1960 Anthony Boucher, renowned as both a mystery writer and as a founding editor of *The Magazine of Fantasy & Science Fiction*, stressed the commonalities underlying Conan Doyle's "detective" and "science" fictions. He was not surprised that many science fiction writers were also Holmes devotees, or that there was "a noticeable overlap between the membership of the Baker Street Irregulars and that of any World Science Fiction Convention."[67] (Boucher himself wrote mysteries that incorporated supernatural and science fictional elements.)[68] Since the turn of the century, readers drawn to science fiction, fantasy, and detective stories were seeking to be enchanted through the gratification of their reason.

Thus, whereas mass culture has often been characterized as an "irratio-
nalist" expression of modernity, the New Romance and its succeeding
genre forms usually extolled rationality. The American writer H. P. Lovecraft's interwar tales of horror, for example, replaced discredited notions of
the supernatural with possibilities derived from modern science. In 1945 a
fan enthused about this distinctive attribute:

> When we think of [Lovecraft's] Azathoth as ruling all space and time at the center of
> Ultimate Chaos, we do not experience the same feeling as we did when confronted by
> the vague, spiritual entities of an older supernaturalism. We feel somehow that Azathoth
> is explicable in terms of modern astronomy and physics. He seems nearer to our rational,
> scientific minds than the misty ghosts and purely spiritual forces of a past age . . . this is
> the leitmotif of Lovecraft's peculiar art, the core of his philosophy of the weird: that all
> these vast and mysterious aspects of the universes around us should be regarded in the
> light of the supernormal rather than the supernatural.[69]

The Oxford philologist Tolkien's epic fantasy *The Lord of the Rings* also
owed much of its appeal to its logical rigor and empirical detail. Its maps,
glossaries, chronologies, and other scholarly elements fostered an analytic
mindset as well as a sense of wonder. Tolkien himself insisted that "fantasy
is a rational not an irrational activity"; that "it does not either blunt the appetite for, nor obscure the perception of, scientific verity. On the contrary:
the keener and the clearer is the reason, the better fantasy will it make."[70]

The New Romance and its successive marketing genres not only
embraced rationality: they made it appealing—indeed, enchanting—to a
mass audience. The writers in this tradition consciously opposed the
narrow, instrumentalist conception of reason associated with materialist
thought, which Weber identified with disenchantment.[71] For them, rationality need not be defined solely in terms of logical procedures and mathematical calculations. They returned to a conception of cognition held by
philosophers such as David Hume and Immanuel Kant in the eighteenth
century, and by romantic poets such as William Wordsworth and Samuel
Taylor Coleridge in the early nineteenth, which conjoined reason with
imagination, analysis with intuition, thought with feeling.[72] In so doing,
writers of the New Romance and the marketing genres derived from it provided an alternative to instrumental reason, one that was capable of reconciling modernity with enchantment.

This more expansive definition of rationality, which I call *animistic reason,* was exemplified by Sherlock Holmes and was arguably the primary reason for his enormous popularity during the fin-de-siècle and after, as we
shall see. Animistic reason was intrinsic to science fiction as well, which
became an identifiable marketing genre in 1926 when Hugo Gernsback

published *Amazing Stories*. This was the first magazine devoted exclusively to what he called "scientifiction" (and later "science fiction"). Gernsback and many early contributors to his growing roster of science fiction magazines were influenced by the New Romance, adhering to the aim of reconciling reason and the imagination. In a 1928 editorial for Gernsback's *Amazing Stories Quarterly*, the author Jack Williamson defined the distinctive tenor of the new genre: "scientifiction . . . takes the basis of science, considers all the clues that science has to offer, and then adds a thing that is alien to science—imagination. It lights the way. And when science sees the things made real in the author's mind, it makes them real indeed."[73]

During the interwar period, this combination of reason and imagination was advanced by many who rejected the artificial sundering of the two in utilitarian and positivist epistemologies, resulting in what T. S. Eliot called the "dissociation of sensibility."[74] Whereas in the late nineteenth century, Western anthropologists had condescendingly associated animistic thinking with so-called primitive peoples, by the early twentieth century scholarly and popular writers alike began to recover animism as a universal attribute of human thought, derived from the natural interplay of reason and the imagination. The philosopher R. G. Collingwood, who enjoyed inventing imaginary worlds as a youth, was one prominent advocate for their reunification. In the 1930s he wrote a series of essays on folktales, published posthumously as *The Philosophy of Enchantment*, arguing that the commingling of reason and imagination was common to both "civilized" and "primitive" cultures. It was dangerous to disaggregate reason and the imagination, for modern progress actually depended on animistic reason: "It is only in a society whose artistic life is healthy and vigorous that a healthy and vigorous scientific life can emerge."[75] Collingwood went on to observe that, "the mind here discovers its true nature as the creator not only of imaginary worlds but of the real world."[76] By demonstrating the underlying commonalities between imaginary and real worlds, the new emphasis on animistic reason enabled readers to use the former to reimagine the latter.

We shall see that it became possible to inhabit such imaginary worlds communally and persistently as a result of new *public spheres of the imagination* that emerged alongside the New Romance at the turn of the century.[77] Letters pages in fiction magazines became public forums for debates about imaginary characters and worlds, which often elided into discussions about the real world. Similarly, associations, publications, and conventions devoted to imaginary characters and worlds were also sites for the collective discussion of fictions and their relations with the real. These public spheres had antecedents in reading groups of the eighteenth and nineteenth centuries, but marked a genuine departure in their overall orientation. They were dedicated to not only discussing the meanings and mechanics of fiction, but also to enhancing the "reality effects" of fantasy: to make the imaginary world more virtually "real" by probing its details, reconciling its apparent contradictions, and filling in its lacunae. Public spheres of the imagination fostered a synergy of multiple minds to bring the imaginary world to life and to perpetuate it as an evolving territory transcending any single reader's involvement, transforming it thereby into a virtual reality. This collective effort often heightened each individual's emotional investment in an imaginary world, as the world became a shared, ongoing project rather than a transient, private encounter.

These fantastic, cohesive, and virtual worlds had personal, social, and political consequences. They provided new social networks, countering the disenchanting effects of isolation and anomie that modernity could engender. A Sherlock Holmes fan gratefully recalled his first encounter with the world of Sherlockian studies, "a world full of fine writers who were having the time of their lives playing a game that they enjoyed so much that it was obvious that anyone with any sense ought to be a part of that strange world."[78] Here was an instance of what some have called "elective belonging" in a global, cosmopolitan age, in which communities need not be defined in terms of geographical boundaries: they can be "more fluid, seeing places as performing identities."[79] If modernity lent itself to deterritorialization, there was a corresponding recourse to new homelands of the imagination. Public spheres of the imagination belied the widely held notion that living in imaginary worlds was solipsistic, an antisocial flight from community. On the contrary: the turn to those worlds was often an act of fellowship, an involvement with and concern for others rather than mere escapism.

Contact with fellow readers could alter individual opinion, even character. The cliché that reading expands horizons is often difficult to reconcile with the tenacity of individual prejudices and predilections. After all, books are silent partners in the prosecution of their arguments, and what a solitary reader actually pays attention to is usually influenced by long-standing presuppositions. At times not even the rational detachment of the ironic imagination is sufficient to challenge one's most cherished opinions. When confronted by others who do not necessarily share one's outlook, however, a genuine and potentially transformative conversation can transpire. Reading can become truly "dialogic" within public spheres of the imagination. Modern enchantments are least likely to delude when they are experienced conjointly via the ironic imagination and diversely constituted public spheres of the imagination.

As we shall see, discussions about imaginary worlds often segued into discussions about the real world. Public spheres of the imagination provided playful spaces in which controversial views about society were debated critically yet with mutual respect. While it might be inadvisable to discuss politics or religion in a bar, debating them in the context of Mordor provides the critical distance that eases the airing of differences. Fantasy worlds become even more relevant when the issues to be confronted defy conventional description, as has been the case for so many of the ineffable tragedies of the past century. Tom Shippey notes that many of the central metaphors used to understand them derive from contemporary works of fantasy: "Sauron and the Ringwraiths, Big Brother and the Party, the pig's head and the choirboys: these have been the defining images of evil . . . for a culture and a century, which have had too close a contact with evil for more traditional images of it to seem any longer entirely adequate."[80]

The alternative realities posited by these virtual worlds had their own ambiguities, and the conflicting interpretations generated in public spheres of the imagination habituated readers to see narratives as complex, provisional, and pragmatic, rather than as transparent, essential, and unchanging. Tolkien, for example, initially intended his tales of Middle-earth to convey nationalist and Christian messages. Despite his professed dislike of allegory, he embedded essentialist convictions in the text of *The Lord of the Rings*. Yet numerous readers who discussed the book together in fanzines and gatherings arrived at quite different interpretations. As a result, many came to appreciate the provisionality not only of fictional texts, but also of normative interpretations of reality. Public spheres of the imagination often compelled members to acknowledge the constructed dimension of identities as well as the liberating capacity to juggle multiple allegiances. Imaginary worlds could help their visitors realize that something as seemingly natural as the nation, for example, was in important respects an "imagined community" brought to life through many of the same social mechanisms used to maintain the virtual existence of Middle-earth or the Starfleet Federation.[81]

Such realizations, and their repeated iterations in public spheres of the imagination, were among the most important practical contributions of modern imaginary worlds to everyday life. These worlds trained their inhabitants not only to think divergently but also to be self-reflexive about the socially constructed dimensions of experience: to perceive one's subjective existence as resulting from the dynamic interaction of material realities and contingent stories, a "mixed reality" combining the virtual and the real.[82] Max Weber mourned the disappearance of stable and shared meanings that allegedly distinguished the premodern, enchanted world, but that was to see modernity as half-empty. Rather than experiencing disenchantment from the loss of universal meanings, one could find a specifically modern enchantment arising from an outlook that embraced pluralistic, provisional, and contingent interpretations. As Marie-Laure Ryan noted, "If we live a 'virtual condition' . . . it is not because we are condemned to the fake but because we have learned to live, work, and play with the fluid, the open, the potential."[83]

In presenting a "half-full," optimistic interpretation of this form of modern enchantment, I don't mean to deny the dangerous uses of fictions for manipulative ends. But such cases, and the argument that mass culture in particular can mislead, are well known, having been rehearsed repeatedly since the advent of mass culture. The central problem with the discourse of disenchantment since the nineteenth century is that it does not take into account the inherently ambivalent properties of enchantment: the capacity to delight and to delude. It was not either/or, but both/and: the price of living with enchantment was always the possibility of being captivated by it.

For that reason, the strategies developed in mass culture to reconcile modernity and enchantment, such as imaginary worlds and their virtual expressions, are important. By emphasizing self-reflexivity, these worlds undercut enchantment's potential to beguile. By stressing public participation and a more capacious definition of rationality, they enlisted the wonders of the imagination in the service of a pluralistic and more tolerant world, one that is continuing to adapt to virtuality in many guises. The anthropologist Arjun Appadurai makes a relevant observation in this regard:

> Until recently . . . fantasy and imagination were residual practices, confined to special moments or places. In general, imagination and fantasy were antidotes to the finitude of social experience . . . As the deterritorialization of persons, images, and ideas has taken on a new force, this weight has imperceptibly shifted. More persons throughout the world see their lives through the prisms of possible lives offered by the mass media in all their forms. That is, fantasy is now a social practice; it enters, in a host of ways, into the fabrication of social lives for many people in many societies.[84]

"Fantasy as social practice": an enchanting—and specifically modern— idea.[85]

FROM THE "JUST SO" TO THE "AS IF"

This book is a selective exploration of large topics. It is not a synoptic account of imaginary worlds or of virtual realities: the former are too numerous to cover in any depth, and the latter are in an ongoing flux of development. Rather, I sketch a broad picture of how a "big bang" of imaginary worlds flared into existence at the fin-de-siècle to re-enchant modernity without rejecting its central tenets, and of how some of these worlds became effectively virtual, anticipating in important respects the emergence of technologically mediated virtuality during our own fin-de-siècle.

As I noted, we shall see that an important consequence of the turn to imaginary worlds during the past century was an emphasis on rationality conjoined with the imagination: from the thrilling cogitations of Sherlock Holmes to the emphasis on communal problem-solving skills in online gaming environs such as World of Warcraft. Just as important, however, is the increasing comfort with the notion that the real world is, to some degree, imaginary, relying on contingent narratives that are subject to challenge and change. Imaginary worlds, in other words, have trained their inhabitants to question essentialist interpretations of the world.

This is a critical contribution, especially if human beings are "natural born essentialists," as psychologist Paul Bloom argues.[86] By this he means that we are predisposed by evolution to interpret all aspects of experience in terms of underlying, often invisible essences that comprise their fundamental natures.[87] He contends that some essentialist outlooks, such as scientific theories, have effective explanatory and predictive powers, and thus it would be a mistake to reject the idea that there are "deep commonalities" in nature that we can identify. He cautions, however, that this "essentialist bias" also "leads us to see deep commonalities even when none exist."[88] The destabilizing processes of modernity, together with the anxieties they engender, have certainly resulted in the creation of new myths taken as essential truths, including a wide stripe of religious, political, and cultural fundamentalisms.

Yet the cultural practice of the ironic imagination was also an outgrowth of modernity, challenging such essentialist narratives. By the fin-de-siècle, essentialist "just so" stories were challenged by a competing faith in provisional, "as if" narratives, notably those of imaginary worlds. The self-conscious practice of dwelling in these worlds through the ironic imagination and public spheres of the imagination promoted an understanding of myths as useful artifices and "truths" as provisional tools. This pragmatic orientation did not exclude scientific theories, spiritual beliefs, or secular commitments. It simply bracketed them as potentially fallible and incomplete, to be accepted with a dose of humility and an openness to alternative interpretations. Thus, while it is tempting to concur with Bloom that "Society makes us less essentialist, not more so," it is important to add that that is only true in certain cultures at certain times.[89] The contemporary West's turn to the virtual is one of these periods, although essentialist outlooks, many empirically unsupportable, remain prevalent.

In the first two chapters, we will survey the cultural contexts for the emergence of imaginary worlds as well as the ironic imagination, animistic reason, and public spheres of the imagination. Chapter 1 discusses changing

attitudes toward fiction and the imagination in the West since the eighteenth century and the expanding recourse to the ironic imagination. Chapter 2 examines the proliferation of realistic yet fantastic imaginary worlds
that appeared at the turn of the century and explores the concomitant development of public spheres of the imagination, which enabled adults to
inhabit these worlds communally and persistently.

The succeeding three chapters are case studies of specific imaginary
worlds that became virtual through sustained and shared participation. The
worlds of Sherlock Holmes, the Cthulhu Mythos, and Middle-earth epito-
mize the core components of the literary prehistory of virtual reality as I am
defining it. (Later imaginary worlds from other media, such as film, radio,
television, comics and so on, derive from this tradition and extend it.)
Conan Doyle, Lovecraft, and Tolkien were among the most important figures who contributed to this history, and they shared certain preoccupations that distinguish it. All three intended their imaginary worlds to
re-enchant modernity in ways compatible with modern reason and secularism. They expected their worlds to be enjoyed through the double consciousness of the ironic imagination. Further, they believed that reason and
the imagination were inextricable, and consciously used their imaginary
worlds to advance animistic reason as an alternative to the narrow instrumental reason decried by cultural pessimists. At the same time, they also
exemplified some of the psychological difficulties involved in substituting
"as if" for "just so" outlooks. Finally, all three created imaginary worlds of
such wide appeal that they were among the first to be rendered virtual
through public spheres of the imagination dedicated to them.

Each chapter will highlight a particular facet of these interrelated issues.
Chapter 3 examines the importance of animistic reason to Conan Doyle as
a way to re-enchant modernity on its own terms, and argues that it was this
dimension of the Sherlock Holmes stories that contributed to the detective's iconic status. Conan Doyle himself was ultimately unable to accept
this strategy, however, and toward the end of his life proclaimed his faith in
the "just so" existence of fairies and spirits. In contrast, fans of his rationalistic detective adopted the stance of modern enchantment, believing in
Sherlock Holmes "as if" he existed.

Chapter 4 explores Lovecraft's use of the ironic imagination to reconcile
modernity and enchantment and discusses its limitations when it came to
identifying and challenging his biases. Lovecraft was very good at imagining fictional "others," but less capable of empathizing with those from ethnic and class backgrounds other than his own. Public spheres of the
imagination helped Lovecraft to attenuate many of his deep, essentialist
prejudices. His example suggests that a combination of the ironic imagination and diversely constituted public spheres of the imagination is most

effective at maintaining a disenchanted form of enchantment, one that successfully challenges the "just so" with the "as if."

Chapter 5 underlines the importance of "as if" narratives in the creation and reception of Tolkien's *The Lord of the Rings*. Although Tolkien was a Catholic and often criticized modernity, he nevertheless intended to re-enchant it by creating new myths compatible with rational and even secular outlooks. He was not only the premier theorist of the ironic imagination; he exemplified its double-minded orientation, which was reflected in his life and works. Tolkien believed in both essential truths and provisional fictions: his imaginary world was simultaneously a "just so" and an "as if" account. These dual outlooks stimulated debates in public spheres of the imagination devoted to Middle-earth, where it was shown that they weren't necessarily incompatible. Many readers—secular and religious alike—came to affirm the centrality of provisional interpretations to the generation of meaning and enchantment in modernity.

Imaginary and real worlds overlap, as Alberto Blanco observed in the epigraph to this chapter. But they are also conceptually distinct. The semanticist Alfred Korzybski, who was to influence the imaginary worlds of Robert Heinlein, A. E. van Vogt, and William S. Burroughs, insisted in 1931 that "the map is not the territory."[90] Let us now embark from this schematic overview into the more rough-and-tumble territory of imaginary worlds and their specifically modern enchantments.

CHAPTER 1

Living in the Imagination

As people mature, they ought to move from one kind of enchantment to another, from fear-driven fantasies to free yet disciplined exercises of the imagination. Imagination so exercised is actually quite commonplace, a fact that we tend to overlook because our attention is too narrowly focused on exceptionally talented individuals and their works.
—Yi Fu Tuan

It's more than true: It actually happened.
—Gogol Bordello

I. A PRELIMINARY RECONNAISSANCE OF IMAGINARY WORLDS

Modern "imaginary worlds" are different from the "imagined worlds" of fiction that have been with us for as long as humans have told stories. The imaginary worlds explored in this book first appeared during the late nineteenth century in Europe and America: fantasy realms presented in a realist mode, cohesively structured, empirically detailed, and logically based, often accompanied by scholarly apparatus such as footnotes, glossaries, appendices, maps, and tables. Despite their apparent realism, they were explicitly marked as fictions, differing thereby from those worlds and characters presented in religions, legends, and myths, whose epistemological status can be more ambiguous. Individuals began to spend a great deal of time residing in imaginary worlds, heightening their emotional investment in them by participating in collective exercises of world building. In so doing, they became ex post facto collaborators with the author, using references from the original text to reconcile its contradictions, fill in gaps, extrapolate possibilities, and imagine prequels and sequels. A number of readers chose to downplay or ignore the original author, whose mundane existence could be seen as an impediment to their belief in the autonomous existence of the fantasy worlds. As the author and critic Anthony Boucher wrote in 1944:

> Most of the BSI [Baker Street Irregulars] would agree with me in considering Sir Arthur Conan Doyle a singularly dull and stuffy gentleman who happened to transcribe the immortal Canon of Baker Street . . . And I think the same goes for [H. P. Lovecraft] . . . [His] . . . Mythos is one of the extraordinary imaginative achievements of our times, and I want to know everything I can about it. But I don't care much what HPL thought about life and manners and things. It is as the transcriber of the Myth that he looms incomparable.[1]

Sometimes readers enhanced their identification by dressing in the attire of the world or of a specific character.

This intense imaginative identification with the textual imaginary world, coupled with the synergistic effects arising from group involvement, effectively reconfigured the world. It was no longer confined to a set text brought to temporary life in individual imaginations; it became a sustained virtual world transcending any particular text or reader. Middle-earth, to take one well-known example, remains an imaginary world when a reader engages with it through Tolkien's works. Should the reader want a more immersive and prolonged experience, however, there is a virtual version awaiting him or her, accessible through societies, fanzines, and websites in which the world is continuously elaborated by a community. In this chapter and the next, we will explore this historically novel practice by which an imaginary world is transformed into a virtual world, enabling individuals to dwell in it communally and relate it to actual life. We will also address why rational individuals would want to engage in such behavior to begin with, and why it became more acceptable to do so by the late nineteenth century.

A more immediate concern ought to be addressed at the outset: why should we even care if adults engage in intense pretense? Isn't this a trivial issue about an even more trivial pastime, especially when funny costumes are involved? After all, creating and inhabiting imaginary worlds are merely hobbies. *Hobby,* according to the *Oxford English Dictionary,* first became a common term in the nineteenth century, when many among the middle classes had more leisure time and disposable income. We should be no more surprised that adults turned to imaginary worlds at that time than that they turned to stamp collecting.[2]

The panoply of imaginary worlds that dawned at the turn of the century represents more than just a new hobby, however: this bright new constellation casts light on several significant issues. One concerns the historical development of specifically modern forms of "enchantment" to counter the prevalent account of modernity as inherently "disenchanted." A related issue involves the vastly expanded role assumed by the imagination in Western thought since the eighteenth century, which has been crucial for the emergence of the concept of *virtual reality* and related terms. For example, the communal and persistent habitation of imaginary worlds is a form of vicarious existence enabled by the imagination. The earliest usage of *vicarious* in this sense (again courtesy of the *OED*) was 1929, approximately the same time that Sherlock Holmes societies and organized science fiction fandom arose on both sides of the Atlantic.[3] Modern imaginary worlds emerged concurrently with notions of the virtual and the vicarious, as well as discussions about disenchantment and re-enchantment. Their popularity during the fin-de-siècle and after is thus a prism through which we can examine the centrality of the imagination to modern enchantment and its increasing sway over everyday life.

In particular, we will explore how the emergence of modern imaginary worlds was part of a broader fictionalist turn in Western culture, in which existence is understood in terms of contingent and provisional narratives: an outlook of "as if." This fictionalist turn is sometimes attributed to the postmodern emphasis on language as the constitutive basis of reality. Its onset, however, can be traced back at least to the eighteenth century and its popular diffusion to the nineteenth—especially during the fin-de-siècle.

Before this cultural embrace of "Fictionalism," a word coined by the philosopher Hans Vaihinger in 1911, individuals certainly had recourse to their imaginations, which were stimulated by a range of narrative forms.[4] They distinguished between reality and appearance, fact and fancy. They also constructed imaginary dwellings as mnemonic devices, although such "memory palaces" were utilitarian, quite different from the escapist functions of modern imaginary worlds.[5] But speaking generally, we can claim that prior to the onset of the fictionalist turn in modernity, individuals tended to dwell within the dimensions of the sacred and the profane rather than the real and the fictional.[6] When the novel became an identifiable literary form in the eighteenth century, conceptual distinctions between reality and fiction sharpened, and the fictional was accorded an important, if ambivalent, place in everyday life. This is not to say that the traditional abodes of the sacred and the profane disappeared, to be replaced by the real and the fictional; the two pairs coexist within the pluralistic orientation of Western modernity. But the option of self-reflexively inhabiting both real and fictional worlds, and observing how they interpenetrate, is a distinctly modern practice.

Modern imaginary worlds, therefore, reflected new concepts of the imagination, expressed an increasing comfort with the fictional, and provided a specifically modern form of enchantment. In addition, they helped acclimatize their adherents to virtual reality long before the creation of data gloves, headsets, and other VR technologies in the late twentieth century. There are of course significant differences between today's virtual realities mediated through such technologies and virtual realities that arise from the collective imagining of a group. Through graphical interfaces and other sensory stimuli, the former can provide a more embodied experience of a virtual world than text-based imaginary worlds.[7] Yet there are also significant similarities. Both types of virtual experiences are consciously understood to be artificial creations, and both depend on imaginative participation. Both are "consensual hallucinations," the phrase used by William Gibson to define the virtual reality of "cyberspace."[8] Indeed, many of today's technological virtual worlds are direct descendants of textual imaginary worlds.

Modern imaginary worlds created since the late nineteenth century have two distinguishing features. First, while they are understood to be explicitly fictional, they are also taken to be real, often to such an extent that they continue to be "inhabited" long after the tale has been told. As we shall see, such imaginary worlds do not exist through the "willing suspension of disbelief," but rather through the willing activation of pretense. Second, they combine fantasy with realism, wild imagination with sober logic. They began to proliferate in the 1880s as a conscious reaction to the disenchanting orientation of literary realism. While their authors rejected the realists' disenchanted perspective, they incorporated the realists' mimetic techniques in their narratives.[9] These fin-de-siècle texts became paradigmatic for subsequent imaginary worlds, including those in other media.

In a pioneering study devoted exclusively to *Imaginary Worlds* (1973), Lin Carter defined an imaginary world as a

> story laid in settings completely made up by the author, whether such settings consist of a single country or an entire world, or even an imaginary period of the remote past or the distant future.[10]

He claimed that William Morris "invented the imaginary-world novel" with his pseudo-medieval fantasies, such as *The Well at the World's End* (1896). These were set within internally consistent, highly detailed geographies of Morris's own invention. The appearance of such realistic, yet fantastic, geographies inaugurated a new approach to fantasy.[11]

Carter's definition is sufficiently capacious to incorporate works whose fantastic element consists solely of the creation of a new continent, such as Austin Tappan Wright's *Islandia* (1942).[12] It also encompasses the wholly invented planets of science fiction, such as Frank Herbert's *Dune* (1965).

However, by insisting on "settings completely made up by the author," Carter's definition would exclude other important works in the modern imaginary-world tradition, such as the London of Sherlock Holmes, and thus is not capacious enough. Imaginary worlds can be constructed primarily around fantastic characters no less than fantastic settings: we wouldn't claim that because Batman lives in Gotham City his is an imaginary world, but because Spiderman lives in New York City his isn't. Arthur Conan Doyle, no less than William Morris, was among the late nineteenth-century originators of modern imaginary worlds, in which the fantastic was limned with the "thick description" of the contemporary realists.

Imaginary worlds could not be occupied persistently and communally until the imagination was deemed a safe territory in which to reside. Shifts in attitudes toward the imagination in the course of the eighteenth and nineteenth centuries led to a greater toleration, and even celebration, of the role of the imaginary in everyday life. The early Victorians were ambivalent about the imagination, but by the Edwardian era of the "New Imperialism" the imagination had become domesticated as a topographic space awaiting colonization; by the mid-twentieth century imaginary worlds were readily available as places of prolonged mental habitation. In 1946, a literary critic surveyed recently published works of fantasy literature and found that this turn toward the imagination as a habitable space arose partly from the realization, at the turn of the century, that "the old material solidity of our world is gone and many of the distinctions we used to make between 'matter' and 'spirit,' 'real' and 'unreal,' 'natural' and 'supernatural' have gone with it." As a salutary consequence:

> The countries of the mind are real countries, legitimate to build, legitimate to inhabit. Here is the creed; here is the justification of the "new fantasy." The narrow world of the naturalists has crumbled; it was merely the dusty abiding place of theories which quickly shrank to the ghost of theories.[13]

Although he was correct to state that the boundary between the real and unreal had been challenged by new epistemologies, in another important respect the boundary had been fortified. Adults could now reside safely within carefully mapped geographies of the imagination without compromising their reason—going native, as it were—because the necessary distinction between fantasy and reality was securely reinforced through the distancing power of irony.

In the remainder of this chapter, we will focus on the expanding role of the imagination from the eighteenth century through the twentieth, and on how it was increasingly utilized in an ironic fashion. We will then examine how this new estimation of the imagination led to a wider recognition, by the fin-de-siècle, of the importance of imaginary worlds to human subjectivity, cognition, and ordinary life.

II. THE IRONIC IMAGINATION

Imaginary worlds are inhabited through the ironic imagination, a double-minded consciousness that became widespread in Europe and America by the late nineteenth century. It permits an emotional immersion in, and rational reflection on, imaginary worlds, yielding a form of modern enchantment that delights without deluding. The ironic imagination is different from Samuel Taylor Coleridge's well-known formulation of how fantasy is apprehended in an enlightened age. In 1817, he asserted that readers engage poetic fictions through "the willing suspension of disbelief."[14]

Coleridge's view reflected the early nineteenth-century ambivalence about the powers and the pleasures of the imagination. The imagination had become a central yet contested faculty during the eighteenth century, when it was recognized for its signal contributions to human cognition and everyday life in a capitalist market economy. Critics argued that the imagination did not just re-present the existing world: it also helped to produce it through recourse to fictions. Credit, finance, and currency were analyzed as fictions that had material effects on the world; laws were fictions that governed practical life; the novel incited visceral desires through imaginary characters and scenarios.[15] Because the imagination was apparently unlimited, exceeding the parameters of the material world it effected in crucial ways, some sought to delimit its expression. As Jean Jacques Rousseau argued in *Emile* (1762), "the real world has its limits, the imaginary world is infinite. Unable to enlarge the one, let us restrict the other."[16] Reason and the will were called upon as checks and balances to the imagination: Coleridge's formulation concerning the "willing suspension of disbelief" reflected them. To prevent the imagination from misleading, a default position of critical skepticism was assumed in the reader. One started with disbelief, which was then willingly suspended in order to partake of the unreal.

Those who turned to the ironic imagination in the late nineteenth century, however, did not so much willingly suspend their disbelief in fictional characters or worlds, as willingly believe in them with the double-minded awareness that they were engaging in pretense.[17] Imaginary worlds were considered analogous to hoaxes, a term used by Lovecraft to describe his realistic tales of frightening yet wondrous creatures who invade our world from other dimensions of time and space. As he wrote to a correspondent in 1930, "My own attitude in writing is always that of a hoax-weaver. One part of my mind tries to concoct something realistic and coherent enough to fool the rest of my mind & make me swallow the marvel."[18] In the interwar period, Lovecraft recast "supernatural fiction," which he believed had been discredited by modern science, into the literature of "cosmic fear," which he felt was compatible with scientific rationality. He described how what I am calling the ironic imagination enabled him to attain a sense of wonder without compromising the rational and secular tenets of modernity:

> [I get a] big kick . . . from *taking reality just as it is*—accepting all the limitations of the most orthodox science—and then permitting my symbolizing faculty to *build outward* from the existing facts; rearing a structure of *indefinite promise and possibility* . . . But the whole secret of the kick is *that I know damn well it isn't so.* I'm probably trying to have my cake and eat it at the same time—to get the intoxication of a sense of cosmic contact and significance as the theists do, and yet to avoid the ignorant ostrich-act whereby they cripple their vision and secure the desiderate results.[19]

Here we see an example of the conjunction of enchantment and modernity through the ironic imagination. It was also evident among the educated professionals who professed "belief" in the existence of Sherlock Holmes, as a *New York Sun* reporter found in 1946: "These Sherlock worshippers have developed a world of the imagination bolstered by enthusiasm and biographical researches rarely given to flesh and blood characters past or present, and they have a stronger belief in him than those who believe from ignorance."[20]

Tolkien also upheld a notion of the ironic imagination, which he described as "Secondary Belief" in "Secondary Worlds." He explicitly criticized Coleridge's formulation in 1939, a time when the imagination had largely freed itself from the religious and utilitarian strictures of Coleridge's era.[21] For Tolkien, "the willing suspension of disbelief" was an inadequate description of a reader's deep emotional and intellectual investment in worlds of fantasy. Further, Coleridge did not perceive that an individual could wholeheartedly "believe" in a fantasy world while concurrently being aware that it was fictional. Tolkien argued:

> [The willing suspension of disbelief] does not seem to me a good description of what happens. What really happens is that the story-maker proves a successful "sub-creator." He makes a Secondary World which your mind can enter. Inside it, what he relates is "true": it accords with the laws of that world. You therefore believe it, while you are, as it were, inside. The moment disbelief arises, the spell is broken; the magic, or rather art, has failed. You are then out in the Primary World again, looking at the little abortive Secondary World from outside. If you are obliged, by kindliness or circumstance, to stay, then disbelief must be suspended (or stifled), otherwise listening and looking would

become intolerable. But this suspension of disbelief is a substitute for the genuine thing,
a subterfuge we use when condescending to games or make-believe, or when trying . . .
to find what virtue we can in the work of art that has for us failed.[22]

Tolkien thus emphasized that "Secondary Belief" in Secondary Worlds simultaneously fostered complete immersion ("you therefore believe it,
while you are, as it were, inside") and ironic distance: one accords Secondary Belief to Secondary Worlds, and Primary Belief to the Primary
World of reality.[23] The ironic imagination, analogous to Tolkien's Secondary
Belief, was at once a more committed, immersive state of mind than the
"willing suspension of disbelief," while retaining a degree of critical detachment. It was not similar to dreaming, but to lucid dreaming.[24] It was also
intrinsic to the "consensual hallucination" that is one defining aspect of virtual reality.

Many imaginary worlds of the period drew attention to their status as
ironic Secondary Worlds even as they labored to convince the reader of
their autonomous reality. Tolkien's own example of "sub-creation" exemplified this. His Middle-earth was a marvelous example of world building,
providing more detail and consistency than many genuine works of history. But the reader was also reminded of the artificial nature of this world
through subtle cues. Take, for example, the dialogue between Sam and
Frodo in *The Two Towers* about how lived experience is made coherent
through narratives and how such narratives in turn affect life. Sam wonders
"if we shall ever be put into songs or tales . . . told by the fireside, or read out
of a great big book, with red and black letters, years and years afterwards.
And people will say: 'Let's hear about Frodo and the Ring!'"[25] If this
weren't enough to alert readers, the dust jackets of the first British editions
of *The Lord of the Rings* were printed with red and black lettering, pace
Sam's wishes.

Not all imaginary worlds attract a devoted following who, through their
persistent and communal dedication, transform them into virtual worlds. It
remains an interesting question why some worlds are more amenable to
prolonged and ironic habitation than others: why that of Sherlock Holmes
rather than that of Professor Challenger, Middle-earth rather than Narnia,
Star Trek rather than *Voyage to the Bottom of the Sea*? The answers must be
sought in the reception history of specific worlds, but imaginary worlds
that attained a virtual existence shortly after their appearance do share
common features. Those most amenable to prolonged habitation straddle a
delicate balance between ironic self-reflexivity and sober realism. Irony
must not be so pronounced as to overwhelm immersion, which is often the
case with metafictions.[26] Immersion can also be stymied by overt moral-
izing and didacticism, which redirects attention away from the imaginary

world to the real world. Tolkien eschewed allegory in Secondary Worlds partly for this reason. His friend C. S. Lewis inflected his Narnia series with Christian allegory; as a consequence, Narnia in its initial print incarnation did not garner as large a fan base for the communal habitation of its imaginary world as did Middle-earth. One fantasy fan reflected in 1967, "I think one of the most beautiful things about Tolkien, and lacking, for instance, in the Narnia tales, is that Middle-earth—well, you can always enter into it. Narnia is always connected to this world—you always have the door and there are references to the other world. But Middle-earth is an entity unto itself."[27]

Conan Doyle's tales of Sherlock Holmes also attained this delicate equilibrium between irony and immersion, autonomy and realism. The world he created, like that of Middle-earth, was at once untethered to mundane reality and empirically grounded. 221B Baker Street was of this world, yet also unworldly: Holmes's adventures were not allegorical, and his imaginary milieu was as cozily self-contained as a snow globe. Like Middle-earth, Holmes's world was replete with convincing minutiae, making effective use of what Roland Barthes called the "reality effect" to establish verisimilitude.[28] And like Tolkien, Conan Doyle enhanced the reader's imaginative participation in the world by alluding to intriguing, unpublished events that gave the world additional depth and mystery.[29] (As Tolkien observed, "A story must be told or there'll be no story, yet it is the untold stories that are the most moving.")[30] This "absence effect" provoked the reader to speculate about the imaginary world, in the process becoming more involved. Indeed, if evolutionary psychologists are right to argue that humans naturally gravitate toward finding mysterious essences of reality, both the idiosyncratic details and the strategic gaps of an imaginary world might serve as irresistible lures for ongoing explorations of its underlying foundations. Many readers of the Holmes stories soon discovered the pleasures of filling in the lacunae and explaining the anomalies of what they affectionately called "the Canon." Conan Doyle also winked ironically at the reader. By having Holmes profess ignorance "of the Copernican Theory and of the composition of the Solar System," or by referring to an unwritten case associated with "the giant rat of Sumatra, a story for which the world is not yet prepared," he attracted and distanced simultaneously.[31]

While the ironic imagination is related to the early romantics' attempts to redress a seemingly disenchanted world through the imagination, it is also different from the romanticist project in three important respects. First, the romantics tended to define the imagination in metaphysical terms, whereas the ironic imagination is not metaphysical: it emphasizes the provisional, the contingent, and the artificial.[32] The second distinction follows from the first: whereas the early romantics stressed sincerity and authenticity, the ironic imagination is comfortable with the artifices of mass culture, and the phantasmagoria of symbols and representations that accompany a capitalist economic order. Finally, the early romantics' hope that the imagination might restore enchantment to a disenchanted world was not widely shared by the middle classes in the first half of the century, whereas the ironic imagination of the latter half of the century became an important resource of enchantment for many.

As we saw with Rousseau, the widespread ambivalence about the imagination during the eighteenth and early nineteenth centuries led numerous critics to find ways to constrain, rather than unleash, the imagination.[33] The rise of evangelical religious movements in both Britain and the United States, as well as the increasing influence of utilitarian thought among elites throughout nineteenth-century Europe and America, made prolonged immersion in fictional worlds even more problematic for the middle classes. They shackled the imagination to moral, religious, and utilitarian imperatives. Novels continued to be evaluated in these terms through the mid-nineteenth century: praiseworthy if they inculcated benevolent sentiments and an appreciation of duty; pernicious if they competed with life, seducing their readers to prefer fantasy over reality.[34] The eponymous heroine of Gustave Flaubert's *Madame Bovary* (1857) was destroyed by her penchant for the hard stuff (racy romances), which only inflamed her discontent with her mundane existence: "Nowadays, I'm all for stories that rush you along breathlessly and make you frightened. I hate commonplace heroes and moderate feelings such as are to be found in life."[35]

Emma Bovary's consequent descent into adultery and suicidal despair was neatly avoided by the sanitary reading program of Isabel Gilbert, the model heroine of Mary Elizabeth Braddon's *The Doctor's Wife* (1864), which was intended as a rebuke to *Madame Bovary*. Isabel, like Emma, is a married woman addicted to works of romance. It is her misfortune to be seduced by an aristocratic rake, but Providence intervenes in the form of his library, well-stocked with titles that would have delighted the Society for the Diffusion of Useful Knowledge. Isabel's fitful browsing inadvertently serves as the chaste kiss that awakens her from the beguiling enchantments of romance:

> Until now she had lived too entirely amongst poets and romancers, but now grave volumes of biography opened to her a new picture of life . . . It is impossible to live in the constant companionship of great writers without growing wiser and better in their grave and genial company . . . Isabel Gilbert went home . . . with a cheerful countenance, and greeted her husband pleasantly, and was tolerably reconciled to a life whose dull monotony was in some manner counterbalanced by a leisure that left her free to read delightful books.[36]

Braddon does not attribute Isabel's salvation to fictional worlds or characters, but to the "grave and genial company" of "great writers." The Victorians often judged the value of fiction by the moral character of its author,
just as John Ruskin estimated the quality of art by the moral character of the
society in which it was created. When turning to a novel, George Eliot
hoped to "[commune] with a large as well as a beautiful mind," irrespective
of the plot.[37] Fictional worlds and characters would not become autonomous from their authors, or from the moral, religious, and utilitarian codes
these Eminent Victorians represented, until the second half of the nineteenth century.

In the early to mid-nineteenth century, fictional worlds dissociated from
the real world were strictly for children, and even then many middle-class
parents tried to dissuade them from too much self-indulgent play. The
Brontë siblings' creation of imaginary worlds is a revealing case. As children
in 1826, they began to create autonomous fictional worlds, developing
them into the highly detailed realms of "Gondal" and "Angria." Charlotte
Brontë, like Emma Bovary and Isabel Gilbert, was fond of inhabiting imaginary worlds and spent much of her leisure time fantasizing about her creations. She may have mentioned this to the poet Robert Southey in 1837,
when she sent him some of her poems for evaluation. In his response
Southey admonished her to keep her imagination corseted:

> You live in a visionary world . . . There is a danger of which I would, with all kindness and
> earnestness, warn you. The day dreams in which you habitually indulge are likely to
> induce a distempered state of mind; and, in proportion as all the ordinary uses of the
> world seem to you flat and unprofitable, you will be unfitted for them without becoming
> fitted for anything else.[38]

She had received comparable words of wisdom from her father: "The sen-
sual novelist and his admirer . . . are diligently and zealously employed in
creating an imaginary world, which they can never inhabit, only to make
the real world, with which they must necessarily be conversant, gloomy and
unsupportable."[39]

The "day dreams" Southey discussed may not have referred specifically
to Charlotte's imaginary world of Angria, but rather to her professed desire
to be a writer. Women, children, the working classes, and "primitive" peoples were presumed to be deficient in the rationality and fortitude required
to resist the seductive blandishments of the imagination. In this spirit,
Southey warned her that "literature cannot be the business of a woman's
life, and it ought not to be."[40]

Like so many of her generation, Charlotte Brontë was highly ambivalent
about imaginary worlds. On the one hand, the visionary world of Angria

had attracted her since adolescence. She and her brother Branwell wrote stories about it, embellishing them with maps, chronicles, and illustrations. On the other hand, she feared that her devotion to a fantasy world was a form of idolatry that threatened her eternal soul, "losing sight of the *Creator* in idolatry of the *creature.*"[41] Eventually she renounced Angria, focusing instead on writing social novels addressing "adult" issues. Just as Flaubert claimed that Madame Bovary "c'est moi," Charlotte Brontë might have recognized aspects of herself in Isabel Gilbert.

The Brontë family's early biographers slighted their creation of imaginary worlds as juvenilia that had little bearing on their adult works. Both Elizabeth Gaskell and Clement K. Shorter, for example, had access to the original manuscripts devoted to Angria and Gondal but gave them short shrift. These exuberant imaginary worlds, and their formative place in the Brontë siblings' literary gestation, first received serious attention in the 1930s, when imaginary worlds of literature, as well as those of radio and film, had become more respectable venues for adults.[42] Subsequent biographers have argued that the Brontë sisters' published oeuvre was indeed beholden to these early writings.[43]

The Brontë's experience was paradigmatic for their period. Responsible adults did not immerse themselves in imagined worlds persistently or communally during the eighteenth and early decades of the nineteenth centuries. This is not to say that they didn't think about or discuss the fictions they read, identify closely with the characters, or find themselves swept away by narratives. These responses to fiction had become well established among elites in Western Europe and America in the eighteenth century, a period that witnessed challenges to traditional religious ideas among the educated classes and a corresponding empathetic identification with fiction.[44] The serial publication of popular novels beginning in the nineteenth century may have encouraged readers to persistently dwell on (if not in) the imagined world while they anxiously awaited the next installment.[45] Novels were read and discussed within families and at social gatherings; authors received passionate letters of praise or censure for how they handled their characters; and these characters were often the subject of reflection and debate.[46] Authors became celebrities, particularly from the mid-nineteenth century on, when societies devoted to them, and commemorations of them, multiplied.[47]

But neither in the eighteenth century nor the early nineteenth do we find anything comparable to the sustained obsession with the evidently fantastic character, Sherlock Holmes, a phenomenon that began in the 1890s. For the first time, a fictional character entirely supplanted the author who created him: Holmes was said to be real, Conan Doyle was said to be fictional; scholarly monographs and the first journals devoted exclusively to a fictional character were published to prove these ironic claims; and associations on both sides of the Atlantic were formed to study the "Sacred Writings" of John H. Watson with Talmudic zeal. (Or was it "James" H. Watson? And what did the "H" stand for?)

Instances that could be cited as precedents to this phenomenon differed not only in degree but in kind. In the eighteenth century, some wrote sequels to popular works such as Swift's *Gulliver's Travels* and John Gay's *The Beggar's Opera*, and there was a brief fad for all things *Pamela* following the publication of Samuel Richardson's novel. The suicide of Goethe's Werther allegedly inspired some readers to follow suit, dressed in the blue and yellow of Werther's suit. Such episodes, however, were anomalous. They were restricted to a limited public for a short time, and ardent interest in the fiction was not divorced from an equally ardent interest in its author or the real-world issues the work raised.[48]

This was true for much of the nineteenth century as well. The early nineteenth century certainly witnessed a widespread engagement with fiction, owing to the expansion of literacy, cheaper books made possible by the new steam presses, and the spread of circulating libraries and other literary resources.[49] The fates of Dickens's Little Nell and Paul Dombey excited tremendous popular interest in Britain and America; Wilkie Collins's *The Woman in White* (1860) was but one of the "sensation" novels to cause a sensation among readers, inspiring commercial tie-ins ranging from cloaks and bonnets to waltzes and quadrilles.[50] Readers also associated actual environs with the fictions that made them memorable, thanks in part to the literary information provided in the new tourists' guidebooks published by Karl Baedeker and John Murray.[51] Yet for all the public attention to these fictional worlds, readers remained as concerned—if not more so—with the moral, political, and social biases of the author. And popular fictional worlds were never far removed from the practical and ethical concerns of everyday life. Imagined worlds had yet to find a room of their own. It is likely that an early nineteenth-century reader who claimed that Werther existed but that Goethe didn't, or who wrote a lengthy biography of Little Nell, replete with footnotes, would have received a similar reception to that which greeted the unfortunate Don Quixada when he proclaimed he was really Don Quixote.[52]

The restrictive attitude toward the imagination began to change during the mid-nineteenth century, owing to the spread of secularism, the greater diffusion of economic prosperity, the increase in leisure time, and the irresistible allures of the new mass culture. By the end of the century, there were more venues available for people to exercise their imaginations, including museums, music halls, amusement parks, and the cinema in its nascent form. Novels and illustrated fiction magazines became more affordable than ever before in America and Britain thanks to the dynamics of mass-publishing that accompanied the expansion of literacy. These new attractions joined earlier resources of popular enchantment, such as street fairs, carnivals, circuses, panoramas, phantasmagorias, magic lantern shows, conjuring acts, and similar amusements, which Simon During has called "magical assemblages."[53] Taken together, these social changes and new attractions gradually undermined the Victorian ethic of "rational recreation" and inculcated a more ironic, self-reflexive attitude toward the representations of everyday life.[54]

While this form of the imagination became dominant by the late nineteenth century, it was emergent in earlier decades. James Cook has demonstrated that in antebellum America the public enjoyed playing with the "artful deceptions" they encountered in magic shows, carnivals, and dime museums, even when they knew or suspected that fakery was being perpetrated. This was recognized by P. T. Barnum when he stated in his autobiography, "The public appears to be disposed to be amused even when they are conscious of being deceived."[55] As Cook observed:

> It seems clear that artful deception in the Age of Barnum routinely involved a calculating intermixing of the genuine and the fake, enchantment and disenchantment, energetic public expose and momentary suspension of disbelief... In the nineteenth-century arts of deception, then, illusionism and realism were always interconnected... There was no need to *choose* between illusionism and realism. The public was amused even when it was conscious of being deceived.[56]

The popularity of Barnum's hoaxes reminds us that there was not a simple, black and white shift between an earlier, moralistic imagination and a later ironic one. Early Victorian mores could promote an ironic outlook, given the obvious disparities between the high-minded Victorian moral code and the less scrupulous ways it was often observed in practice.[57] But in terms of nineteenth-century, middle-class culture, the relative valences shifted in the course of the century: from a more restrictive attitude toward the imagination to a more relaxed and playful one, from a moralistic to an ironic imagination.

An early indication of this new tolerance for a less encumbered imagination was the emergence of a new form of children's literature in the mid-nineteenth century. Until then, books for children tended to be didactic and moralistic or, in the case of the "penny dreadful," were simply proscribed by the middle classes. Children's literature of the 1860s and after was more accepting of the whimsical free play of a child's imagination and less burdened by overt homilies. Works by Charles Kingsley, George MacDonald, Lewis Carroll, and others absorbed their young readers in autonomous worlds of fantasy, and the generation that came of age in the 1880s was anxious to recapture the enchanted spheres they had inhabited in their youth.[58] Many authors of the fin-de-siècle who created notable imaginary worlds, including Conan Doyle and Robert Louis Stevenson, acknowledged that their childhood reading influenced the fictions they wrote as adults; they hoped to restore the sense of wonder they had experienced as young readers.[59] (Conan Doyle famously dedicated *The Lost World* (1912) "To the boy who's half a man / Or the man who's half a boy.")[60] The spirit of make-believe encouraged by the new children's literature sowed the seeds for the fantastic texts of the New Romance, written for children and adults alike starting in the 1880s.[61]

This less inhibited imagination assumed an ironic cast. Scientific skepticism was part of the tenor of the times, but the sheer profusion of visual representations of the new mass culture, abetted by the concomitant rise of professional advertising at the end of the century, contributed to a mounting appreciation of artifice. This in turn imparted an enhanced momentum to the relativistic and ironic attitude toward this new society of the spectacle that had been developing for decades.[62] As Michael North noted:

> Even by the turn of the century, irony had become less a defense against commercialized modernity and more a way of participating in it . . . As society becomes progressively aestheticized . . . as audiences begin to consume imaginative and symbolic materials as they had previously consumed material goods, then everyday life acquires an inherent ironic distance from itself.[63]

Ironic distance functioned as an important prophylactic against the beguiling potential of modern enchantment; the ideal was to be delighted, not deluded. By the early decades of the twentieth century, motion pictures—the most widely disseminated form of mass culture—circulated the ironic apprehension of waking dreams. The phenomenon of movie stars, which originated at the turn of the century, was a notable spur to this double-minded consciousness. They were at once real people and fantastic personae manufactured by studio publicists.[64] Many fans acknowledged the deliberate blurring of the "reel" and "real" worlds even as they engaged with the fairy-tale scenarios promoted by gossip columnists and movie magazines.

This double-minded pretense, and the possibility that a few naïve fans might not understand the game, was captured nicely in a scene from the Ernst Lubitsch comedy *To Be or Not to Be* (1942). Carole Lombard plays a famous actress, Maria Tura, who is visited by an ardent male fan who recounts all sorts of fanciful events from her life that he has read in gossip columns. Tura is puzzled, until she realizes that the fan naïvely believes in her movie-star persona, which, thanks to the creative imagination of her publicists, carries on a romantic existence quite different from the genuine Maria Tura. She politely goes along with the naïve believer, becoming an ironic believer in the fictitious life she is supposed to have led. Those watching *To Be or Not to Be* knew enough about the star system to appreciate the joke. Even actors appreciated the irony of movie stardom. Cary Grant (formerly Archibald Leach) admitted that, "Everybody wants to be Cary Grant. Even I want to be Cary Grant."[65]

III. SUBJECTIVITY, COGNITION, AND INTERIOR WORLDS

Other aspects of the Victorian moral and social codes were being redefined in the course of the nineteenth century, imparting greater latitude to the imagination and a heightened sensitivity to the existence of multiple "selves" and interior "worlds." These changes, like those we have already discussed, facilitated the self-reflexive habitation of imaginary worlds by the fin-de-siècle. Scientific investigations of the unconscious during the second half of the century posited the existence of "double consciousness," undermining the Victorian ideal of a unified self as well as contributing to the growing acceptance of a double minded, ironic imagination.[66] As early as 1844, one psychologist explained that an individual could be consciously aware that he experienced illusory perceptions because humans in effect had "two distinct and perfect brains: One brain was, as we so often see, watching the other, and even interested and amused by its vagaries."[67] In *Human, All-Too-Human* (1878), Nietzsche discussed double consciousness, which allowed one to entertain illusions while remaining rational at the same time, in similar corporeal terms. "A higher culture must give man a double-brain," he wrote, "as it were a brain with two chambers, one for the reception of science, the other for that of non-science."[68]

The early nineteenth-century stress on "character," connoting a coherent self and consistent conduct, was increasingly opposed in the final decades of the century by the more individualistic notion of "personality," which suggested ongoing self-fashioning.[69] The Austrian physicist Ernst Mach, for example, argued that the notion of a stable self was a fiction, masking the continuous flux of sensations that comprised individual consciousness.[70] Other writers also celebrated the self as a fluid, variegated space—a universe encompassing multiple personae and worlds.

Walt Whitman anticipated, and helped promote, this outlook when he acclaimed "Walt Whitman" as a "kosmos" in "Song of Myself" (1855), exulting, "I am large, I contain multitudes."[71] Robert Louis Stevenson's *Strange Case of Dr. Jekyll and Mr. Hyde* (1886) similarly represented individual subjectivity as a heterogeneous "polity":

Man is not truly one, but truly two. I say two because the state of my own knowledge does not pass beyond that point. Others will follow, others will outstrip me on the same lines: and I hazard the guess that man will be ultimately known for a mere polity of multifarious incongruous and independent denizens.[72]

The Portuguese poet Fernando Pessoa (1888–1935), himself an Anglophile, embodied this polity more literally than most. In addition to writing poems under his own name, he wrote them under at least seventy-two other names. These were not pseudonyms, however, but what Pessoa called "heteronyms": they represented distinct fictional selves, with their own unique biographies, languages, literary styles, and philosophies.[73] Like Whitman and Stevenson, Pessoa embraced the plurality of personae harbored within a single individual:

Each of us is several, is many, is a profusion of selves. So that the self who disdains his surroundings is not the same as the self who suffers or takes joy in them. In the vast colony of our being there are many species of people who think and feel in different ways.[74]

Such multiple selves in turn generated heterogeneous worlds. Henry Adams observed, "The child born in 1900 would, then, be born into a new world which would not be a unity but a multiple," indicating that the self not only accommodated different perspectives, as Nietzsche insisted, but also alternative worlds, manifold geographies of the imagination.[75]

In an age of rising nationalism and imperialism, readers were encouraged to imagine new homelands and to envision the imagination as one of them. Metaphors abounded likening the imagination to a geographical territory waiting to be colonized by readers.[76] Camille Flammarion's 1864 *Les Mondes Imaginaires et Les Mondes Réels* is notable in this regard. Earlier works of proto-science fiction, from the classical world through the early nineteenth century, tended to focus on imaginary "journeys" or "voyages."[77] Flammarion's later survey, however, highlighted the geographical destination rather than the journey: imaginary worlds themselves, rather than the voyages to them, had now become central. (Similarly, fantastic narratives of underground worlds during the nineteenth century also shifted from places to be visited to places to be inhabited.)[78] In H. Rider Haggard's *She* (1887), the immortal queen Ayesha informs the intrepid explorers who discover her hidden African realm that she rules by psychologically intimidating the natives: "my empire is of the imagination."[79] Ayesha refers to a common technique of imperial domination, but there is another meaning to her claim. *She* was one of the first examples of the New Romance of the 1880s, a fantastic narrative composed in a realist mode and supported by photographs, footnotes, and other scholarly appurtenances. Through such "objective," documentary means, the imaginary world of the novel became as legible as any colonial space mapped by agents of the New Imperialism. In the act of reading *She,* the reader's mind was transformed from a *terra incognita* into a virtual "empire of the imagination." Tolkien also likened imaginary worlds to imperial possessions. As a young man he read the Finnish national epic *Kalevala* and enthused about it in terms of discovery and colonization: "You are at once in a new world and can revel in an amazing new excitement. You feel like Columbus on a new Continent."[80]

Scholars and scientists joined novelists in representing the mind as a repository of multiple worlds rife for exploration and habitation. In *The Interpretation of Dreams* (1899), Sigmund Freud pointedly distinguished his representation of the unconscious from preceding ones because he alone had provided its cartography. Psychoanalysis, he declared, was the "royal road" to the unconscious, and he would provide its "map."[81] In *Civilization and its Discontents* (1930), he likened the mind to a Roman archaeological site consisting of overlapping strata of civilizations, tiered temporal worlds that continued to affect the present.[82] His one-time colleague Carl Jung argued for the continued presence of ancient archetypes within the unconscious, leading the English writer Owen Barfield to observe in 1944 that "the Unconscious, as Freud and Jung have conceived it, really is a sort of *place,* an interior space where there are, shall we say, all sorts of things going on."[83] Barfield was a member of the Inklings, an informal association that included Tolkien, Lewis, and other creators of imaginary worlds; he may have been especially attentive to such metaphors as a result.

Jack London presaged Freud's archaeological image in *The Star Rover* (1915), in which an American prisoner endures his harsh captivity by recovering previous lives that lie buried in his mind. By putting himself into a trance state, he is able to inhabit the other worlds in which he once lived, including ancient Rome, medieval Korea, and early modern France. He asserts that these worlds were all contained within him, distinct territories of the imagination: "These things were in the content of my mind, and in my mind I was just beginning to learn my way about."[84] Interior worlds were also central to the thought of French political theorist Georges Sorel. In presenting myths as spurs to revolutionary activity, Sorel likened them to imaginary worlds: "When we act, it is because we have created an entirely artificial world, in advance of the present, consisting of movements which depend on us."[85] Similarly, the German phenomenologist Edmund Husserl analyzed the "Lifeworld" (*Lebenswelt*) present to consciousness, just as Ludwig Wittgenstein, in his later philosophy, investigated how languages generated their own life worlds: "And to imagine a language is to imagine a form of life."[86] (Tolkien's creation of Middle-earth was an unlikely proof of this. He had first invented artificial languages, and then found they required an imaginary world in which they could "live." The organically developing languages in turn suggested the "forms of life" for his imaginary world.) Fin-de-siècle sociologists also identified the mind as a congeries of "worlds" enabling individuals to cope with new and stressful social formations, such as the city and the crowd. Georg Simmel, for example, argued that the increased sensory stimuli of urban living prompted individuals to find protective shelter in interior worlds; for him, reality was merely "one of many possible worlds."[87]

Turn of the century occult movements, new religions such as Christian Science, and adherents of more secular "mind cure" strategies likewise highlighted the centrality of the imagination and its interior worlds. They maintained that the imagination played a significant role in effecting both spiritual and somatic changes; for some, it even afforded access to existent "Other Worlds" populating the astral plane.[88] Many readers who enjoyed literary imaginary worlds were intrigued by these allegedly real Other Worlds, although it is likely that they entertained them in a skeptical, "as if" fashion. Occultists themselves could hold their beliefs ironically, as was often the case with Aleister Crowley. In one of his works he stated, "In this book it is spoken of the Sephiroth and the Paths, of Spirits and Conjurations; of Gods, Spheres, Planes and many other things which may or may not exist. It is immaterial whether they exist or not."[89] Crowley created a fictional psychic detective who appeared in short stories and the 1927 novel *Moonchild*: his name, revealingly, was "Simon Iff." (Would that he had an antagonist named "Justin So.")

The imagination and imaginary worlds received further legitimation at this time as idealist philosophers, and scientists influenced by them, contended that reality itself was imaginary to some degree. In reaction to the mid-nineteenth century school of materialist psychology, which reduced consciousness to physiological processes, neo-Kantian and neo-Hegelian thinkers in the second half of the nineteenth century illustrated the complex role played by the imagination in the formation of concepts representing the real. Idealist philosophers in Britain and America at the turn of the century identified the real world as, in significant ways, an imaginary world. In the 1930s, R. G. Collingwood recalled that "in the last quarter of the century, there arose . . . a new school of philosophy, in revolt against naturalism and materialism and positivism, asserting the freedom of mind to create an orderly life of its own and a world in which to dwell."[90]

Exponents of non-Euclidean geometry and relativistic physics similarly employed imaginary worlds to convey their counterintuitive understandings of reality.[91] Edwin A. Abbott's *Flatland: A Romance of Many Dimensions* (1884) was on one level a modern imaginary world in the mode of

the New Romance, written by "A. Square" and accompanied by illustrations and a map—but it was also a serious account of mathematical dimensions beyond those perceived by the human senses.[92] (See figure 1.1)
Contemporary scientists forthrightly embraced the imagination and imaginary worlds when they endorsed Ernst Mach's technique of conducting
Gedankenexperimenten or "thought experiments" to represent reality by
imaginary means. (The term was first translated into English in 1897.) Einstein's reliance on the Gedankenexperiment influenced his view that scientific theories are "free inventions of the human mind," having a "purely
fictitious character."[93]

Thus science and art, reason and the imagination, kept separate by mid-
nineteenth century positivism, began their rapprochement in the final third
of the nineteenth century, becoming conjoined alongside worlds real and
imaginary. The imagination, long subordinate to reason in Western history,
was now hailed as its necessary complement. Whereas studies of the imagination as a delimited human faculty had been largely the preserve of
romantic and esoteric thinkers in the early nineteenth century, by the early
decades of the twentieth the imagination was being investigated more
widely, especially among Francophone thinkers.[94] French surrealists, for example, made the imagination the cardinal point of their aesthetic and political projects. Andre Breton enthused that Freud's investigations into the
unconscious signaled that the "imagination may be about to gain its
rights."[95] His remark certainly applied to French philosophy: Jean-Paul Sartre's *L'Imagination* (1936) was the first work of Western philosophy devoted exclusively to this faculty, and Jacques Lacan's elaboration of the
"imaginary" influenced later concepts of the "social imaginary" developed
by Guy Debord and Cornelius Castoriadis, among others.[96]

The French surrealists and their fellow travelers joined the mounting
chorus of those who proclaimed that imaginary worlds, however fantastical, were inextricable from the apprehensions of the real, and that the condition of modernity itself was partly defined by the recognition of this fact
and the ability to sojourn freely between these domains. As Max Ernst
explained,

> When the Surrealists are said to be the painters of a continually mutable dream-reality,
> this should not be taken to mean that they simply paint their dreams (that would be
> descriptive, naïve naturalism) or that they all build their personal little worlds from
> dream elements in which they can play a good or evil role (that would be escapism). It
> means that they move freely, daringly, and naturally on the physically and mentally quite
> real ("surreal"), if still largely undefined, frontier between interior and exterior world,
> registering what they see and experience there, and intervening where their revolutionary
> instincts suggest.[97]

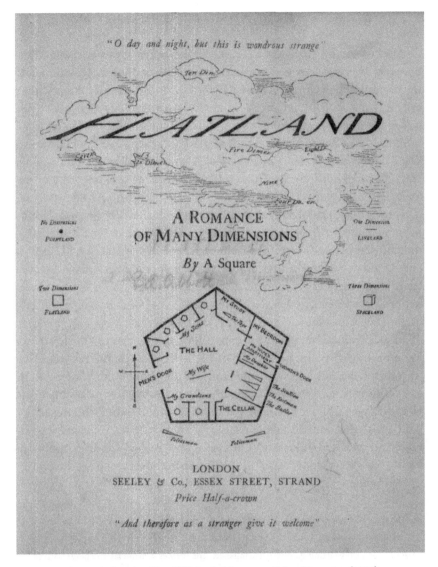

Figure 1.1 Cover of Edwin A. Abbott's *Flatland: A Romance of Many Dimensions* (1884).

This estimation of the creative agency of imaginary worlds, their inherent capacity to defamiliarize the status quo and provide alternative visions of the real, has had a considerable impact on modern politics as well. One of the most notable instances, which can stand for many others, transpired in 1968 when French students made "All Power to the Imagination" their revolutionary slogan, one embraced by many counterculture activists in the West.[98]

IV. FICTIONALISM AND THE IRONIC IMAGINATION

Our discussion by no means exhausts the fin-de-siècle preoccupation with the fuzzy overlaps between the worlds of reality and the imagination, and the corresponding elevation of imaginary worlds as a central category. They can be subsumed under an "aestheticist" epistemology that effectively ended the Western tradition of subordinating the imagination to reason.[99] Emblematic of this aestheticist turn of thought was the 1911 publication of *The Philosophy of "As If,"* a manifesto of "Fictionalism" by the philosopher Hans Vaihinger. Inspired by Kant and Nietzsche, he examined the prevalence and utility of fictions in science, aesthetics, religion, jurisprudence, and ethics. Vaihinger distinguished "fictions," which were acknowledged to be unreal, from "hypotheses," which could be tested by the scientific method. Hypotheses were probable concepts whose match with experience could be verified by logical analysis and experimentation, whereas fictions were explicitly understood to be empirically false. Nevertheless, fictions were expedient ways to comprehend those vast areas of experience that were not amenable to testable hypotheses.

In addition to being useful constructs, fictions were the source of higher aspirations and morals, positing concepts such as "freedom" that were inspiring but had no firmer foundation than an "as if" existence. For Vaihinger, fictions included thought experiments, metaphors and similes, myths, allegories, and parables: all were among the necessary "untruths" that individuals consciously employed for practical knowledge and spiritual guidance. Thus he distinguished the "relatively objective ideational constructs" of science and "those which are subjective or fictional":

> The real difference between the two is that the fiction is a mere auxiliary construct, a circuitous approach, a scaffolding afterwards to be demolished, while the hypothesis looks forward to being definitely established. The former is artificial, the latter natural. What is untenable as an hypothesis can often render excellent service as a fiction.[100]

Vaihinger admitted that it was often difficult in practice to distinguish fictions from hypotheses, as both originated in the human mind, with its admixture of reason and imagination.[101] Fictions themselves might lead to testable hypotheses; they were therefore both distinct from the "relatively objective" expositions of science, and also intrinsic to the pursuit of "real" as well as provisional truths.[102] He also cautioned against assuming that either fictional or more verifiable hypothetical constructs matched experience exactly. Both were human artifices that represented experience, but neither corresponded fully with what they attempted to picture.

His philosophy of "as if" exemplified the double consciousness of the ironic imagination. It allowed for ironic belief in useful fictions that were empirically unverifiable, as well as for the scientific method to establish normative propositions that were testable. Vaihinger was wary, however, of extending essentialist claims beyond the narrow limits established by institutionalized science and cautioned against reifying hypotheses. Contingent fictions, rather than essential truths, were his answer to Weber's crisis of meaning in an allegedly disenchanted world. He believed that an "as if" orientation to existence would preserve value and purpose in a self-reflexive modern age.

Rudyard Kipling also challenged the Victorian habit of essentialist thinking in his 1902 *Just So Stories*.[103] Many of these delightful fables explained the origins of animal and human characteristics, such as how the leopard got its spots. Yet they were also a gentle parody of the fundamentalist claims of traditional myths, religions, and folktales. Kipling's stories were told in the authoritative voice of an oral bard; the omniscient narrator addressed the reader as "O, my beloved" and disavowed any ambiguity or provisionality while relating the tales. The narrative events might seem incredible, fantastic, impossible: nevertheless, they happened "just so." Kipling's ironic deflation of essentialist thinking in this work joined Vaihinger's elevation of a fictionalist approach at the fin-de-siècle; the "as if" perspective of the ironic imagination directly confronted "just so" accounts.

Fictionalism as a state of mind was assisted by the state of play of published fiction at the turn of the century. The economic logic of mass-production created a situation in which fictional characters began to overshadow their corporeal authors, as publishers increasingly promoted lucrative, brand name characters whose public visibility overshadowed that of their authors. (Conversely, authors became fictions themselves when publishers brought out works under house-names, a common practice of "fiction factories" in America and Britain at this time.)[104] The advent of film, radio ("the theater of the imagination"), comic strips, and comic books contributed to the torrent of popular fictional characters and worlds that were effectively dissociated from their original creators.[105] An interesting instance of this is "crossover" fiction, in which an author brings together fictional characters created by other authors; it first became popular at the turn of the century. Jess Nevins traced "the first truly modern crossover" to Mary Cowden Clarke's *Kit Bam's Adventures* (1849), but examples don't proliferate until the late nineteenth century.[106] By the early twentieth century, fantastic environs and their inhabitants had become emancipated, worlds unto themselves that readers were encouraged to visit repeatedly. Michel Foucault has analyzed the decline of the "author function" in the modern world, and to this we can add the corresponding rise of autonomous fictional characters and worlds.[107]

The establishment of English literature as an academic discipline at the turn of the century in Britain and America further contributed to the autonomy of fictional characters and worlds. This was ironic, since an underlying purpose of the new field was to create a canon of authors and texts that would link literature closely to an essentialist idea of the "nation."[108] However, by receiving formalist scrutiny within respected havens of knowledge, fictional characters and worlds were legitimated as objects of critical attention in their own right. In Britain, educators started to use literary maps to instruct primary and secondary school students about the history of the real world, inadvertently reinforcing the idea that fictions could be understood as autonomous Secondary Worlds with cohesive cartographies.[109]

Secondary sources devoted to fictions as Secondary Worlds began to appear outside of the academy as well. In 1910, George Routledge of London and E. P. Dutton of New York jointly issued "dictionaries" of the characters to be found in the novels of Sir Walter Scott, Charles Dickens, William Thackeray, and George Meredith. The author of the volume dedicated to Scott justified it somewhat anxiously as a scholarly work intended for researchers, but allowed that it could be useful to recreational readers: "This book is intended as a work of reference for the student and lover of the Waverley novels, and, in a minor degree, for the humanist who sees in Scott a noble nature worthy of closer acquaintance."[110] In other words, rest assured dear reader: this dictionary dedicated to nonexistent people and worlds is not frivolous; nor has the Victorian idealization of the author been entirely forgotten. Despite such an earnest disclaimer, the appearance of the series indicated that fictional worlds could be taken as independent realms deserving of their own Baedekers.

Twentieth-century philosophical approaches, such as pragmatism and existentialism, continued to underline the vital role of Fictionalism in the modern Western world. (Later in the century, fictional worlds became an important tool for philosophers and literary critics concerned with the epistemological status of "possible worlds.")[111] Revisionist Marxists likewise attributed greater autonomy and agency to fiction, and culture more generally, even if they did not welcome all of its modern manifestations.[112] The ethnographic turn taken by Anglo-American anthropology in the interwar period similarly underscored the contingent, symbolic dimensions of "culture"; practitioners were enjoined to inhabit the subjective "worlds" of their subjects. (As an anthropologist who recently studied Second Life observed, "Ethnography has a special role to play in studying virtual worlds because it has *anticipated* them. Virtual before the internet existed, ethnography has always produced a kind of virtual knowledge.")[113]

V. "THE WORLD WILL BE TLÖN": IMAGINARY WORLDS
AS DELUSIVE ENCHANTMENTS

Much more could be said about the modern history of the imagination and its ironic deployment. I hope that this sketch establishes that by the turn of the century the imagination had attained a degree of freedom from earlier Victorian social and moral strictures, often assuming an ironic form. An active fantasy life had become more permissible for adults than it had been only a century before. This greater freedom facilitated the prolonged habitation of imaginary worlds, which themselves had become widely discussed by the end of the century.

The double consciousness of the ironic imagination enabled one to shuttle back and forth between actual and imaginary worlds, retaining critical detachment while gratifying a craving for wonder. Such a disenchanted form of enchantment was praised by the editor of the American science fiction magazine *Wonder Stories* in 1930:

> We all yearn to travel to far distant places, to escape for awhile the boredom of the sameness of our lives, and live in a newer and more glorious existence. And we ask ourselves, how can we do that and still remain here, as we must? Then the answer comes—through the imagination. For the half hour or hour that one is immersed in a gripping story of new worlds and new ages, he is really living in that new world and new age. Science fiction then, we believe is a new method of transportation. Only the passage is made instantaneously both ways.[114]

We must acknowledge, however, that residual Victorian prejudices against, and anxieties about, the imagination continued well into the twentieth century. Fantasy fiction, and the sensibility of enchantment more generally, could still be associated with immaturity. The fin-de-siècle discourse of disenchantment marginalized the fantastic as the irrational "other" of reason, and the discourse continued to be perpetuated well into the new century. In interwar Britain and America, this discourse, together with a lingering Protestant discomfort with the pleasures of the imagination, branded the new marketing genre of science fiction as a "guilty pleasure" if not "that crazy Buck Rogers stuff."[115] It is no wonder that science fiction fans could be torn between a desire for enchantment on the one hand and respectability on the other. In 1928, an adult reader of *Amazing Stories Quarterly* expressed his discomfort with the magazine's title in a letter to the editor: "It has always seemed to me a little childlike, for a person of normal intelligence, to wish to be amazed. It is a hard thing to explain, but I have had the feeling myself, when picking up your publication, that I was afraid someone was watching me—like a grown man playing with his small son's toy train."[116] The pervasive rhetoric of disenchantment seemed to outlaw the sentiment of wonder from a properly mature outlook, making it difficult to challenge the alleged opposition between modernity and enchantment.

This situation was exacerbated by the bias of intellectuals against mass culture for much of the century. Many dismissed it as irrelevant at best, irresponsibly escapist at worst. Some disliked mass culture because its consumer-driven popularity challenged their role as self-appointed guardians of cultural standards, and because much of it was foreign to their more traditional education in the classics.[117] And some disliked it because much of it was sensationalistic, formulaic, and vapid. A great deal of it could be complex, self-reflexive, and stimulating as well—but few intellectuals were willing to meet mass culture halfway in the first half of the century. The American critic Edmund Wilson was a representative figure, and he was especially withering about imaginary worlds. Reviewing Lovecraft's stories in 1945, he impatiently derided Lovecraft's pseudo-mythology: "The 'Cthulhu Mythos' and its fabricated authorities seem to have been for him a sort of boy's game which Lovecraft diverted his solitary life."[118] He was even more appalled that adults would form communities dedicated to imaginary worlds: "the Lovecraft cult, I fear, is on even a more infantile level than the Baker Street Irregulars and the cult of Sherlock Holmes."[119] (Wilson never discussed the "cult" dedicated to *The Lord of the Rings*, although he complained that the books themselves were infantile: "Certain people—especially, perhaps, in Britain—have a lifelong appetite for juvenile trash." This from a man who liked to be called "Bunny.")[120]

While imaginary worlds and states of enchantment continued to face an uphill battle for acceptance in the first half of twentieth century, the gradient was less steep than it had been in the nineteenth. In the second half of the century, postmodern critiques of cultural hierarchies helped to further erode elite prejudices against mass culture. The mass media, largely indifferent to critical opinion but sensitive to market forces, continued to provide fantasy fodder, which contributed to gradual changes in critical opinion. Successive generations of critics weaned on mass culture generated a more tolerant, and even appreciative, reception for imaginary worlds and their persistent habitation. By the turn of the twenty-first century, imaginary worlds had gone from being the tiny purview of dedicated fantasy fans to attracting millions of inhabitants all over the world.

Critics of mass culture, however, did raise important questions about the imagination's potential to undermine the necessary critical detachment established by its more ironic form. As we shall explore in subsequent chapters, the double consciousness of the ironic imagination requires ongoing practice to maintain. And even with such practice, there are powerful countervailing forces that make it difficult to retain an ironic stance, especially during periods of personal or social instability.[121] Seductive fantasy can too easily become self-evident reality: the imagined community that is the nation has often been mistaken as preordained and natural, for example, and fascism's success as an interwar political movement was partly beholden to its canny appeals to the imagination alongside its deliberate undermining of critical reason. Even those who pride themselves on being coolly impartial are not immune from the irrational enticements of the imagination. Thomas Mann, for example, was a vocal proponent of the ironic imagination in the first decade of the twentieth century, and yet found himself being swept away by the tide of jingoistic nationalism in Germany during the First World War. (Afterward he repudiated his chauvinistic attitude, but not the importance of an ironic outlook to prevent its recurrence.)[122]

While some worry that virtual reality might eclipse corporeal reality, given the former's ability to gratify desires that are difficult, if not impossible, to obtain in the real world, this is an unlikely scenario. According to Paul Bloom, psychological studies suggest that, "When it comes to nature, we want the real thing; we are uncomfortable with substitutes."[123] In fact, fantasy can lead to an increased appreciation for the real. Readers of *The Lord of the Rings* often comment that an imaginary sojourn among the natural beauties of Middle-earth enhances their esteem for nature and desire to preserve it, and this is but one instance of the fruitful interchanges between imaginary and real worlds that we will explore.

Nevertheless, imaginary worlds can still become confused with reality when the protections of the ironic imagination are undercut—not only by the desires these worlds fulfill, but also by the security they provide. Unlike the messy contingencies of ordinary experience, imaginary worlds, for all their exoticism, are manageable and safe, appealing sanctuaries from life's uncertainties. Jorge Luis Borges brilliantly identified their dangerous attractions in "Tlön, Uqbar, Orbis Tertius" (1940). In this cautionary tale, a secret society creates the imaginary world of Tlön, whose every detail is laid out in a multivolume encyclopedia that took generations to create. Copies of the encyclopedia, as well as invented artifacts of the imaginary world, are seeded throughout the world by a mysterious group in order to persuade people that Tlön is real. Not only do individuals start to believe in the planet's reality, they do so at the expense of ordinary reality. The marvels of Tlön are too beguiling to be withstood; soon, the narrator fears, "The world will be Tlön."[124] He understands that an imaginary world, no matter how estranging and mysterious, will always be more legible and coherent than ordinary experience—and therefore more appealing:

How could the world not fall under the sway of Tlön, how could it not yield to the vast and minutely detailed evidence of an ordered planet? It would be futile to reply that reality is also orderly. Perhaps it is, but orderly in accordance with divine laws (read: "inhuman laws") that we can never quite manage to penetrate. Tlön may well be a labyrinth, but it is a labyrinth forged by men, a labyrinth destined to be deciphered by men.[125]

Lest this sound implausible, the narrator reminds the reader of other systems "with an appearance of order" that evinced a similar fatal attraction: "dialectical materialism, anti-Semitism, Nazism."[126]

The psychoanalyst Robert Lindner provided another admonitory example, this time factual rather than fictional, of how imaginary worlds can delude while delighting, effacing the borders set by the ironic imagination. One of his patients, a brilliant scientist, had created a detailed futuristic universe inspired by the patient's extensive reading of science fiction. He not only documented this universe in great detail but also believed it to be real; without any irony, he spent many waking hours "visiting" it in his imagination to the detriment of his work and personal life.

Lindner's therapeutic strategy was to enter into his patient's fantasy in order to wean him from it. He steeped himself in the world's details, initially from an ironic perspective. But he unexpectedly found himself nearly as captivated by the imaginary world as its creator: "My condition throughout was . . . that of enchantment developing toward obsession."[127] The wish fulfillments provided by this imaginary realm proved too entrancing for Lindner, its wonderfully vast scope permitting him to be "geologist, explorer, astronomer, historian, physicist, adventurer" instead of the sedentary, middle-aged analyst he had become. This beguiling form of enchantment overtook him at a vulnerable period in his life, when he was most susceptible to its blandishments. Soon he was involved in an "intense pursuit of error and inconsistency in the 'records' . . . with the obsessive aim of 'setting them straight,' of 'getting the facts.'"[128] Lindner awoke from his fixation through the intervention of his patient, who had grown uneasy about Lindner's peculiar interest in his world and drew his attention to it: the physician had to heal himself. Lindner's account of "The Jet-Propelled Couch" is a classic example of how the ironic imagination can lose its prophylactic distance from the immersion it makes possible.

The science fiction genre itself has long been alert to the ambiguous enchantments of imaginary worlds. Authors such as Philip K. Dick, William S. Burroughs, and J. G. Ballard have focused on the complex relationship between the imaginary and the real, anticipating many of the questions we currently raise about virtual reality. (Ballard coined the phrase "inner space" to denote "the meeting ground between the inner world of the mind and the outer world of reality.")[129] The theme has been a staple of television series like *Star Trek,* with its accommodating Holodeck, and films like *The Matrix* and *Avatar.*[130] Among the most nuanced reflections are those by Poul Anderson, who justifiably prided himself on the creation of coherent imaginary worlds compatible with current scientific knowledge. Anderson wrote nuts-and-bolts essays on the mechanics of creating plausible imaginary worlds, but several of his own tales were meditations on their uses and abuses.[131] He was familiar with their effects not only as a creator but also as a participant; he was an active member of the Baker Street Irregulars and one of the founders of the Society for Creative Anachronism, which was dedicated to reenacting the Middle Ages (in its most appealing aspects).

In "The Queen of Air and Darkness" (1971), Anderson reflected on humanity's predilection for believing comforting illusions in the face of rational knowledge. Ironic detachment is shown to be relatively helpless in preventing the acceptance of enchanting explanations over more banal, factual interpretations. Take the following exchange about the nature of stars between a biologist named Barbro and a detective named Sherrinford:

> "I suppose it's just something left over from my . . . childhood, but do you know, when I'm under them I can't think of the stars as balls of gas, whose energies have been measured . . . No, they're small and cold and magical; our lives are bound to them; after we die, they whisper to us in our graves." Barbro glanced downward. "I realize that's nonsense."
>
> "Not at all," [Sherrinford] said. "Emotionally, physics may be a worse nonsense. And in the end, you know, after a sufficient number of generations, thought follows feeling. Man is not at heart rational. He could stop believing the stories of science if those no longer felt right."[132]

In the story, which takes place on a distant planet colonized by humans, Barbro's child has been snatched by what the colonists think are the equivalent of elves or fairies, ruled by their eponymous Queen. It transpires that the planet was not devoid of life as the colonists believed when they decided to settle there. The indigenous population, confronted by this invasion of their home, use their telepathic abilities to read and manipulate the colonists' thoughts. By tapping into the colonists' archetypal fears and desires, the creatures hope to enchant the unwelcome interlopers into giving more credence to magic and spells than to science and technology, which will then place the colonists within their power.

Human children, like Barbro's, are kidnapped by the creatures to become changelings, similar to those described in human folklore, anticipating the eventual conversion of the entire earth colony to the weird ways of the planet's natives. "Yes," Sherrinford ponders, "our Queen of Air and Darkness knew well what sights to let lonely people see, what illusions to spin around them from time to time, what songs and legends to set going among them."[133] He wonders if most might even be happier living in the illusions crafted for them. But he rejects that option for himself: "Nevertheless, I believe in choosing one's destiny."[134] Emulating the detective from Baker Street who is his own chosen archetype, Sherrinford foils the natives' schemes. Rational disenchantment, represented by Sherrinford, is thus victorious in the end, although the story concludes with a mournful coda for the intoxicating visions spun by the indigenous creatures for their human victims. And while beguiling enchantments have been shown to be stronger than rational reflections—"Man is not at heart rational"—the viability of disenchanted enchantments aren't ruled out entirely. After all, Sherrinford has consciously modeled his own life on a fictitious character, while firmly upholding the distinction between fantasy and reality.

A similar ambivalence colors "The Saturn Game" (1981), although this later story presents virtual reality in a more positive light than "The Queen of Air and Darkness." In the far future, astronauts on lengthy space voyages stave off boredom by playing "psychodramas" or collective role-playing games. The narrator relates that these first developed in the mid-twentieth century, as a creative alternative to more passive entertainments like television. Role-playing games initially relied solely on the imaginations of their participants, but over time more embodied, three-dimensional virtual realities were produced by computer technologies. Experienced players, however, tended to reject these technologically mediated imaginary worlds for the pleasures of the unaided imagination: "It seemed that, through practice, they had regained the vivid imaginations of their childhoods, and could make anything, or airy nothing itself, into the objects and the worlds they desired."[135]

The astronauts thus inhabited imaginary worlds through their ironic imaginations; unlike the colonists in Anderson's earlier story, they seem able to maintain their critical detachment. When the fictional personae of two astronauts become lovers in their shared virtual world, neither of the real-world astronauts feel the need to come into physical contact with each other: "After all, this was a story they composed about two fictitious characters in a world that never was."[136]

Yet there are moments when the enchantments of the fantasy world have the potential to bleed into and interfere with reality. When three of the astronauts exit their ship to explore one of the moons of Saturn, they are delighted to find that its glaciers and snowdrifts resemble features of the imaginary world they've communally inhabited during their eight-year voyage. But the astronauts' unexpected comfort with the terrain may have led them to be incautious. They miss the signs of an impending avalanche and, in the ensuing disaster, one is killed while the other two are injured.

Anderson is careful not to directly attribute the accident to the psycho-drama. He leaves the real-world effects of the imaginary world ambiguous. And the game clearly has beneficial as well as negative repercussions, which he makes apparent as the two surviving astronauts slip in and out of the shared imaginary world while struggling to secure the safety of their ship. Their fictional world helps them cope with their desperate situation, grant-ing them breathing space and imparting courage and hope: "Without that respite, they would not have gone as long as they did."[137] After their rescue, the astronauts assess the relative effects of the psychodrama on both the accident and their survival. They determine that, while the fantasy world may have led them to misread the realities of their situation initially, they could prevent similar misapprehensions in the future through exerting stricter control over the game and learning to stop if necessary.[138] Indeed, the astronauts had already proven they could do this as they struggled to return to their ship: at that point they were in control of their illusions, using them strategically to survive. Whereas "The Queen of Air and Dark-ness" embraced rational disenchantment, "The Saturn Game" advocated disenchanted enchantment.

If the ironic engagement with imaginary worlds that we will explore in subsequent chapters is any indication, Anderson's second story better cap-tures how many individuals balance the virtual and the real. The double-minded consciousness of the ironic imagination permits greater control over virtual fantasies. This is a skill that must be practiced, but it has been part of the cultural repertoire for well over a century now. With the advent of virtual realities mediated by technology, such as online gaming worlds, the ironic imagination continues to be exercised just as it had been for lit-erary virtual worlds. Most players recognize that such high-tech versions of psychodramas are, in the end, only games. The practical distinction between reality and fantasy appears to be reinforced through the ongoing habitation of virtual spaces, even as philosophical quandaries about their interrela-tions are heightened.

It is true that in virtual realities mediated by technology, the human nervous system can be fooled by cues to react in automatic ways beyond one's conscious control. Ironic self-reflexivity may be powerless against physical reflexivity, especially when much of it occurs at an unconscious level. Further research on the effects of technologically mediated virtual worlds will be necessary before any definitive conclusions can be made. What we can say now is that the self-reflexive practice of living in virtual worlds of the imagination has inculcated the ability to abide in real and vir-tual worlds without confusing the two. The fears of Borges, and the examples of Mann and Lindner, are important reminders that elisions are always pos-sible. But the equally salient examples of millions of pilgrims to imaginary worlds, from the London of Sherlock Holmes to the computer-generated World of Warcraft, suggest that the continued exercise of the ironic imagination permits enchantments that delight without deluding.

We can further refine our analyses of how imaginary worlds became sites of communal and persistent habitation in terms that would be familiar to Sherlock Holmes: motivation, method, and means. As we have seen, a central motivation was the desire for the re-enchantment of the world; a central method was the ironic imagination. The specific means whereby imaginary worlds came to be inhabited by adults are the focus of the next chapter. These included the "spectacular texts" inaugurated by the "New Romance," and new "public spheres of the imagination." Taken together, they established the literary prehistory of virtual reality.

CHAPTER 2

Delight without Delusion

The New Romance, Spectacular Texts, and Public Spheres

As for Mr. Rider Haggard, who really is, or had once, the makings of a perfectly magnificent liar, he is now so afraid of being suspected of genius that when he does tell us anything marvelous, he feels bound to invent a personal reminiscence, and to put it into a footnote as a kind of cowardly corroboration.

—Oscar Wilde

In dreams begin responsibilities.

—Delmore Schwartz

I. AESTHETICISM, THE NEW ROMANCE, AND THE RISE OF IMAGINARY WORLDS

We have seen that by the late nineteenth century individuals found greater freedom to indulge their imaginations, which often took a double minded, ironic form. The imagination was frequently defined as a discrete place in which multiple selves and territories coexisted. It was also at this time that a new type of imagined world—a fantastic yet realist "imaginary world"— evolved to populate this newly defined inner space. Imaginary worlds became conceptual possibilities at this time, but they were also conceptual necessities, called into being as antidotes to disenchantment. Their creators were influenced by two seemingly antagonistic literary camps: Aestheticism (which encompassed different artistic movements, such as Symbolism and

Decadence) and the New Romance of popular literature. Both movements, however, had much in common, and their mutual focus on imaginary worlds established these domains on a new footing. With the concurrent emergence of public spheres of the imagination that encouraged communal participation in their ongoing elaboration, certain textual imaginary worlds were transformed into virtual worlds, anticipating the technologically mediated virtual realities of the late twentieth and early twenty-first centuries.

Of the two literary movements that gave birth to imaginary worlds in the late nineteenth century, Aestheticism is better known. On the whole, it was created by and for the elite and is often associated with the creed "art for art's sake."[1] Aestheticism embraced different political tendencies, ranging from the aristocratic rejection of mass democracy by many of the Decadents, to the varieties of socialism espoused within the English Arts and Crafts movement.[2] There was greater consensus about its core mission, however: aesthetes celebrated the artifices of the imagination as the source of enchantment in a disenchanted world. They judged art an autonomous and spiritual preserve from the rationalism, materialism, and commercialism of modern life. Many sought transcendence in what the poet Charles Baudelaire called "artificial paradises."[3]

J.-K. Huysmans's *Against Nature* (1884), "the breviary of decadence," pursued the logic of this position to its embittered end.[4] Des Esseintes, the novel's wealthy protagonist, rejects the world and retreats to his home, which he has designed as a haven of artificial paradises. Each room stages an imaginary world, and he also surrounds himself with luxurious books, rare perfumes, exotic pets, and glittering jewels, all intoxicants to his imagination. Within this hermetic sanctuary from the disappointments of a disenchanted modernity, Des Esseintes literally inhabits his imagination. He prefers virtual geographies to actual ones:

> Travel, indeed, struck him as being a waste of time, since he believed that the imagination could provide a more-than-adequate substitute for the vulgar reality of actual experience ... one can easily enjoy ... imaginary pleasures similar in all respects to the pleasures of reality; no doubt, for instance, that anyone can go on long voyages of exploration sitting by the fire ... by dipping into some book describing travels in distant lands.[5]

Against Nature was partly a satire on aesthetic extremism; Des Esseintes carried the aesthetes' inversion of life and art to its logical if bizarre conclusions, such as taking nutriments artificially through an enema. But Huysmans, like many other aesthetes, believed artifice provided a spiritual recourse in a secularizing age for "the Christian who doubts ... the unbeliever who would fain believe."[6]

Aestheticism thus accorded with Max Weber's claim that art would provide a compensatory sphere to the "iron cage" of rationalized and bureaucratized modernity: "Art becomes a cosmos of more and more consciously grasped independent values which exist in their own right. Art . . . provides a *salvation* from the routines of everyday life, and especially from the increasing pressures of theoretical and practical rationalism."[7] Like Weber, many contemporary thinkers interpreted the aesthetes' artificial paradises as a characteristic response to modern disenchantment: the rational was countered by the irrational, materialism by sensualism, secularism by spiritualism, and populism by elitism. Enchantment was cast as the opposite of disenchantment, an understandable but atavistic response to the triumph of modernity.

Yet there was another literary response to the discourse of disenchantment that explicitly opposed this binary logic and attempted to reconcile the rational and secular tenets of modernity with enchantment. Because it appeared within mass culture, this response was met with condescension by numerous critics, but the imaginary worlds it produced were popular with the public throughout Europe and America. It was a literary movement I call the "New Romance," following contemporary usage of the phrase.[8] The New Romance arose in Britain in the 1880s, with the expressed intention of combining the objective style of realism with the fantastic content of romance.[9] To many readers, the innovative works by Robert Louis Stevenson, H. Rider Haggard, Rudyard Kipling, Arthur Conan Doyle, Bram Stoker and others redressed the pessimistic outlook of literary realism and the general reductivism of scientific naturalism during the last third of the century. "The world is disenchanted," admitted the author and critic Andrew Lang in an 1887 sonnet dedicated to Haggard's recently published *She*. But, he continued, it could become re-enchanted through the sort of imaginative worlds exemplified by Haggard's epic.[10] Another prominent critic, W. E. Henley, promoted both Haggard's *King Solomon's Mines* (1885) and *She*, observing that, "just as it was thoroughly accepted that there were no more stories to be told, that romance was utterly dried up, and that analysis of character . . . was the only thing in fiction attractive to the public, down there came upon us a whole horde of Zulu divinities and the sempiternal queens of beauty in the caves of Kor."[11] The first salvo of the New Romance, Stevenson's *Treasure Island* (1883), might have appeared an anomaly, a work of romantic adventure written to please the sensibilities of adults as well as children, if it weren't for the enormous success of Haggard's two novels that immediately followed. Taken together, critics felt that a new literary trend had emerged, and their opinions were confirmed by the subsequent publication of many other works in the same mode. Writing in 1892, the critic George Saintsbury noted, "we have revived the romance . . . on a scale which a whole generation had not seen. We have wound ourselves up to something like the pitch of Romantics of sixty or seventy years ago."[12]

But this pitch was a distinctively new note in literature, not simply a refrain from the operatic extravagances of gothic romances of the past. The New Romance was distinguished by its appropriation of realist techniques for its expressions of the fantastic, allowing it to command the attention of adults schooled in scientific naturalism yet yearning for the marvelous. A contemporary reviewer of Haggard's novels, for example, singled out his "hybrid species of invention—jolting you at every step from the naturalistic to the fantastic and back again."[13] Another reviewer called *She* "a marvelously realistic tale of fantastic adventures," and *Blackwood's Edinburgh Magazine* praised its author as "the avatar of the old story-teller, with a flavour of the nineteenth century and scientific explanation."[14] Haggard, explained *The Scots Observer*, "describes his fabulous action with a realistic minuteness and full relative truth."[15] This combination of naturalistic style and fantastic content defined the New Romance as a whole, according to another critic: "The methods of the new *raconteur* are not refined . . . His object is to work in as many marvels as possible, with so many realities as to make the whole look as if it might have been."[16] The merger of these two modes inspired heated debates in the late 1880s about the relative merits of "Realism and Romance," attracting wide publicity to the New Romance. According to Lang, "a new Battle of the Books is being fought."[17]

Regardless of the positions writers took in the debate, their essays drew attention to the pervasive climate of intellectual disenchantment that seemed to preclude the existence of marvels and wonders in everyday life. One critic wondered if, in a world governed by scientific rationality, "we shall ever find anything really marvelous, anything which will deflect the whole current of human thought, or even make us question the accuracy of what we know. We doubt it greatly. One can dream of such things."[18] The imagination would be the source for modern enchantment, just as it had been for the tiny coterie of the early romantics, although the writers of the New Romance emphasized analysis as much as fancy, the factual no less than the transcendental. In a culture that valued positivism and materialism, even the enchantments of the imagination required grounding in realism. *King Solomon's Mines,* according to a critic, was popular because it met that criterion, addressing modern readers' demands "that the lust of wonder should be fully and, so to speak, honestly satiated." Previous generations had been satisfied with tales of the supernatural or chivalric romances, but "their descendants, unable to believe in magic . . . seek a similar gratification in discovery—scientific, antiquarian, or geographical."[19] The modern cartographer of imaginary worlds was advised to steer a fine course between the Scylla of fantasy and the Charybides of realism, or risk alienating his or her audience. As Haggard himself reflected, "adventure in this constricted world of ours is a limited quality, and imagination, after all, is hemmed in by deductions from experience. When we try to travel beyond these the results become so unfamiliar that they are apt to lack interest to the ordinary mind . . . The lines which close in the kingdom of romance are very narrow."[20]

By delimiting the "kingdom of romance" to an autonomous sphere of the imagination, adults were enabled to actively engage in the pretense that the marvels described were real, while simultaneously acknowledging this mental sleight of hand. The novels created a space where mature readers were authorized to play. Their immersion in these fantastic worlds was enhanced because the authors of the New Romance stressed plot alongside verisimilitude, eschewing the estrangements of more overt metafictions and the implausible contrivances of gothic and sensationalist fictions. Romances, Stevenson argued, were distinguished from other forms of fiction by their emphasis on a compelling narrative, which was the most powerful element in captivating readers: "It is not character but incident that woos us out of our reserve. Then we forget characters and plunge into the story without reserve—then we are reading romance."[21]

The New Romance's focus on linear narratives full of fantastic incidents, often supported by "paratexts" (footnotes, charts, appendices, photographs, etc.) connoting scientific objectivity, more than offset the texts' sly ironies, at least in terms of capturing and maintaining the reader's attention.[22] Nevertheless, experienced readers knew they were reading an extravagant fiction even as they gave themselves over to it wholeheartedly. In this respect, these works were akin to the "hoaxes" of American popular culture perpetrated by P. T. Barnum and others earlier in the century, their scholarly paraphernalia the equivalent of a trickster's props.

The authors of the New Romance cited earlier models for the art of elaborating a convincing literary hoax, especially the works of Edgar Allan Poe and Jules Verne. Both authors were acclaimed by Stevenson, Haggard, Conan Doyle, and others for their innovations in making the fantastic plausible through the use of scientific detail, which imparted such apparent authenticity to the narratives that some readers believed them to be real.[23] (In turn, some works of the New Romance also fooled naïve or less experienced readers: Haggard reported receiving a fair amount of correspondence from those who believed that *King Solomon's Mines* was true, just as Conan Doyle received similar letters about Sherlock Holmes.)[24]

Poe had been fascinated by hoaxes, exposing some while perpetuating his own literary versions.[25] These relied on minute, corroborative details drawn from nonfictional sources, as well as "ingenuity, audacity, *nonchalance*"—the elements he cited in his 1843 jocular essay on hoaxes, "Diddling Considered as One of the Exact Sciences."[26] He presented a realistic account of a balloon journey across the Atlantic that fooled some readers into believing it genuine; others were fooled into believing that *The Narrative of Arthur Gordon Pym* (1838) was what it professed to be, a nonfiction account of harrowing sea-voyages by Pym himself.[27] In this work, Poe's name does not appear on the title page and is only referred to briefly in the preface, which is signed "A. G. Pym." Pym thanks a "Mr. Poe, lately editor of the *Southern Literary Messenger*," for his advice in preparing the manuscript. (Pym adds that he previously allowed Poe to publish a portion of his adventures "under the garb of fiction," because he didn't think his fantastic account would be believed. Because so many took it to be true, Pym was emboldened to publish the whole "true" narrative himself. The ironic reversals used are wonderful.) Poe's employment of realistic detail to make the fantastic events he relates not merely plausible but "actual"—in the sense of a hoax meant to be taken as real—was a departure from the preceding gothic mode of narration. As Adam Roberts noted, "When Mary Shelley writes the fantastic elements of *Frankenstein,* she adopts a strained, elevated gothic sublime tone of voice; when Poe writes about the fantastic [in "Hans Pfaall"] he does so in as matter-of-fact a manner as he can."[28]

Poe's deliberate blurring of the line between scientific fact and imaginative fantasy was in turn admired by Jules Verne. He acknowledged that his first book, *Five Weeks in a Balloon* (1863) had been influenced by Poe's merging of wild invention and empirical detail.[29] Verne partially discharged his debt to Poe by writing an affectionate essay about his life and works, including praise for his literary hoaxes.[30] He also wrote a sequel to Pym's adventures, *An Antarctic Mystery* (1897), treating Poe's novel as if it were nonfiction, just as Pym claimed it to be.

Verne's "extraordinary voyages" of the 1860s and after continued Poe's melding of the marvelous and the documentary and were important influences on the New Romance. The lavish editions issued by Verne's publisher Hetzel included maps, charts, and footnotes as well as numerous full-page illustrations.[31] These sumptuous volumes lacked the photographs that were to impart a greater degree of realism to many of the works of the New Romance. Nevertheless, from their colorful bindings to their graphic interiors, they exuded a theatrical quality that framed the narratives as artificial worlds unto themselves. (See figures 2.1 and 2.2) The evident materiality of the Hetzel editions underscored the notion that the reader was entering into a domain of the imagination distinct from the everyday, which in turn facilitated the ironic belief in the fantastic adventures that Verne documented with such scientific precision. In his autobiography, Jean-Paul Sartre recalled how the spectacular nature of the Hetzel editions he read as a child transported him to an autonomous world of the imagination:

I adored the works in the Hetzel series, little theatres whose red cover with gold tassels represented the curtain; the gilt edges were the footlights. I owe to these magic boxes . . . my first encounters with Beauty. When I opened them, I forgot about everything. Was that reading? No, but it was death by ecstasy. From my annihilation there immediately sprang up natives armed with spears, the bush, an explorer with a white helmet. I was *vision,* I poured forth light . . . on Phileas Fogg's sideburns. Freed from himself at last, the little wonder became pure wonderment.[32]

Beauty and wonder were also the desiderata of the aesthetes, and many hailed Poe, and at times Verne, as important influences. But unlike the writers of the New Romance, the aesthetes were highly ambivalent about modern science, empiricism, and "ratiocination." [33] They also were ambivalent about mass culture, including the popular fiction of the New Romance. When they entertained consumer culture, it was for their own artistic purposes. Taking a cue from contemporary advertisers, they viewed the self as a site of display and truth as delightful pretense.[34] But theirs was an aristocratic assimilation

Figure 2.1 Hetzel edition of Jules Verne's *Vingt Mille Lieues sous les Mers.* Jean-Paul Sartre remembered these editions as "little theatres whose red cover with gold tassels represented the curtain; the gilt edges were the footlights. I owe to these magic boxes . . . my first encounters with Beauty."

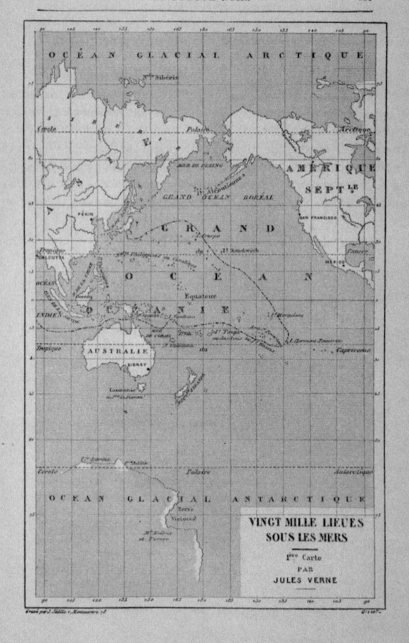

Figure 2.2 Map from the Hetzel edition of Jules Verne's *Vingt Mille Lieues sous les Mers*.

of the consumerist ethos that transmuted it into aesthetic self-fashioning. When it came to the actual products of mass culture, many aesthetes shivered in distaste; for them, commodity culture represented the detritus of a disenchanted world. Conversely, numerous proponents of the New Romance enjoyed mass culture and disparaged Aestheticism as elite, effete, and degenerate.[35] Partisans of each movement sniped at one other. Oscar Wilde complained that writers of the New Romance went too far in tethering their fantasies to scientific detail: "Facts are not merely finding a footing-place in history, but they are usurping the domain of Fancy, and have invaded the kingdom of Romance. Their chilling touch is everywhere."[36] In turn, Andrew Lang defended the New Romance creed as "stories told for stories sake"—a clear rejoinder to the aesthete's credo of "art for art's sake."[37]

Despite these differences, the two literary movements shared important elements in common.[38] Like the aesthetes, the writers of the New Romance fashioned their imaginary worlds as wellsprings of wonder. And like the aesthetes, these writers found that such worlds could be inhabited ironically: both camps praised Poe's efforts to capture the marvelous through self-conscious artifice.[39] Several writers straddled both literary movements. Huysmans, for example, did not share his fellow aesthetes' disdain for realist fiction; he accepted the New Romance writers' aim of combining the marvelous and the empirical, resulting in what he called a "supernatural realism" or a "spiritual naturalism."[40] Stevenson, a defender of popular literature, the common reader, and the New Romance, nevertheless dressed himself (and at times his prose) in a dandy's raiment, appearing to some as a precious aesthete, to others a hardworking hack. Using the language of sensory stimulation and aesthetic autonomy favored by the aesthetes, he described how reading popular fiction could transport readers into a separate sphere of consciousness:

> The process itself should be absorbing and voluptuous; we should gloat over a book, be wrapt clear out of ourselves, and rise from the perusal, our mind filled with the busiest, kaleidoscopic dance of images, incapable of sleep or of continuous thought. The words, if the book be eloquent, should run thenceforward in our ears like the noise of breakers, or the story, if it be a story, repeat itself in a thousand coloured pictures to the eye. It was for this last pleasure that we read so closely and loved our books so dearly in the bright troubled period of our boyhood.[41]

Other authors of the New Romance, as well as those influenced by it, signaled that they too had affinities with Aestheticism and its pursuit of artificial paradises. Conan Doyle limned Sherlock Holmes as an aesthete as well as a man of action. Lovecraft, self-described rationalist and materialist, intended his realist tales of "cosmic fear" to evoke the enchanting sensations cultivated by the aesthetes. He declared that he and several of his fellow writers for the pulp *Weird Tales* "belong to the wholly aesthete-pagan tradition of Keats, Poe, Swinburne, Walter Pater, Oscar Wilde, Baudelaire ... Art for art's sake only is our motto."[42] Tolkien too was influenced by Aestheticism, particularly that of the Pre-Raphaelites, in both his paintings and writings.[43] He combined deep Catholic convictions with the aesthetes' creed of art for art's sake. As we shall see, he tried to reconcile the apparent tensions between Catholicism and Aestheticism by envisioning God as the supreme Artist, and individuals as expressing the divine through their role as "sub-creators." This reconciliation appealed to the equally narrative-besotted C. S. Lewis. He too had been torn between the aesthetes' celebration of endless artifice and a craving for religious certitude. Writing to a correspondent about Tolkien's "imaginary world" and "private mythology," Lewis acclaimed Tolkien's solution, because "private worlds have hitherto been mainly the work of decadents or, at least, mere aesthetes. This is the private world of a Christian. He is a very great man."[44]

Lewis was right: many creators of imaginary worlds shared the aesthetes' more secular understanding of life as artifice, and their celebration of provisional narratives as the source of meaning in the modern age. E. R. Eddison is a representative example. A British civil servant, he wrote *The Worm Ouroboros* (1922) and several other fantasies; Tolkien declared that Eddison was "the greatest and most convincing writer of 'invented worlds' that I have read."[45] An enthusiast of Nietzsche, Théophile Gautier, and Marcel Proust, Eddison insisted, "I am no dogmatist, being very certain that Truth is protean, & her shapes or dresses infinite, & that all I can ever hope to get a glimpse of is her shape for *me*."[46] It was this attitude, as well as Eddison's preference for paganism over Christianity, which led Tolkien to qualify his praise for Eddison's imaginary worlds: "Corrupted by an evil and indeed silly 'philosophy,' he was coming to admire, more and more, arrogance and cruelty."[47]

In the following section we shall examine several "spectacular texts" of the New Romance and the marketing genre of science fiction that developed from it, to see how their rhetorical strategies and physical layouts facilitated imaginative immersion and ironic distance. Like the "artificial paradises" of the aesthetes, the imaginary worlds of the New Romance and the marketing genres it influenced were autonomous habitations that provided a refuge from a disenchanted modernity. Unlike those of the aesthetes, however, the worlds of the New Romance were usually receptive to the rational, scientific, and consumerist trends of modernity. Readers never simply "escaped" by turning to these worlds. Instead, they found new ways to think about modernity and about themselves.

II. SPECTACULAR TEXTS IN AN AGE OF THE SPECTACLE

Contemporaries cited Stevenson's 1883 *Treasure Island* as inaugurating the New Romance; Haggard recalled that it inspired him to write *King Solomon's Mines*, which appeared two years later. Both novels were published with elaborately detailed, fold-out maps. Publishers' artifices such as these were critical to the project of the New Romance. Metonymically, the maps signaled that the text itself was to be taken as a "geography of the imagination," subject to imaginative habitation. More prosaically, they underlined the author's commitment to literary realism, no matter how fantastic the narrative.

Stevenson's map began as a spontaneous sketch he did in the course of improvising his story for a young friend. He later confessed that the more "realistic" map that was eventually published lacked the naïveté he associated with the narrative's genesis:

> It is one thing to draw a map at random, set a scale in one corner of it at a venture, and write up a story to the measurements. It is quite another to have to examine a whole book, make an inventory of all the allusions contained in it, and with a pair of compasses, painfully design a map to suit the data. I did it, and the map was drawn again in my father's office, with embellishments of blowing whales and sailing ships, and my father himself brought into service a knack he had of various writing, and elaborately forged the signature of Captain Flint, and the sailing directions of Billy Bones. But somehow it was never "Treasure Island" to me.[48]

The engineer's exactitude that went into the creation of the later map was important, however, in transforming the tale from yet another adventurous romance into a naturalistic account of the fabulous. (See figure 2.3) While missing the innocence of his original map, Stevenson did perceive the corresponding benefit of accuracy for imaginary worlds and commended it to aspiring writers. He admitted that he himself even resorted to an atlas: "The author must know his countryside, whether real or imaginary, like his hand; the distances, the points of the compass, the place of the sun's rising, the behavior of the moon, should all be beyond cavil."[49] The built environment of Stevenson's island was laden with pirates' treasure, but also with the rational tropes of science, the latter facilitating ironic "belief" in the former.

Other writers of the New Romance would follow Stevenson (and important predecessors like Poe and Verne) in creating enchanting worlds of the imagination distinguished by the indexical idioms of scientific objectivity. Maps in particular were important for establishing the imaginary world as a virtual space consistent in all its details. Like Stevenson, Tolkien noted

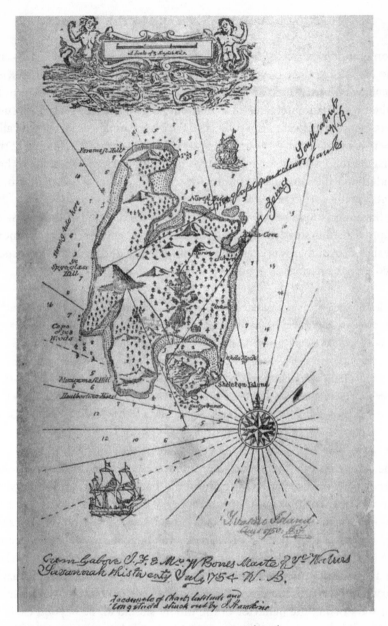

Figure 2.3 Map from Robert Louis Stevenson's *Treasure Island* (1883).

that in writing his epic, "I wisely started with a map, and made the story fit (generally with meticulous care for distances). The other way about lands one in confusions and impossibilities."[50] Similarly, when E. R. Eddison wrote *The Worm Ouroboros,* he made wax reliefs to guide him in the literary delineation of his imaginary world. When the book was published in 1922, some readers were disturbed by the absence of maps in the volume itself (which did contain a lengthy "historical" chronology), especially since they intuited that Eddison's imaginary world was internally consistent: maps would have added to the rational glamour they were seeking. Gerald R. Hayes, one of Eddison's professional colleagues, informed readers of *Civil Service Arts Magazine* in 1930 that he had established conclusively that Eddison's fantastic world was as empirically grounded as any survey commissioned by Whitehall:

> Guided only by the internal evidence, I constructed a series of maps, both on small scales, and large enough to show all the details. Everything fell in happily and even latitudes were available from references to stars. Some time after, I found that the author, with characteristic thoroughness, had made relief models in wax when planning his book. The agreement of my maps with these, proved the realism of his scenes.[51]

(Hayes sent a copy of one of his maps to C. S. Lewis, who replied that he was entranced by it: "I have a passion for imaginary maps & look forward to hours of amusement with yours.")[52] Three American readers unwittingly emulated Hayes in 1932 when they too reconstructed a map from the details in Eddison's novel. They sent Eddison their "cartographic conception of Demonland and Impland," noting that it had been a diverting game: "It was fun! Notes were taken, roughs were drawn and redrawn, directions became the point of bitter argument, distances were bandied, compromises effected—and finally the maps were finished."[53] Their communal practice transformed the imaginary world into a virtual one that they could inhabit together. Hilaire Belloc confessed to a similar impression of the world's habitability when he reviewed the novel: "Its landscapes are magnificent. One lives in it."[54]

Writers of the New Romance were assisted in their efforts at fantastic realism by new printing technologies of the 1880s, such as half-tone lithography. This process permitted the reproduction of photographs and detailed drawings containing fine gradations of shadow and tone. According to Neil Harris, half-tone lithography rendered illustrations more "objective" than earlier forms of lithography and wood-cuts, which drew attention to the hand of the individual artist. With the half-tone improvement, "the illusion of seeing an actual scene, or receiving an objective record of such a scene, was immeasurably enhanced."[55] The illusion of objectivity was also induced through other paratextual elements traditionally associated with scholarship, such as footnotes, glossaries, and appendices. Instances of the New Romance that combined these diverse elements deserve to be called "spectacular texts" for the contemporary "Society of the Spectacle," presenting empirically detailed imaginary worlds appealing to adults no less than children.[56]

H. Rider Haggard's *She* (1887) is an exemplary spectacular text. He had taken great pains with the map for his earlier book *King Solomon's Mines*, commissioning Agnes Barber to fabricate a weathered map that looked as if it had been etched in blood on linen.[57] (See figure 2.4) Many were fooled into thinking the map real, which encouraged Haggard to create an even more elaborate set of visual and verbal deceptions for *She*. The front matter contains photographs—a contemporary indicia of truth—of a "Facsimile of the Sherd of Amenartas," Haggard's invented potsherd that provides the protagonists with key information for their fantastic quest in search of She-Who-Must-Be-Obeyed. (See figure 2.5) Haggard had Barber create an actual sherd, and then had two scholars compose the classical Greek, Latin, and Old English translations inscribed on it, to ensure the texts' accuracy. (See figure 2.6) (In addition to being visible in the photos of the sherd, these inscriptions were also presented typographically within the text, figure 2.7) When Haggard showed the completed sherd to the antiquarian Sir John Evans, Evans thought it would make an effective hoax: "All I can say is that it might possibly have been forged."[58]

Haggard also used footnotes throughout the work, attributed to two distinct authors. The book begins with the framing device of an introduction by an "Editor" (presumably Haggard, as it is claimed that the Editor has written an earlier "Central African adventure"). The Editor receives a manuscript from "L. Horace Holly," who insists that his text is "a real African adventure."[59] The rest of the novel consists of this manuscript, with footnotes by either the "Editor" or "L. H. H." The footnotes elaborate on the events of the novel or provide factual support or emendations to statements in the text. (Thus one early footnote, attributed to "L. H. H.," begins "The Kallikrates here referred to by my friend was a Spartan, spoken of by Herodotus [Herod. Ix.72] as being remarkable for his beauty. He fell at the glorious battle of Plataea [September 22, B. C. 479].")[60]

There are several remarkable aspects about these footnotes. Haggard uses them extensively, to drive home the effect intended by his frontispiece: *She* is an objective account of a genuine adventure. However, the very prominence of sober footnotes in such a fanciful narrative, like the incredible elaboration of the sherd, has the opposite (and intended) bathetic effect—to remind the reader again and again that the text is a fiction. At the same time, this estranging technique is undercut by having two authors write the footnotes. The reader assumes that Holly is fictitious, but is not sure about the Editor, who is implied to be Haggard; and the Editor's notes indicate he accepts the reality of Holly's manuscript. Haggard has been criticized for being a poor stylist, but his techniques for inducing a double-minded consciousness in the reader are brilliant. While other novelists might use framing devices, or illustrations, or occasional footnotes, Haggard combined them all in a spectacular package, facilitating imaginative immersion while encouraging ironic detachment.

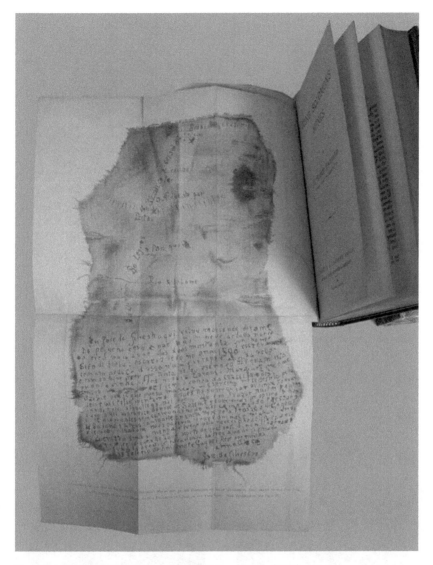

Figure 2.4 Map from H. Rider Haggard's *King Solomon's Mines* (1885).
Photo by J. P. Morgan. Reproduced by permission of the Heritage Bookshop.

There is little doubt that Haggard's use of irony in *She* was intentional, although this is an aspect that critics tend to underplay or ignore. Contemporary readers were often aware of it, however. His friend Andrew Lang read a draft of *She* and suggested Haggard prune some of the facetious remarks in the citations: "I'm sure the note about a monograph on Ayesha's Greek pronunciation for the use of public schools, will show the Public you are laughing—a thing I can never help doing, and the B[ritish] P[ublic] hate it."[61] Haggard's ironic self-parody encouraged others to write parodies and pastiches of his works, which would also hold true for Conan Doyle

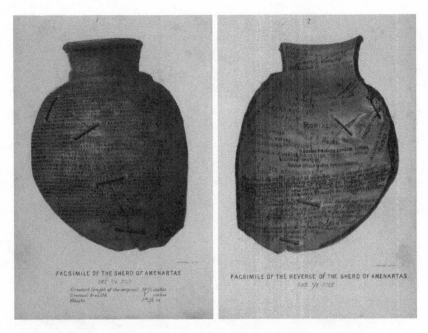

Figure 2.5 Front matter photos of the "Sherd of Amenartas," *She* (1887).

Figure 2.6 Agnes Barber's "Sherd of Amenartas," commissioned by H. Rider Haggard for use in *She*.
Reproduced by permission of the Norfolk Museums & Archaeology Service.

when he created Sherlock Holmes.[62] Through such affectionate tributes an imaginary world could become ubiquitous and hence autonomous from its original source. It assumed a virtual life of its own that transcended any single author or reader's interpretation of it.

Lang and Walter Herries Pollock wrote an anonymous parody of *She*, titled *He*, also published in 1887. (The cover proclaims the book is "by the author of *It*.") The text directed attention to the ironic, realist, and spectacular aspects of Haggard's work. For example, paralleling the footnotes by two authors in *She*, there is throughout *He* a running dialogue in footnotes between the "PUBLISHER" and the "EDITOR" about the realist aspects of such a fantastic narrative, such as the lengthy translations from ancient Greek and Latin:

Don't you think this is a little dull? The public don't care about dead languages.

—PUBLISHER.

Story can't possibly go on without it, as you'll see. You *must* have something like this in a romance. Look at Poe's cypher in the *Gold Beetle*, and the chart in *Treasure Island*, and the Portuguese scroll in *King Solomon's Mines*.

—ED.[63]

Highlighting the spectacular nature of the new mass-consumer society and its role in fostering an ironic imagination among the public, the two discuss ways to sell advertising within the story. Here is an example of one such footnote exchange, instigated by the following line of the story:

The wine was procured, as I would advise every African traveler to do, from Messrs.———[1]

[1]. Messrs. Who? Printers in a hurry.

—PUBLISHER

Suppressed the name. Messrs.———gave an impolite response to our suggestions as to mutual arrangements.

—ED.[64]

He has many other references to advertising. In fact, the entire plot revolves on an elaborate confidence trick, in which a man claiming to be an ancient wizard (the "He" of the title) bilks the female versions of Holly and Leo, Polly and Leonora, out of their money. The satire also mocks the typographical tricks Haggard employed in *She*, once again drawing attention to the spectacular nature of that text and situating it within the context of the modern society of the spectacle. (See figure 2.8)

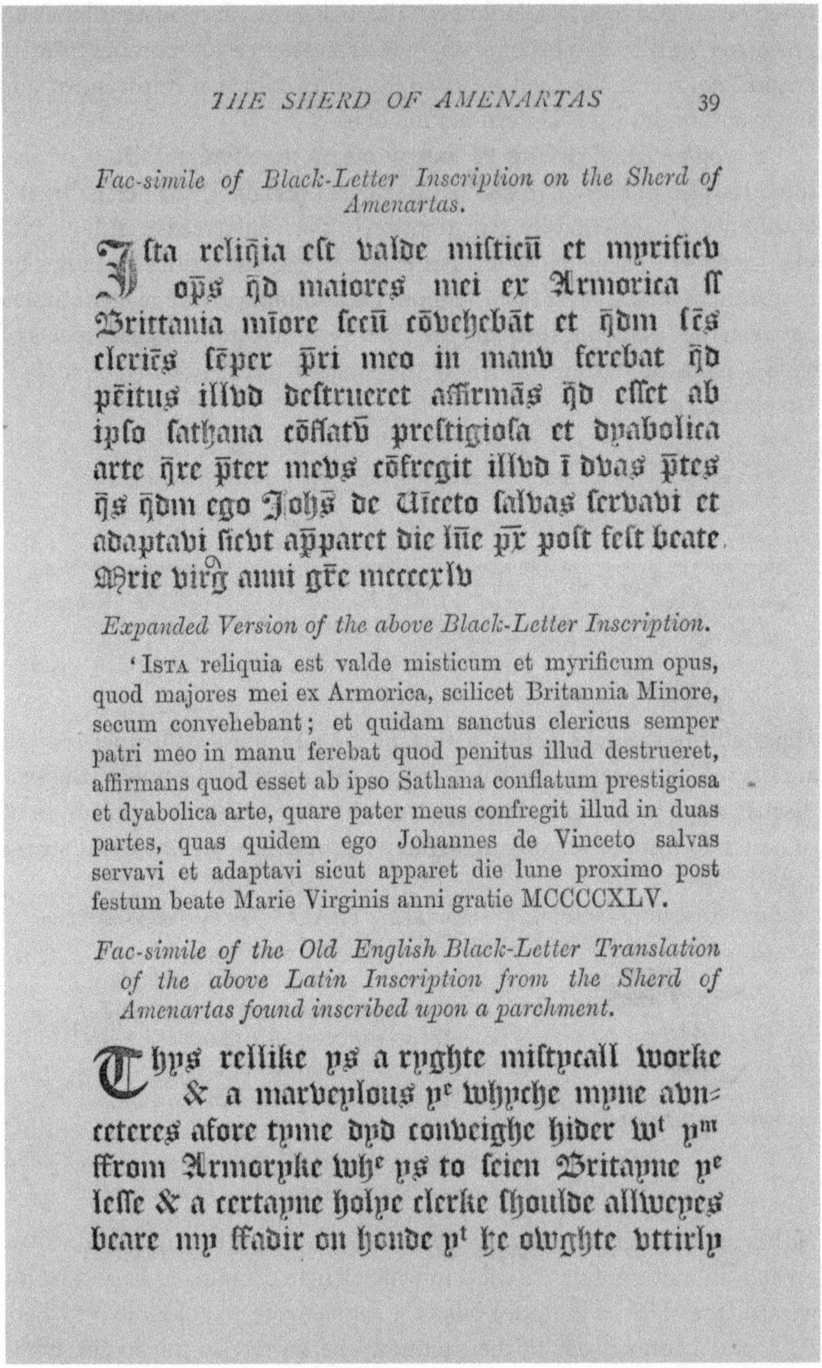

Fac-simile of Black-Letter Inscription on the Sherd of Amenartas.

Ista reliqia est valde misticū et myrificu ops q̄d maiores mei ex Armorica ſſ Brittania miore secū cōvehebāt et q̄dm ſc̄s clerīc̄s ſc̄per p̄ri meo in manu ferebat q̄d p̄itus illud destrueret affirmās q̄d esset ab ipso sathana cōſſatu prestigiosa et dyabolica arte q̄re p̄ter mevs cōfregit illud ī dvas p̄tes q̄s q̄dm ego Johꝫ de Uiceto salvas servavi et adaptavi sicut apparet die lūe p̄r post feſt beate Marie virg̃ anni g̃c̄e mccccxlv

Expanded Version of the above Black-Letter Inscription.

'Ista reliquia est valde misticum et myrificum opus, quod majores mei ex Armorica, scilicet Britannia Minore, secum convehebant; et quidam sanctus clericus semper patri meo in manu ferebat quod penitus illud destrueret, affirmans quod esset ab ipso Sathana conflatum prestigiosa et dyabolica arte, quare pater meus confregit illud in duas partes, quas quidem ego Johannes de Vinceto salvas servavi et adaptavi sicut apparet die lune proximo post festum beate Marie Virginis anni gratie MCCCCXLV.

Fac-simile of the Old English Black-Letter Translation of the above Latin Inscription from the Sherd of Amenartas found inscribed upon a parchment.

Thys rellike ys a ryghte mistycall worke & a marveylous p^e whyche myne aun= ceteres afore tyme dyd conveighe hider w^t y^m ffrom Armoryke whᵉ ys to scien Britayne p^e lesse & a certayne holpe clerke shoulde allweyes beare my ffadir on honde p^t he owghte vttirly

Figure 2.7 Transcript of medieval black letter inscription on "Sherd of Amenartas" in *She*.

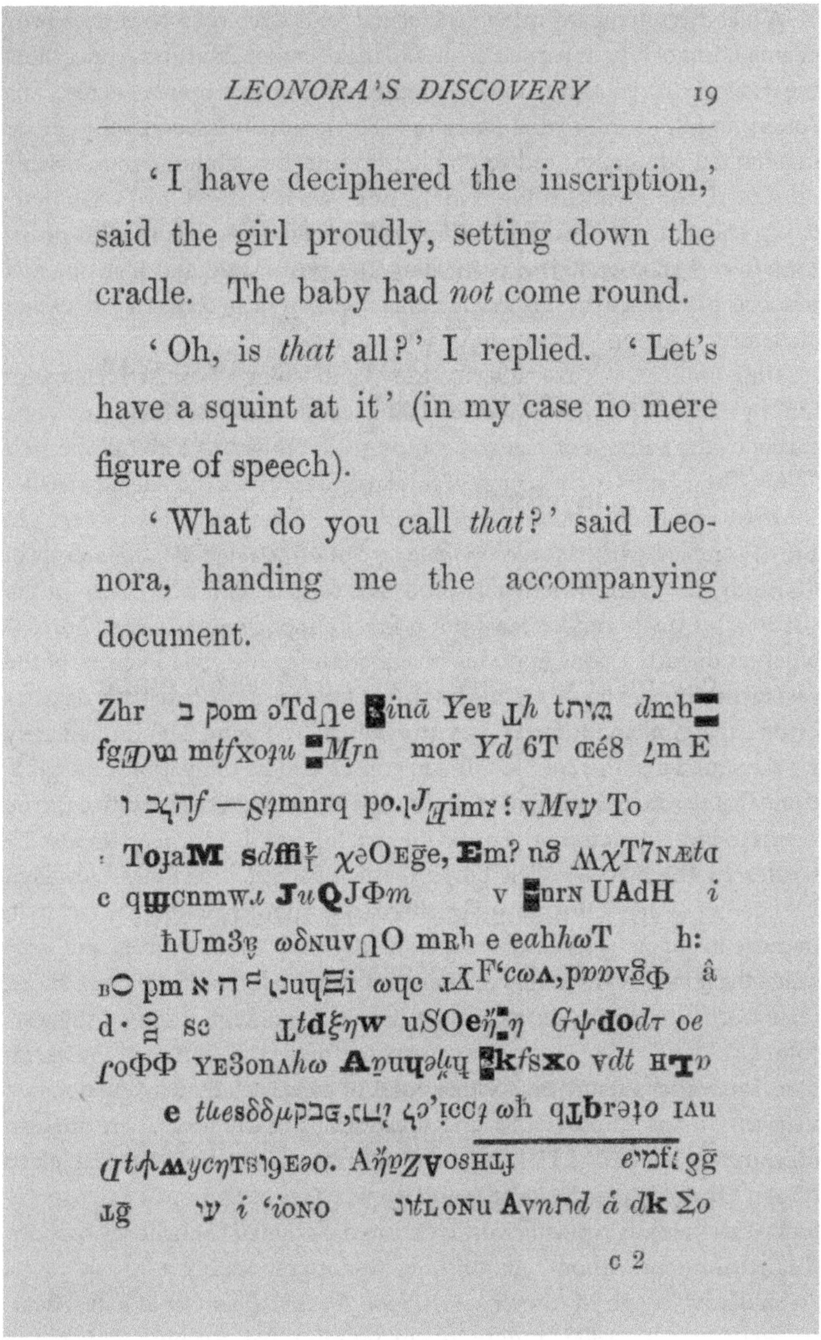

'I have deciphered the inscription,' said the girl proudly, setting down the cradle. The baby had *not* come round.

'Oh, is *that* all?' I replied. 'Let's have a squint at it' (in my case no mere figure of speech).

'What do you call *that*?' said Leonora, handing me the accompanying document.

Zhr ⊐ ꝓom oTd∩e ▪inā Yeʋ Ɪh tⁿⴼ⟨ dmb▪
fg⊞ꟺ mt∫xoʈu ▪M∫n   mor Yd 6T œé8 ꞮmE

⟩ ⵣꬵ∫ —S∤mnrq po.⎸J⊞imⴽ∶ vMvⲩ To

ᛙ Toja▪ sd∯∮ꞏⵡ χ∂OEḡe, ▪m? n⫰ ⋀⋀χT7ɴæta
c q⬛cnmw⟋ **J**u**Q**J⏀m   v ▪nⴽɴ UAdH   *i*

hUm3ꞑ ⍵δꝧuv∩O mʀh e eahhωT   h∶

ᴮᴑ pm א ꞓ Ꞓ ⎹꙰uq⨱i ⍵꬗c ꞮχF‘cωʌ,pⲩⲩⲩ⫰⏀ â

d ꞏ ⟨∘ sc   Ɪtdξ∩w uSOeꞧ꞊∩ G𝜓do dⴛ oe

ꝓoⲫⲫ ⲩE3onʌhω **A**ⲩu𝜂∂ꟿ ▪k∫s⨯o vdt Hꞇⲩ

e tℓesδδμꝓ⊐ɢ,꞊u∤ ꞡ∘’ɪcc∤ ⍵h q꞊brꙩo Ɪʌu

⨗t⨼⋀⋀yc∩Tꜱ⁊9E∂o. A𝜂ꞷZꝞosʜꞺ   e⁊∩∫ꞎ ꝯḡ

Ɪḡ   ’ⲩ *i* ‘ꞽoɴo   Ꞽꞎ꞉LoNu Avnꝧd *á* d**k** Σo

Figure 2.8 Parody of the typographical tricks in *She* in Andrew Lang and Walter Herries Pollock's satire *He* (1887).

While there are many other spectacular texts that could be cited, a brief examination of four in particular should make earlier assertions concerning the ironic, artificial, and rational elements of these texts more concrete. The American John Uri Lloyd's *Etidorpha* (1895), initially issued by the author in a limited edition, proved so popular it went through numerous lavishly illustrated, commercial editions in the next two decades. Lloyd was a practicing scientist who was dismayed by the narrow materialism of his peers. *Etidorpha* was intended to re-enchant the positivistic and instrumental practice of science by illustrating the metaphysical concerns of earlier alchemists and non-Western approaches to nature.

The complex frame narrative has Lloyd publishing a manuscript left with him by a "Mr. Drury," who himself had been entrusted with it many years earlier by the narrator of a fantastic journey into the earth who calls himself "I-Am-The-Man." (In the course of this latter narrative the reader learns that the earth is actually a hollow sphere harboring a multitude of wonders.) In Lloyd's preface, which is accompanied by a photograph that is apparently of his study, he states "whether I stood face to face with Mr. Drury in the shadows of this room, or have but a fanciful conception of his figure,—whether the artist drew upon his imagination for the vivid likeness of the several personages figured in the book that follows, or from reliable data has given us facsimiles authentic,—is immaterial."[65] (Figure 2.9) Immediately we are situated in the double-minded consciousness of the ironic imagination. That we are encouraged to doubt that anything in the narrative is true seems to be evident from the prologue that follows the preface, supposedly written by the man who left Lloyd the manuscript, "Johannes Llewellyn Llongollyn Drury." Drury describes his background, including the fact that, because his name is so cumbersome, he decided "to select from and rearrange the letters of my several names, and construct therefrom three short, terse words" to use for casual acquaintances: a moment's thought suggests John Uri Lloyd.[66] But Drury also insists on the factual nature of the narrative. The reader's sympathy for this point of view is elicited by the detailed diagrams, maps, photographs, and illustrations in the text. There are also footnotes by the real "J. U. L." that corroborate statements in the text left to him by Drury. In the spectacular and ironic pages of *Etidorpha* a rigorously logical yet patently fantastic world is created, designed to challenge modern disenchantment without relinquishing modern rationality.

Similarly, Joseph M. Brown's *Astyanax: An Epic Romance of Ilion, Atlantis, and Amaraca* (1907) undergirds its premise that northern and central American civilizations were founded by survivors of the Trojan war and

"SKELETON FORMS OPPOSE MY OWN."

thought-expressions destined to become energetic intellectual forces? I sit in such a weird library and meditate. The shades of grim authors whisper in my ear, skeleton forms oppose my own, and phantoms possess the gloomy alcoves of the library I am building.

With the object of carrying to the future a section of thought current from the past, the antiquarian libraries of many nations have been culled, and purchases made in every book market of the world. These books surround me. Naturally many persons have become interested in the movement, and, considering it a worthy one, unite to further the project, for the purpose is not personal gain. Thus it is not unusual for boxes of old chemical or pharmacal volumes to arrive by freight or express, without a word as to the donor. The mail brings manuscripts unprinted, and pamphlets recondite, with no word of introduction. They come unheralded. The authors or the senders realize that in this unique library a place is vacant if any work on connected subjects is missing, and thinking men of the world are uniting their contributions to fill such vacancies.

Enough has been said concerning the ancient library that has bred these reflections, and my own personality does not concern the reader. He can now formulate his conclusions as well perhaps as I, regarding the origin of the manuscript that is to follow, if he concerns himself at all over subjects mysterious or historical, and

Figure 2.9 Photo-documentary "realism" in John Uri Lloyd's fantastic *Etidorpha* (1895).

Atlantis with four fold-out maps ("prepared by the hand of the author, of the greatest interest and importance to the reader"), an appendix, a calendar, many illustrations, footnotes, and "about 40 tailpieces, almost as fascinating as the illustrations themselves."[67] (See figure 2.10) The spectacular nature of the text as at once real and artificial is further emphasized by the inclusion of a photograph of a woman in costume, captioned "Columbia." On a tissue overleaf, the author has written: "Miss Maxine Elliott, fitting the author's ideal of Princess Columbia. Miss Elliott's personality has, with her gracious consent, been embodied in the various drawings of Princess Columbia in this work. The author thus considers it fitting that one of the most charming of Miss Elliott's photographs should preface the work."[68] (Figure 2.11) The succeeding illustrations of a fictitious character modeled after a photograph of a real woman dressed as a fictitious character nicely encapsulates the ongoing juxtaposition of the genuine and the virtual, the objective and the artificial, which typify these spectacular texts.

We see this as well in Conan Doyle's *The Lost World* (1912). He took care that the photographs and illustrations for the book appeared realistic, going so far as to don makeup, wig, and beard for photographs of himself as Professor Challenger that appeared in the text, shown in figure 2.12. (These were captioned as being by "William Ransford, Hampstead." Ransford was the actual photographer.) Conan Doyle scrupulously supervised the creation and placement of other photographs, sketches, and illustrations of the Lost World and its prehistoric inhabitants. Several of the illustrations were captioned as from the sketchbook of one of the novel's characters, and others were photographs of the Lost World these characters discovered in South America. In a letter to the actual illustrator, Conan Doyle stated, "I feel that we shall make a great joke out of this ... I look forward with great interest to see your first studies of fakes."[69] When the novel was first published in installments in *The Strand*, editor H. Greenhough Smith told Conan Doyle he loved the serial, "especially when it has the trimmings of faked photos, maps and plans."[70] Conan Doyle had created a fantastic imaginary world as an ironic hoax, a tradition going back to Poe that characterized the New Romance and its twentieth-century successors.

Our final example concerns the hardcover edition of Rudyard Kipling's tale about postal delivery by dirigibles in the twenty-first century, *With the Night Mail* (1909), published as if it were a nonfiction account from a magazine of the future. The story was accompanied by other departments of the spurious magazine: "Correspondence"; "Reviews"; an "Aerial Board of Control Report" on weather conditions, accidents, and pilot infractions;

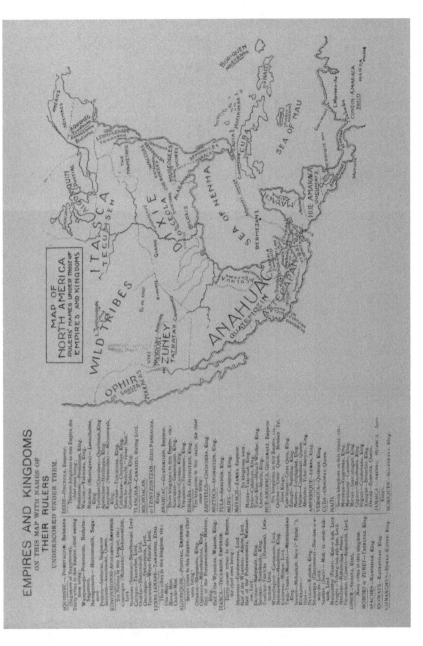

Figure 2.10 One of several foldout maps in the "spectacular text" of Joseph M. Brown's *Astyanax: An Epic Romance of Ilion, Atlantis, and Amaraca* (1907).

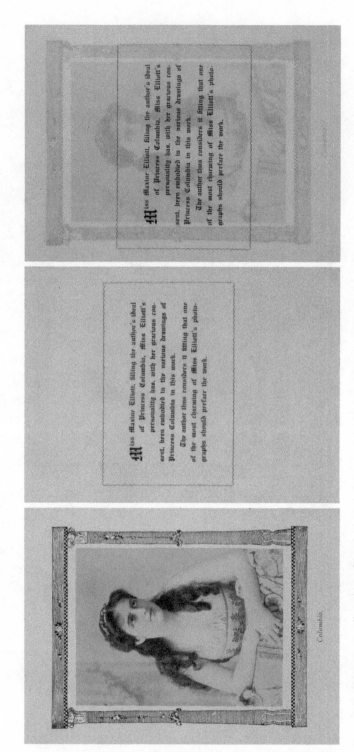

Figure 2.11 "Miss Maxine Elliott, fitting the author's ideal of Princess Columbia." From Joseph M. Brown's *Astyanax*.

Professor Challenger in his Study
(From a photograph by William Ransford, Hampstead)

Figure 2.12 Arthur Conan Doyle portrayed his creation, Professor Challenger, in *The Lost World* (1912). The editor of *The Strand* wrote Conan Doyle to commend him on the novel, "especially when it has the trimmings of faked photos, maps and plans."

an advertising section offering dirigible parts and custom-designed dirigibles; a "Help Wanted" section, and more. (Figure 2.13)

The story was a straightforward futuristic adventure charting a voyage of a mail-ship between London and Quebec. In the course of its evening run it encounters damaged dirigibles, inconsiderate pilots, an aerial hospital ship, and an electrical storm. Kipling managed to present a detailed imaginary world in this short compass, which he continued to explore in a later story set in the same world, "As Easy as A. B. C." (1912). The reader of *With the Night Mail* who scrutinizes the "magazine back matter" as well as the story itself will learn in passing many intriguing details of this world. These are not all necessary to the plot, but do construct a convincing, autonomous imaginary realm. The incidental facts reveal how dirigibles supplanted airplanes as major modes of conveyance; how all air transport (and thus nearly all commerce) is governed by a worldwide organization known as the Aerial Board of Control, whose motto is "Transportation is Civilization"; how the average human lifespan has been extended thirty years due to the beneficial consequences of traveling in the thinner air of high altitudes; and other internally consistent features of this imaginary world.[71]

Kipling utilized the rational rhetoric of aviation and engineering to impart verisimilitude to this world. He also portrayed a secular environment in which commerce is more evident than religion, rendering his modern enchantment consonant with capitalism as well as science. In the course of describing an electrical storm buffeting the dirigible, the narrator made this clear in his choice of metaphors: "If one intrudes on the Heavens when they are balancing their volt-accounts; if one disturbs the High Gods' market-rates by hurling steel hulls at ninety knots across tremblingly adjusted electronic tensions, one must not complain of any rudeness in the reception."[72] The numerous advertisements reproduced in this spectacular text reinforced the idea that consumer capitalism and romantic adventure were intertwined. (Figures 2.14 and 2.15) The ads were often gently ironic, helping the reader maintain the delicate balancing act between immersion and distance. Kipling deftly captured the tone and layout of contemporary newspaper advertisements in his copy for the year 2000, as in this listing under the "Wants" column:

FAMILY DIRIGIBLE.

A COMPETENT, steady man wanted for slow speed, low-level Tangye dirigible. No night work, no sea trips. Must be a member of the Church of England, and make himself useful in the garden.

—M. R., The Rectory, Gray's Barton, Wilts.[73]

Correspondence

Skylarking on the Equator

To THE EDITOR — Only last week, while crossing the Equator (W. 26.15), I became aware of a furious and irregular cannonading some fifteen or twenty knots S. 4 E. Descending to the 500 ft. level, I found a party of Transylvanian tourists engaged in exploding scores of the largest pattern atmospheric bombs (A. B. C. standard) and, in the intervals of their pleasing labours, firing bow and stern smoke-ring swivels. This orgie — I can give it no other name—went on for at least two hours, and naturally produced violent electric derangements. My compasses, of course, were thrown out, my bow was struck twice, and I received two brisk shocks from the lower platform-rail. On remonstrating, I was told that these " professors " were engaged in scientific experiments. The extent of their " scientific " knowledge may be judged by the fact that they expected to produce (I give their own words) " a little blue sky " if " they went on long enough." This in the heart of the Doldrums at 450 feet! I have no objection to any amount of blue sky in its proper place (it can be found at the 2,000 level for practically twelve months out of the year), but I submit, with all deference to the educational needs of Transylvania, that "sky-larking" in the centre of a main-travelled road where, at the best of times, electricity literally drips off one's stanchions and screw blades, is unnecessary. When my friends had finished, the road was seared, and blown, and pitted with unequal pressure-layers, spirals,

[68]

Figure 2.13 A "correspondence page" from Rudyard Kipling's *With the Night Mail* (1909).

Figure 2.14 A page of display ads from Kipling's *With the Night Mail*.

The rational rhetoric deployed by these New Romance texts and the accompanying paratextual markers of "objectivity" were also characteristics of the succeeding marketing genres of "science fiction" and "detective fiction."[74] They became established as distinct genres largely through the emergence of American pulp magazines dedicated to them in the early decades of the twentieth century. (The British lacked a thriving pulp-magazine industry, but they imported American magazines.) The intellectual genealogies of these marketing genres are complex and contested, but Poe, Verne, and the New Romance were integral to their development. In an address commemorating Poe's centenary in 1909, Conan Doyle acclaimed him as the fount of diverse tributaries of fiction: "[his] tales have been so pregnant with suggestion, so stimulating to the minds of others, that it may be said of many of them that each is a root from which a whole literature has developed."[75]

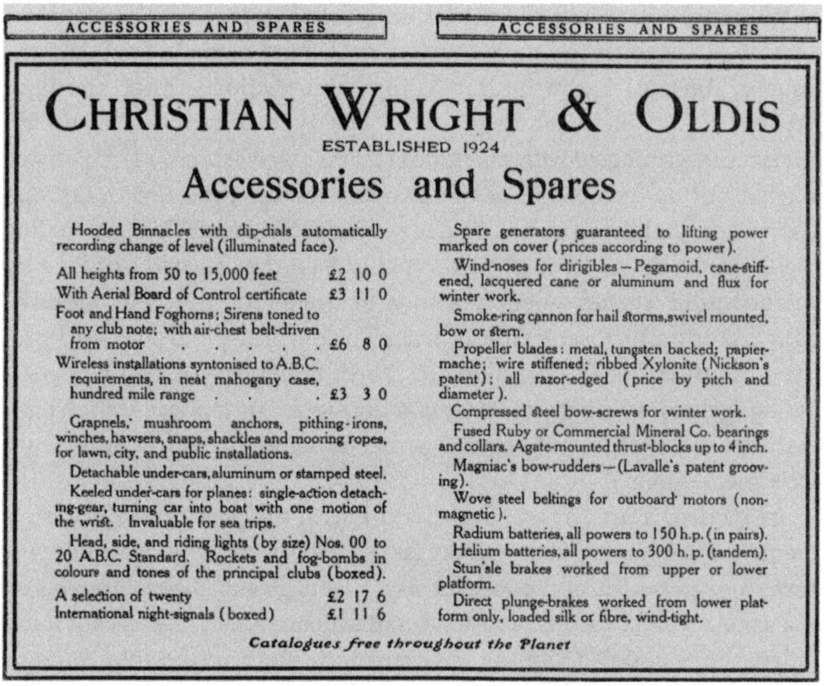
ACCESSORIES AND SPARES | ACCESSORIES AND SPARES

CHRISTIAN WRIGHT & OLDIS

ESTABLISHED 1924

Accessories and Spares

Hooded Binnacles with dip-dials automatically recording change of level (illuminated face).

All heights from 50 to 15,000 feet	£2 10 0
With Aerial Board of Control certificate	£3 11 0
Foot and Hand Foghorns; Sirens toned to any club note; with air-chest belt-driven from motor	£6 8 0
Wireless installations syntonised to A.B.C. requirements, in neat mahogany case, hundred mile range . . .	£3 3 0

Grapnels, mushroom anchors, pithing-irons, winches, hawsers, snaps, shackles and mooring ropes, for lawn, city, and public installations.

Detachable under-cars, aluminum or stamped steel.

Keeled under-cars for planes: single-action detaching-gear, turning car into boat with one motion of the wrist. Invaluable for sea trips.

Head, side, and riding lights (by size) Nos. 00 to 20 A.B.C. Standard. Rockets and fog-bombs in colours and tones of the principal clubs (boxed).

A selection of twenty	£2 17 6
International night-signals (boxed)	£1 11 6

Spare generators guaranteed to lifting power marked on cover (prices according to power).

Wind-noses for dirigibles—Pegamoid, cane-stiffened, lacquered cane or aluminum and flux for winter work.

Smoke-ring cannon for hail storms, swivel mounted, bow or stern.

Propeller blades: metal, tungsten backed; papier-mache; wire stiffened; ribbed Xylonite (Nickson's patent); all razor-edged (price by pitch and diameter).

Compressed steel bow-screws for winter work.

Fused Ruby or Commercial Mineral Co. bearings and collars. Agate-mounted thrust-blocks up to 4 inch.

Magniac's bow-rudders—(Lavalle's patent grooving).

Wove steel beltings for outboard motors (non-magnetic).

Radium batteries, all powers to 150 h.p. (in pairs).

Helium batteries, all powers to 300 h. p. (tandem).

Stun'sle brakes worked from upper or lower platform.

Direct plunge-brakes worked from lower platform only, loaded silk or fibre, wind-tight.

Catalogues free throughout the Planet

Figure 2.15 Advertisement for dirigible spare parts, from Kipling's *With the Night Mail.*

Conan Doyle was probably thinking of Poe's pivotal role in the creation of detective fiction, especially his stories featuring the cerebral Auguste Dupin.[76] In "The Sign of the Four" (1890), Holmes himself paid indirect tribute to Poe's foundational role when he credited Dupin as one of the first consulting detectives.

Hugo Gernsback, the creator of the new marketing genre of science fiction, also identified Poe and Verne as seminal influences on this branch of literature. In 1926 he published *Amazing Stories,* the first publication devoted entirely to narratives that Gernsback called "scientifiction" (modified by him in 1929 to the more euphonious science fiction). There were precedents for this mode of fiction, some extending back to antiquity, which took disparate forms, including extraordinary voyages, utopias, and social satires.[77] Several umbrella terms were used to identify these types of stories in the nineteenth century, including the "New Romance," the "weird tale," and the "scientific romance." But prior to Gernsback there was little sense of a distinct genre with its own preoccupations and traditions.[78] Even the New Romance indiscriminately lumped together all fantastic tales cast in a realist mode, including extravagant adventures (*Treasure Island*); the supernatural (*Dracula*); lost races (*She, The Lost World*); and future fantasies (*With the Night Mail*).

With missionary zeal, Gernsback articulated science fiction's aims and genealogy, leaving it to others to refine or dispute them. In the inaugural issue of *Amazing Stories* he stated, "By 'scientifiction' I mean the Jules Verne, H. G. Wells, and Edgar Allan Poe type of story—a charming romance intermingled with scientific fact and prophetic vision." [79] Poe was singled out as forebear in advertisements for his collected works that Gernsback ran in early issues. Under a caption blazoned "Edgar Allan Poe the Father of Scientifiction," he was praised as "the originator of the first 'scientifiction' stories—fiction with a plausible scientific background." (The ad copy also observed that Conan Doyle was inspired by Poe's detective tales to create Sherlock Holmes, thereby linking the two new marketing genres in their mutual commitment to modern rationality; Gernsback soon brought them together in another pulp title, *Scientific Detective Monthly*.) [80]

In another issue, Gernsback enlisted Poe in the project of re-enchantment: Poe was "one whose views are far removed from the disagreeable pessimism so prevalent of the present day." [81] This genial assessment ignored Poe's melancholia and his occasional ambivalence about science, but it did reflect the "can-do" optimism of Gernsback, who had come to America from Luxembourg and made his fortune by popularizing electronics, the radio, and modern "sexology" as well as scientifiction. [82] Gernsback concurred with Poe's view that a tale of scientific wonder should be imbued with such authenticity it could be deemed a hoax and enjoyed through the ironic imagination. [83] This sentiment was shared by many of the initial readers of the new genre. When one asked the editor of the 1930s fanzine *Fantasy Magazine* why the magazine devoted a column to scientific hoaxes, he was told that since "all these hoaxes were fakes, frauds, fiction, and based on scientific or pseudo-scientific principles [they] did not conflict with the spirit or purpose of *Fantasy Magazine*." [84]

As it incubated in the pulp magazines, the embryonic science fiction genre became a distinct resource for modern enchantment. Gernsback believed that science fiction would foster a sense of wonder by conjoining science and imagination. Reason would no longer be alienating or purely disenchanting; by combining it with imagination it could be redefined as a vital force that would not just analyze the world but vivify and transform it. Gernsback believed that this combination, which I call "animistic reason," could be trained on current scientific findings to prescribe possible avenues for scientists to follow. His vision for the new literature was extolled on the *Amazing Stories'* masthead: "Extravagant Fiction Today—Cold Fact Tomorrow." The stories created virtual worlds that could have real world effects, as a reader observed in 1928: "Scientifiction should mean . . . a statement of virtual possibilities that after they have become . . . actual, science can and will classify, dissect, and otherwise take credit for this 'discovering.'"[85]

Gernsback's magazines—*Amazing Stories, Science Wonder Stories, Air Wonder Stories, Scientific Detective Monthly,* and *Wonder Stories*—were thus meant to educate and inspire as well as entertain, to heal the "dissociation of sensibility" that cultural pessimists like T. S. Eliot complained of, while also teaching basic scientific concepts. Like the works of the New Romance, these magazines were spectacular texts, augmenting the rational rhetoric of the narratives with informative paratexts, including charts, graphs, and footnotes. Gernsback's magazines boasted of having scientific consultants on the editorial staff that vetted the stories for factual accuracy. They also included scientific columns and quizzes on the scientific facts embedded in individual stories. ("What is a 'tesseract'? The answer is to be found in 'The Great Four Dimensional Robberies.'")[86] As the first periodicals devoted to this newly defined genre, they became the templates for succeeding science fiction magazines in the interwar period, although many of Gernsback's competitors abandoned his scientific didacticism in favor of uninhibited adventure stories.[87] Nevertheless, the enchanting possibilities of modern science, and the animating use of reason, were never abandoned as the field expanded in the interwar period; they remained the raison d'être of the genre.

In fact, Gernsback's promotion of the wonders of science and the magic of reason was often achieved in spite of the fiction he published. While some of his writers were scientists, or had degrees, or had even graduated high school, this was not always the case: many of the extravagant fictions were built on few cold facts. Readers were quick to spot mistakes and outlandish postulates; some preferred to label the genre "pseudo-science" stories. Correspondents to the magazines' letters pages frequently identified embarrassing scientific errors, and there were a fair number of complaints that the fiction did not live up to Gernsback's rather exalted ideals. "The Lizard Men of Bu-Lo," protested one reader, was "rotten, impossible, and hackneyed in plot. A disgrace." (He also criticized the scientific content of other stories, demanding that "the next sham to get rid of is that board of science editors. They don't pass on the stories and don't tell me different.")[88] Another complained that *Amazing Stories* published "scientific bunk." With admirable sangfroid, the editor responded that the magazine "certainly contains what you term scientific bunk, but along with it is also a quantity of good, natural science."[89]

And this was the fundamental point. Science fiction didn't have to be accurate all the time, but it did have to uphold the principles of rational analysis and extrapolation from known scientific fact.[90] If these were generally adhered to—or at least gestured at—then writers were often forgiven for employing, in H. G. Wells's phrase, "an ingenious use of scientific patter."[91] As one author explained, "one of the main functions of scientifiction is to give its readers the correct atmosphere of any science."[92] This broad orientation helped modern readers to enjoy the stories with the double consciousness of the ironic imagination, affirming on the one hand what they knew was incredible on the other. "We admit that many of our stories may be impossible," the editor of *Amazing Stories* stated in the letters pages, "but the right kind of impossibility is the basis for the best kind of stories."[93]

While the principle, if not always the practice, of the scientific method was enshrined in the fiction, the practice was to be found regularly in the magazines' editorials, scientific columns, articles, and the letters pages, where readers and editors debated scientific theories and discussed the latest scientific developments.[94] (The Lorentz-Fitzgerald contraction theory "is much more complex than it sounds," opined the editor of *Wonder Stories*, prior to discussing it in detail.)[95] In a period when few readers attained more than a secondary school education, the science fiction pulps provided a rudimentary introduction to scientific findings and the scientific method alongside their more outlandish wonders. As a result of reading science fiction, one reader asserted, "A whole new world was opened up to me . . . I became interested in everything pertaining to science. I got out of my rut. I thought again."[96]

Science fiction, like Vaihinger's philosophy of as if, allowed for the enchantments of imagination, but balanced these with an allegiance to science and its critical method. Pseudoscience was not absent from the pages of the science fiction pulps, but many readers enjoyed playing with these ideas in a skeptical manner. They could become outraged when pseudoscientific claims went beyond the joking confines of an ironic hoax to being presented as unimpeachably real. In the mid-1940s, for example, *Amazing Stories* published accounts by Richard Shaver claiming that ancient Lemurians were secretly influencing the modern world. Editor Ray Palmer presented the "Shaver Mystery" as authentic, either to generate sales or because he believed in Shaver's theories. Many science fiction fans objected strongly to Palmer's presentation, critiquing the tales for their lack of verifiable evidence and poor science, and organized a boycott of *Amazing Stories*. (Some treated the affair as a hoax; one letter to *Amazing Stories* defended Shaver by citing information found at Miskatonic University, a fictional institution in Lovecraft's imaginary world.) The boycott may have had an effect: Palmer suddenly left the magazine in 1947, while he was still running Shaver's works. According to Shaver (admittedly not the most reliable of sources), the publishers fired Palmer after a reader pointed out that Shaver's theory contradicted Einstein's general theory of relativity.[97]

An editor of *Astounding Stories* emphasized in 1936 that the new genre combined imaginative wonder with scientific analysis: "Perhaps we dream—but we do so logically, and science follows in the footsteps of our dreams."[98] By openly embracing this fusion, science fiction helped displace the cliché that science exclusively disenchanted the world. Readers knew that science both disenchanted and enchanted simultaneously. According to one, science fiction "fills my yearning for both knowledge, and dreams of the unknown."[99] Philip K. Dick recalled that when he first read a science fiction magazine at the age of twelve in 1940, he immediately associated science with enchantment: "At once I recognized the magic which I had found, in earlier times, in the *Oz* books—this magic now coupled not with wands but with science . . . In any case my view became magic equals science . . . and science (of the future) equals magic."[100]

Like the New Romance, interwar science fiction pulps relied on graphic displays no less than rational rhetoric to foster the illusion that the imaginary worlds they presented were real. Thus in the May, 1941, issue of *Astounding Science-Fiction,* editor John W. Campbell published, "in semigraphical form," portions of a large and complex chart that Robert Heinlein created for his Future History sequence of stories that appeared in the magazine. (See figure 2.16) The chart included notable dates (ranging from 1940 to 2140), flagged key characters as well as technological and sociological changes, and provided summary remarks about important developments along the timeline. Campbell's editorial praised Heinlein's ability to create an imaginary world that was so detailed and cohesive that it could be taken as a virtual space of imaginative habitation. To this end, Campbell emphasized the "lived" reality that Heinlein's overarching Future History imparted to its component tales:

> Heinlein is a Grade A writer to begin with, but by giving himself the added help of a carefully worked out history, building up in his mind a picture of the world of tomorrow that's "lived in," his stories have achieved manifold greater reality.[101]

Campbell also contributed to the readers' emotional investment in this imaginary world by associating it directly with their lived lives. He encouraged them to "trace in on this suggestion for the future your own life line . . . Where does your life line fall? Where will your children's end?"[102] Heinlein's Future History was positioned simultaneously as an autonomous and fanciful world of the imagination, and as one that could conceivably jibe with actual developments in history.

Science fiction fans admitted that they engaged in a double minded form of pretense, shifting back and forth between worlds real and imagined through the ironic imagination. In the March 1938 fanzine *Imagination!* a reader

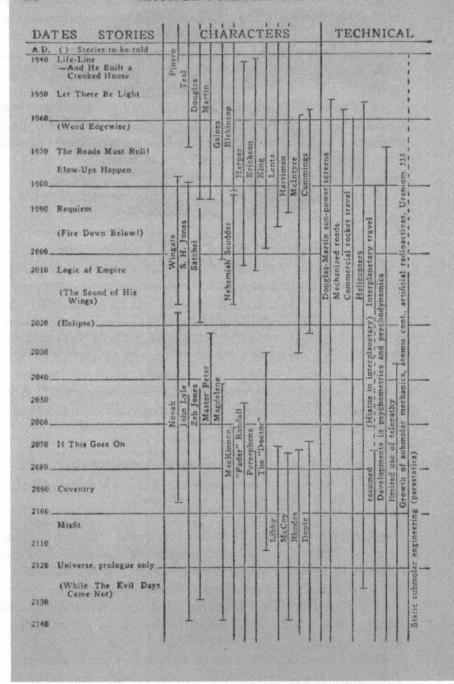

Figure 2.16 Robert Heinlein's "Future History" chart, *Astounding Science-Fiction*, May 1941.

DATA	SOCIOLOGICAL	REMARKS

	Collapse THE
	    — of — "CRAZY
	    Europe YEARS"
		Considerable technical advance during this period, accompanied by a gradual deterioration of mores, orientation, and social institutions, terminating in mass psychoses in the sixth decade, and the Interregnum.

—Transatlantic rocket flight	Strike of '60 The "FALSE DAWN," 1960-70 First rocket to Moon, 1978	
Antipodes rocket service		The Interregnum was followed by a period of reconstruction in which the Voorhis financial proposals gave a temporary economic stability and chance for re-orientation. This was ended by the opening of new frontiers and a return to nineteenth-century economy.
	Space Precautionary Act Harriman's Lunar Corporations — Luna City founded PERIOD OF IMPERIAL EX- PLOITATION, 1970-2020 Revolution in Little America Interplanetary exploration and exploitation American-Australasian anschluss	

Bacteriophage
—The Travel Unit and
    the Fighting Unit
	Rise of religious fanaticism
	The "New Crusade"
	Rebellion and independence for
	    Venusian colonists
		Three revolutions ended the short period of interplanetary imperialism; Antarctica, U. S., and Venus. Space travel ceased until 2072.

Commercial stereoptics		
	Religious dictatorship in U. S.	Little research and only minor technical advances during this period. Extreme puritanism. Certain aspects of psychodynamics and psychometrics, mass psychology and social control developed by the priest class.
—Booster guns —		
Synthetic foods	THE FIRST HUMAN CIVILI- ZATION, 2075 et seq.	Re-establishment of civil liberty. Renascence of scientific research. Resumption of space travel. Luna City refounded. Science of social relations, based on the negative basic statements of semantics. Rigor of Epistemology. The Covenant.
—Weather control Wave mechanics		
The "Barrier"		
Atomic "tailoring," Elements 93-416 Parastatic engineering		Beginning of the consolidation of the Solar System.
		First attempt at interstellar exploration.
Rigor of colloids Symbiotic research Longevity		Civil disorder, followed by the end of human adolescence and beginning of first mature culture.

claimed that the charge of "escapism" properly rested with religious believers rather than science fiction devotees. The former escaped into a world of "mumbo jumbo" without acknowledging it as such, whereas the latter "realized" they were pretending while remaining fully engaged in their play.[103]

Science fiction magazines didn't allow readers to forget this double consciousness, periodically perpetrating in-jokes and hoaxes. In early 1943, for example, newsstand browsers would have spotted a wonderfully garish cover illustration by Virgil Finlay for that month's *Super Science Stories*. Finlay's cover depicted a yellow giant with green eyes, scratching an eyebrow in puzzlement as he hefted a rocketship to his face to peer at a diminutive astronaut threatening him with a raygun. (Figure 2.17) As pulp covers went, this one wasn't unusual, but it did advertise an unusually titled story: "Reader, I Hate You!" by Henry Kuttner. The story began, "Reader, I hate you. I don't know what your name is—Joe or Mike or Forrest J.—but I mean you, the little guy who buys all the magazines with Finlay pictures and Kuttner [stories]."[104] (As dedicated fans would have recognized, Forrest J. no doubt referred to Forrest J. Ackerman, a well-known fan whose numerous letters appeared in most of the contemporary science fiction pulps.)

The story turns out to be an infinitely recursive one, involving a self-described superman who meets Finlay and Kuttner in a bar and places them under his hypnotic control. Finlay is compelled by the superman to paint the cover illustration, which captured an adventure the superman actually had with a yellow giant with green eyes. Kuttner is forced to write the story alluding to this adventure, as well as describing how he and Finlay became involved with the superman. Finlay assures the superman that he will see to it that the cover and story are published. Why should the superman go to all this trouble? Because an unnamed science fiction reader had inadvertently taken an important item from him, and he wants it back. Because the reader had revealed that he was a devoted fan of Finlay's art and Kuttner's fiction, the superman reasons that an issue of a science fiction magazine with an eye-catching cover by Finlay and a headline story by Kuttner would likely attract the reader into buying it, reading Kuttner's contribution, getting the message that the item must be returned, and doing so via the offices of *Super Science Stories*. Kuttner relates in the story that even after he and Finlay finished their individual assignments, they are compelled to repeat them, for the hypnotic commands won't cease until the reader with the item contacts the magazine. Hence the aggrieved title of the story, as well as its conclusion, which ends as it began, "Reader, I hate you. I don't know what your name is . . ."

By addressing the reader directly, this tale gently mocks the fantasy fan's desire to participate in imaginary worlds. (Fredric Brown devoted an

Figure 2.17 Virgil Finlay's cover for the May 1943 issue of *Super Science Stories*.
Reproduced by permission of the copyright holder, Lail M. Finlay.

entire novel to this conceit in his 1949 *What Mad Universe*.) Kuttner and Finlay's confection also pokes fun at the standard conventions of the genre, from the contents (superman, giant, rocket, raygun) to the forms (preposterous covers, insider references). At the same time, the story also renders its own imaginary world more "real" by becoming a tangible token of it: the reader is, after all, holding a physical object that has the exact cover and story that the story claims were created at the behest of the superman.

The November 1949 issue of *Astounding Science-Fiction* must have been also surprising—and perhaps disconcerting—to those who read the November 1948 issue. The 1949 issue boasted a stellar roster of popular authors, including Isaac Asimov, Robert Heinlein, Theodore Sturgeon, and A. E. van Vogt. This lineup was a fan's dream—quite literally, it turned out. In the November 1948 issue, Campbell had published a letter from a reader that praised the November 1949 issue and listed the titles of the stories and their eminent authors' names. Campbell's published response to this reader's hoax in 1948 was a laconic, "Hm-m-m—he must be off on another time track."[105] But hoaxes and other virtual stratagems were part of science fiction's life-blood and were hard to resist. Hence a year later, Campbell published nearly all of the stories by nearly all of the writers listed in the 1948 letter. His accompanying editorial addressed the value of science fiction as a literature of prophecy—an ironic wink at Gernsback's "extravagant fiction today—cold fact tomorrow." Readers appreciated the irony and probably appreciated that irony was intrinsic to the genre.[106]

In such ways, the spectacular texts of the New Romance, and the marketing genres it inspired, facilitated the readers' immersion in imaginary worlds, while also eliciting a degree of ironic distance. These innovative texts were attended by new spaces that enabled imaginary worlds to be inhabited communally and persistently: "public spheres of the imagination." These spheres helped transform certain imaginary worlds into virtual ones through the "consensual hallucination" of a group agreeing to pretend the worlds were real. In addition to fostering the communal and prolonged habitation of imaginary worlds, public spheres of the imagination encouraged debates about how these worlds were to be interpreted. As an unintended consequence, these spheres reinforced the fictionalist perspective that interpretations of reality, no less than fantasy, were provisional, subject to contestation and change. Public spheres of the imagination enabled their participants to relate the virtual world to the real world in a critical manner, turning fantasy into a social practice. In what follows we will examine these public spheres in general terms; succeeding chapters will examine them in the light of particular authors and specific imaginary worlds.

III. PUBLIC SPHERES OF THE IMAGINATION

In the history of reading practices in the West, some scholars claimed that reading was "intensive" prior to the mid-eighteenth century, but became more "extensive" afterward, owing to the greater profusion of reading material.

Critics of this model responded that extensive reading does not necessarily preclude intensive reading, an observation sustained by the near-devout interest inspired by certain fictions of the fin-de-siècle and after, notably those of Conan Doyle's Sherlock Holmes stories.[107]

The success of these stories owed much to Conan Doyle's intrinsic gifts as an author. His plots were clever, his characters intriguing, his style brisk and engaging. Holmes was a larger than life character, but he was also appealingly human; he made mistakes, and sometimes owned up to them. But extrinsic factors, having to do with the dynamics of mass publishing at the end of the nineteenth century, were also important in the character's popularity and longevity. Increased competition for readers led periodical writers and publishers to forge innovative strategies aimed at securing reader loyalty. As an unexpected byproduct, several of these strategies resulted in sustained reader engagement with the fiction itself, helping to transform some imaginary worlds into virtual worlds.

For example, Conan Doyle's Holmes stories in *The Strand* were self-contained, permitting new readers to become involved with the characters in any given issue. Yet they also had elements of a serial narrative: each successive story reinforced the depth and familiarity of this particular imaginary world, heightening readers' anticipation for the next installment of Holmes's credibly incredible adventures. Conan Doyle asserted that he pioneered this technique of combining the addictive elements of serial fiction with the immediate accessibility of self-contained narratives. The technique also enhanced his readers' immersive experience by situating the individual stories within an overarching imaginary world as their referent, just as Heinlein's Future History chart framed his stories as part of a cohesive world. When Watson rattled off the titles of Holmes's previous adventures that had been published, readers familiar with them felt a thrill of complicity. And those not familiar with these earlier adventures were given a tantalizing glimpse of a complex world whose history they too could master. In so doing, they would become members of an in-group whose enjoyment of the stories was enhanced by the knowledge of its most arcane details. Few wished to remain mere tourists in a country they had grown to love.

George Newnes, the publisher of *The Strand* (intended for upper- and middle-class audiences) and *Tit-Bits* (intended for lower-middle and working-class audiences), capitalized on the series' popularity by running the Holmes stories in both magazines, sponsoring contests around them, and encouraging and publishing inquiries regarding them. This promotion of a continuing public dialogue in the pages of a magazine about that magazine's fiction, in which readers were rewarded for paying careful attention to the stories' details, was another innovation of the fin-de-siècle. Earlier, readers might have written directly to an author or editor, but magazines did not usually solicit or publish at length readers' opinions concerning the fiction. (An editor might comment on the letters received, but this was very different from the direct exchanges among readers that were to become commonplace by the interwar period.)

Newnes's publicity innovations were followed by similar attempts by other publishers to secure the opinions and loyalty of their readers. American "pulpwood" periodicals devoted to fiction, such as *Munsey's Magazine, The Argosy,* and *Adventure,* established letters pages in which readers were encouraged to discuss the fiction with one another, the editor, and the writers.[108] Editors initially did this as a marketing device, to discover what their readers preferred, but the letters pages became popular among readers, who actively contributed to discussions about the fictions' plausibility, style, and other attributes. These sections also fostered a sense of community that redressed the anomie of modernity.[109] Arthur S. Hoffman, the editor of the American pulp magazine *Adventure,* recalled how he originated the popular letters-section, the "Camp-Fire," in 1912:

> Gradually it grew on me that here was something more than a fiction magazine . . . Here . . . was a certain community of interest. Among people who had hitherto had no common meeting-place, no means of communication among themselves. Why not make that magazine that had collected them their meeting place? . . . Our 'Camp-Fire' represents human companionship and fellowship.[110]

Similarly, the editor of *Astounding Stories* told his readers in 1936 that "We have something in common, something binding us together—for we *see,* eye to eye, standing in a solid phalanx, shoulder to shoulder."[111] Readers reciprocated these sentiments. They enjoyed having their minds stretched as much by discussions about the fiction as the fiction itself. As one "youthful reader" remarked on the letters pages in a 1928 *Amazing Science Quarterly,* "I believe that it is the best feature of the whole magazine. Not only does it give me the opinion of others, but it also gives me an enjoyable hour comparing my ideas with the ideas of the contributors to the discussions."[112] The modern enchantments derived from imaginary worlds need not be solipsistic: many readers found their "sense of wonder" amplified when it was shared with others.

The idiosyncratic personalities who populated these letters pages also compensated for the concept-driven nature of science fiction. Some critics complained that science fiction lacked credible characters and human interest—a fair charge in the early years of a genre that was defining itself as a literature of ideas and that was further constrained by the pulp audience's demand for action and adventure. What critics didn't realize was that the world of fandom inspired by the genre provided its enthusiasts with much of the human interest that mainstream readers found in more conventional fiction. In "The Vizigraph," the lively letters pages of *Planet Stories*, a reader observed insightfully that "Stories give us imaginary characters to think about, but The Vizigraph gives us *real people* [who] sound like level-headed folks who take their fandom seriously, but are not above a bit of humor, even caustic humor, when it is apropos."[113] (Similarly, science fiction fanzines, as they flourished from the 1930s on, often focused on the everyday trials and tribulations of fans rather than on the fiction that had been their original inspiration.)

Letters pages reflected and supported the growing tendency to inhabit imaginary worlds through the ironic imagination in at least three ways. First, they facilitated readers' immersion in imaginary worlds by encouraging them to contribute their own perceptions about the worlds. By writing to one another about the fiction, many became more engaged with it. Even those who only read these exchanges could be caught up in the communal elaboration of the fictional world, which began thereby to assume a virtual existence.

But if the first effect of letters pages was to enhance imaginative immersion and communal participation, the second effect was to reinforce in readers' minds the artificiality of such imaginary worlds—that they were aesthetic constructs, the creations of authors whom the letters pages had turned into recognizable personalities. Letters pages in fiction magazines were thus a manifestation, and facilitator, of the double-minded consciousness of the ironic imagination. Within them, readers became active participants in the elaboration of imaginary worlds and detached critics of them as well.

Finally, letters pages linked imaginary worlds to the real world, in effect becoming "public spheres of the imagination." In using this phrase, I am adapting the concept of the "public sphere" first advanced by the philosopher Jurgen Habermas. He charted the emergence of new public venues in late seventeenth- and early eighteenth-century Europe, such as coffeehouses, salons, fraternal organizations, and newspapers.[114] The nascent middle classes used these sites to exchange ideas about politics and society, and to bring the resultant "public opinion" to bear on contemporary governance. For Habermas, the public sphere approximated the Enlightenment ideal of unconstrained, rational, and equal exchanges, although in practice it often reflected the social exclusivities of the eighteenth century. Nevertheless, in the short term it helped undermine the traditional order through the reasoned inquiry and informed public opinion it promoted, and in the long term it became a defining feature of modernity. Pulp fiction readers were probably unaware that the letters pages they enjoyed had such a lofty pedigree, but they did discuss them in terms reminiscent of the public sphere. "I like *Astounding*," a reader wrote in 1939 to "Brass Tacks," the magazine's letters section, "chiefly because the fans, authors, artists and editor seem to work together and discuss things—a sort of meeting."[115]

Public spheres of the imagination, like the venues Habermas described, were not always egalitarian in practice. Science fiction fandom in Britain and America was comprised largely of white males for much of the twentieth century, and numerous Sherlock Holmes societies in America did not admit women until century's end.[116] Despite their exclusions and unwitting biases, however, many of these spheres were intended to foster unconstrained, egalitarian, and rational deliberations on topics of public concern. Arthur S. Hoffman, for example, believed in an engaged citizenry, and deliberately fashioned the letters pages of *Adventure* as an inclusive public sphere, as he made clear in the "Camp-Fire": "We believe that *public opinion* . . . is a mightier influence than any force man can raise against it, that this force has been systematically used only by the few and generally by the worst, and that, by right endeavor, it can be made a restless weapon in the hands of the many."[117] An editor of *Wonder Stories* also spoke proudly in 1931 of his letters pages' "policy of free and open discussions . . . Friends in newspaper and magazine circles tell us that we have one of the most interesting readers' columns in the city and that some of them buy the magazine chiefly to read this fascinating department."[118]

Some readers were disconcerted by the sharp retorts and unconventional views that could ensue from these discussions. One expressed concern that *Wonder Stories* published "several bitterly antagonistic missives . . . Your sense of fair play induced you to print them, but why must you heed this minority."[119] Similarly, the editor of *Planet Stories* was chided in 1949 by a reader for printing letters advocating racism: "Certainly, *Planet Stories* should not serve as a medium for its propagation."[120] The editor responded that the letters pages reflected a gamut of opinion, which was their purpose as a public sphere: "*Planet Stories* has propagated no prejudices. *Planet Stories* has allowed both sides to air their views. Is this wrong?"[121] As much as the didactic nature of the stories, these exchanges could be educational experiences. They accustomed readers to the give-and-take of debate and the expression of divergent views.

The initial public spheres of the imagination rapidly expanded from magazine letters pages to societies, fanzines, and conventions. Those spheres devoted to science fiction increased enormously when *Amazing Stories* began publishing the addresses of the letter writers along with their letters in the late 1920s. Gernsback encouraged fans to contact one another directly, which fostered international communications as well as more local correspondence. Fans soon exchanged fanzines and letters, created clubs (or joined the transatlantic "Science Fiction

League," which Gernsback established in the mid-1930s), and organized regional conventions, as well as the first of many "world" science
fiction conventions in 1939. Public spheres of the imagination helped
institutionalize science fiction fandom in both Britain and the United
States during the 1930s.[122] It was also during this decade that Sherlock
Holmes fandom became formally organized through the creation of
similar spheres, such as the Baker Street Irregulars in America and the
Sherlock Holmes Society of London.

Adults were encouraged to exercise their fancy and their reason within
these spheres by relating imaginary worlds to the real world. In this way,
imaginary worlds became "good to think with" about topical social and
political concerns. By extrapolating current social trends and scientific
findings into the future, science fiction provoked debates about the directions contemporary societies were taking, goading its readers to explore
alternatives to the status quo. The literary critic Darko Suvin famously
defined science fiction as the literature of "cognitive estrangement," in
which novel concepts set in the future stimulate readers to view the present from unfamiliar vantages.[123] Early readers of science fiction were
proud of the independent thinking it could provoke, although they spoke
of its estranging effects in homelier terms. As one reader commented in a
1936 issue of *Astounding Stories:*

> It is a well-known fact that science fiction fans comprise the most enthusiastic group of
> readers in the entire magazine fiction field. In no other magazines can one find, for
> instance, such lengthy readers' departments, where one is able to discuss the magazine
> and its stories or criticize scientific theories, expounding one's own views.[124]

Of course, fantastic literature could also reinforce prevailing stereotypes.
The New Romance and interwar science fiction often indulged in the sort
of sexist, racist, imperialist, and xenophobic attitudes rampant in Western
cultures at the time.[125] Yet the ironic imagination could lend a self-subvert-
ing dimension to such texts, as we saw in the case of Haggard's *She.* Debates
about these attitudes in the letters pages could further destabilize unitary
textual interpretations and challenge normative views.

Indeed, by encouraging multiple interpretations of fictional narratives, public spheres of the imagination inculcated in many readers a
greater tolerance for difference and an appreciation of pluralism. The
range of diverse opinions expressed naturally depended on the social
constitution of a public sphere; those that were homogeneous were more
likely to reinforce ingrained attitudes of their members than challenge
them. Yet during the interwar period, many of the American science fiction pulp magazines boasted about their diverse readership, a claim that

was usually supported by the range of individuals who contributed to the letters pages: male and female, professional and working class, old and young, well off and impoverished. The editor of *Wonder Stories* in the early 1930s noted that "our daily mail furnishes us with a good cross section of all classes, all types, and all possible attitudes, not only toward us but toward the world as a whole." As a consequence, the letters section of the magazine "allow[s] our readers to present their views of the vital questions of today and tomorrow, and in general to stimulate the mind to search out from the mists of deception, illusion, superstition, and narrowness those paths of existence that will promote their personal happiness."[126] The editor of *Astounding Stories* also celebrated the variety of views expressed in a civil fashion in its letters pages: "We are a great army without discord. Debate? Of course! Differing opinions? Certainly. But with an inspiration visualized by dreams of the future, based on known facts of the present."[127]

Readers came to appreciate that provisional, self-reflexive, "as if" meanings could be no less enchanting than the stable "just so" narratives that allegedly distinguished the premodern world. Writing to *Planet Stories* in 1949, one reader asserted that the genre was marvelous precisely because it embraced contingency and novelty: "If science fiction has anything to offer other than mere escapism, its value lies in promoting a receptive, questioning attitude and freeing the mind from the narrow, superstition-bound, taboo-ridden ruts of accustomed thought channels."[128]

In terms of modern enchantment, then, these new spheres produced important effects. They enabled individuals to collectively inhabit an imaginary world for prolonged periods, transforming it into a virtual world that generated more immersive states of enchantment. Escapism, however, was allied to social engagement, for public spheres often used these worlds as touchstones for interpreting the real world. And the plurality of opinions expressed stimulated participants to reflect on the contingent and provisional facets of all interpretations. If normative claims about an imaginary world were challenged within these spheres, then normative claims about the real world might come under similar scrutiny—as they often did.

Further, public spheres of the imagination became vital adjuncts to the ironic imagination. The latter can establish a critical perspective on one's assumptions and beliefs, but often in a less sustained and searching way than within public spheres of the imagination. When composed of a diverse membership, these spheres augmented the perspectival effects of the ironic imagination: they forced participants to contend with unpalatable interpretations and to provide justifications for self-evident views. Taken together, the ironic imagination and public spheres of the imagination advanced a modern form of enchantment that tended to delight but not delude.

The advent of the Internet has resulted in a vast proliferation of public spheres of the imagination, including newsgroups, blogs, web pages, and social networking sites. Online gaming worlds are among the most prominent (and profitable) of contemporary imaginary worlds, and they too have generated public spheres of the imagination to support them. As Jane McGonigal observed in 2011, "Hundreds of millions of people world-wide are opting out of reality for larger and larger chunks of time."[129] (World of Warcraft alone had twelve million players in October 2010.)[130] There is a direct lineage between these computer-generated virtual worlds and the textual virtual worlds of the fin-de-siècle and after that we have been examining. Many of the initial creators of online worlds were devo-tees of Dungeons & Dragons (D&D), a paper-and-pencil fantasy role-play-ing game that appeared in 1974. In turn, the creators of D&D were inspired by the empirically detailed fantasy texts of Robert E. Howard, H. P. Love-craft, Fritz Leiber and others, which had developed in the marketing genres indebted to the documentary fantasies of the New Romance.[131]

D&D players inhabited imaginary worlds communally through prac-tices similar to those used by fantasy fans earlier in the century. Game play relied on a "Dungeon Master" who carefully mapped out the imaginary world and players who were willing to engage in the group pretense that this fantastic world existed. Fantasy was accompanied by strict rationality: players followed complex rules laid out in dauntingly thick rulebooks. (To say nothing of the use of twenty-sided dice, which could be bewildering to initiates and noninitiates alike.) This combination of logic and fancy was pursued in the name of modern enchantment, as players imagined them-selves as heroic warriors, clever thieves, or subtle mages exploring a myste-rious world teeming with adventure and danger. In the 1970s, the typical players were adolescent males who enjoyed the camaraderie the game of-fered as much as the sense of wonder it generated.[132]

Some of the players would go on to create the first virtual worlds on the Internet. These ranged from text-based Multi-User Dungeons (MUDs) devel-oped in Britain and the United States in the late 1970s, to the visually rich, Massively Multiplayer Online Role-Playing Games (MMORPG) of the 1990s.[133] The latter took advantage of new graphic interfaces and more pow-erful computer networking to present extensive virtual worlds that could be inhabited communally by thousands of players at any hour of the day or night. Many of the pioneering online game designers hoped to replicate the immer-sive enchantments they had experienced as readers of fantasy fiction: as one explained, "We were all in it out of a sense of wonder."[134] The games usually required players to complete quests that called for critical thinking as well as swift reflexes; mindless slashing and hacking, while perhaps gratifying in the short term, were likely to slow advancement and result in an early "death."[135]

Computer game designers also intended to replicate the social community that had been integral to Dungeons & Dragons and the textual virtual realities that preceded them.[136] Online role-playing games, such as Everquest, World of Warcraft, and Ultima Online, permitted players to socialize with one another within the imaginary worlds as well as to engage in quests and adventures. The fellowship generated in the virtual world became so important that many players continued to meet "face2face" outside of the game.[137] Similar communities emerged spontaneously out of online, multiplayer action games, such as Doom and Quake, whose initial design parameters had not included them. According to one account:

> Most of the games and the online services that rose to support them included a text-chat function, which tended to start with lines like 'EAT LEAD SUCKAH!' but often moved on to actual conversations about the game and game play and then other topics, until players realized they'd crossed some line to become genuine acquaintances or even close friends, often without even meeting face to face.[138]

It is clear that many inhabitants of online virtual worlds were not the solitary, antisocial misfits of media lore. "The Daedalus Project," which has been surveying online role-playing gamers, since 1999, found that 80 percent frequently played with someone they know.[139]

Online virtual-world communities gradually became diversified, not only in terms of gender but also age, profession, and nationality.[140] As public spheres of the imagination, they complemented the narrow, instrumental logic of the game rules with broader perspectives, becoming playful spaces in which players could experiment with alternative identities and values, political structures, and social mores. Amidst the diversion there was also utopian thinking and experimentation; along with an escape to marvelous environs there was a rational engagement with everyday life. The science fiction world of Eve Online, for example, hired a Ph.D. in economics to issue a quarterly newsletter about the game's virtual economy, and in 2007 gamers proposed creating an elected council of players to represent themselves, "with ideas drawn from philosophers from Aristotle to John Rawls."[141] A corporate executive behind World of Warcraft indicated that his company viewed the imaginary world as a public sphere of the imagination: "I look at World of Warcraft not so much as a game but as game meets social networking... It has as much in common with Yahoo message boards or MySpace or Facebook as anything else, and it's very powerful once you start thinking of games in that way."[142]

This concept is central to Second Life, an online imaginary world that was designed for social networking when it appeared in 2002. Its creators, Linden Labs, provide the infrastructure that allows its inhabitants to generate personalized virtual selves, domiciles, communities, art, businesses, and nearly anything else that can be imagined (and is in accord with company policies). Here too fantasy and reality, enchantment and reason commingle. On first impression, Second Life appears little different from other online fantasy worlds. Inhabitants design their own personas, or avatars (a concept made popular by Neil Stephenson's 1992 science fiction novel *Snow Crash* and then worldwide by James Cameron's 2009 film *Avatar*). The options available for avatar expression range from the bland to the incredible. One visitor thought he was being daring by decreasing his love handles, until he found that daring is a relative term in this fantastic world: "There were robot-headed monsters, cartoon-faced clowns, spiky-haired punks, leather-clad dominatrices. There were flying figures, with fairy wings instead of arms."[143] He too learned how to fly, a standard means of transportation in Second Life—alongside teleportation.

Yet the interactions within Second Life can be serious as well as fanciful, and the virtual experiences are often directly connected to the real world. Individuals and corporations conduct actual business, scholars engage in research, artists display and sell their works. Many individuals freely create alternative identities and lifestyles that may or may not affect their everyday lives. Like textual and online fantasy gaming worlds, Second Life is an autonomous imaginary world that generates a "sense of wonder," but its enchantments are often intimately intertwined with the practical, rational affairs of the modern world. At the same time, it is a fluid space of possibility, where normative conventions are always subject to question.

Online virtual worlds are the contemporary heirs of the fin-de-siècle imaginary worlds, but they lack the marginal status that had been ascribed to their predecessors for generations. Whereas the earlier, literary virtual worlds had been limited to fantasy fans and dismissed by intellectuals for much of their history, virtual worlds like Second Life indicate that genre labels are no longer as relevant when it comes to living in the imagination. They demonstrate that Vaihinger's Fictionalism, with its "philosophy of 'as if,'" has become a widespread stance of modernity, and the practice of inhabiting imaginary worlds communally through the ironic imagination has expanded beyond the habits of fan coteries. There are online virtual spaces for every genre, including "mainstream literature." (Or simply "lit-fic," to place it on par with "sci-fi.") Earlier, I distinguished realist "imagined worlds," such as those of Balzac, Zola, and Powell, from fantastic "imaginary worlds," such as those of Conan Doyle, Lovecraft, and Tolkien. Imaginary worlds were the first to become virtual worlds—they provided the modern enchantments readers craved—but today even imagined worlds have taken virtual flight.[144]

The type of reason exercised in imaginary worlds is not the "instrumental rationality" that Weber and others blamed for disenchanting the world. This was a functional form of reason, which worked within empirical constraints as it pursued the most efficient means to attain delimited ends. Late nineteenth-century bureaucrats excelled at this means-ends rationality, as did positivist scholars and scientific naturalists. They often denigrated anything that could not be measured or observed, including the imagination.

Yet the imaginary worlds of the New Romance and the succeeding marketing genres of science fiction, detective fiction, and fantasy fiction proffered an alternative form of rationality, which combined reason and the imagination. It transformed critical thinking into a quasi-magical process that, while proceeding within logical parameters and relying on empirical evidence, also enlivened the facts on which it operated. Because of its vivifying power, it was an animistic form of reason. It re-enchanted the modern world without abjuring modernity's commitment to rational critique.

Poe's Auguste Dupin was the first fictional character to endorse animistic reason, but its most charismatic exponent was Sherlock Holmes. By exemplifying an alternative to the disenchanting instrumental reason of the late nineteenth century, he became enormously popular and has remained so over a century later. Not just a quintessentially modern character, Sherlock Holmes is also the first virtual reality character of modern fiction. Some of his most ardent fans have playfully written his creator out of the picture, or relegated him to the role of Watson's literary agent. But Conan Doyle cannot be neglected, because the issues of disenchantment and re-enchantment were crucial to him, just as they were for the consulting detective of 221B Baker Street—our next (imaginary) destination.

◦◊◦

CHAPTER 3

Clap If You Believe in Sherlock Holmes

Arthur Conan Doyle and Animistic Reason

[Imagination] is a power in the human mind which is at work in our everyday perception of the world, and is also at work in our thoughts about what is absent; which enables us to see the world, whether present or absent, as significant, and also to present this vision to others, for them to share or reject. And this power, though it gives us "thought imbued" perception . . . is not only intellectual. Its impetus comes from the emotions as much as from reason, from the heart as much as from the head.

—Mary Warnock

Yet as more and more the interest of the world centers upon the life of Mr. Sherlock Holmes, every item of his association becomes enchanting.

—Vincent Starrett

I. DISENCHANTMENT, ANIMISTIC REASON, AND THE IRONIC IMAGINATION

In 1920, Sir Arthur Conan Doyle published an article in *The Strand* magazine affirming his belief in the existence of fairies. Accompanying the article were several photographs of the alleged sprites, taken by two young girls from Yorkshire in 1917, which had convinced Conan Doyle of a discovery he termed "epoch-making."[1] "Obvious faking" was the preferred term of many of his readers, however. Fans of the rationalist detective Sherlock Holmes were appalled that his creator, a trained physician, could display such credulity. Didn't Conan Doyle wonder why many of the preternatural creatures in the photos were wearing contemporary evening dresses and had their hair cut in the fashionable "bobbed" style?[2] Conan Doyle had already come under public criticism for his wholehearted adoption of spiritualism in 1917, but with his acceptance of fairies even the spiritualists began to keep their distance.[3] In the "Adventure of the Chuckle-Headed Doctor," one of Conan Doyle's critics had Sherlock Holmes confess to being as baffled as the public: "But how," Holmes asks, "did a sober-minded and apparently abstemious doctor, last seen at midnight at the National Sporting Club, came to be found at four a.m. on the Mendip Hills, bereft of his wits and professing to have spent the night dancing with fairies?"[4]

The wonderful irony of the situation is that at the same time that Conan Doyle was criticized for claiming that fairies were real, many of his readers were claiming that Sherlock Holmes was real. Indeed, Holmes was the first character in modern literature to be widely treated as if he were real and his creator fictitious.[5] Since his appearance in *The Strand* magazine in 1891, many either believed Holmes existed or at least claimed that they did. The interwar period witnessed an outpouring of articles in prominent magazines and books from respectable publishers that treated Holmes and Watson as real, but never mentioned Conan Doyle. For example, scholarly "biographies" of both Holmes and Watson appeared in 1932, inspiring equally scholarly reviews and leading articles debating such fine points as which college Holmes attended or how many wives Watson had. Looking back years later, the author of the Watson biography stated he was "amazed at the number of columns which editors allotted to reviews of these two books."[6] He wasn't alone in his surprise. Conan Doyle, who clearly was willing to countenance many unusual ideas, nevertheless thought it was "incredible how realistic some people take [this imaginary character] to be."[7] G. K. Chesterton observed, "The real inference [of these works] is that Sherlock Holmes really existed and that Conan Doyle never existed. If posterity only reads these latter books it will certainly suppose them to be serious. It will imagine that Sherlock Holmes was a man."[8]

Was this simply a further peculiarity of the English? One English reviewer thought so: "Does anything puzzle a foreigner more . . . than the enthusiasm with which our learned men . . . investigate the character and career of two purely imaginary persons?"[9] But the fancy that Holmes and Watson were real was an international phenomenon. Americans also published articles and books treating Conan Doyle's characters as real. *The Saturday Review of Literature* in the 1930s and 1940s published many pieces asserting the reality of the characters, as did *The Bookman* and the *Chicago Tribune* (via Vincent Starrett's popular "Books Alive!" column).[10] Indeed, the Sherlock Holmes "cult" attracted eager devotees in Canada, France, and Japan, among other countries, creating a worldwide audience for works of nonfiction devoted to works of fiction that were taken to be true.

These "studies in Sherlock," or "Sherlockiana," helped establish an imaginary world that could be accepted as both real and fictional through the ironic imagination. Such ironic play was highlighted in the studies themselves. The epigraph to a collection of essays, *Profile by Gaslight: An Irregular Reader About the Private Life of Sherlock Holmes* (1944) read, "The characters in this book are real persons. Any resemblance to fictional characters, living or dead, is purely accidental."[11] A mystery novel of 1940, Anthony Boucher's *The Case of the Baker Street Irregulars,* injected a note of "realism" into the fictional proceedings: "All characters portrayed or referred to in this novel are fictitious, with the exception of Sherlock Holmes, to whom this book is dedicated."[12] And W. S. Baring-Gould's full-length biography, *Sherlock Holmes of Baker Street* (1962), cautioned readers that "No characters in this book are fictional, although the author should very much like to meet any who claim to be."[13]

Sherlock Holmes was the first fictional creation that adults openly embraced as real while deliberately minimizing or ignoring its creator, and this fetishization of Holmes has continued for over a century. The cult of Holmes focuses not just on a singular character, but on his entire world: fans of the "canon" obsess about every detail of the fictional universe Conan Doyle created, mentally inhabiting this geography of the imagination in a way that was never true for partisans of earlier characters. And the Holmesian phenomenon has continued for over a century, far longer than the intermittent eighteenth-century vogues for Samuel Richardson's *Pamela,* let alone the more restricted generational enthusiasms for Werther, Little Nell, and others. Sherlockian devotion is thus a departure from preceding public infatuations with fictional characters and a template for subsequent public infatuations for imaginary worlds and their protagonists. The popular fascination with Holmes commenced the transformation of certain imaginary worlds into virtual worlds. The question is, why Holmes?

There are several answers to this question, but the most important has to do with the discourse of disenchantment that circulated among intellectuals during the waning decades of the nineteenth century and early decades of the twentieth. Many mourned the apparent absence of communal beliefs and higher ideals in an age that seemed dominated by positivism and materialism, and turned to alternative sources of spiritual sustenance. These ranged from the nostalgic medievalism of the Arts and Crafts movement, to a fascination with non-Christian beliefs and non-Western art, to attempts to reconcile science and religion through spiritualism, occultism, and psychical research.

However, these and other efforts to escape from the "iron cage" of rationality that Weber imputed to the modern West were uneasy compromises between the past and the present that left many unsatisfied. Modernity was widely associated with progress toward the rational and away from the supernatural, and efforts by believers to impart the veneer of scientific respectability to the supernatural were frequently greeted with skepticism if not outright disdain by contemporary commentators. Thus psychical research and spiritualism, both nineteenth-century efforts at finding a *via media* between science and religion, tended to be marginalized by established science at the turn of the century. Several of the prominent scientists in the Society for Psychical Research who supported spiritualism, such as Sir William Crookes, Sir W. F. Barrett, and Oliver Lodge, were viewed by most of their professional peers as credulous believers who tried to legitimate their faith with scientific rhetoric but without compelling scientific evidence— just as Conan Doyle's belief in fairies was to be viewed.[14] And while the efflorescence of spiritualism at the popular level in Britain during and immediately after the Great War was an understandable emotive reaction to the tremendous losses suffered by many, it too was often represented as a "traditional" rather than "modern" phenomenon (using the binary oppositions common to the period) and one that was diminishing by the 1930s.[15]

The character of Sherlock Holmes, however, represented and celebrated the central tenets of modernity adumbrated at the time—not just rationalism and secularism, but also urbanism and consumerism. The stories made these tenets magical without introducing magic: Holmes demonstrated how the modern world could be re-enchanted through means entirely consistent with modernity. Because Holmes represented the values of modernity in ways that addressed the criticisms of the cultural pessimists, he spoke to the dissatisfactions and hopes of adults as well as to the imaginations of children. Like many of his readers, Holmes yearned for enchantment, confessing to his "love of all that is bizarre and outside the conventions and humdrum routine of everyday life."[16] But Holmes was also able to gratify his sense of wonder by embracing modernity, rather than turning nostalgically to the past: "for strange effects and extraordinary combinations we must go to life itself, which is always far more daring than any effort of the imagination."[17] As in the case of H. P. Lovecraft's later fictions, Holmes finds the marvelous not in the supernatural, which science has discredited, but in the natural made sublime: "The world is big enough for us," he tells Watson. "No ghosts need apply."[18]

Sherlock Holmes became a modern icon partly because he utilized reason in a manner magical and adventurous, rather than in the purely instrumental fashion that many contemporaries feared was the stultifying characteristic of the age. Science and art, which had been associated from the Renaissance through the Enlightenment, as well as in the writings of early romantics such as Goethe, Wordsworth, Coleridge, and Shelley, appeared to be severed by the mid-nineteenth century.[19] Holmes restored their vital interchange, rendering science creative and art enlightening. He expanded the definition of rationality beyond a narrow, means-ends instrumentalism to include the imagination, resulting in the more commodious form of "animistic reason" that imbued its objects with meaning. It was through his animistic reason that Holmes the private detective bested professional detectives on cases, as he often boasted. (In one case he confides to Watson that "Inspector Gregory, to whom the case has been committed, is an extremely competent officer. Were he but gifted with imagination he might rise to great heights in his profession.")[20] Holmes solved cases by relating seemingly discrete facts to a more encompassing and meaningful configuration, whose integuments were derived from a combination of rigorous observation, precise logic, and lively imagination. The professional investigators whom Holmes trumps in these cases tend to be unimaginative positivists who miss everything that is not presented directly before their senses, or are unable to interpret creatively those that are:

> "Is there any point to which you would wish to draw my attention?"
> "To the curious incident of the dog in the night-time."
> "The dog did nothing in the night-time."
> "That was the curious incident," remarked Sherlock Holmes.[21]

Holmes's dramatic use of animistic reason was the mass-culture exemplification of a complex of ideas that circulated as part of the fin-de-siècle revolt against the dominant discourses of positivism, materialism, and scientific naturalism. In creating Holmes, Conan Doyle had been influenced by Poe, who stressed the inseparability of reason and the imagination in his pioneering detective tales featuring Auguste Dupin. In "The Murders in the Rue Morgue" (1841), Dupin opines that "the *truly* imaginative [are] never otherwise than analytic."[22] He continues in this vein in "The Purloined Letter" (1844). Refuting the narrator's contention that "mathematical reason has long been regarded as *the* reason par excellence," Dupin insists that imagination is vital to the ratiocinative process: "As poet *and* mathematician, [the mathematician] would reason well; as mere mathematician, he could not have reasoned at all."[23] While Sherlock Holmes made some disparaging remarks about Dupin, it is evident that Conan Doyle's frequently expressed admiration for Poe included Poe's definition of ratiocination: Holmes represented it. He explains to Watson that his abilities are in part hereditary; his grandmother was the sister of the French painter Vernet, and "art in the blood is liable to take the strangest forms."[24] Many of Conan Doyle's contemporaries—figures as diverse as Friedrich Nietzsche, Henri Bergson, Stéphane Mallarmé, Oscar Wilde, Henri Poincaré, and William James—were among those who maintained that reason and the imagination were inextricable, sharing Richard Wagner's call for "the emotionalization of the intellect."[25] By advocating the integration of reason and the imagination, these thinkers gainsaid the fashionable cultural pessimism of the period and made it possible to see modernity and enchantment as compatible rather than antagonistic.

While writers like Poe and Verne, and the later marketing genres of detective and science fiction, celebrated the romance of reason, it was arguably Holmes who made this romance most explicit and attractive to a mass reading public in sixty narratives published over the course of four decades. These tales made analysis an adventure, quotidian facts an infinite source of astonishment. "Depend upon it," insists Holmes, "there is nothing so unnatural as the commonplace."[26] When Watson suggests that Holmes's analytical methods are the most exciting aspects of the stories he narrates, Holmes demurs: "Pshaw, my dear fellow, what do the public, the great unobservant public, who could hardly tell a weaver by his tooth or a compositor by his left thumb, care about the finer shades of analysis and deduction!"[27] Perhaps this was true before Holmes came into their lives. But it was his example that helped thousands of readers to perceive the romance of reason, ranging from elites disillusioned with the means-ends form of cognition that seemed to signify the spirit of the age, to ordinary readers who might not have associated reason with disenchantment—but probably didn't associate it with enchantment, either. After encountering Holmes, many of them did.

Indeed, numerous fans of the great detective emulated his methods by bringing their intellects and imaginations to bear on Conan Doyle's stories, scrutinizing every particular as if Holmes himself was a mystery to solve. Some actually believed that Holmes existed—"naïve believers"—but most were "ironic believers," who were not so much willingly suspending their disbelief in a fictional character as willingly believing in him with the double-minded awareness that they were engaged in pretense. By emulating Holmes's deployment of animistic reason, adults could immerse themselves in imaginary worlds without relinquishing their practical reason: they could believe in Holmes in an enchanted yet rational way. *The Times* noted in 1932 that the authors who treated Holmes and Watson as real did so with the greatest sobriety, but that this was "only their fun—the single-minded fun of spiritually young Sherlockians at play."[28]

"Play" was precisely what many cultural pessimists thought had been driven out of the modern world by the ineluctable advance of an impoverished instrumental reason. Johan Huizinga, in his classic survey of the role of play in the creation of civilization, *Homo Ludens* (1938), ended on a morose note: "More and more the sad conclusion forces itself upon us that the play-element in culture has been on the wane ever since the eighteenth century."[29] But the widespread "belief" in Sherlock Holmes is a telling illustration that precisely the opposite situation prevailed in Western culture at the time of Huizinga's assertion.

Thus a widespread form of modern rationality became the animistic reason employed by Sherlock Holmes, and a prevailing form of the modern imagination was the ironic imagination affirmed by many of his devotees.[30] Together they yielded rational and secular enchantments that provided an alternative to the supernatural enchantments of the premodern period. They are distinguished by an "as if" orientation—as we shall see by comparing Conan Doyle's "just so" faith in preternatural fairies with his readers' ironic belief in Sherlock Holmes.

Many readers of the early Sherlock Holmes stories assumed that his creator must have shared the attributes that made Holmes so quintessentially modern: his secularism, his rationalism, his skepticism. But from an early age, Conan Doyle expressed ambivalence about modernity. He was raised as a Catholic and educated by Jesuits, but as a young man he renounced Catholicism and gravitated toward the rationalist and positivist outlook of his medical school instructors at the University of Edinburgh. Yet he was not comfortable with modern atheism and materialism either; his disenchantment with these aspects of modernity and dissatisfaction with agnosticism led him to explore Theosophy in 1884 and spiritualism shortly thereafter, before he wrote the first Holmes story.[31] His spiritualist convictions increased over the decades, and he announced his full-fledged conversion to spiritualism in 1917 (before either his son Kingsley or his brother Innes died as a consequence of the Great War).

The Holmes stories reflect Conan Doyle's ambivalence about modernity. Critics often remark that Holmes's continued popularity is beholden to the nostalgic vision of the late Victorian era the stories convey. T. S. Eliot, for example, claimed, "Sherlock Holmes reminds us always of the pleasant externals of nineteenth-century London."[32] But aside from the occasional reference to a cozy fire in the hearth or buttered toast on the table at 221B Baker Street, Conan Doyle's stories tend to emphasize the unpleasant rather than pleasant externals of nineteenth-century London. In the first Holmes tale, "A Study in Scarlet," London is described by Watson as "that great cesspool" and "the great wilderness"; other descriptions of the urban environment focus on dank fog, murky clouds, "mud-colored streets," "dingy streets and dreary byways," and so on.[33] In "The Sign of the Four" the externals remain the same: in London the "mud colored clouds dropped sadly over the muddy streets. Down the Strand the lamps were but misty splotches of diffused light which threw a feeble, circular glimmer upon slimy pavement."[34] Once you notice this trend, which continues through the series, it is difficult to imagine "pleasant externals" in the London of Conan Doyle's imagination. Many projected their own nostalgia for a distant era onto the stories, but the stories themselves often depict the squalor and anomie of modern urban existence.

Conan Doyle's ambivalence is also reflected in the character of Holmes, who is as much a victim of modern reason as he is, in Watson's words, "the most perfect reasoning and observing machine that the world has seen."[35] Holmes is often trapped in the iron cage of reason: the banal routine of modern life bores him, and at times he resorts to cocaine for stimulation. As he tells Watson in "The Adventure of Wisteria Lodge," "Life is common-place, the papers are sterile; audacity and romance seem to have passed for ever from the criminal world."[36] Yet when an interesting case does arrive, Holmes snaps out of his lethargy: mystery has been restored to the world, however briefly, and as Holmes notes, "mystery stimulates the imagina-tion"[37] and returns romance to the world. But this is a modern form of romance in which reason provides the magic, and indeed Holmes's use of reason is so uncannily effective that Watson remarks, "You would certainly have been burned, had you lived a few centuries ago."[38] In the Holmes stories, rationality is the problem, but also the solution.

Conan Doyle was not satisfied with the romance of reason, however. He grew tired of Holmes and tried to end the series in 1893 by having Holmes and his arch-nemesis Professor Moriarty plunge into the Reichenbach Falls.[39] Public demand, as well as a lucrative contract from his publisher, led Conan Doyle to revive Holmes a decade later. But he had few good words to say about his most famous character, and believed that his enduring novels would be his medieval romances *The White Company* (1891) and *Sir Nigel* (1906). Conan Doyle was not simply bored with Holmes, as he main-tained; rather, Holmes's ambivalence about the modern world were those of his creator, but Holmes's solution—the use of reason to re-enchant the world—was not one that Conan Doyle found satisfactory. Like Holmes, Conan Doyle had been trained to be analytical and skeptical, but unlike Holmes (as far as we can tell), Conan Doyle had also been brought up in a religious environment, and he continued to crave the unambiguous cer-tainties, along with the traditional mysteries, that religion provided.

Holmes gave rare expression to Conan Doyle's deeper fears and hopes in two unusual remarks that have long puzzled readers because they are so foreign to the detective's materialist orientation. In the conclusion of "The Adventure of the Cardboard Box" (1892), Holmes reflects on the existen-tial terrors of an apparently random cosmos:

> What is the meaning of it, Watson? . . . What object is served by this circle of misery and
> violence and fear? It must tend to some end, or else our universe is ruled by chance,

which is unthinkable. But what end? There is the great standing perennial problem to which human reason is so far from an answer as ever.[40]

This was the problem Conan Doyle wrestled with, one that was all the more compelling as a result of his firsthand experience of human suffering as a physician. And Holmes's apparent epiphany in "The Naval Treaty" (1893) foreshadows the conclusion that Conan Doyle would eventually adopt. Holmes reflects on the gratuitous beauty of a rose to deduce the possibility of a beneficent plan to existence: "[The rose's] smell and its colour are an embellishment of life, not a condition of it. It is only goodness which gives extras, and so, I say again that we have much to hope from the flowers."[41]

These remarks, starkly anomalous in terms of Holmes's secular orientation in the other stories, are readily explained by Conan Doyle's spiritual yearnings, which he appeased through a fascination with psychical research in the 1900s. Late in World War I he converted to the faith of spiritualism, and in 1920 he eagerly accepted the photographic evidence of fairies: "these little folks . . . will become familiar," he proclaimed in his article for *The Strand*. "The recognition of their existence will jolt the material twentieth-century mind out of its heavy ruts in the mud, and will make it admit that there is a glamour and a mystery to life."[42] But Conan Doyle's belief in fairies and supernatural spirits, a premodern form of enchantment, no longer had a future. Instead, many of his readers believed in Sherlock Holmes as a way to re-enchant the world without rejecting the secular and skeptical tenets of modernity.

II. NAÏVE BELIEVERS, IRONIC BELIEVERS, AND THE WEB OF CAUSATION

Most readers of the Holmes stories approached them as entertaining fictions, but some believed in Holmes's existence from his earliest appearance. After the second Holmes story was published in 1890, Conan Doyle wrote to his editor, surprised that "a . . . tobacconist actually wrote to me under cover to you, to ask me where he could get a copy of the monograph in which Sherlock Holmes described the difference in the ashes of 140 different types of tobacco."[43] There were two types of Holmes believers: the "naïve believer" and the "ironic believer." Let me take each in turn.

The naïve believer genuinely believed that Holmes and Watson were real. The press had a field day when reporting on the naïve believers, who wrote letters to Holmes requesting his assistance or scoured Baker Street looking for his residence. Conan Doyle received numerous letters addressed to Holmes, as did the magazines that ran the stories.[44] Editors

responded coyly to their earnest inquirers; in 1892 the penny weekly *Tit-Bits* remarked, "Buttons wishes to know whether Sherlock Holmes, the detective genius . . . is or is not an actual person. We cannot positively say . . . [I]f . . . we should find that no such person is in existence, we shall then be very much disappointed indeed."[45] (Although a note of exasperation could also be detected in the editor's comments, as in the following to reader H. L.: "It is not true that Oliver Wendell Holmes was the father of Sherlock Holmes; as a matter of fact, they were not related at all.")[46] Interestingly, the press identified many of these naïve believers as foreigners, perhaps reflecting unease with the idea that British common sense could in practice be so uncommon. In 1926 a leader in *The Times* noted that "In certain backward countries, it is said, full obituaries of the great Sherlock were published as of a real man; and those who spent any time on the Continent about twenty years ago may recall seeing . . . what seemed to be whole libraries of apocryphal Holmes literature, not by any means translations, but the free creations of a mythological fancy, rather like the Eastern legends of Alexander the Great."[47] And in 1930 a writer to *The Times* claimed that "thousands of people" believed Holmes was real, citing among the thousands the Turks in Constantinople.[48] But press reports of naïve believers weren't simply an instance of Orientalism; in 1937 *The Times* also enjoyed reporting on an elderly Danish couple who had written a respectful letter to Holmes requesting financial assistance.[49]

The naïve belief in Sherlock Holmes can be explained in part by the dynamics of mass publishing and the beginning of celebrity culture at the turn of the century. The Holmes stories quickly garnered a wide readership among an increasingly literate population. Conan Doyle's talents as an author and Holmes's distinctiveness as a character were, of course, central to the popularity of the series. Several commentators stressed how lifelike Holmes was in comparison with the detectives of Edgar Allan Poe and Émile Gaboriau, or of Conan Doyle's contemporary imitators.[50] As we have seen, Conan Doyle also maximized the size of his audience by writing the continuing adventures of his character as self-contained short stories rather than serial chapters, permitting new readers to become involved with Holmes at any point in the series and established readers to anticipate avidly his next adventures. George Newnes, the publisher of *The Strand* and *Tit-Bits*, promoted the Holmes stories vigorously in both mass-circulation magazines. In addition, Holmes received enormous media exposure when Conan Doyle tried to end the series by killing him in 1893, and when Conan Doyle found it financially advantageous to write new Holmes narratives starting in 1901.

Holmes was also one of the first characters to become ubiquitous through the new mass media. He was visually recognizable through Sidney

Paget's remarkable illustrations in *The Strand*. Conan Doyle said of Paget, "he illustrated the stories so well that he made a type which the whole English-reading race came to recognize."[51] He was also recognizable through William Gillette's portrayal of Holmes in a very popular stage dramatization that toured America and Britain at the turn of the century; through numerous short films that commenced in 1900; and through radio dramatizations as well as feature-length films in the 1930s.

Thus Holmes became a media celebrity in his own right, in a period when the culture of celebrity was new and not yet fully understood. The synergistic effect of all this attention devoted to Holmes may have encouraged less sophisticated readers to approach the stories as nonfictional rather than fictional. Working within the tradition of the New Romance, Conan Doyle wrote the stories in a realist style, with allusions to contemporary events and earlier "case-histories"; readers who were unused to distinguishing among different modes of writing might easily have fallen into the trap of believing Dr. Watson's compelling, "factual" narratives.[52]

This befuddlement was exacerbated when Conan Doyle became a celebrity alongside his celebrated creation. He was featured in many of the gossipy interviews then being pioneered by the New Journalists, in which he and his interlocutor casually referred to Holmes as a real person. Holmes returned the favor, granting his first interview to the *National Observer* in 1892 and then to other publications. As celebrities Conan Doyle and Holmes were thus linked, and often confused, in the public mind, especially as Conan Doyle himself attempted to solve several highly publicized crimes. He recalled one unnerving lecture engagement when the audience seemed visibly disappointed at his appearance at the lectern: "they all expected to see in me a cadaverous looking person with marks of cocaine injections all over him."[53] When Holmes received obituary notices in 1893, many thought that Conan Doyle had died;[54] after Conan Doyle ran for Parliament, a newspaper ran a story headlined "How Holmes Tried Politics."[55] When Conan Doyle announced his belief in fairies, one headline read "Poor Sherlock Holmes, Hopelessly Crazy?"[56] At a time when celebrity culture itself was beginning to efface distinctions between reality and appearance, naïve readers might be forgiven for mistaking Conan Doyle for Holmes, or Holmes for a real person.

The second type of believer was the ironic believer, who pretended that Holmes was real—but for whom this pretense was so earnest that the uninitiated might not recognize it as pretense. Like the naïve believers, the ironic believers appeared in the early 1890s. But the tenor of the ironist's writings changed over time, from outright parodies to more solemn, quasi-scholarly investigations. Beginning in the 1890s, the ironists published parodies and pastiches of the stories in college magazines, *Punch,* and *Tit-Bits.*

The "game" of Sherlockian scholarship commenced in the same spirit as early as 1902. In that year, Frank Sidgwick wrote an open letter to Dr. Watson in the *Cambridge Review* inquiring about the apparently contradictory details in the recently published *The Hound of the Baskervilles;* and Arthur Bartlett Maurice, an editor of the American magazine *The Bookman,* published ongoing queries about the work as well. The first well-known example of parodic scholarship, or "Sherlockiana," was Ronald Knox's "Studies in the Literature of Sherlock Holmes," published in 1912. In this piece Knox lampooned the German Higher Criticism of the Bible by applying similar methods to the numerous discrepancies in the stories. Questions about whether Watson's name was John or James, whether he was shot in the shoulder or the leg, ad infinitum, were resolved by reference to the multiple authors of the canon: the Deutero-Watson, the Proto-Watson, and so on.[57]

Knox's essay was not only funny: it used Holmes's methods to solve the mysteries of Holmes's history, enabling the ironist to play at being his favorite character while reading his exploits. When Knox's essay was republished in 1928, a year after the final Sherlock Holmes story appeared in print, it proved to be a key inspiration for a host of more solemn studies of the series on both sides of the Atlantic.[58] Other influences included the renewed attention to Holmes sparked by Conan Doyle's death in 1930 and the publication that year of the first one-volume collection of all the tales. The early 1930s witnessed a torrent of works devoted to the premise that Holmes existed, including S. C. Robert's *Doctor Watson: Prolegomena to the Study of a Biographical Problem, with a Bibliography of Sherlock Holmes* (1931); T. S. Blakeney, *Sherlock Holmes: Fact or Fiction?* (1932); H. W. Bell, *Sherlock Holmes and Dr. Watson: A Chronology of Their Adventures* (1932); and Vincent Starrett, *The Private Life of Sherlock Holmes* (1933). The authors of these and other works engaged in a "game" whose cardinal rule, according to Dorothy Sayers, "is that it must be played as solemnly as a county cricket match at Lord's: the slightest touch of extravagance or burlesque ruins the atmosphere."[59]

Sherlockian studies tended to adhere to the cardinal rule. Many of them were analytical and carefully documented, epitomizing sober scholarship. The writers included some of the most prominent figures in Britain and America: journalists like Desmond MacCarthy and Christopher Morley; novelists and critics like Dorothy Sayers and Vincent Starrett; academics like Jacques Barzun and S. C. Roberts; broadcasters like Elmer Davis; scientists like Buckminster Fuller and Norbert Wiener, statesmen like Lord Gore-Booth and President Franklin Delano Roosevelt (who argued that Holmes was really an American); and businessmen like Edgar W. Smith, a senior executive with General Motors. In 1934 the Baker Street Irregulars (BSI) was founded in New York and the Sherlock Holmes Society was established in London, both celebrating the memory of the greatest detective who ever "lived." The *Baker Street Journal* first appeared under the BSI's auspices in 1946, and the Sherlock Holmes Society of London commenced publication of the *Sherlock Holmes Journal* in 1952: the first magazines dedicated to the ironically held proposition that a fictional character was real. They continue to thrive today.[60]

The aspect of Holmes that made him into a modern icon for all those who professed belief in him, to whatever degree, was that he re-enchanted modernity without compromising the central tenets of modernity: rationalism, secularism, urbanism, and mass consumerism. Holmes believed that every detail of modern life, ranging from the footprints of a giant hound to advertisements in mass-circulation newspapers, was charged with meaning.[61] By 1920, Conan Doyle no longer believed that; only the existence of the supernatural could imbue modernity with enchantment. But Holmes, and the conventions of the detective genre he represented, could assuage the modern craving for the magical without ever reverting to the supernatural. In a 1942 interview Jacques Barzun stated, "We believe in Holmes because he believes in science and we do too."[62] Vincent Starrett observed that "Conan Doyle . . . created the *fictional* Holmes for our enchantment."[63]

But Holmes's science of observation was not the same as positivistic science. It re-enchanted the world by imbuing everything with hidden import. Holmes demonstrated that profane reality could be no less mysterious or alluring than the supernatural realm; the material world was laden with occult meanings that could be revealed to those with an observant eye and logical outlook. When Watson remarks that Holmes has made deductions based on clues "quite invisible to me," Holmes replies in irritation, "not invisible but unnoticed, Watson. You did not know where to look, and so you missed all that was important. I can never bring you to realize the importance of sleeves, the suggestiveness of thumb-nails, or the great issues that may hang from a boot-lace."[64]

While Holmes is obviously gifted in his powers of observation, the implication of the tales is that such skills can be practiced by anyone. In "The Red-Headed League," this democratic message is made explicit. The client of this tale is initially dumbfounded when Holmes scrutinizes him and determines that the man has engaged in manual labor, takes snuff, is a Freemason, has visited China, and has recently done a great deal of writing. Holmes then explains how he deduced each point from the man's appearance, and the client is pleasantly surprised at the apparent simplicity of the detective's methods: "I thought at first that you had done something clever, but I see that there was nothing in it, after all."[65] The client reveals his ignorance, of course, since Holmes is supremely clever, but readers could nevertheless share his delight that the method is accessible to the common individual. (Watson's occasional successes in its practice are further confirmations of this enthralling possibility.) Joseph Bell, the Edinburgh physician who was one of Conan Doyle's models for Holmes's uncanny inductive and deductive skills, served as living proof that real people could find the extraordinary in the ordinary. Holmes's methods, Bell noted, "are at once so obvious, when explained, and so easy, once you know them, that the ingenious reader at once feels, and says to himself, I also could do this; life is not so dull after all; I will keep my eyes open, and find out things."[66]

G. K. Chesterton perceived both this reinscription of supernatural glamour into the profane world and the democratic implications of the detective genre Conan Doyle helped establish. He observed in 1901 that these narratives were the modern equivalent of fairy tales, which trained ordinary readers to perceive marvels in the commonplace:

> No one can have failed to notice that in these stories the hero or the investigator crosses London with something of the loneliness and liberty of a prince in a tale of elfland, that in the course of that incalculable journey the casual omnibus assumes the primary colours of a fairy ship ... It is a good thing that the average man shall fall into the habit of looking imaginatively at ten men in the street even if it is only on the chance that the eleventh might be a notorious thief.[67]

Contemporaries agreed with Chesterton, arguing that the Holmes tales should not be considered mere escapism, because they encouraged readers to emulate Holmes's rational scrutiny of everyday life. Writing to *Tit-Bits* in 1894, one physician said that the stories "make many a fellow who has before felt very little interest in his life and daily surroundings, think that after all there may be much more in life, if he keeps his eyes open, than he has ever dreamed of in his philosophy."[68] *Tit-Bits* reported on readers like F. W. B. who "has been applying the principles of this great detective in various matters connected with actual private life."[69] The stories have continued to motivate readers to find wonder in the everyday through observation and logic. When students at West Virginia University established a Sherlock Holmes society in 1956, their mission statement read, "In promoting the study of Sherlockian material, the group hopes to develop the faculty of observation and deduction, which only Mycroft Holmes possesses in larger degree than his younger brother."[70]

Holmes's method provided a much sought alternative to the purely means-ends rationality that cultural pessimists believed characterized modernity and rendered it sterile. Rather than practicing this instrumental reason, Holmes brought reason and imagination together into an animistic reason, one that was congruent with aesthetic intuition. While Holmes may have been a thinking-machine, he was also a fin-de-siècle aesthete who arose late in the morning, kept his tobacco in the toe of a Persian slipper, thought best while smoking or playing his Stradivarius, and, of course, had his occasional recourse to cocaine. In one of the first "biographies" of Holmes, T. S. Blakeney noted that "this [combination of reason and imagination] was one of Holmes' strongest assets as a detective—he called it the scientific use of the imagination."[71] Animistic reason of the sort practiced by Holmes clearly was important to the ironic believers; it was precisely this union of logic and fancy that enabled them to maintain that he existed. Referring to the Baker Street Irregulars' scholarly exegesis of what they called the "Canon" (as distinct from "Conanical" writings about Conan Doyle), Edgar W. Smith stated that, "what we do in probing out the inner things is done ... in emulation of [Holmes's] approach to life, and as a tribute to his master mind."[72]

Readers also appreciated that Holmes's animistic reason restored a holistic import to the world. Cultural pessimists feared modernity was fragmented and looked back to the premodern period as a time of organic unity they believed might be forever lost; Conan Doyle's spiritualism and belief in fairies were attempts to restore such unity through reestablishing premodern beliefs in a modern guise.[73] But Holmes's form of reason revealed subtle links to modern existence that did not require supernatural intervention. He always managed to ascertain logical, but not necessarily obvious, connections among the empirical facts that he observed. Through careful scrutiny, analytical reasoning, and imaginative insight, Holmes demonstrated that modern experience could be holistic and legible, while remaining wonderfully variable. He argued that "all life is a great chain, the nature of which is known whenever we are shown a single link of it."[74] (At other times he refers to existence as a "web"; this metaphor negated the deterministic implications of a "chain" of causation.)[75]

Writing in 1894 to *Tit-Bits*, a reader praised the Holmes stories for highlighting life's mysterious yet decipherable interconnections. He stated, "The glory of all 'The Adventures of Sherlock Holmes' is that in them a due proportion is preserved for every link in the chain. In Holmes' examination of [a] room, every action and every deduction appears, not as an isolated phenomenon, but as one of a series of events, and the gradual evolution is ... the greatest charm of all to me."[76] Decades later the same point was made by Marshall McLuhan, who likened Holmes's use of reason to the organic holism of the romantics and contrasted it to the narrow instrumental reason of bureaucrats, whose "technique is serial, segmented, and circumstantial. They conclude effect immediately from preceding cause in lineal and chronological order. They do not dream of totalities or of the major relevance of details." While cultural pessimists sought but were unable to find an alternative to the instrumental reason of the modern bureaucratic state, Sherlock Holmes was practicing one, which is why McLuhan concluded that "the ordinary man finds a hero in Holmes."[77] The detective's use of animistic reason implied that the world was resonant with holistic meanings and replete with endless surprises.

Thus Holmes became an icon precisely because he provided the means to re-enchant the modern world without rejecting it. By combining reason and imagination in a tight synthesis he was able to vivify inert facts and reveal underlying correspondences; his readers could apply this example of animistic reason to their own lives, and many—the ironic believers— certainly applied it to the Holmes canon itself. In so doing, they helped to legitimate the idea that Western adults could indulge their imaginations without losing their reason. By engaging in such imaginative play they could bring the two together, as Holmes himself did. Edgar W. Smith, Vice-President of General Motors Overseas Operations, recognized this. No one could call this chief executive officer an escapist, except in the sense that he and other Holmes enthusiasts were escaping the narrow scientism and instrumentalism that many identified as modernity's essence. To Smith, Holmes "is Galahad and Socrates, bringing high adventure to our dull existences and calm, judicial logic to our biased minds . . . That is the Sherlock Holmes we love—the Holmes implicit and eternal in ourselves."[78]

While there were those, like Arthur Conan Doyle, who found modernity disenchanting and turned to the security of premodern beliefs, others were content to relegate those premodern beliefs to imaginary fancies, and then to embrace imaginative fancy as a distinctly modern form of enchantment. As Dorothy Sayers asked in 1934, "Why, if mere creatures of the imagination, like Peter Pan, are to be commemorated with statues, this honour should be withheld from national figures such as Sherlock Holmes"?[79]

III. HOLMES'S PUBLIC SPHERES OF THE IMAGINATION

Not everyone was amused by the spectacle of seemingly responsible adults devoting their leisure to the fiction that Holmes was not fiction. Conan Doyle's son Denis, a trustee of the Conan Doyle Estate, indicated his "grave disapproval" when he attended a Baker Street Irregulars' dinner in 1940. According to one account, he listened with perplexity to the numerous toasts to Holmes and to the short papers explicating aspects of Holmes's life. Turning to a member, he whispered, "I don't understand this! My father's name has not been mentioned." The member explained that this was the highest compliment an author could obtain: not even

Shakespeare created characters that were seen as more real than their creator. When Denis asked the member how the Baker Street Irregulars defined his father's role, he was told that Conan Doyle was usually identified as Watson's literary agent.[80] By the end of the decade Denis and his brother Adrian were sending messages to the Baker Street Irregulars to "Cease, Desist, and Disband."[81]

While Conan Doyle's sons had a certain proprietary interest in establishing that Holmes was fictional and their father factual, there were others who felt that the spectacle of adults pretending to believe in a fictional character was unbecoming. S. C. Roberts, the Vice-Provost of Cambridge University, recalled that when news of his election as President of the Sherlock Holmes Society of London was published in *The Times,* he received a chiding letter: "I could hardly believe the evidence of my eyes when I read about [your election]. Sherlock Holmes and Watson were two ficti[t]ious characters invented by Conan Doyle. All there is about these two invented people is what Conan Doyle wrote. There is nothing more to it and very little at that!"[82]

Many weren't sure what to make of the Sherlock Holmes Society of London's weeklong tour of Switzerland in 1968, which included a carefully choreographed reenactment of Holmes and Moriarty's fight at the Reichenbach Falls. (See figures 3.1 and 3.2) Over forty members, all dressed in period costume, were led by the Society's President, Paul Gore-Booth, who was disguised as Holmes. (British journalists reminded their readers that his day job was that of Permanent Under-Secretary of State at the Foreign Office. The *Evening Standard* published a cartoon of him returning to Whitehall in his Holmesian garb, only to be informed by an official that "your job's been taken, we heard you'd had been killed at the Reichenbach Falls!")[83] A French observer could only comprehend their visit in national terms: "To come all this way to make fools of themselves so delightfully—such a British thing to do."[84] Some of the local Swiss were bemused, others perplexed. When a professor of forensic medicine at Lausanne University was asked if members of the Society could address his class, he anxiously cabled Interpol for a profile of the visitors. He was assured that "the group was made up of highly influential personalities . . . endowed with a sense of humour."[85] His students, however, weren't informed of the impending visit and unexpectedly found themselves being addressed by Sherlock Holmes, Colonel Sebastian Moran, and Professor James Moriarty, among others:

> After the professor [finished a serious presentation], the Sherlockians climbed up on to the rostrum to lecture. The industrious note-taking of the Swiss students gradually ceased, and a look of incredulous horror spread across their earnest young faces.[86]
> (Figure 3.3)

Figure 3.1 Members of the Sherlock Holmes Society of London in Victorian garb, about to board a modern jet at Heathrow Airport for their 1968 tour of Switzerland. Reproduced by permission of the Sherlock Holmes Society of London.

Figure 3.2 "Sherlock Holmes" struggles with "Professor Moriarty" near the very real Reichenbach Falls during the Sherlock Holmes Society of London's 1968 tour of Switzerland.
Reproduced by permission of the Sherlock Holmes Society of London.

For all the good-natured mockery they received over the years, however, the Sherlock Holmes enthusiasts in Britain and America were less subject to the dismissive scorn commonly endured by fantasy fans between the 1930s and 1980s. This is not because detective fiction was thought to be more mature than other marketing genres—although it was a twentieth-century nostrum that "intellectuals" weren't averse to relaxing with a good mystery. The virtual world of 221B Baker Street was distinguished from other literary virtual worlds on the basis of social status: many of those who created and joined Sherlock Holmes societies were eminent professionals who couldn't be dismissed as maladroit teenagers, dreamy escapists, or hopeless cranks. The London *Sun* discerned this during the 1968 Swiss tour: "it is all tolerated because it has a literary (and slightly upper-class) respectability. It is not working-class dimness; rather middle-class eccentricity."[87] The *New*

Figure 3.3 "After the professor [finished a serious presentation to his class], the Sherlockians climbed up on to the rostrum to lecture. The industrious note-taking of the Swiss students gradually ceased, and a look of incredulous horror spread across their earnest young faces."
Reproduced by permission of the Sherlock Holmes Society of London.

York World-Telegram made a similar point, albeit in a more American accent: the Baker Street Irregulars was "a super-duper Holmes fan club with a highbrow membership."[88] A reporter from the *New York Sun* observed dryly in 1946 that "there are no professional detectives in the [Baker Street Irregulars], although there are writers, doctors, lawyers, and other professional men—including a psychiatrist."[89] It would have been clear to most observers that such generally accomplished people inhabited their fantasy world in an ironic, tongue-in-cheek manner, as it was to the *Chicago Tribune* in 1944: "The Sherlock Holmes cult is not too serious; it's a game and those who play it have fun."[90] When Simon & Schuster issued their publicity release for *Profile by Gaslight* (1944), a collection of essays edited by Edgar W. Smith presenting Holmes and Watson as real, they stressed Smith's bona fides as a CEO: "Thus, as editor, he combines the ability to keep both executive feet on the ground while fixing idolatrous eyes on the sun that never sets on Baker Street."[91]

The tenor of respectability surrounding Holmes fandom permitted the mainstream media to play at the "game" when they weren't reporting on it. *The Times* of London devoted leaders to Sherlock Holmes as if he were real and published letters from his associates. Charles Honce, a correspondent of the Associated Press, enjoyed issuing reports featuring Holmes as a real person over the wire service, "reaching, I like to believe, a reading public of untold millions."[92] Reputable magazines also treated Holmes as an existing person: "Was Sherlock Holmes a Drug Addict?" appeared in the *Lancet;* "Sherlock Holmes, Sportsman" appeared in *Sports Illustrated;* "Sherlock Holmes: Spectacular Diagnostician" appeared in the *Marquette Medical Review;* "Sherlock Holmes and Dermatology" appeared in *Skin*—and the list continues. (Perhaps the world's only review of Professor Moriarty's monograph, *The Dynamics of an Asteroid,* appeared in the June 1962 issue of *Air Force and Space Digest.*) The media's participation in the "Great Game" thereby contributed to the establishment of Holmes as the first virtual reality character in modern fiction, and also legitimized the practice of the ironic imagination and the habitation of public spheres of the imagination.

The professional ambience of Sherlockian (or, as the more formal British sometimes prefer, Holmesian) fandom has had other effects on the public spheres of the imagination devoted to maintaining this virtual world. The Baker Street Irregulars, the Sherlock Holmes Society of London, and their many affiliated "scion societies" have a scholarly cast to their meetings and publications, celebrating the animistic reason that distinguished Holmes. Their scholarship is conducted with humor, but also with rigor. Edgar W. Smith, the founder and editor of the *Baker Street Journal,* maintained that, "if we approach our task of writing about the Writings with the sincerity and objectivity Holmes himself would have liked . . . we shall, after all, have more fun than if we try heavily to be funny."[93] Many of the first members in 1934 of both the American and British Sherlock Holmes societies had received a classical education and delighted in displaying their intellectual prowess; some of the toasts at annual meetings were delivered in Latin and Greek. The societies' journals published essays on a range of topics, many of which were extensively footnoted. Social gatherings of members could resemble medieval oral examinations, if we take as representative a 1953 meeting of "The Sons of the Copper Beaches of Philadelphia":

> Dr. Klauder . . . read a paper, accepted for publication in the American Medical Journal, entitled "Sherlock Holmes and Dermatology." Dick Dalzell followed by detailing his research on the "nice little brougham" of the Hereditary King of Bohemia, and exhibited a beautiful model of it which he had built. Neophyte Ball then read his paper, "Early Days in Baker Street," in which he discussed the errors due to Dr. Watson's abominable handwriting, and went on to demonstrate that, thanks to Mycroft, Sherlock Holmes was a King's Messenger . . . The final bit of business was the quiz upon the assigned subject of "The Red-Headed League." Barristers Morris and Simpson led with perfect scores.[94]

(Perhaps another medieval aspect of such meetings was the carousing, as suggested by the reported tally of drinks imbibed at the 1946 Baker Street Irregulars' Annual Dinner: "The liquor consumption on Friday was 96 cocktails, 243 scotches, 98 ryes, and 2 beers"—not to mention the wine served with dinner.)[95]

In addition to animistic reason, the public spheres of the imagination dedicated to Holmes have been defined by a resolute antiquarianism. Nearly all the Sherlockian efforts focused on maintaining, in the words of Vincent Starrett, "a nostalgic country of the mind: where it was always 1895."[96] For the Sherlockians of the troubled decades of the 1930s and 1940s, nostalgia was a significant factor in their idealization of 1895. Many of them fondly recalled the fin-de-siècle as the golden years of their childhood, which had been enlivened by reading Conan Doyle's stories as they first appeared or soon after.[97] Smith, born in 1896, captured the sentiments of his generation when he described the attraction of this particular imaginary world in 1944:

> [Holmes] lived and had his being, in sober truth, in that nostalgic gas-lit London of the late nineteenth century which saw the realization of a snug and peaceful world that never would be any worse and never could be any better. It was a world we would all give our hearts to capture and to know again; yet the nostalgia it raises up is not so much for the pervading charm of the age and time itself as for the age-less, timeless man who stands before us as its brightest symbol.[98]

This desire to recapture and preserve in amber a magical past helps explain why the Sherlockian scholarship during these decades rarely associated Holmes's world with contemporary concerns.

But it doesn't explain why this habit continued, with few exceptions, through subsequent decades. In postwar issues of the American *Baker Street Journal* and the London *Sherlock Holmes Journal,* there is a silence more ostentatious than that of the dog who did not bark about the Cold War and Suez Canal crisis of the 1950s, the counterculture and political turmoil of the 1960s, Watergate and stagflation of the 1970s, and Reaganism and Thatcherism of the 1980s. At times there were gestures toward current events: Smith, an internationalist in politics, occasionally asserted that Holmes could function as a symbol of Anglo-American unity in this new era; a few Sherlockians made half-hearted associations between Mycroft Holmes and computers, or a bohemian Holmes and the hippie movement. But these and other attempts at contemporary relevance were rare, the clear exceptions to the unstated rule. The effective *cordon sanitaire* surrounding 221B Baker Street led one younger reader to protest in 1962: "With all due respect to Mr. Starrett . . . I humbly submit that the Master Detective not only would, but does, play a prominent and contemporary part in the modern hustle-bustle-'get-to-the-moon-first' race of the 1960s."[99] Nevertheless, this imaginary world existed for most Sherlockians as Watson existed for Holmes: "the one fixed point in a changing age."[100]

Imaginary worlds in the science fiction and fantasy genres usually did not evince a similar isolation from topical references or debates. While on one level they were created as autonomous realms, and enjoyed as such, on another level they were "good to think with" about contemporary issues. As we shall see in the next chapter on H. P. Lovecraft, fans were drawn to the social and political implications of the imaginary worlds of science fiction, engaging in passionate debates about their applicability to the present. Fantasy worlds could also excite similar discussions, especially when these worlds dealt overtly with moral and spiritual questions, as I'll explain in the case of Tolkien's *The Lord of the Rings* (Chapter 5). But most Sherlockian scholarship intentionally kept the virtual world of Holmes autonomous, blissfully free of relevance to any issues that did not impinge directly on the period when he thrived (roughly between his birth in the 1850s, to his final recorded case in 1914). Why should this be the case?

The answer has to do with Holmes's own aestheticism. Just as his readers adopted his animistic reason, using it to re-enchant the world, they also emulated Holmes's freedom from utilitarian concerns—at least when it came to inhabiting his imaginary world. Conan Doyle's stories dwell repeatedly on Holmes's aestheticism: as Watson explains in "The Adventure of Black Peter," "Holmes . . . like all great artists, lived for his art's sake."[101] He can afford to take only those cases that captivate him, "working as he did rather for the love of his art than for the acquirement of wealth."[102] Holmes confirms this in "The Adventure of the Red Circle," when he concedes of the case that "There is neither money nor credit in it, and yet one would wish to tidy it up."[103]

Holmes's independence from instrumental purposes evidently appealed to Conan Doyle, who often complained that he wrote the detective stories only for money and wished he could devote the time to more serious, artistic work, such as his medieval romances. But it would have been attractive to his middle- and working-class readers as well, for Holmes made Aestheticism appear less *louche* and more respectable. In the 1880s and 1890s, Aestheticism was widely associated with aristocratic elitism and artistic perversity; by the latter decade, largely as a result of Oscar Wilde's trial for homosexuality, it had become indistinguishable from moral and physical "degeneration" in the minds of conservative critics.[104] Yet Aestheticism's ideal of living for transcendental moments of freedom and creativity retained a powerful attraction in an increasingly utilitarian age. Holmes represented a wonderful compromise for those who were drawn to independence but equivocal about bohemianism. Let Holmes play his violin at all hours, fire bullets into Mrs. Hudson's walls, and lounge in his dressing gown: no matter; here was a responsible hero who knew right from wrong, respected Queen and country, was implacable to his foes, chivalrous (if chilly) to women, and loyal to his friends. Like other adventure heroes, Holmes undertook dangerous and thrilling exploits that his readers experienced vicariously. But he had the additional merit of enabling them to play at being aesthetes in the realm of the "as if"—and, for those readers who took the extra step and became Sherlockians, actually participating in that form of life by writing about his. Holmes lived for freedom rather than necessity, and in the public spheres of the imagination devoted to his virtual world, so did his fans.

Certainly the professionals who were the founding members of the Sherlock Holmes societies found his aestheticism irresistible. Christopher Morley spoke for them when he declared that Holmes was "the triumphant illustration of art's supremacy over life."[105] These fans were respectable and industrious, living "instrumental" lives to greater or lesser degrees. Holmes had already made reason, the tool of their trades, into something magical rather than disenchanting. Now, by inhabiting his imaginary world and contributing to its virtual existence through their freely chosen efforts, they had the opportunity to become aesthetes. Indeed, in this virtual world they had the best of both worlds: like Holmes, they were productive detectives, solving the riddles of his existence; like Sherlock, they were self-determining artists, delineating his character solely out of love.

There is nothing surprising, then, in the Sherlockians' decision to keep their imaginary world autonomous. They were only following their hero and his credo of art for art's sake. This was the case for Ivor Gunn, whose obituary in the *Sherlock Holmes Journal* commended him for showing fellow members "how to play the game for the game's own sake."[106] Edgar W. Smith too found 221B a haven of aestheticism. The *Baker Street Journal* he edited in spare moments was a labor of love. Unlike General Motors, it was not pursued for profit and sometimes ran in the red. He was joined in this enterprise by many others who contributed lengthy, scholarly articles for no pay, no professional credit, and little acclaim. (Christopher Morley quipped, "Never was so much written by so many for so few.")[107] Smith noted in a 1954 editorial for the *Baker Street Journal:* "'I play the game for the game's own sake,' Sherlock Holmes said. And that, for better or for worse, is the philosophy to which the JOURNAL is dedicated."[108]

In the late eighteenth century, the poet and critic Friedrich Schiller anticipated this aesthetic orientation and believed that it would induce unity and spontaneity in the modern age. In his *On the Aesthetic Education of Man, in a Series of Letters* (1794), he argued that the frequently opposed aims of social harmony and individual freedom could be reconciled if citizens were infused with the spirit of art.[109] For Schiller, art manifested the organic combination of spontaneous, sensuous particulars with organized, conceptual form—the free play of imagination and reason, freedom and structure. Encounters with art, he believed, would inspire individuals to cultivate a similar psychic integration, which in turn would contribute to social integration: individuals would be more at home with themselves and the world.

We don't know what sort of education Holmes had (Sherlockians have their theories), but he did embody the ideals of an aesthetic education in Schiller's sense, attractively combining analysis and imagination, duty and liberty, individualism and community. When his fans came to play in his imaginary world, they sought a comparable balance. By modeling themselves after Holmes and his Secondary World, his devotees might imbue their Primary World, to some degree, with his moral autonomy and holistic cognition; they had already re-created the sodality of 221B Baker Street within the tightly knit Sherlockian societies. In this important way, the virtual world of 1895 did interact with the real world even as it preserved its own gas-lit glamour. As Howard Haycraft observed of the Sherlock Holmes "cult" in 1944:

[It] is certainly defensible as the most innocent and least harmful of its kind. Its unashamed insistence that what-never-was always-will-be stands in oddly human fashion for a Higher Sanity in a too-real world.[110]

CHAPTER 4

✇

From "Virtual Unreality"
to Virtual Reality

H. P. Lovecraft and Public Spheres
of the Imagination

The reasons to opt for unbelief go beyond our judgments about religion, and the supposed deliverances of "science." They include also the moral meanings which we now find in the universe and our genesis out of it. Materialism is now nourished by certain ways of living in, and further developing, our cosmic imaginary; certain ways of inflecting our sense of the purposelessness of this vast universe, our awe at it, and sense of kinship with it.

—Charles Taylor

From even the greatest of horrors irony is seldom absent.

—H. P. Lovecraft

I. PUBLIC SPHERES AS MEDIATORS BETWEEN PRIMARY
AND SECONDARY WORLDS

As we have seen, enchantment traditionally signified both delight and delusion. Ideally, the modern "disenchanted enchantment," embracing reason, imagination, and irony, should secure wonder without beguiling the mind. But how well does this work in practice? The ironic imagination and animistic reason are powerful bulwarks against deception, but they have not always been effective in warding off the insidious spells cast by modern politicians, advertisers, and prophets. In a globalizing world, prejudice against difference of all sorts remains endemic, despite the explosion of information about the lives of others available through media both old and new. Some claim that greater tolerance and understanding will accrue through an increased exposure to variegated narratives, which would highlight the contingent nature of different world views. According to the philosopher Richard Rorty:

> [The] processes of coming to see human beings as "one of us" rather than as "them" is a matter of detailed description of what unfamiliar people are like and of what we ourselves are like. This is a task not for theory but for genres such as ethnography, the journalist's report, the comic book, the docudrama, and, especially the novel . . . That is why the novel, the movie and the TV programs have, gradually but steadily, replaced the sermon and the treatise as the principal vehicles of moral change and progress.[1]

But there is no necessary reason to believe this is true. We usually interpret incoming information through our personal predilections ("confirmation bias") and social conditioning ("cultural cognition").[2] In our private communion with texts, "us" and "them" can remain distinct.

Public spheres of the imagination do seem to have concrete effects on how their participants construe fictions, however, by providing an arena where interpretations are open to contestation. Opinions may not always change as a result, but implicit assumptions will often have been made explicit and alternative possibilities broached. Because discussions in these arenas frequently elide from interpretations of fictions to interpretations of actuality, public spheres of the imagination can perform the functions that Rorty optimistically assigned to the texts themselves.

We can see the importance of public spheres of the imagination as complements to the ironic imagination and animistic reason by examining the life and works of the American writer of "weird fiction," Howard Phillips Lovecraft (1890–1937). Lovecraft created a cohesive imaginary world that became virtual during his lifetime; after his death it was dubbed the "Cthulhu Mythos."[3] Through this Secondary World, Lovecraft grafted the wonders and terrors once evoked by the supernatural onto the secular and scientific understandings of the cosmos.[4] He was an atheist and materialist who intended to re-enchant the world through the ironic imagination, creating what he called an "artificial mythology" for the age of artifice.[5] Like the imaginary worlds of Conan Doyle and Tolkien, Lovecraft's Cthulhu Mythos has become a virtual reality shared by successive generations. The Mythos has an extended literary genealogy—a 1999 concordance lists 2,631 works—and has also inspired films, comics, games, pseudo-histories, occult philosophies, and even a colorful line of plush toys.[6]

Lovecraft hoped that his fictions would evoke a mood of "adventurous expectancy" or "outsideness" to redress the routinized existence of modernity, and his best stories do induce a powerful sense of wonder at the marvels specific to a scientific worldview. Many feature scholarly narrators who, like Sherlock Holmes, use their animistic reason to unravel frightening mysteries. (Thus, in "The Case of Charles Dexter Ward" [1927], the investigators "strove to exercise deduction, induction, and constructive imagination to their utmost extent.")[7] Scraps of newspapers, passages from myths and religions, and ambiguous—usually hysterical—accounts from witnesses must be deciphered to clarify the origin of bizarre events.

While in the Holmes stories the wonders become fully explicable by the conclusion (except for the ultimate wonder of Holmes himself), in Lovecraft's tales there remain vaster mysteries associated with the relativistic understanding of time and space that may never be comprehended. In these stories, rather than exorcising enchantment, the sublime implications of modern science lead to its unlimited unfolding. In "The Colour out of Space" (1927), for example, a meteorite strikes farmland in quiet Arkham, Massachusetts, releasing a strange gas in a color never perceived before, one that has a unique spectrographic signature. The gas insinuates itself into the land with unsettling results:

> All the orchard trees blossomed forth in strange colours, and through the stony soil of the yard and adjacent pasturage there sprang up a bizarre growth which only a botanist could connect with the proper flora of the region. No sane wholesome colours were anywhere to be seen except in the green grass and leafage; but everywhere those hectic and prismatic variants of some diseased, underlying primary tone without a place among the known tints of earth. The Dutchman's breeches became a thing of sinister menace, and the bloodroots grew insolent in their chromatic perversion.[8]

Soon animals, and then humans, are horribly affected, their tribulations receiving no more explanation than those of Job—except that theirs is viewed within a scientific framework:

> This was no fruit of such worlds and suns as shine on the telescopes and photographic plates of our observatories. This was no breath from the skies whose motions and dimensions our astronomers measure or deem too vast to measure. It was just a colour out of space—a frightful messenger from unformed realms of infinity beyond all Nature as we know it; from realms whose mere existence stuns the brain and numbs us with the black extra-cosmic gulfs it throws open before our frenzied eyes.[9]

Lovecraft's stylistic excesses are evident in these passages—he seems never to have met an adjective he didn't like—but his genuine knack for evoking wonder is as well. The cosmos he represents is not the purely quantifiable one of Max Weber's disenchanted vision; for Lovecraft, the iron cages of space and time have been rent asunder by the new cosmology of the early twentieth century. And it is worth threshing through his occasionally over-wrought prose to discover such kernels of visionary eloquence as "the bloodroots grew insolent in their chromatic perversion."

Lovecraft's narratives have been called nihilistic, and he does revel in shattering humanistic illusions.[10] His mythology insists that anthropocen-trism is of no import when viewed from a cosmic perspective. As he wrote in 1917, "I thought of the inconsequentiality—the virtual unreality—of mankind, and of the surging, unfathom'd, half-hideous forces in whose grasp he vainly and impotently writhes."[11] This disillusioned truth may come as a shock to Lovecraft's naïve protagonists, especially those who end up being mauled by inscrutable aliens from other dimensions. (It could also be coldly comforting to those, like Lovecraft, who never achieved their own ambitions in this world and rejected the idea of a better life to come.)

He was more of a modern Stoic than a nihilist, however. Despite his pro-fessed disdain for humanity, he was capable of discovering wonder and value in ordinary existence even as he charted the vaster sublimities of the universe, which is one reason for his continued appeal. His tales start from the familiar world, often lovingly described, and gradually reveal an inef-fable cosmos, shattering all terrestrial conceptions. A key to his success is his ability to connect the domains of the materially human and the immate-rially transcendent, a strategy he consciously pursued:

> I begin with the individual & the soil & think outward—appreciating the sensation of spatial & temporal liberation only when I can scale it against the known terrestrial scene . . . All I want to do is to kick off the bondage of immediate time & space & natural law without losing touch with the particular corner of the universe in which I happen to be thrown. It is significant that I always think of the cosmic gates of the sunset as glimpsed beyond the familiar spires & roofs & elm-boughs of the old Rhode Island country. If one is to step off into space, one must have a starting point.[12]

The infinite universe revealed to Lovecraft's narrators is mind expanding. He believed that "only in the direction of the outside can our sense of *mys-tic spaciousness & expectant adventurousness* be titillated to the fullest extent."[13] In his fiction, knowledge shatters anthropocentrism, but com-pensates for such a wrenching loss with the marvelous perspective of a sci-entific "cosmicism."

True, escaping from mundane reality by steeping oneself in tales of havoc wreaked by monsters and their human minions may not sound particularly "enchanting." Lovecraft, however, believed that horror could elicit delight as well as fear, and most of his protagonists find the combination irresistible. The narrator of "The Lurking Fear" has a harrowing encounter with a horrible creature, and while he "experienced virtual convulsions of fright . . . that fright was so mixed with wonder and alluring grotesqueness, that it was almost a pleasant sensation."[14] Better the devil you don't know than the devil you do, explains another wonder-besotted character as he eagerly pursues a potential horror after dark: "to my soul nothing was more deadly than the material daylight world."[15]

Lovecraft's most characteristic tales were richly empirical and internally consistent, signaling their affinities with the hoaxing tradition established by Poe, Verne, and the New Romance. His locales, extraterrestrials, and ancient tomes were invested with such verisimilitude that some took them to be real, while others were inspired to make them so. (His fabricated volume of "eldritch lore" that drives its readers mad, the *Necronomicon*, cited briefly in some of his stories and poems, is now available in several full-length versions, including paperback editions for the cost conscious.) An enthusiastic antiquarian, Lovecraft compiled voluminous notes and drawings from his research into New England history, which were reflected in his fictional locales and events. He fashioned detailed maps of his fictional towns, provided his characters (including the nonhuman ones) with lengthy ancestries, and even noted the chronologies—down to the hour—of when events happened. "As against romanticism I am solidly a realist," he wrote to a correspondent in 1930. "My conception of phantasy, as a genuine art-form, is *an extension rather than a negation of reality*. Ordinary tales about a castle ghost or old-fashioned werewolf are merely so much junk."[16]

Fans debate which of Lovecraft's stories fit into a coherent Secondary World; some find nearly all of his narratives are applicable, while others use more stringent criteria. Brian Lumley, who has contributed his own stories to the Mythos, offers an appealingly concise and vivid synopsis of its narrative core:

> That this earth and its neighboring "dimensions" conceal centuried (aeonian?) . . . slumbering, or hibernating alien creatures . . . whose telepathic dreams infest the minds of certain artistic, sensitive, and often mentally "fragile" human beings, to the extent that they are caused to meddle with seals real and metaphysical that confine these Great Old Ones in their forgotten (drowned, buried, or extradimensional) tombs or "houses."[17]

(In the spirit of fannish, or academic, persnicketiness, it should be noted that many among Lovecraft's ghastly pantheon are not confined, and that his cosmology was resolutely materialist rather than metaphysical. Some of his characters resort to metaphysical explanations in their desperate efforts to understand the inexplicable.)

The Cthulhu Mythos was, on the one hand, a meta-myth that incorporated preceding global myths and religious traditions within its broader ambit. In this respect it was similar to Tolkien's *The Lord of the Rings*, which claimed that Middle-earth represented the prehistory of our contemporary world, leaving its traces in subsequent folkloric traditions and Indo-European languages. On the other hand, David E. Schultz plausibly defined this approach as an "anti-mythology," because it reframed apparently supernatural events from a modern, scientific perspective.[18] Lovecraft's protagonists discover that traditional tales of gods and monsters expressed humanity's earliest attempts to account for the presence of extraterrestrials in their history. (A deflating revelation in "At the Mountains of Madness" is that aliens created human beings "as jest or mistake.")[19] Lovecraft maintained that myths and religions were merely fictions, but less truthful than his mythos tales, which declared themselves to be fictions. Whether meta-myth or anti-myth, his Cthulhu Mythos represented a distinctly modern form of enchantment. It conveyed the centrality of "as if" narratives to human existence, while at the same time capturing the sense of wonder betokened by contemporary science. Lovecraft's answer to modern disenchantment was to embrace the virtual realities of the imagination as a way to cope with the "virtual unreality" of modern life.

He praised the ironic imagination in particular as a prophylactic against dogmatic beliefs and irrational creeds, stating that "all opinion should be wholly *provisional,* & subject to revision."[20] He knew that fictional enchantments could delude as well as delight, but "the wise man will use the misconceptions decoratively & intelligently when he can get pleasure or stimulation thereby, but he will be able to *undermine their associated emotions* through reflection on their meaninglessness & triviality when such emotions tend to operate against his larger well-being."[21] Recalling a friend who was drawn to "freak cults from Rosicrucians to Theosophists," Lovecraft mused that "there is surely . . . a tremendous pathos in the case of those who clutch at unreality as a compensation for inadequate or uncongenial realities. The fortunate man is he who can take his phantasy lightly—getting a certain amount of kick from it, yet never actually believing in it—and thus being immune from the possibility of devastating disillusion."[22] Yet was the ironic imagination sufficient to expose and rectify his own prejudices, especially when they buttressed his "larger well-being"?

The question becomes unavoidable when we see the appalling discrepancy between Lovecraft's imaginative investment in fictional aliens and the nugatory empathy he accorded to actual human beings different from himself. He was quite attentive to the uniqueness of "others"—that is, of extraterrestrial others. But when it came to imagining human beings, particularly those from a different class or ethnicity, for most of his life Lovecraft upheld the racist stereotypes of his white, middle-class, Protestant upbringing. Those who did not share his Anglo-Saxon background could be as frightening to him as the creatures from outer space that beset his nervous narrators, but received far less understanding or scrutiny. As a young man he flaunted his political and cultural conservatism and avoided coming to terms with the complex social realities of his time. As late as 1930 he proclaimed, "I am too much of an antiquarian ever to feel a citizenship in a swollen, utilitarian national enterprise whose links with the past are cut, and whose instincts and sources have to do with scattered and alien people and lands and things—people and lands and things which have no connection with me, and can have no interest or meaning for me."[23]

Despite this unequivocal assertion, over the years Lovecraft gradually questioned and revised his attitudes. Before his death in 1937, he had undergone remarkable changes in many of his political, intellectual, and social views. These resulted as much from spirited exchanges within the new public spheres of the imagination as through his private recourse to the ironic imagination. The ever-present "alien people and lands and things" that he had found marvelous only in his Secondary World could now be entertained more empathetically, and with fewer frissons of fear, in his Primary World.

Lovecraft's legacy is therefore twofold. He demonstrated how it was possible to re-enchant modernity while retaining its disenchanted perspective. And, as an enthusiastic exponent of the ironic imagination, he inadvertently demonstrated through his own life that an ironic stance alone may be insufficient to allay the powerful beguilements of the imagination. Lovecraft came to admit that he needed interchanges with others as well as ironic detachment to remain enchanted in a disenchanted way. Both helped him come to terms with those conditions of modernity that initially terrified him and that defined many of his most horrifying creations: difference, hybridity, and liminality.

II. LOVECRAFT'S GEOGRAPHIES OF THE IMAGINATION

For most of his life, Lovecraft the cosmic visionary lived a provincial existence in Providence, Rhode Island. He was born there in 1890, the only child of Winfield Lovecraft, a traveling salesman, and Sarah Susan Phillips, daughter of a prominent local businessman. He was proud of his parents' genteel status in the city and their English ancestry, but elements of the southern gothic were intermixed with this Yankee heritage. When Lovecraft was two, his father began to exhibit dementia from syphilis and died insane in a mental asylum when the boy was seven. His mother was a high-strung, possessive woman who remained a domineering figure in his life until she too died in an asylum in 1921. Lovecraft was largely self-educated. His school attendance was sporadic due to unspecified illnesses, and a nervous breakdown prevented him completing high school, ending his long-cherished dream of attending Brown University. He continued to live with his mother, and then with his two aunts after her death, while he eked out a marginal living revising the writings of others and occasionally selling one of his own stories to pulp magazines such as *Weird Tales* and *Astounding Stories.* (He boasted that as a "gentleman" he did not write for the market but rather for his own aesthetic satisfaction, an attitude that condemned him to penury.)

His contact with other people, like that with money, was at arm's length. "I am essentially a recluse who will have very little to do with people wherever he may be," he wrote in 1926. "I think that most people only make me nervous."[24] He began to emerge from his introverted shell when he joined an amateur press society in 1914, where he exchanged essays and stories with other members and garnered friendships through correspondence. He also attracted a devoted following when he began publishing in the pulps in the early 1920s. Many of those who became his regular correspondents developed an enduring affection for him without ever meeting him. After his mother's death he felt freer about traveling to meet some of these epistolary friends, although trips were limited because he never had much money, preferred to venture forth at night and sleep during the day, and couldn't abide temperatures below seventy degrees.

Certainly his boldest attempt at personal intimacy occurred when he married Sonia Greene in 1924, living with her for a year in New York. He had met her through the amateur press society in 1921 and they continued to see each other during some of Lovecraft's infrequent trips away from home. Enthralled by his intellect, Sonia was willing to support his literary endeavors with her own income; he appreciated her energetic devotion to his needs, especially because he was recently bereft of his attentive mother. She said she loved him, and he replied that he was "fond" of her; their wedding night was spent retyping a manuscript he had lost earlier that day. The year in New York was trying for them both. Sonia's heroic devotion to Lovecraft did not prevent her from objecting to his anti-Semitic and xenophobic comments, which he continued to make even though she was a Jewish immigrant from Russia. (In her memoir she recalls Lovecraft ranting about the "alien hordes" polluting New York. "When I protested that I too was one of them, he'd tell me I 'no longer belonged to those mongrels. *You are now Mrs. H. P. Lovecraft of 598 Angell St., Providence, Rhode Island!'"*)[25] Sonia had instigated the relationship and did her best to preserve it, but the couple's incompatibilities led Lovecraft to return to his aunts' Providence home in 1926 and to later file for divorce.

Next to Providence, Lovecraft felt most at home in his mind. He began to read when he was two, recalling that "the mellowed tomes of the family library became my complete world."[26] As a child he loved fairy tales, classical mythology, and stories of the Arabian Nights. He constructed toy villages, forerunners of the imaginary world he would build and inhabit as an adult: "There was a kind of intoxication in being lord of a visible world (albeit a miniature one) and determining the flow of its events."[27]

He soon developed passions for horror fiction, modern science (notably astronomy, which awakened his awe of the cosmos), and history (especially that of classical Rome and the neo-classical eighteenth century). These divergent interests led him to yearn for the enchantments of the past but not to renounce the present, no matter how disenchanting currents of modern thought might be. Science, he lamented in an essay of 1922, "has stripped the world of glamour, wonder, and all those illusions of heroism, nobility, and sacrifice which used to sound so impressive when romantically treated."[28] Nevertheless, he was proud to be "archaic in my personal tastes, emotions, and interests, but so much of a scientific realist in philosophy that I cannot abide any intellectual point of view short of the most advanced."[29]

Lovecraft retreated to his imagination not only as a way to escape the tense dynamics of his personal life, but also because he believed the imagination was the only way to re-enchant modernity without denying its tenets. As a youth he had rejected his family's Protestant religion and identified himself as an agnostic who acceded to the "mechanistic materialism" and cultural pessimism held by many thinkers during the last third of the nineteenth century. In this "age of standardization, and decreased variety and adventurousness," he wrote, "*all* sensitive men have to call in unreality in some form or other or go mad from ennui. That is why religion continues to hang on even when we know it has no foundation in reality."[30] (Later he would identify as an atheist, although characteristically he kept this identification provisional, open to refutation from experience: "In theory I am an *agnostic,* but pending the appearance of rational evidence I must be classed, practically and provisionally, as an *atheist.* The chance's of theism's truth being to my mind so microscopically small, I would be a pedant and a hypocrite to call myself anything else.")[31] He turned to a form of imagination that frankly acknowledged its unreal nature—the ironic imagination—and that adhered to the rationalist and secular currents of modernity. Defending himself against the charge that he was inconsistent in being "a complete agnostic and materialist on the intellectual side, and a confirmed fantasiste and myth-weaver on the aesthetic side," Lovecraft responded, "The reason I *want* to write about circumventions of time, space, and natural law is that I *don't* believe in such! If I *believed* in the supernatural, I would not need to create the aesthetic illusion of belief."[32]

Lovecraft insisted that both the real and the imagined, while conceptually distinct, were inseparable in terms of everyday experience. As a self-professed materialist and aesthete, he believed in the primacy of sensations, which were evoked by intangible ideas and images no less than by concrete reality. Thus all conscious experience was, ultimately, subjective: and if this phenomenological perspective were accepted, one could never truly escape from, or to, the imagination; at best one consciously shifts from a normative, consensus "reality" to a more subjective one.[33] "Surely," he observed, "the strange excrescences of the human fancy are as real—in the sense of real phenomena—as the commonplace passions, thoughts, & instincts of everyday life."[34]

Many of Lovecraft's protagonists wonder if they have dreamed the fantastic events they narrate, and they usually discover that there is only a fine line between dream and reality, one often effaced in ordinary experience. The narrator of his early story "The Tomb" (1917) states that "men of broader intellect know that there is no sharp distinction betwixt the real and the unreal; that all things appear as they do only by virtue of the delicate individual physical and mental media through which we are made conscious of them."[35] In "Beyond the Wall of Sleep" (1919), the narrator ponders the epistemological status of his fantastic dreams. He inverts the hierarchy of "primary" and "secondary" worlds, finding reality to be the less substantial, "virtual" existence: "Sometimes I believe this less material life is our truer life, and that our vain presence on the terraqueous globe is itself the secondary or merely virtual phenomenon."[36] A later Cthulhu Mythos tale, "The Shadow out of Time" (1934–35), is also a meditation on the interchange between Primary and Secondary Worlds. In this story, the narrator's personality is involuntarily switched with that of a time-traveling alien from the early years of earth's prehistory. While he is confined in the alien's body in the past, the alien uses his in the present to study the contemporary world. When the narrator is restored to his own body after several years, he has vague, partial, and troubling dreams of his prehistoric existence. He initially assumes these reflect a psychological breakdown rather than a genuine case of mind transference, calling his detailed yet fantastic dreams a "secondary state" enveloping his "secondary personality."[37] He then discovers tangible remnants of the prehistoric world of his dreams, proving that his "secondary" life was in fact a "primary" one. This realization triggers the double-minded consciousness of the ironic imagination: "I was awake and dreaming at the same time."[38]

This was precisely the effect Lovecraft sought to evoke in himself and his readers. His own grasp of Primary and Secondary Worlds was never as confused as that of his beleaguered narrators, but like them he could find these worlds to be of equal weight. He did not "have the maniac's or religious mystic's tendency to *confuse* reality with unreality" but he did have "the cynic's and analyst's inability to recognize any difference in *value* between the two types of consciousness-impacts, *real* and *unreal*. I know which are which, but cannot have any prejudice in favour of either class."[39]

Lovecraft thus demarcated the real from the imaginary, but in practice found that the two interpenetrated, rendering both realms equally habitable, equally "rational." On the one hand he claimed that his cosmic fictions were realistic, with the exception of the single "marvel" that was at best a remote possibility in reality. He lived a "real" life in his fictional worlds, visiting "strange places which are not upon the earth or any known planet."[40] On the other hand, in his "actual" existence, he maintained the self-conscious fiction that he was an eighteenth-century English gentleman, writing poems in the style of Pope and concluding his letters with the salutation, "God save the King!": "I love to fuse myself into the old times—to become an actual part of them with all the strength of a not entirely inactive imagination."[41] He was therefore acutely conscious of the constructed nature of all experience and tried to view himself with the same ironic detachment that he applied to everything else. As he acknowledged to a friend, "A sense of humour has helped me to endure existence . . . In a way, I am supremely ridiculous with my pompous verses, heavy prose, overweighted words, and self-important pseudo-philosophy!"[42]

In his eyes this "as if" double consciousness made him a genuine modern, unlike those literary modernists who thought they could speak for, and perhaps recover, a "just so" past. Like T. S. Eliot, for example, Lovecraft valued tradition and considered himself a royalist and a classicist. But he took pride in his ironic awareness that these allegiances were imaginary, and therefore more authentically modern than the essentialist claims of certain modernists:

> I object to the feigning of artificial moods on the part of literary moderns who cannot even begin to enter into the life and feelings of the past which they claim to represent . . .
> I feel I am living in the 18th century, though my objective judgment knows better, & realizes the vast difference from the real thing. The only redeeming thing about my . . . remoteness from reality is that I *am fully conscious of it*, hence . . . make allowances for it, & do not pretend to an impossible ability to enter into the actual feelings of this or any other age.[43]

Following Nietzsche, Lovecraft enjoyed piercing illusions even as he consciously used them to re-enchant the world.

Like the authors of the New Romance, Lovecraft artfully combined seemingly antithetical strands of late nineteenth-century thought, such as realism and Aestheticism, in his quest to create virtual worlds of the imagination that he could inhabit. He circulated short stories to members of his amateur press association during the war years, many reminiscent in style and content to the stories of Poe, whom he admired. These were fledgling efforts, but his works began to elaborate their own distinct cosmology after he discovered the fantasy fiction of Lord Dunsany in 1919. In his life, Dunsany was many of the things Lovecraft wished he could be—British aristocrat, scholar, fighter, writer—and in his creation of an autonomous fictional universe that could be inhabited imaginatively, Dunsany provided an initial model for what Lovecraft would attempt.

He read Dunsany's early, interlinked fantasy stories that revolved around an invented cosmology, which began with *The Gods of Peganā* (1905) and continued in several other volumes published through the First World War. Dunsany's tales appealed to Lovecraft because their fantastic visions were nevertheless logically coherent and self-reflexive about their own status as aesthetic constructs. He later compared Dunsany's works to the fairy tales of another Irish aesthete, Oscar Wilde. Both used exotic imagery to transport their readers to imaginary worlds of beauty and desire that were in pointed contrast to sordid realism, while maintaining "a certain humorous doubt of their own solemnity and truth."[44] Dunsany created an autonomous aesthetic realm that both alluded to and mocked traditional religions and myths. Adults could appreciate the playfulness of the individual stories while immersing themselves in the carefully wrought universe they provided. It was precisely this combination of detachment and immersion that so inspired the young Lovecraft:

> [Dunsany's] main work belongs to what modern critics have called the "literature of escape"; the literature of conscious unreality created out of an intelligent and sophisticated conviction that analysed reality has no heritage save of chaos, pain, and disappointment. He is thus a conservative and a modern; a conservative because he still believes that beauty is a thing of golden rememberings and simple patterns, and a modern because he perceives that only in arbitrarily selected fancy can we find fixed any of the patterns which fit our golden rememberings. He is the supreme poet of wonder, but of intelligently assumed wonder to which one turns after experiencing the fullest disillusion of realism.[45]

Lovecraft wrote several fantasies influenced by Dunsany's disenchanted enchantments, but he admitted that they were unoriginal, lacking the subtleties of their progenitors. In crafting these early works, he was influenced by fin-de-siècle Aestheticism as well as by Dunsany. Like the Symbolists, whom he admired, he attempted to evoke fantastic images and associations that would create moods of "adventurous expectancy," a liberating escape into the imagination from the deterministic laws of time and space, "the indefiniteness which permits me to foster the momentary illusion that almost any vista of wonder and beauty might open up, or almost any law of time or space be marvelously defeated or reversed or modified."[46] Closure of any sort would terminate the sense of wonder that Lovecraft hoped to perpetuate; the iron cage of modernity was what he was trying to elude.

But his attempts to emulate the diaphanous styles of the aesthetes didn't satisfy his need for plausible imaginative alternatives to reality. It was not just that his work was derivative of others, while lacking their stylistic flair; it was that Lovecraft was too rational, and too enraptured by science, to turn away entirely from the known to the mystical unknowns of the Symbolists. When he was most under the influence of the aesthetic movement, between the late nineteen-teens and early nineteen-twenties, he had disparaged science as inimical to art and pleasure, but this was a youthful pose he soon abandoned. Since childhood he had loved science, and as an adult the explorations and discoveries of astronomers, physicists, geologists, and biologists continued to captivate him. Science might reveal a universe stripped of meaning or purpose, but it still dealt in mysteries: its explorations stimulated in him a profound sense of wonder. In the interwar period he modified his "mechanistic materialism" to incorporate the relativistic findings of Planck, Einstein, and Heisenberg. He wanted to capture in his fiction the counterintuitive vistas revealed by the new physics, the unconventional marvels and sublime perspectives uncovered by the new cosmology. He realized that his own work would have to be realist in execution, its fantastic elements plausible complements rather than contraventions of known reality.

Thus, in the mid-1920s, Lovecraft shifted from writing baroque fantasies and more traditional horror stories to writing tales of "cosmic fear" that dismissed the supernatural and fully embraced the rational. He continued to enjoy fantasy as a genre, particularly admiring those fantasy worlds, like Dunsany's, whose internal cohesiveness and detail lent them verisimilitude. And he continued to defend Aestheticism, arguing in 1929 that art's purpose was to evoke sensations and moods that would transport its audience out of a disenchanted world.[47] But, as he also wrote to another correspondent in the same year:

> You are fundamentally a *poet*, & think first of all in symbols, colour, & gorgeous imagery, whilst I am fundamentally a *prose realist* whose prime dependence is on building up atmosphere through the slow, pedestrian method of multitudinous suggestive detail & dark scientific verisimilitude. Whatever I produce must be the somber result of a deadly, literal seriousness, & almost pedantic approach . . . I have to see a thing or scene with clear-cut visual distinctness before I can say anything whatever about it—then I describe it as an entomologist might describe an insect. Prose realism is behind everything of any

importance that I write—a devilishly odd quality, when one stops to think about it, to exist in conjunction with fantastic taste & vision![48]

Apart from fantasy, he admitted, his favorite writers were the realists: Balzac, Flaubert, Zola, and Proust. He quite literally lived for flights of fancy, but was proud of being able to inhabit two worlds simultaneously. He felt sorry for those who refused or were unable to make this distinction, such as the Theosophists and spiritualists, because they were incapable of reconciling modernity with enchantment. The wonders they embraced were of the beguiling sort, clouding their reason; his detached, ironic form of enchantment was compatible with modern rationalism and secularism, and therefore was one of delight rather than delusion: "Much as I'd like to live in a cosmos full of my favorite Cthulhus, Yog-Sothoths, Tsathogguas, and the like, I find myself forced into agreement with men like Russell, Santayana, Einstein, Eddington, Haeckel, and so on. Prose is less attractive than poetry, but when it comes to a choice between probability and extravagance, I have to let common sense be my guide."[49]

The literature of cosmicism, Lovecraft argued in "Supernatural Horror in Literature" (1927), would no longer depend on the supernatural, which had been rendered superfluous by science. If tales of vampires, werewolves, ghosts, and the like continued to affect modern readers, that could be explained as an atavistic response dictated by physiology: such tales remained attractive due to ingrained memory traces of our primitive fears of the unknown. And despite the ostensible subject of the essay signaled by its title, Lovecraft very quickly dropped the term "supernatural" and replaced it with "cosmic fear" or "cosmic terror," which more accurately describe the sensations he hoped to evoke in his work.

The purpose of this literature was to induce an aesthetic emotion that would imbue the modern world with wonder. He insisted that "A serious weird tale is, necessarily, not so much a chronicle of events as simply a picture or crystallization of a certain human mood."[50] Next to his antiquarian pursuits, Lovecraft found such fiction to be a satisfying means of attaining the desired "impression of *liberation* & *strangeness*" that countered the routines and constraints of a disenchanted age.[51] The "protagonists" of weird fiction were awe-inspiring phenomena or concepts, not human beings; its aim was to provide the reader with visions of an infinite and strange universe remote from human finitude.

Such aesthetic aims could only be attained by the strict use of realism, for modern readers would no longer accept the extravagances of conventional romance. A successful tale must be realist in every detail, with the sole exception of the marvel at its core—and even that, ideally, ought to be a plausible extension of reality rather than its negation. Like Poe and authors of the New Romance such as Conan Doyle, Lovecraft believed that in the modern world tales of wonder must be "devised with all the care & verisimilitude of an actual *hoax*. The author must . . . build up a stark, simple account, full of homely corroborative details, just as if he were actually trying to 'put across' a deception in real life—a deception clever enough to make adults believe in it. My own attitude in writing is always that of a hoax-weaver. One part of my mind tries to concoct something realistic and coherent enough to fool the rest of my mind & make me swallow the marvel."[52]

Realism and Aestheticism combine to create a modern form of enchantment that is not, in Lovecraft's view, qualitatively different from the traditional enchantments of religion and myth: it is simply more compatible with a secular, rationalistic worldview, honoring reason in its spirit of ironic play. His constructed mythology might be taken as childish by some critics, a point Lovecraft readily conceded: "I agree that *Yog-Sothoth* is a basically immature conception and unfitted for serious literature. The fact is, I have never approached serious literature as yet." But, he continued, "I consider the use of actual folk-myths as even more childish than the use of new artificial myths, since in employing the former one is forced to retain many blatant puerilities and contradictions of experience."[53] His, at least, was an enchantment intended to delight but not delude.

Lovecraft did not plan from the outset to create a Secondary World of extraterrestrials that infest sleepy New England towns. He adopted his realist approach in the mid-1920s and found himself referring to the same set of creatures, locales, and artifacts in different stories; as he became conscious of this he decided to impose some consistency on this developing "artificial mythology."[54] He enhanced the reality effect of his imaginary world by including references to characters, places, beings, and objects from story to story, a technique he borrowed from fin-de-siècle writers of weird fiction such as Dunsany, Robert W. Chambers, Ambrose Bierce, and Arthur Machen. (He also included references to their fictional creations, creating a shared constellation of modern Secondary Worlds.) Such intertextual links among his stories gave them cohesion and, in the case of references to works by other writers, served as ironic winks to readers in the know. Lovecraft accentuated the virtual reality of his imagined universe by steeping his stories in the results of his own antiquarian research, which included visits to many New England towns. Arkham, Innsmouth, Dunwich and other fictional abodes were all based on places he had visited: "I take pains to make these places wholly and realistically characteristic of genuine New England seaports—always being authentic concerning architecture, atmosphere, dialect, manners and customs &c."[55]

He also took great pains with the names of his alien entities to enhance their verisimilitude. Some of the names reflected the cultures of those humans who first recorded their encounters with the entity in question—thus "Nyarlathotep" was the name coined by ancient Egyptians. Other names of aliens found in the *Necronomicon* reflected the language of its original author, the "mad Arab" Abdul Alhazred. (Lovecraft wrote in 1927 that the *Necronomicon* was a translation of the "original" Arabic text, *Al Azif*; while he derived the Arabic title from Samuel Henley's notes to William Beckford's *Vathek*, he might also have been playfully alluding to Vaihinger's *The Philosophy of "As If*," first translated into English in 1924.)[56] He explained to a friend, "Thus when I cite the name of some wholly non-human thing supposed to be mentioned in the *Necronomicon*, I try to have the *foundation* of the word absolutely unearthly and alien, yet give it an outwardly *Arabic* aspect to account for the transmitting influence of the mad Arab Abdul Alhazred. Typical *Necronomicon* names are *Azathoth*, *Yog-Sothoth*, *Shub-Niggurath*, etc."[57] (But, he added, in one of his stories he "cited" an Aztec document that indicated the extent of the cultural transmission of these alien terms—Yog-Sothoth had become Yog-Sototl.)[58] Names like "Cthulhu" were simply an approximation of the sounds made by alien vocal apparatus, for he strived to include "details & . . . imputations of geometrical, biological, & physico-chemical properties definitely outside the realm of matter as understood by us."[59] Some critics found these names ridiculous, but Lovecraft countered that "a coined word which has been shaped with great care from just the right associational sources" could be effective, evoking sensations like Symbolist poetry.[60] "Cthulhu" was self-evidently *le mot juste*.

Lovecraft's realist means were thus enlisted for aestheticist ends: the creation of an artificial pattern of symbols and allusions that would evoke virtual realities to offset the virtual unrealities of much of modern life. He was playing "the old game of blindman's buff with the mocking atoms and electrons of a purposeless infinity."[61] The artful deception of his invented universe allowed him to live in reality and fantasy simultaneously:

> Thus my wish for freedom is not so much a wish to put all terrestrial things behind me & plunge forever into abysses beyond light, matter, & energy. That, indeed, would mean annihilation as a personality rather than liberation. My wish is perhaps defined as a wish for *infinite visioning & voyaging power*, yet without loss of the familiar background which gives all things significance.[62]

His friends observed him living capably in both worlds. One noted the "amused twinkle in his eye" as he discussed his invented mythology or tried to approximate Cthulhu's guttural dialect. Another friend remarked that "he had it all spelled out; he drew maps, and locations of the cities. You'd think he was drawing a map of Rhode Island."[63]

Writers of Lovecraft's acquaintance, including Clark Ashton Smith, Fritz Leiber, Robert Bloch, and Robert E. Howard, were inspired by him to create their own Secondary Worlds, replete with forbidden tomes, bizarre creatures, and cohesive backgrounds. They cited facets of his Secondary World in their published fiction, just as he used elements of theirs; he encouraged this practice as "our black pantheon acquires an extensive publicity & pseudo-authoritativeness it would not otherwise get."[64] He found that "This pooling of resources tends to build up quite a pseudo-convincing background of dark mythology, legendry, & bibliography, though of course none of us has the least wish actually to mislead others."[65] Like the Sherlockians, he and his friends were simply creating a virtual reality in the spirit of adult play: "I think it is rather good fun to have this artificial mythology given an air of verisimilitude by wide citation."[66]

He enhanced the virtual effects of his Secondary World by citing real works of magic alongside his fictional ones, traditional mythological deities alongside his newer ones. He also slyly inserted his inventions into stories by others that he was asked to revise, several of which were published in his primary outlet, *Weird Tales*. Both he and *Weird Tales* received letters from readers inquiring if the *Necronomicon* or the "Old Ones" were real, because they had been mentioned so often by disparate authors in the magazine. One letter published in the March 1930 issue of *Weird Tales* is representative of the burgeoning virtual life assumed by Lovecraft's imaginary world:

> I was very much interested in tracing the apparent connection between the characters of Kathulos, in Robert E. Howard's "Skull Face," and that of Cthulhu, in Mr. Lovecraft's "The Call of Cthulhu." Can you inform me whether there is any legend or tradition surrounding that character? And also Yog-Sothoth? Mr. Lovecraft links the latter up with Cthulhu in "The Dunwich Horror" and Adolphe de Castro also refers to Yog-Sothoth in "The Last Test." Both of these stories also contain references to Abdul Alhazred the mad Arab, and his *Necronomicon*. I am sure this is a subject in which many readers besides myself would be interested.[67]

When Lovecraft died of cancer in March 1937, readers wrote to *Weird Tales* mourning his loss and the apparent demise of this shared imaginary world, which the editor dubbed "the Lovecraft mythology."[68] In the July issue, Robert Bloch, who had also contributed to it, lamented, "There's an end of the world—the world of Arkham, Innsmouth, Kingsport; the world of Cthulhu, Yog-Sothoth, Nyarlathotep, and Abdul Alhazred; the finest world of fantasy I know."[69] But news of this world's demise was greatly exaggerated. Clark Ashton Smith accurately predicted in his letter in that issue that Lovecraft's virtual world would transcend its creator: "Leng and Lomar and witch-ridden Arkham and sea-cursed Innsmouth are part of my mental geography; and dreadful, cyclopean R'lyeh slumbers somewhere in the depths. Others will venture into the realms that the Silver Key of his mastery has unlocked."[70] Indeed, in the August 1937 issue, Manly Wade Wellman published "The Terrible Parchment," a story centered on the *Necronomicon*, and other tales by other hands were soon to follow. Two of Lovecraft's young acolytes, August Derleth and Donald Wandrei, established the publishing firm of Arkham House in 1939 to issue the first omnibus collection of Lovecraft's fiction, *The Outsider and Others*. They referred to the "Cthulhu Mythology" in their joint introduction. Derleth in particular became a zealous proponent of the Mythos, writing stories elaborating it and using Arkham House to keep Lovecraft's work in the public eye.

The Mythos continued to acquire a mythic reality of its own. New fiction, films, role-playing games, computer games, comic books, and other forms of mass culture have extended Lovecraft's Secondary World, amplifying it while usually remaining true to the rational and secular parameters he established.[71] "Like the world of Tolkien," one fan stated in 1976, "the work of Lovecraft . . . allows the reader to build for himself a world of his own imagination's enchantment which will very likely never leave him."[72] Although Lovecraft called the Mythos "artificial," it was precisely this quality that made it an "authentic" mythology for an age that condones the virtual without relinquishing the real.

III. EMBRACING THE INNSMOUTH LOOK:
COMING TO TERMS WITH DIFFERENCE

In the 1940s, Edmund Wilson condemned the Mythos as jejune, "a sort of boy's game."[73] It is ironic that Wilson, one of the earliest celebrants of the Symbolist movement, was unaware of Lovecraft's own aestheticist aims, but he wasn't incorrect about the potential for mass culture to be a soporific rather than a stimulus to life. In theory, the ironic imagination should provide a counterweight to the allures of mass culture, by inculcating a detached perspective and an inquiring attitude toward other possibilities of being. Lovecraft believed that this attitude enabled him to remain detached and responsive to difference. But in practice, he was a close-minded bigot for much of his life, proud to be "the essential provincial as opposed to cosmopolitan."[74]

Lovecraft upheld the ethnic stereotypes shared by many from his middle-class, Protestant background. These were exacerbated by his anxieties about his own liminal status in a period of rapid social and economic change, as well as his unstated dread that he might share a hereditary predisposition to the "degeneracy" that landed both of his parents in an asylum.

This fear is literally reflected in his early story "The Outsider" (1921). It is a first-person narrative of an individual who, after living alone for his entire life, leaves the stark confines of his castle and enters another dwelling where he encounters a grotesque monstrosity, from which others flee in terror. The lurid punch line reveals that the narrator encountered this horror within an "unyielding surface of polished glass."[75]

Lovecraft projected his own frustrations, fears, and antipathies onto other "Outsiders." His early poems and stories are marred by racist images, and his letters in the nineteen-teens and twenties, while laden with wit, kindness, and erudition, often inveigh against the incursions of immigrants into "Anglo-Saxon culture." He enjoyed provoking others with his ironic poses; some of his xenophobia may have been exaggerated in his letters to particular individuals. Nevertheless, his cultural chauvinism was marked through the 1920s, a decade in which American insularity seemed to ratify his own outlook. In 1924, the U. S. Congress passed legislation restricting immigration to America, a fact that Lovecraft used to support his claim two years later that "to permit or encourage [immigration] is suicide—as you can clearly see in that hell called New York where a chaos of scum has raised a stench intolerable to any self-respecting white-man."[76]

Lovecraft clung tenaciously to alleged Anglo-Saxon traditions because he believed culture remained an important source of stability amidst the flux of modernity. Like many conservatives, he turned to the continuity of the past as a refuge against the forces of change; roots must be nourished, and borders maintained, to counteract modern anomie and homogenization. In a world that no longer relied on commonly shared meanings, culture provided the necessary psychological bastion against the ever-present turbulence of modernity:

> Religious people seek a mystical identification with a system of hereditary myths; whereas I, who am non-religious, seek a corresponding mystical identification with . . . the continuous stream of folkways around me . . . I follow this acceptance purely for my own personal pleasure—because I would feel lost in a limitless and impersonal cosmos if I had no way of thinking of myself but as a dissociated and independent point.[77]

Hybridity challenged these defensive boundaries and therefore terrified him. Most of the horrors in his fictions are described as "fluid," lacking clear demarcations. The sea-dwelling Cthulhu is a hideous amalgam, "a monster of vaguely anthropoid outline, but with an octopus-like head whose face was a mass of feelers, a scaly, rubbery-looking body, prodigious claws on hind and fore feet, and long, narrow wings behind."[78] The New England seaport of Innsmouth is overrun by fish-like aliens who interbreed with humans, producing a degenerate population distinguished by "the

Innsmouth look."[79] "The Thing on the Doorstep" (1933) was once human, but is transformed by the story's end into a "liquescent horror" by an evil sorceress.[80]

Critics are understandably attracted to interpreting Lovecraft's fiction in terms of his sheltered existence and peculiar psyche. While this approach can be reductive, there is no doubt that part of his intolerance of the foreign stemmed from his apprehension that he too was an "Outsider." He could not avoid occasional admissions of hybridity, as when he confessed to being "a sort of hybrid betwixt the past and the future."[81] But for much of his life he prided himself on his cosmic disdain for mere humanity and refused to sympathetically imagine others outside of his narrow social and cultural experience: firm demarcations counteracted his own fragile sense of status. When it came to blacks, he never relinquished his belief in a "colour-line" to prevent miscegenation and enthused about the original Ku Klux Klan.[82]

This sad history of prejudice would seem to belie Lovecraft's claims to follow reason wherever it led without preconceptions. Yet his admirers may find some comfort in the fact that Lovecraft did change many of his views in the later 1920s and the 1930s. Whereas people tend to become more conservative as they age, Lovecraft became more liberal. Late in his life, he described himself as evolving from a reactionary conservative to a socialist who admired Norman Thomas.[83]

This shift in political orientation was indeed remarkable, given Lovecraft's anxieties and the indoctrinations of his upbringing. Although he continued to insist that minority cultures assimilate to the dominant culture, he also expressed a more tolerant attitude toward cultural difference in the 1930s. He suggested there should be a split between the public sphere, in which certain norms apply to all for the purpose of coexistence, and the private sphere, in which individuals should be left alone to pursue their own aestheticist projects of self-creation. As Lovecraft explained, "All that anyone of us has to bother about is to obey such practical laws as are generally agreed upon, to be true to the traditions of beauty as perceived through the lenses of one's own personality, and to leave others free to follow their visions as one follows one's own."[84] Such a position testifies to the ironic imagination's potential for entertaining other possibilities and challenging illusions of homogeneity.

But Lovecraft's example also suggests that the ironic imagination, when nurtured by books alone, may be insufficient to imagine other possibilities. Near the end of his life he acknowledged that "the picture one gets from books is unreal and distorted."[85] By the 1930s, he had come to the conclusion that interchanges with others holding divergent views were often necessary to contest self-gratifying illusions fostered by selective reading. In 1932, he praised debate as an "indispensible" condition of life because it enables us to test our own opinions and amend them if we find them in any way erroneous or unjustified. One who never debates lacks a valuable chart or compass in the voyage for truth—for he is likely to cherish many false opinions along with sound ones for want of an opportunity to see each opinion viewed from every possible angle. I have modified many opinions of mine in the course of debate, and have been intensely grateful for the chance of doing so.[86]

His growth through intersubjective exchanges began with his participation in amateur journalism when he was twenty-four. Years later he acknowledged that "The more completely one is absorbed in his aspirations, the more one needs a circle of intellectual kin. . . . [Amateur journalists] alone have furnished me with the incentive to explore broader and newer fields of thought."[87] The hobby arose in America in the second half of the nineteenth century to assist individuals in publishing and circulating their writings to fellow members. Between the foundation of the National Amateur Press Association in 1876 and the United Amateur Press Association in 1895, amateur journalism had become an established institution, one of the new public spheres of the imagination that emerged at the turn of the century. (In Britain, the first amateur press association appeared in the 1890s; members also engaged in interchanges with their American counterparts.)[88]

Lovecraft joined the United in 1914 and credited it with easing him out of the reclusive state brought on by a nervous collapse in 1908. Soon he became a prominent participant, issuing his own magazine, contributing essays, fiction, and poems to the publications of others, and serving in various administrative capacities. He discovered that "the correspondence of members is one of its most valuable features" because "persons of opposed ideas may mutually gain much breadth of mind by hearing the other side of their respective opinions discussed in a genial manner."[89] Amateur journalism literally opened up new, nonimaginary worlds to him. When he attended a convention in Boston in 1920, it marked the first time he had slept away from home since 1901. He thanked the movement for giving him "the very world in which I live."[90]

As he widened his circle of correspondents among amateur journalists and fantasy fiction enthusiasts, at times visiting them in person, Lovecraft found himself reassessing his opinions and beliefs, questioning what he had once taken for granted as a solitary reader: "Books make one credulous and extravagant and soft-headed if not temper'd by sound, brisk, argument."[91] The two years he spent in "cosmopolitan" New York as a married man had been a difficult time for him emotionally; he wrote two of his most racist stories, "The Horror at Red Hook" and "He" (both 1925) and often complained about the city's "stinking, amorphous hybridism."[92] But when he returned to the comforts of his beloved Providence in 1926, he acquired a greater degree of equanimity and self-reliance. He took extended trips to see friends and acquaint himself with other ways of life. Interchanges with others led to a broadening of horizon: he now could laugh "at the piety, narrowness and conventionality of the New England background which I love so well and find so necessary to contentment."[93]

His political and social views also shifted remarkably in the early 1930s as a result of the social and economic effects of the Great Depression. By 1937, he had abandoned his affected eighteenth-century "Tory" political conservatism to welcome Roosevelt's New Deal, although he continued to believe that an intellectual aristocracy was necessary to preserve cultural standards in a democratic society. Rejecting most of his earlier deterministic biological beliefs, he accepted that people could be as influenced by nurture as by nature. The malleable influences of culture now replaced, for the most part, his earlier faith in the clear and ineradicable laws of biological racism.

Lovecraft came to this conclusion partly as a result of a lengthy and at times heated interchange in the early 1930s with Robert E. Howard on the relative merits of civilization versus barbarism. Lovecraft had always championed civilization and was forced to admit that, despite his "Saxon blood," he instinctively took the side of the ancient Romans against the Goths because the Romans stood for an ordered way of life. Acknowledging that he might be committing "blood-treason," Lovecraft concluded from his own sympathies that "At all times, the force of *cultural environment* . . . is a potent competitor of biological instinct; so that when the two are opposed, it is hard to say which will win the tug-of-war. When no *radical* race difference is involved . . . I think that cultural heritage is often more powerful than blood."[94] In a 1934 letter to another correspondent, he argued for the equality of the sexes, noting that "many qualities commonly regarded as innate—in races, classes, and sexes alike—are in reality results of habitual and imperceptible conditioning."[95]

His writings from this period reflect a far greater tolerance for difference than he had shown previously. He even appeared to have forgotten his own anti-Semitic remarks of the 1920s as he witnessed the persecution of the Jews by the Nazi regime. In a 1936 letter, he seemed genuinely surprised to learn that a friend had become anti-Semitic as well as a Nazi supporter and criticized these outlooks: "The general Jewish question has its perplexing cultural aspects, but the biologically unsound Nazi attitude offers no solution."[96] Even cultural hybridity, he now maintained, could have positive aspects:

What is more, it is silly to *belittle* even the admittedly hybrid art of Judaeo-Germans or Judaeo-Americans. It may not represent genuine German or American feeling, but it at least has a right to stand on its own feet as a frankly exotic or composite product—which may well excel much of our own art in intrinsic quality.[97]

The creatures he invented for his fiction during the nineteen-teens and twenties had been monstrously "other." They were no less horrifying than the "brachycephalic South-Italians & rat-faced half-mongoloid Russians & Polish Jews & all that cursed scum" that he lambasted at the time for threatening "his" traditional society.[98] But in the 1930s, he reversed course and accepted that alterity was necessary for human maturation: "We act first & instinctively with *the sort of people whose tastes and background are like our own*. Only with difficulty & in mature years are we generally able to think & act independently of our hereditary-culture-milieu—& all too few of us can achieve this independence."[99]

Lovecraft had not achieved complete independence, but he had come far. His more inclusive imagination is reflected in some of the major stories he wrote in this decade. In "At the Mountains of Madness" (1931), the alien race of "Old Ones" is ultimately credited by the narrator with admirable properties:

> Poor devils! After all, they were not evil things of their kind. They were the men of another age and another order of being . . . Scientists to the last—what had they done that we would not have done in their place? God, what intelligence and persistence! What a facing of the incredible, just as [their] . . . forebears had faced things only a little less incredible! Radiates, vegetables, monstrosities, star spawn—whatever they had been, they were men![100]

True, in this tale there exist other aliens whose abhorrent nature is linked to their hybridity. These "shoggoths" were created by the Old Ones as slaves, but end as their terrifying masters. They are described as "Formless protoplasm able to mock and reflect all forms and organs and processes—viscous agglutinations of bubbling cells—rubbery, fifteen-foot spheroids infinitely plastic and ductile—slaves of suggestion, builder of cities—more and more sullen, more and more intelligent, more and more amphibious, more and more imitative!"[101] Likened to resentful servants with ideas above their station, they seem modeled on the immigrant barbarians at the gate whom Lovecraft often derided. But what is striking about the story is the degree of empathy accorded to the Old Ones, for all their leather-like wings and pseudopods. Indeed, "At the Mountains of Madness" is the first tale in the Mythos in which aliens are presented sympathetically, and this trend continued in a lengthy tale of 1935, "The Shadow out of Time."

In another story written late in 1931, "The Shadow over Innsmouth," the issue of hybridity is confronted directly, with surprising results. The narrator visits the eponymous fishing village, which has been shunned for decades by its neighbors because of the peculiar people—resembling fishes—who live there, and who are rumored to be engaged in vile practices. Innsmouth natives, it turns out, have a history of miscegenation, one of the most horrible acts in the Lovecraftian imaginary: first with the Africans and Chinese, who came to the town as laborers, and later with fish-like aliens, who have dwelt below the sea for millennia and who wish to settle the land. The narrator learns that in the mid-nineteenth century, these creatures began to colonize Innsmouth by mating with its human inhabitants. After several harrowing adventures he manages to escape the stricken village, but not before he discovers that he might not have come to it by chance. His frightening experiences trigger repressed memories. In a dream he recalls the undersea world of the creatures, envisages his grandmother inhabiting this realm of "marvels," and understands that "I would never die, but would live with those who had lived since before man ever walked the earth." Awakening, he stares at himself in the mirror and is forced to acknowledge the truth: part of his ancestral line was from Innsmouth, and he indeed bore *"the Innsmouth look."*[102]

Whereas the narrator of Lovecraft's 1921 story "The Outsider" had screamed in horror when he encountered his own monstrous form in the mirror and remained hopelessly isolated from others, the narrator in this 1931 story accepts his hybrid nature and the hybrid community from which he came. In fact, he finds his mixed nature to be a wellspring of wonder, enabling him to transcend the oppressive laws of time and space, those iron cages of existence that Lovecraft had sought to escape through the ironic imagination:

> The tense extremes of horror are lessening, and I feel queerly drawn toward the unknown sea-deeps instead of fearing them. I hear and do strange things in sleep, and awake with a kind of exaltation instead of terror ... Stupendous and unheard of splendours await me below, and I shall seek them soon ... [I] shall go to marvel-shadowed Innsmouth ... and in that lair of the Deep Ones [I] shall dwell amidst wonder and glory for ever.[103]

Rather than capitulate to fear and self-loathing, the narrator is willing to descend into the depths, psychically as well as physically, and join a community defined by difference and the amorphous plasticity represented by the sea. Lovecraft's repeated use of "marvels" and the promise of immortality, his lifelong desiderata, suggest an optimistic interpretation of this narrative, as does the fact that it was written while he was becoming more tolerant of diversity in others, and perhaps within himself.

Lovecraft's greater forbearance for difference in his fiction at this time was matched by his greater outgoingness; the limits to his travels were more

financial than psychological. His earlier avowal that "life has never interested me so much as the escape from life" seemed no longer the case.[104] As
a young man he had re-enchanted a "virtually unreal" modernity through
inhabiting the virtual realities of his imagination, and while that did provide
him with an antidote to cultural pessimism, it ultimately proved limiting in
its solipsism. He had escaped the iron cage of reason only to find himself in
a funhouse mirror of fancy, whose distortions, while diverting, remained
multiple versions of himself. Lovecraft experienced a more multifaceted
and profound enchantment when he combined the ironic imagination with
public spheres of the imagination and direct encounters. In the last year of
his life he felt ashamed about views he had held only a decade before:

> There was no getting out of it—I really *had* thrown all that haughty, complacent,
> snobbish, self-centered, intolerant bull, & at a maturer age than anybody but a perfect
> damned fool would have known better! That earlier illness had kept me in seclusion,
> limited my knowledge of the world, & given me something of the fatuous effusiveness of
> a belated adolescent when I finally *was* able to get about more . . . is hardly much of an
> excuse . . . It's hard to have done all one's growing up since 33—but that's a damn sight
> better than not growing up at all.[105]

This is not to say that by the time of his death H. P. Lovecraft was an entirely different person; such dramatic transformations happen only in pulp
fiction. While he had become more receptive to difference and social democracy, he retained remnants of his earlier racism and elitism. His readers
should recognize, however, how far he developed when he left the confines
of his imagination and recognize also how those confines stretched to
incorporate his more vigorous interchanges with others. The ironic imagination allowed him to render enchantment compatible with the rational
and secular tenets of modernity, though it proved less effective in warding
off enchantment's propensity to delude. For that, he required encounters
with actual rather than imagined difference.

The lessons he learned were replicated regularly within public spheres of
the imagination, no matter how unpropitious they might at first appear.
Take, for example, the letters pages of the pulp magazine *Planet Stories*,
which specialized in "space operas," exuberant adventure stories with little
claim to social relevance. Nevertheless, its raygun-besotted readers during
the 1940s and 1950s insisted that its tales expanded their outlooks: one
argued in the letters section, "The Vizigraph," "If science fiction has anything to offer other than mere escapism, its value lies in promoting a receptive, questioning attitude and freeing the mind from the narrow,
superstition-bound, taboo-ridden ruts of accustomed thought channels."[106]
This comment was typical for science fiction fans, who often congratulated

themselves on their exceptional intelligence and receptivity to different ideas and ways of life—just as Lovecraft did.

And, just like Lovecraft, they could be blind to their own prejudices even as they exercised regularly the "cognitive estrangement" critics attribute to the genre. The public forum of "The Vizigraph" exposed and challenged these biases, leading readers to reflect on their unconscious assumptions about worlds real as well as imaginary. When a few writers to "The Vizigraph" stated in 1943 that a race of aliens in Leigh Brackett's "Citadel of Lost Ships" should be "liquidated" and "fumigated," Brackett responded in no uncertain terms:

> If that isn't totalitarian reasoning, I never saw it. Under democratic law, any and every minority, so long as it functions within legal limits, is guaranteed a right to live, think, and worship as it sees fit. You might as well say that we ought to LIQUIDATE the Mennonites, the Amish, or any other decent, peaceable group simply because they're different.

Brackett acknowledged that while her aliens were "pure fiction . . . the reaction to them shows a dangerous point of view. It's well to remember one thing, when you are planning the liquidation of minorities. Human society is a fluid and unstable thing. And it's frightfully embarrassing to wake up one morning and find that all of a sudden *you* have become—a minority."[107]

A story published in 1947 provoked another set of letters advocating racist beliefs. The writers insisted that "Caucasians" were superior to other human "races" and that harmony among different racial groups was impossible. (As one put it, the shoot-the-Martian-plot might be overused, but it is "the only sensible way to deal with an alien race." By the latter phrase he was not limiting himself to extraterrestrials.)[108] Many opposing viewpoints were printed in subsequent issues, adducing evidence from anthropology, biology, and history to combat racism. Even the findings of psychology came into play, which were used to explain the psychodynamics behind racist thinking. A Temple University biologist provided citations to contemporary scientific literature refuting racism, and a medical doctor denied that there was an innate difference in intelligence between Caucasians and all others. One reader went beyond criticizing the original writers to criticizing the entire genre: "no source has been more active in perpetuating the clichés of the races than [SF] pulps," which were rife with "Kiplingesque imperialism and Dixonesque racism."[109]

It is not clear if the original letter writers who provoked the controversy were persuaded by the flood of counterarguments. One appeared to qualify his original racist assertion, stating that "I do not know whether it is true, but I do know that plenty of evidence could be gathered to indicate it."[110] The debate did effect other readers, however. Some realized that their views about science fiction fandom had been too idealistic. ("It's a little disconcerting to realize that such as they enjoy science fiction," said one writer of those who kindled the debate. "Who was the halfwit who said fans were broadminded?" asked another.)[111] They were now more aware that science fiction had its own implicit ideological positions that required interrogation. Like Lovecraft, participants in this debate were forced to reflect on their preconceptions concerning the "alien." The letter writer who argued that science fiction promoted "Kiplingesque imperialism and Dixonesque racism" convinced another reader to see the genre anew: "You have a point there; I've never thought much about it before but most heroes are American or at least Anglo-Saxon. Why doesn't dear old *Planet Stories* run a story with a Chinese hero or something?"[112]

The editor of "The Vizigraph" appreciated this comment. He had been criticized during the long-running debate for printing letters propagating racism and had gamely defended his role as an impartial host of a public sphere of the imagination. *Planet Stories,* he insisted, took no sides, but simply aired divergent views.[113] Still, it must have been gratifying for him to respond that he had already scheduled for publication a story with a Martian as the hero.[114]

J. R. R. Tolkien famously defined imaginary worlds as "Secondary Worlds," autonomous from the "Primary World" of the everyday. However, as we have seen in the case of H. P. Lovecraft and his Cthulhu Mythos, imaginary worlds were never completely autonomous from the Primary Worlds of their creators or readers. Lovecraft's prejudices informed his invented world from the outset, and his interpretations of other imaginary worlds were also filtered through these preconceptions. No matter how "alien," exotic, or different from the quotidian they might be, the imaginary worlds he inhabited for much of his life conformed to the essentialist, "just so" categories of race, class, and gender informing his upbringing. As he gradually became exposed to more diverse perspectives through public spheres of the imagination, Lovecraft reconsidered many of his unquestioned beliefs and the Cthulhu Mythos changed as a result. By the mid-1930s, it had become an imaginary world more open to pluralism than it had been a decade earlier: a "secondary" world in the sense that it interrogated a number of the hierarchies of difference that he had formerly accepted as unquestionably primary.

A public sphere comprising diverse perspectives could thus undo spells cast by fiction by reminding participants of the multivalent dimensions of all narratives. It could also remind them that the "as if" nature of fiction was not restricted to Secondary Worlds but was often inextricable from the apprehension of the Primary World: that the "real" was in important respects a contingent and subjective construction, one open to ongoing revision. Secular and religious discourses alike shared these interpretive and provisional dimensions; both were capable of delighting without deluding if their fictionalist aspects were acknowledged. We shall now see that such a middle-way characterized the disenchanted enchantments of Middle-earth.

CHAPTER 5

✦

The Middle Positions
of Middle-earth

J. R. R. Tolkien and Fictionalism

The salient feature of Western societies is not so much a decline of religious faith and practice, though there has been lots of that . . . but rather a mutual fragilization of different religious positions, as well as of the outlooks both of belief and unbelief . . . The cross pressures are experienced more acutely by some people and in some milieu than others, but over the whole culture, we can see them reflected in a number of middle positions, which have drawn from both sides.

—Charles Taylor

I. PLURAL AND PLURALISTIC WORLDS

J. R. R. Tolkien knew that collective imagining, a synergy of many minds, was necessary to transform an imaginary world into a virtual world. When he started to write his mythology during the First World War, he dreamed of having collaborators who would contribute to its longevity as a shared entity. In his 1945 story "The Notion Club Papers," a character explained that myths derive their "daimonic force" and persistence "from the multiplication of them in many minds."[1] Tolkien certainly got his wish. Beginning in the mid-1960s, Middle-earth went from being an imaginary world redolent of Tolkien's sense of Englishness to a virtual world distinguished by its cosmopolitanism, the site of lively debates among people from different nations, cultures, and religions.[2] In public spheres of the imagination dedicated to Middle-earth, readers prolonged the sense of wonder that drew them to it in the first place, but they also negotiated different understandings of this world, often through rational and respectful debate. Many came to appreciate the manifold interpretive possibilities of the text and to see their own lives in fictionalist terms. Through their collective imaginings, Middle-earth became a playful site, one that permitted participants to challenge normative narratives of the Primary World, including those of the nation, religion, and identity.

Like the tales of Sherlock Holmes and the Cthulhu Mythos, *The Lord of the Rings* appealed as a specifically modern form of enchantment. Animistic reason, the union of imagination and rationality exemplified by Holmes and vital to Lovecraft's aesthetic, was also fundamental to Tolkien's outlook. He stated that the "light of Valinor," which originally suffused Middle-earth, "is the light of art undivorced from reason, that sees things both scientifically (or philosophically) and imaginatively."[3] *The Lord of the Rings* radiates such a mixed light: while a lavish fantasy, Tolkien's invented world is also rigorously rational. Its genealogical charts, detailed chronologies and appendices, and scholarly discussions about nomenclature, geography, history, and languages encourage the reader to approach Middle-earth analytically as well as imaginatively. Tolkien maintained that an imaginary world

> does not destroy or even insult Reason; and it does not either blunt the appetite for, nor obscure the perception of scientific verity. On the contrary. The keener and clearer is the reason, the better fantasy will it make ... For creative fantasy is founded upon the hard recognition that things are so in this world as it appears under the sun; on a recognition of fact, but not a slavery to it.[4]

The Lord of the Rings also melds the enchantments of established myths and sagas with expressly modern concerns. It is a traditional epic of mighty heroes vying with supernatural foes, but also one of everyday individuals confronting existential choices.[5] Tolkien stated that he intended to "modernize . . . myths and make them credible."[6] For him, re-enchantment through fantastic Secondary Worlds was not a rejection of modernity, but rather a corrective to its one-sided emphases.

Perhaps the work's most "modern" aspect is its emphasis on the centrality of narratives to impart meaning, order, and enchantment to the incoherence of experience. Fictionalism is at the heart of *The Lord of the Rings*. Tolkien's essay "On Fairy-stories" was a manifesto for the modern practice of inhabiting fantastic imaginary worlds through the ironic imagination. He first presented his views in a 1939 lecture, while he was in the early stage of writing his epic, and published a revised version in 1947, when he was nearly two years away from finishing it. The essay argued that fantasy fiction

produced states of enchantment that were inspirational as well as recreational, a view echoed by several characters in his work. "On Fairy-stories"
celebrated "the seamless Web of Story," and individuals in *The Lord of the
Rings* perceive their own lives as filaments within this greater narrative web.[7]
They invest existence with meaning in terms of the ancient songs and stories
passed down to them. They also take comfort that their own deeds might
survive as narrative, and that the larger narrative of which they are a part
will continue after their demise. "What a tale we have been in, Mr. Frodo,"
comments his friend Sam near the end of the epic. "I wish I could hear it
told! . . . And I wonder how it will go on after our part."[8] Bilbo Baggins also
reflects on the ongoing, open-ended narrative of which he is a part when he
remarks, "Don't adventures ever have an end? I suppose not. Someone else
always has to carry on the story."[9] There is no organized religion in Middle-
earth, but there is a shared faith in the power of narrative to console, redeem,
and inspire. It's as if the characters in Middle-earth were adherents of Hans
Vaihinger's 1911 philosophy of "as if."

Many of Tolkien's arguments in the essay reflect the fin-de-siècle turn
toward the ironic imagination, animistic reason, and imaginary worlds to
re-enchant modernity. By "fairy-stories" he meant tales of fantastic imaginary worlds, "the making or glimpsing of Other-worlds."[10] These Secondary
Worlds address the widespread yearning for enchantment, "the realization,
independent of the conceiving mind, of wonder."[11] They are believed in
with a double-minded awareness that one is engaging in pretense ("Secondary Belief"), and they combine reason and imagination in their form, as
well as their content, to impart "the inner consistency of reality."[12] Although
Tolkien claimed that these traits are characteristic of fairy stories throughout history, his interpretation is in fact historically specific, mirroring the
new ideas about the imagination, imaginary worlds, and the search for specifically modern forms of enchantment prevalent at the turn of the century.
His definition of enchantment is clearly beholden to the "artificial paradises" of late nineteenth-century Aestheticism:

> Enchantment produces a Secondary World into which both designer and spectator can
> enter, to the satisfaction of their senses while they are inside; but in its purity it is artistic
> in desire and purpose. . . . Uncorrupted it does not seek delusion, nor bewitchment and
> domination; it seeks shared enrichment, partners in making and delight, not slaves.[13]

Writer and reader are collaborators in a conscious game that promotes lu-
cidity as well as wonder, a specifically modern form of enchantment that
delights but does not delude. As C. S. Lewis noted in a review of *The Lord of
the Rings,* Tolkien's fantasy stood at "the cool middle point between illusion
and disillusionment."[14]

Tolkien's ideas about the logical coherence of Secondary Worlds, and his belief in the capacity of readers to inhabit pluralities of worlds and identities, has intriguing affinities with current literary and philosophical understandings of "possible worlds." Charles Spinosa and Hubert L. Dreyfus, for example, argue that individuals are able to "cross dwell" in a plurality of "weakly incommensurate worlds." These worlds have their own rules, tasks, and identities: "cultures and past historical epochs of cultures, then, are obvious candidates for worlds."[15] Those dwelling in one world need not find another world entirely unintelligible. They can discover ways to translate the logic of a given world into terms they can understand, or at least determine ways to relate to the world even if they do not understand, or accept, all of its premises. By cross-dwelling in another world, a visitor could benefit from the perspectives and practices that she might not find in the context of her own world. The habit of consciously dwelling in plural worlds, they maintain, is already a feature of Western culture: "To grow up in the West means being socialized into marginal historical practices as well as dominant ones. Thus, we are able to dwell in more than one world and so can see why the distinctions in each world make or made sense to the people living in them."[16]

Spinosa and Dreyfus insist that this practice is important for undermining the essentialist claim that all views accord with "one complete, consistent, comprehensive, and coherent description of reality."[17] Essentialism results in the exclusion or denigration of perspectives that challenge this unitary understanding. By cross-dwelling in plural worlds, one can accept the norms in each world without being committed to the exclusionary principle of an essentialist orientation: "Since we are able to have multiple identities by dwelling in different worlds, the stable distinctions of any world need not be seen as establishing dangerous exclusionary practices. What is excluded from seriousness in one world may be revered in another in which members of the first world already 'cross-dwell.'"[18]

Spinosa and Dreyfus did not discuss fictional worlds, but Tolkien's definition of an imaginary world resonates in important respects with their definition of what can be called a world. Tolkien stated that the author "makes a Secondary World in which your mind can enter. Inside it, what he relates is 'true'; it accords with the laws of that world. You therefore believe it, while you are, as it were, inside."[19] Many of Tolkien's readers determined that Middle-earth was one of the "weakly incommensurate worlds" that was enriching to inhabit not merely as entertainment but because it gave them new perspectives concerning their Primary World. Readers from different ethnicities, cultures, and systems of beliefs found they could entertain the categories and distinctions set up within Middle-earth without having to accept them all. In fact, those issues that generated tensions with their primary beliefs could be the most fruitful ones, forcing them to question their own tacitly held convictions. This was especially true within public spheres of the imagination dedicated to Middle-earth, where contentious issues often resulted in productive discussions.

However, not all readers who encountered Middle-earth via the ironic imagination accepted that narratives were contingent constructs employed for pragmatic purposes. *The Lord of the Rings* appealed as well to those who despised the relativistic, anti-essentialist currents of the contemporary West and desired a return to the alleged stabilities of the premodern world. For example, neo-fascist groups in Europe and America celebrated the epic as a rejection of modernity: in the 1970s, right-wing Italian extremists established summer "Hobbit Camps" to indoctrinate youth, and in the 1980s the British National Front commended what they perceived as the racism of Tolkien's works. (To add insult to injury, they also named their type-setting firm Gandalf's Graphics).[20] When the White People's Party, an American neo-Nazi group, published an analysis of *The Lord of the Rings* as "an Aryan work of art" in 1979, they praised it for its essentialist outlook:

> Tolkien rejected the 20th century world, with its materialism, pollution, moral ambiguities and apathy. The imaginary world he created has none of these; it has heroism and self-sacrifice. It has clear skies and rivers, it has sharply defined concepts of Right and Wrong. It is little wonder that his work struck a resonant note in Aryan young people—those who are young in heart as well as those who are young in age.[21]

These organizations were unlikely to be public spheres of the imagination; given their professed beliefs, it is difficult to imagine that they permitted free discussions conducted on the principles of equality, rationality, tolerance, and mutual respect. But they are a reminder that public spheres of the imagination might be insufficiently diverse to avoid perpetuating homogeneous points of view, in effect rejecting "weakly incommensurate worlds" for those wholly commensurate with one's beliefs. Tolkien belonged to a group of writers known as The Inklings, which could be considered a public sphere of the imagination, although it was hardly a diverse one: it consisted of white, middle-class, male professionals, nearly all of whom were committed Christians.[22] In it, Tolkien was preaching to the converted, and they in turn rarely dissented.

Tolkien's views, like those of Conan Doyle and Lovecraft, expressed the tension between the ironic acceptance of Secondary Worlds and the tenacious hold of essentialist narratives concerning the Primary World. The "as if" vied with the "just so" in his mind, especially during the first half of the twentieth century. As a philologist, Tolkien held an "as if" attitude regarding the historical reconstruction of languages. Like others in the profession, he

recognized that the fragmentary nature of evidence concerning early languages often required provisional hypotheses about their origins. These
were known as "asterisk realities," signaling their contingent status.[23] But for
all his related gestures toward "as if" narratives in "On Fairy-stories," he also
believed that they—indeed, all stories—were essentially True. Humans
were "sub-creators," emulating God's creative power in their fictions; stories
inevitably expressed and furthered God's purposes in the world. In Tolkien's metaphysical notion of "Mythopoeia," all myths were, at some level,
real, with Christianity expressing the highest truth as well as being incarnate within history.[24]

Tolkien also maintained an essentialist belief in nationalist narratives.
For him, the nation embodied a mystical core that expressed itself in the
"tongue and soil" of its native inhabitants.[25] He hoped to create a mythology
for England during and after World War I, and following World War II his
nationalist views only intensified in the light of Britain's relative geopolitical
and economic decline. He stubbornly insisted that aspects of Middle-earth
incorporated an essential Englishness that resisted translation into other
languages and resonated with the English psyche. In effect, he lived in two
imaginary worlds—England and Middle-earth—and he believed that both
existed at a metaphysical level.

How then do we account for Tolkien's apparent acceptance of provisional, open-ended narratives in "On Fairy-stories" and *The Lord of the
Rings?* These countervailing views are not misinterpretations. Tolkien, the
supreme theorist of double consciousness when it came to fiction, was of
two minds when it came to essentialist and provisional orientations. His
essentialist leanings were counterbalanced by his attraction to Aestheticism, which contributed to his understanding of imaginary worlds as artificial constructs habitable through the ironic imagination. In addition, he
was wary of asserting conclusive interpretations as a consequence of his
Roman Catholicism, which led him to maintain that individuals could
never fathom the Lord's ultimate intentions, the essential "ends" of all
stories. Tolkien's famous dislike of allegorical interpretations of *The Lord of
the Rings* reflected his discomfort with unitary points of view, manifested in
the epic by the mesmeric single eye of Sauron and the overly confident rhetoric of Saruman. Theirs was the sin of anyone who would try to impose
limited perspectives on others, ranging from the postwar superpowers to
the puny powers of literary critics.

Tolkien therefore believed in both essentialist truth and provisional perspectives: his acceptance of seeing the world in terms of "as if" at times vied
with an underlying faith that all stories were "just so." His ambivalent attitudes concerning essentialist religion and contingent fiction is a sharply
defined instance of a conflict in Western thought since at least the eighteenth

century, when the cultural origins of the Bible began to be emphasized alongside its origin through divine revelation.[26] By the time that Matthew Arnold presented the Bible as a literary resource for wisdom and morality in *Literature and Dogma* (1873), secular fictions were competing with, and arguably superseding, traditional religious teachings as sources of meaning and enchantment for many in Western Europe and North America. Tolkien tried to reverse the trend that Arnold had codified. Rather than envisioning religious texts as useful fictions, he defined all fictions as being in some way religious, "sub-creations" that inevitably echoed the inscrutable intentions of the supreme creator. Yet this position, which he shared with fellow Christians like C. S. Lewis and G. K. Chesterton, can be seen as a back-handed compliment to the tremendous cultural sway of secular fictions at the turn of the century. Whereas fiction in the early and mid-nineteenth century had to justify itself before religion—the Brontë children's experience was symptomatic—religion now had to respond to the increasing attractions of secular fiction and the imaginary worlds it purveyed.

This suggests that in the modern Western world, religious faith alone might be insufficient to re-enchant the world for many. The competing enchantments from secular mass culture are simply too pervasive, too enthralling, to ignore or reject. (The phenomenal success of the "Left Behind" series of books and video games among evangelical Christians in the United States is partly due to their canny combination of traditional eschatology with secular genre conventions.) This was certainly the case for Tolkien and Lewis, who were as enchanted by pagan myths and secular fictions as they were by religious texts. At times the former seemed more attractive to them than the latter, which might explain why the two men anxiously attempted to incorporate all fictions within a theistic understanding.

Yet Tolkien's imaginary world of Middle-earth, and his theorizations of the importance of fantasy in the modern world, contributed to the worldly trend he and Lewis hoped to forestall. Many readers found in Middle-earth a secular form of spirituality, or at least enchantment. This form of modern enchantment does not preclude traditional religious belief, but it has served as an alternative to it, and the ironic imagination it promotes has challenged fundamentalist interpretations. Since the 1960s, many of Tolkien's fans have been less ambivalent than he about Fictionalism. They extol provisional interpretations and the benefits of cross-dwelling in a plurality of worlds, thanks in part to his discussions of the double-minded consciousness of the ironic imagination. While Tolkien based his theory of Secondary Belief in Secondary Worlds on a metaphysical foundation, it proved conducive to an outlook suspicious of foundations and essences. Modern enchantment, negotiating a path between delight and delusion, acknowledges the siren call of the "just so" even as it cleaves to the slippery slopes of the "as if."

II. A MAN OF TWO MINDS

At the turn of the twentieth century, sociologists associated modern disenchantment with the loss of a religious worldview. Tolkien, however, was a deeply religious man, and he argued that disenchantment had earlier roots, preceding the onset of modernity. As a Catholic, he viewed all of human existence in light of the Fall: in effect, disenchantment began with paradise lost. Even Christianity, in its institutional form, contributed to disenchantment by domesticating the "demonic energy" of paganism as expressed in the northern myths and sagas.[27] In notes for a 1926 lecture about the Norse *Eddas,* Tolkien asserted that the pagan gods were "vanquished, not by the World-girdling serpent or Fenris-wolf . . . but by Marie de France, and sermons, medieval Latin and useful information, and the small change of French courtesy,"[28] resulting in "the dying down of the flame, into the gentle smoulder of the Middle Ages, taxes and trade-regulations, and the jog-trot of pigs and herrings."[29] Like other cultural pessimists, he believed modernity represented the nadir of this ongoing process of historical decline. It was a "robot age" combining "elaboration and ingenuity of means with ugliness."[30]

The most disenchanting losses for Tolkien, however, were personal. They all involved the loss of home, of a stable world he could call his own. Homelessness, he believed, was a fundamental condition following humanity's expulsion from paradise: "We all long for it . . . our whole nature . . . is still soaked with the sense of 'exile.'"[31] But Tolkien had suffered more immediate exiles during his youth that would affect the rest of his life. He was born in 1892 in Bloemfontein, a city in what is now South Africa. His parents, Arthur and Mabel, relocated there from England when Arthur was offered a job as a bank manager. In 1895, Mabel took Tolkien and his younger brother Hilary to England for a visit with relatives; Arthur was to join them, but died unexpectedly of rheumatic fever in 1896.

Tolkien never returned to South Africa, but he retained vivid memories of his first home—now irrevocably lost. More losses followed in rapid succession. His mother settled her small family in Sarehole, a picturesque village adjoining Birmingham in the West Midlands, but this idyll ended abruptly when Mabel's limited finances forced the family to move to Birmingham. Whatever sense of community they found in Mabel's extended family was compromised when she converted to Catholicism in 1900, alienating most of her Protestant relatives. And then came the most devastating loss of all: in 1904 Mabel died of diabetes, leaving her twelve-year-old son to look after his brother. The orphans were put under the care of a Catholic priest; the continuity with Catholicism, at least, was to remain a stable element throughout Tolkien's life.

His already-tarnished Edwardian world was forever shattered a decade later by the outbreak of the First World War. Tolkien fought at the Battle of the Somme, recalling years later that "to be caught in youth by 1914 was no less hideous an experience than to be involved in 1939 and the following years. By 1918 all but one of my close friends were dead."[32] Returning from the muddy hell of no-man's-land, he watched in helpless frustration as bucolic Sarehole was industrialized during the interwar years.

It is no wonder, then, that modernity became inextricably associated in his mind with unsettling flux and painful loss. He yearned for stable worlds that would recover the emotional security and natural beauty that he enjoyed too briefly as a child in the country. In an early draft of "On Fairy-stories," he jotted, "Life of a less changeful kind—humanized. It lies out just beyond the cruel modern world. I was born in a time when it was still recognizable."[33]

Catholicism provided him with one such spiritual home, albeit a mysterious one. Having suffered so much instability, he craved something more tangible and secure, a stable world free from the oscillations of doubt and faith that accompanied religious belief. Like Søren Kierkegaard, Tolkien experienced faith as a leap into the unknown that must be made repeatedly. In 1963, he reminded his son Michael about the importance of regular church attendance, for the "temptation to 'unbelief' (which really means rejection of Our Lord and His claims) is always there within us. The only cure for sagging of fainting Faith is Communion . . . Like the act of Faith it must be continuous and grow by exercise. Frequency is of the highest effect."[34]

Tolkien assuaged his need for a fixed home by creating foundational imaginary worlds where he could dwell. One of these was England, although he did not think of the nation as an "imagined community." England was his Primary World, and he thought of it in essentialist terms, celebrating the unique soil, climate, and psyche of its people. The other was Middle-earth, which he did acknowledge as imaginary: a Secondary World.[35]

Tolkien was at once a nationalist and an aesthete, and these orientations could clash in his thought just as they did in the wider culture at the turn of the century. Nationalism took many forms, including a cultural or "aestheticist" one that identified the nation as a contingent product of historical circumstances. In the late nineteenth century, however, it was more often understood in essentialist terms as it became entangled with contemporary scientific ideas about biological differences among distinct "races." Although Aestheticism could also don an essentialist guise, its adherents gesturing to a metaphysical spirit underlying all creation, it more often emphasized the centrality of artifice, replacing confidence in certitudes with a tolerance for multiple perspectives, multiple truths. At the turn of the century, nationalism tended to be a "just so" story, whereas Aestheticism epitomized the "as if."

Tolkien may have recognized the tension between his professed essentialist views about religion and the nation and his appreciation of the art for art's sake philosophy of Aestheticism. He knew himself to be a man of two minds who could see apparently opposing perspectives as complementary rather than contradictory. "On Fairy-stories" was only the most far-reaching of his reflections on the double consciousness of the ironic imagination that enabled him to dwell simultaneously in primary and secondary worlds. In an unfinished tale of 1945, "The Notion-Club Papers," a character asserted, "it is clear that the mind can be in two places at one time. When you are writing a story, for instance, you can . . . *see* two places at once. You can see (say) a field with a tree and sheep sheltering from the sun under it, and be looking round your room. You are really seeing both scenes, because you can recollect details later."[36]

Tolkien also empathized with earlier writers whom he believed juggled antithetical conceits and maintained a similar double consciousness. Just as he attempted to reconcile divergent views—Victorian essentialism and Edwardian perspectivism, theism and secularism, disenchantment and re-enchantment—he gravitated to writers who lived in transitional times and tried to syncretize past and present, paganism and Christianity, heroism and humility. He admired the poet of the Old English epic *Beowulf*, whom he described as an English Christian witnessing the dying afterglow of the pagan world. *Beowulf* combined the best of both Christian and pagan worldviews: it was not a confused poem, as many critics complained, but a "fusion that has occurred at a given point of contact between old and new."[37] Similarly, he argued that the Norse poems emerged from "a special transition-period—one of poise between old and new, and one inevitably brief and not long to be maintained."[38] *The Lord of the Rings* likewise represented a transitional moment of history, echoing that of Tolkien's own fin-de-siècle. The Third Age of Middle-earth was "a Twilight Age, a Medium Aevum" when one world was dwindling, another about to be born.[39]

Tolkien's self-described "legendarium" of the First and Second Ages of prehistory (known collectively as "The Silmarillion"), and his epic narrative of the Third Age (including *The Hobbit* and *The Lord of the Rings*) expressed the essentialist and anti-essentialist currents vying during his own time. The result was an unstable mixture that gave his work its layered complexities and contributed to its lasting and wide appeal. In order to understand how *The Lord of the Rings* in particular would continue to attract a diverse audience and fuel debates in public spheres of the imagination, we need to examine more closely the intricate interplay among Tolkien's nationalist, aestheticist, and religious views.

III. FROM "NORTHERN" TO "LITTLE" ENGLAND

Tolkien's first imaginary world was not Middle-earth: it was England. His construction of Middle-earth was, in part, an ongoing elaboration of his understanding of Englishness and changed as broader cultural representations of English national identity changed.[40] In its earliest formulations during the First World War, Middle-earth was indebted to a heroic, Anglo-Saxon or "Northern" understanding of English identity that had been prevalent in the country since the mid-nineteenth century. During the interwar period, however, Middle-earth altered, following a shift in English culture that promoted a less heroic, and more bourgeois and domestic, understanding of Englishness. The values of Middle-earth coincided with those of "Little England" in the 1920s and 1930s. Underlying these shifts, however, were certain continuities. Middle-earth always expressed an interpretation of English history that legitimated facets of Tolkien's own background as being quintessentially English, including his alleged Anglo-Saxon genealogy, his Midland ancestry, and even his Catholicism. "Mine is not an 'imaginary' world," he wrote in 1956, "but an imaginary historical moment of 'Middle-earth'—which is our habitation."[41]

Tolkien needed to create an imaginary prehistory of England to authorize his English identity, which he could not take for granted. After all, he had been born on another continent and was not a member of the established Protestant faith, which remained a defining aspect of Englishness for most of his life.[42] Such apparently small differences between him and most of his compatriots assumed great importance in his mind. Like Lovecraft's defensive championing of his own Anglo-Saxon heritage, Tolkien's strident insistence on the purity of his English background reflected his insecurity about his status. He became more English than the English, proclaiming that his national identity was vouchsafed by his heredity or "blood." This inherent connection to the nation had been clear to him from the moment he entered the country as a three-year-old: "I had this strange sense of coming home when I arrived";[43] England was "the place where I belonged but which was totally novel and strange."[44] Throughout his life he asserted vehemently that he was "English," not "British."[45]

He claimed that he was linked to the Anglo-Saxons, and thus to the English, via his maternal ancestry.[46] The Anglo-Saxon language not only formed the "root" of English but also fostered the peculiarly "Northern" outlook that many at the turn of the century thought was intrinsic to the English national character.[47] He also noted that when his paternal ancestors arrived in England from Germany in the eighteenth century they became "quickly and intensely English (not British)."[48]

His mother's family, the Suffields, also became well-established in Birmingham at the same time, and Tolkien adopted the West Midland region as another branch of his English genealogical tree. He felt he had a mystical affinity for the Midland dialect of Middle English because of this ancestry, writing to W. H. Auden in 1955 that he was a "West-midlander by blood (and took to early west-midland Middle English as a known tongue as soon as I set eyes upon it.)"[49] His earliest poems and stories about Middle-earth, beginning in 1915, associated it not only with England but specifically to the environs of the West Midlands.[50] (While he would later claim that Middle-earth represented the northwest of Europe, he continued to defend its essential "Englishness." Middle-earth could just as well be described as Midland-earth.)[51]

Tolkien's early works sprang from his long-standing hobby of inventing languages, his love of fantasy, and his nationalist ambition to create a mythology for England. Since childhood he had enjoyed inventing languages, and as an Oxford undergraduate prior to the war he began to write poems about fairies in one of his artificial tongues. He soon found that his languages were vivified by situating them in their own world of myth and history, which in turn fostered the ongoing development of a Secondary World. Just as his languages became more "real" by being organically associated with their own imaginary environment and history, the world itself exfoliated from them.

It was not surprising that Tolkien set his first works in the realm of faery, as fairy tales were widely popular in Edwardian Britain.[52] He had developed an interest in them as an adolescent, alongside his growing passion for languages.[53] It is likely that he responded to their themes of loss and disenchantment, as many of them recounted the waning of fairies with the onset of modernity. Certainly the earliest poems and stories of his mythology, written during and immediately after the First World War, were redolent with nostalgia for a vanishing world of nobility and magic.[54] But he also intended his early works to promote the "Northern" heroic and spiritual values expressed by certain fairy tales, myths, and sagas. Like many at the turn of the century, he had become preoccupied with finding forms of re-enchantment for a disenchanted age.

He shared this aspiration with a small group of fellow students at King Edward's grammar school in Birmingham, who formed the "Tea Club and Barrovian Society" (TCBS) in 1911. Together they championed the ideals of courage, nobility, and moral purpose, which had attracted Tolkien in his omnivorous readings of myths. In an early lexicon of one of his invented languages, Tolkien noted that "the fairies came to teach men song and holiness"; this was the general agenda of cultural renewal adopted by the TCBS.[55] As one of the Society's few survivors after the Great War, he may have felt morally bound to continue their project of re-enchantment through his developing mythology.

In addition to providing resources for re-enchantment, fairy tales had a distinctly nationalist dimension at this time that jibed with Tolkien's patriotic inclinations. They were among the folklore collected by eighteenth- and nineteenth-century intellectuals to establish founding traditions for the nation.[56] Because of his own anxieties about his English identity, Tolkien was acutely aware that England lacked such a legitimating mythology. As an undergraduate, he delivered a paper on a recently created national myth, the Finnish epic of the *Kalevala*, which had been written in the previous century from surviving fragments of native lore. Tolkien was enthralled by it, and it may have inspired him to create a specifically English mythology. As he reflected decades later:

> I was from early days grieved by the poverty of my own beloved country: it had no stories of its own (bound up with its tongue and soil) . . . I had a mind to make a body of more or less connected legend . . . which I could dedicate simply to: to England; to my country.[57]

He rejected the popular Arthurian myths as "imperfectly naturalized, associated with the soil of Britain but not with English."[58] Instead, he would associate the fairy tradition directly with England.

Thus the project of modern re-enchantment became entangled with a self-consciously nationalist project, which Tolkien commenced during the jingoistic period of the First World War. He enlisted in the war, telling a friend in November 1914 that "The duty of patriotism and a fierce belief in nationalism are to me of vital importance."[59] He later acknowledged that his adolescent taste for myths was "quickened to full life by war."[60]

Tolkien continued to write poems about fairies as he trained in 1915, associating some of the narratives with Warwick, the West Midlands home of Edith Bratt, whom he would marry in 1916. He fought in the Battle of the Somme and became ill with trench fever; during his convalescence he wrote the earliest prose narratives of his legendarium. These focused on the First Age of fairies, soon to be called "Elves." They were the primary "children" of Ilúvatar, the supreme God, who created them with the aid of a lesser pantheon of deities or angels, the Valar.[61] (Humans, the other children of Ilúvatar, awoke on Middle-earth after the Elves and would continue to play a subordinate role in his work until the 1930s.) The Elves were immortal; they were also extraordinary artists. Their excessive pride over the exquisite products of their culture led to a fratricidal conflict, just as Tolkien and his generation were engaging in a war defined in terms of German "Kultur" versus British and French "Civilization."

In these early stories of his legendarium, Tolkien's imaginary world was cast in the heroic mold of Norse mythology.[62] He likewise associated the early history of England with the warrior ethos of the Northern pagan world: "Of English pre-Christian mythology we know practically nothing. But the fundamentally similar heroic temper of ancient England and Scandinavia cannot have been founded on (or perhaps rather, cannot have generated) mythologies divergent on this essential point."[63] He argued that Old English works such as *Beowulf* demonstrated that the pagan code of undaunted courage in the face of insurmountable odds had been brought to England by the Saxons and continued to affect English character.[64] *Beowulf,* however, was a syncretic text, reflecting the establishment of Christianity in England alongside the pagan ethos. For Tolkien the Roman Catholic, *Beowulf* had the distinct merit of combining pagan assertiveness with Christian humility.[65] He was attracted to similar Middle English poems while formulating his own mythology, such as *Sir Gawain and the Green Knight* and *Pearl.* They demonstrated how the English adoption of Catholicism tempered the self-assertiveness of the Northern heroic ideal in beneficial ways.

Finally, he claimed that his English myths were characteristically "Northern" in their clarity and rationality, which distinguished them from the "lavish and fantastical, incoherent and repetitive" myths of the Celtic-British imagination.[66] Tolkien's specifically English project of re-enchantment presented "science and romance" as "integrally related"; England was thus distinguished by the trait of animistic reason.[67] Tolkien's mythology would have the best of all English worlds, embodying pagan courage and Christian compassion, reason and imagination, stoicism and salvation. "Nowhere was [the Northern spirit] nobler than in England, nor more early sanctified and Christianized," he wrote in 1941, adding that he had spent his life trying to "present [it] in its true light."[68]

Tolkien collected these early stories under the title "The Book of Lost Tales," which he continued to augment through the early 1920s.[69] His nascent mythology recounted the civil war among the Elves, as well as their war against Morgoth, one of the Valar who challenged Ilúvatar's supremacy over creation. "The Book of Lost Tales" was as much about the First World War as it was about the First Age of Middle-earth, using traditional materials to represent the indescribable horrors of modern warfare.[70] This rhetorical strategy was widespread in the interwar years, facilitating the mourning process in ways that more abstract, modernistic techniques could not.[71] In Tolkien's early story "The Fall of Gondolin," dragons and other monsters fashioned by Morgoth from iron and steel suggest tanks, airplanes, and flamethrowers; the devastation wreaked on the landscape is reminiscent of the no-man's-land of the Western front. Tolkien recalled vividly the military ambience in which "The Book of Lost Tales" was written: "in grimy canteens, at lectures in cold fogs, in huts full of blasphemy and smut, or by candle-light in bell-tents, even some down in dugouts under shell-fire." These tales processed his war experience, enabling him to come to terms with "good, evil, fair, foul in some way: to rationalize it, and prevent it just festering."[72]

Following the war, Tolkien worked for the *Oxford English Dictionary* and then taught at Leeds University; in 1925 he became professor of Anglo-Saxon at Oxford. Alongside his busy professional and family life he continued to write about the First and Second Ages of Middle-earth. He informally referred to his expanding legendarium as "The Silmarillion," named after the exquisite jewels fashioned by the Elves that had precipitated the conflicts in Middle-earth.[73] Many of the tales remained epic in style, although they could include whimsical elements. The traditional, patriarchal social order they portrayed did not exclude strong and resourceful female characters, some of whom were reminiscent of his mother. (Tolkien claimed that Lúthien was based on his wife, but two of the most capable women in the legendarium, Morwin and Erendis, were in effect single parents.)[74]

When humans, and the human-like hobbits, became more prominent in his legendarium beginning in the 1930s, its style and themes shifted from this Northern, heroic register to a more realist, and certainly a more domestic, mode.[75] The change was partly fortuitous, as the children's story that introduced the hobbits and their bourgeois manners, *The Hobbit* (1937), was not intended to be part of his expanding mythology. Yet the cozy, familial milieu of the hobbit enclave in the Shire also reflected a shift in English conceptions of national identity during the interwar years, one that was to remain an important theme in the book's sequel, *The Lord of the Rings*.

This new conception of Englishness popularized an insular, domestic, and rural image of the nation, in contrast to the more public, masculine, and imperial representations that had been common during the later Victorian and Edwardian periods.[76] The genesis of "Little England" had many causes, including the financial and psychological repercussions of the war, greater ambivalence over empire, discomfort with a growing cosmopolitanism, and a sharper consciousness of a specifically English identity following the creation of the Irish Free State.[77] The blunt, assertive prewar icon of John Bull was replaced by the image of the "Little Man," not dissimilar in character to a hobbit: he was domestic, deferential, and unadventurous, yet also courageous, quick to act in concert with others when the occasion demanded.[78] Little England glorified both the private home and the national community; its citizens cherished their individualism and hard-won freedoms but also acknowledged the claims of fellowship and the commonweal.

Tolkien had expressed similar sentiments even before the new ideology became pervasive in the interwar period. He opposed imperialism, favored Irish Home Rule, loved the English countryside and rarely went abroad, or even beyond the confines of Oxford. But the domestic, Little England perspective of his legendarium became more pronounced in *The Hobbit* and *The Lord of the Rings* than it was in much of "The Silmarillion." *The Hobbit*, he later stated, "proved to be the discovery of the completion of the whole, its mode of descent to earth, and merging into 'history.' As the high Legends of the beginning are supposed to look at things through Elvish minds, so the middle tales of the Hobbit take a virtually human point of view—and the last tale blends them."[79]

The Shire was, as he acknowledged, "based on rural England and not any other country in the world—least perhaps of any in Europe or Holland."[80] The hobbits were intended as an affectionate satire of the English middle-classes, including their philistinism, but they also represented solid English traits: a love of nature, common sense, decency, courage, and a reverence for tradition coupled with irreverence for authority.[81] The Shire was an anchor in the ever-threatened world of Middle-earth, just as Little England became Tolkien's imaginary haven in an increasingly cosmopolitan and industrialized world. Both shared a firm foundation in his mind. As Merry reminds Pippin in *The Lord of the Rings*, "It is best to love first what you are fitted to love, I suppose; you must start somewhere and have some roots, and the soil of the Shire is deep."[82]

But during and after the Second World War, Tolkien feared that his beloved Little England might be uprooted by the flood-tides of globalization. His increasing apprehension of cosmopolitanism could be seen in minor matters, such as his unexpected rejection of Esperanto after the Second World War. Tolkien had been a vocal proponent of this artificial language, which had been created in 1887 to transcend national differences. He wrote an exercise in Esperanto in 1909 and was an advisor to the British Esperanto Association in 1932; in the early 1930s he claimed that an invented language like Esperanto was "the one thing antecedently necessary for uniting Europe, before it is swallowed up by non-Europe."[83] Presumably the non-Europe he meant was the United States, which had become a global financial power and was successfully exporting its industrial and cultural products to Europe.[84] But by 1956, it may have been clear to Tolkien that Esperanto would prove no match for the new hegemony in the West established by the United States. The artificial language now appeared to him as a symbol of inhumanity, perhaps reflecting the regimentation of the world under the aegis of both the USA and the USSR. He repudiated Esperanto, condemning it as a "dead" language, lacking its own myths and traditions.[85] Artificial languages like Esperanto were no longer a "good thing" because "at present I think we should be likely to get an *inhumane* language."[86]

Tolkien disliked allegorical interpretations of *The Lord of the Rings,* and it would be a mistake to read it reductively in the light of his own preoccupations. Nevertheless, it is possible to see in its pages a heart-felt defense of Little England in the face of globalization, particularly the cultural and economic sway of the United States. He started the work in 1937, following the unexpected publishing success of *The Hobbit.* When his publisher asked for a sequel, he was emboldened to submit samples of "The Silmarillion," but the firm didn't know what to make of Tolkien's elaborate cosmogony, which seemed to contain everything but adorable hobbits, and insisted he continue the adventures of these lucrative beings. Tolkien acquiesced, but as he proceeded to write, the narrative gradually became enmeshed in his wider mythology. By the time *The Lord of the Rings* was published in three volumes in the early 1950s, it was no longer a children's story, but a dark and complex work detailing the cataclysmic war besetting Middle-earth during its Third Age. It begins and ends in the Shire, a version of Little England that had been at the heart of his nationalist mythology since the 1930s.

Tolkien commenced the requested sequel with no preconceived plan, but as the Second World War engulfed the Primary World, his Secondary World came to reflect his growing anxieties about the postwar world. Read in the light of his fears that English culture might be eclipsed by a more cosmopolitan one after the war, one can perceive the Shire and its environs being threatened by two inhumane presences. The looming shadow of the United States, no less than that of the dark lord Sauron, menaced the very English topography and temper that informs much of Middle-earth.

The hobbits of the Shire find their way of life imperiled by Sauron, whose unbridled lust for power threatens to transform Middle-earth into a mechanized enclave subject to his command. Tolkien worried aloud that a similar fate awaited England from the United States, and his apprehension can be discerned in *The Lord of the Rings.* In later years he rejected interpretations of the work that equated Sauron and his ring of power with Stalin, Hitler, or the atomic bomb. But after reading the letters he wrote to his son Christopher during the war, it is difficult not to associate the valiant fight of the hobbits with the struggles of Little Englanders resisting the imposition of American hegemony in the postwar years. By 1943 Tolkien was certain that Hitler would be defeated, but he remained wary of the postwar settlement. He wrote his son:

> I wonder (if we survive this war) if there will be any niche left for reactionary back numbers like me (and you). The bigger things get the smaller and duller or flatter the globe gets. It is going to be all one blasted little provincial suburb. When they have

introduced American sanitation, morale-pep, feminism, and mass-production throughout [the globe], how happy we shall be. I do find this Americo-cosmopolitanism very terrifying. For I love England (not Great Britain and certainly not the British Commonwealth).[87]

At the conclusion of *The Lord of the Rings,* which he was still writing after the war, the Shire itself begins to be industrialized by a group of foreign men directed by an ally of Sauron, the evil wizard Saruman. Tolkien had complained as early as 1933 about the similar destruction of Sarehole, which resulted from the ongoing internal industrialization of England and had little to do with America. In the chapter "The Scouring of the Shire," however, it is striking that the agents of devastation are clearly foreigners from the wider world beyond the Shire—and there is an incidental detail that has a distinctly "American" flavor. Saruman has assumed an alias; he is known to the Orcs under his command as "Sharkû" ("Old Man") and to his thug-like human henchmen as "Sharkey." Sharkey connotes an American gangster's nickname, which would have been familiar to British readers of the interwar years through the popular, "American" crime fiction of English writers like James Hadley Chase, as well as through imports of American films and noir fiction. (George Orwell complained about their corrupting influence on the more genteel tradition of English detective fiction in his 1944 essay, "Raffles and Miss Blandish.")

In the postwar years Tolkien continued to oppose his essentialist vision of Little England to a no less essentialist vision of an American behemoth. While he had hoped to create a mythology for England, he was distressed that *The Lord of the Rings* had become the basis for "cults" of fans in America. Two years before his death in 1973 he wrote, "The horrors of the American scene . . . arise in an entirely different mental climate and soil, polluted and impoverished to a degree only paralleled by the lunatic destruction of the physical lands which Americans inhabit."[88] He had the satisfaction of knowing that if Little England continued to dwindle on the global stage, it would at least survive in the imagination as Middle-earth.

IV. IN THE BEGINNING WERE THE WORDS

When Tolkien began his legendarium during the First World War, his aim of establishing a national myth defining the essence of a people might have appeared ambitious, even grandiose, but not inconceivable. "Just so" narratives relating fundamental truths competed with "as if" narratives, especially at the fin-de-siècle. Following the Second World War, however, such essentialist national myths were met with greater skepticism, given their pivotal role in the outbreaks of both World Wars and their centrality to fascism. They were now more often viewed as justifications for exclusionary practices, atavisms in an age witnessing, in Daniel Bell's phrase, *The End of Ideology* (1960). Roland Barthes's deconstructive *Mythologies* (1957) captured the general "hermeneutics of suspicion" toward these and other types of essentialist narratives.[89]

Even Tolkien admitted that his youthful aspiration could appear "absurd" in the chastened circumstances of postwar England.[90] Despite his self-deprecating remarks, however, he continued to believe his legendarium resonated at an archetypal level with the psyche of the English people. For him, the language of his mythology was imbued with an essential Englishness; individual words, no less than themes and symbols, conveyed a national outlook. Although *The Lord of the Rings* was not accepted consciously as a national mythology when it was published in the early 1950s, it could still operate covertly as one. He believed it would strike an unconscious chord with its native English readers, who were predisposed by environment, and perhaps by heredity, to grasp its mystical significance.

Like Lovecraft, Tolkien's views about the hereditary, racial dimension of national identity shifted toward a less essentialist, cultural explanation during the 1930s, as scholars in Britain and America increasingly criticized the concept of race and the National Socialists carried it to its murderous extremes.[91] It is also important to stress that Tolkien's nationalism had never been as explicitly, or as persistently, racist as that of Lovecraft. Tolkien most often linked Englishness to language, climate, and geography rather than race. On the whole, his was a cultural form of nationalism, similar to those pioneered by Enlightenment theorists of the nation like Johann Herder and the Baron de Montesquieu. But as we have seen, he occasionally linked national identity to "blood" as well as soil, coming perilously close to the pseudo-scientific racial understandings of the nation prevalent in late nineteenth-century Europe and America. In 1955, the same year that he wrote to Auden about how his West Midland "blood" enabled him to master the Midland dialect, he also wrote a biographical sketch asserting that "it is . . . as much due to descent as to opportunity that Anglo-Saxon and Western Middle English and alliterative verse have been both a childhood attraction and my main professional sphere."[92]

His evolving representations of the dwarves in the legendarium might be taken as an index of his changing views and firmer commitment to a cultural understanding of ethnic differences. Tolkien long associated the dwarves with the Jews. In a 1955 letter he stated that the dwarves, like the Jews, were "at once native and alien in their habitations," and in a 1965 interview he went further: "The dwarves of course are quite obviously—wouldn't you say that in many ways they remind you of the Jews? Their words are Semitic obviously, constructed to be Semitic."[93] And Tolkien's earliest depiction of the dwarves is reminiscent of the Jews, but only in the most unfortunate way. In "The Nauglafring," one of stories in "The Book of Lost Tales," they conformed to some of the ugliest stereotypes of the "genteel anti-semitism" endemic among the British middle classes during the interwar period.[94] Dwarves in Old Norse literature were subterranean creatures, short, stout, and bearded, miners of precious gems and ores.[95] So too were Tolkien's dwarves: but in addition they were greedy, treacherous, and never heard of the one true God—"or hearing disbelieve."[96] Their appearance, abilities, and appetites corresponded to contemporary caricatures of Jews:

> They are squat in stature, and yet are strong. And their beards reach even to their toes . . . their crafts and cunning surpass that of the Gnomes in marvelous contrivance, but of truth there is little beauty in the works of themselves . . . Indeed all that folk love gold and silver more dearly than aught else on earth.[97]

A decade later, Tolkien began *The Hobbit*. Here the dwarves have more redeeming characteristics than before, although they still are not the sort one would admit to one's club: "There it is: dwarves are not heroes, but calculating folk with a great idea of the value of money; some are tricky and treacherous and pretty bad lots; some are not, but are decent enough people . . . if you don't expect too much."[98] By the time *The Hobbit* was published in 1937, Tolkien was horrified by the situation in Nazi Germany, which he felt was a travesty of the heroic Northern ideals he so admired. In 1938, he drafted a letter to a German publisher, excoriating the National Socialist's racial ideology: "I have many Jewish friends, and should regret giving any colour to the notion that I subscribed to the wholly pernicious and unscientific race-doctrine."[99] The dwarves in *The Lord of the Rings*, completed by 1949, were among the most admirable "races" to inhabit Middle-earth. (But elements of Christian discomfort with the pretensions of the "Chosen People" still linger: in Tolkien's creation myth, the dwarves, unlike Elves and men, are not among the Children of Ilúvatar. They were created in secret by one of the Valar, an offense in the eyes of the One God and only allowed to survive by His grace.)

In the years following the Second World War, Tolkien explicitly disavowed the idea that there were clear distinctions among races, as well as the equation of biological race and nation. In his 1955 lecture "English and Welsh," he argued that "language is the prime differentiator of peoples— not of 'races,' whatever that much-misused word may mean in the long-blended history of Western Europe."[100] He repudiated his earlier belief in distinct racial traits, such as "the wild, incalculable poetic Celt, full of vague and misty imaginations."[101]

Nevertheless, his cultural nationalism continued to represent language in essentialist terms: the reification of race was replaced by the reification of language. He now distinguished between a "cradle-tongue"—one's "customary" language that is learned in infancy—and a "native tongue," one's "buried" and "inherent linguistic predilections."[102] Tolkien claimed that while his cradle-tongue was English, his native tongue was Gothic; he responded profoundly to the sounds of the words without knowing their meaning.[103] One's native tongue was "largely" the product of history "through indefinite generations."[104] This sounds more hereditary than customary, however, and its essentialist tenor is only heightened by Tolkien's claim that a native tongue could be recognized when "it stirs deep harp-strings in our linguistic nature."[105] For Tolkien, the mystical concept of the "native tongue" seemed to replace "blood," or even be synonymous with it. In the published version of "English and Welsh," he continued to refer to "blood," sometimes with sanitizing quotation marks and sometimes without. He delivered the talk the same year in which he wrote to Auden explicitly linking language to "blood."[106]

Tolkien flirted with different ways an essential English nature might be transmitted. In addition to blood he discussed genetic memories, the collective unconscious, and the possibility of reincarnation.[107] But language proved the primary vehicle by which it was conveyed, and this remained true from the inception of his imaginary world to his reconsiderations of it after the publication of *The Lord of the Rings*. The initial spark of his legendarium had been ignited when he read the Anglo-Saxon poem *Crist* and was overwhelmed by the uncanny beauty of the word *éarendel*. We can imagine how this word might have affected him by consulting "The Notion Club Papers," in which a philologist resembling Tolkien recalls the profound impact this and related words in *Crist* had on him: "I felt a curious thrill, as if something had stirred in me, half wakened by sleep. There was something very remote and strange and beautiful behind those words, if I could grasp it, far beyond ancient English."[108] In 1913, Tolkien also determined to discover the word's earliest meaning, deducing that *éarendel* represented the personification of the morning star in an unrecovered myth. He wrote his own poem in the manner of such a myth in 1914, "The Voyage of Eärendel the Evening Star," which he later identified as the inception of the legendarium.[109]

From its commencement then, Tolkien's mythology harbored an essential Englishness in its language that would resound with his compatriots at a primordial level. Tolkien's fictional philologist speculated that *éarendel* "might derive its curiously moving quality from some other world," echoing Tolkien's own sense that his legendarium conveyed metaphysical truths: "[the stories] arose in my mind as 'given' things, and as they came, separately, so too the links grew ... Always I had the sense of recording what was already 'there,' somewhere: not of 'inventing.'"[110]

This belief would explain his furious reaction in 1956 when Dutch translators substituted their own terms for some of the names of people and places in *The Lord of the Rings*. He felt the translators were insensitive to the work's unequivocal Englishness. "After all," he pointed out, "the book is English, and by an Englishman"; its English references "I regard as integral and essential."[111] This imaginary world was for him, at some level, a very real world, and like England it was now being threatened by cosmopolitanism: "These 'translations' are not English," he fulminated, "they are homeless."[112] The translators responded quite reasonably that Tolkien himself had made it clear in the book's appendices that the hobbits did not speak English but rather their own language, which had then been translated into English.[113]

Tolkien's reply would seem bizarre only if *The Lord of the Rings* was to be taken as entirely fictional. He asserted that the appendices should be interpreted as "pseudo-historical" fictions, forms of poetic license, which did not accurately represent the genuine Englishness underlying the entire work:

> That the Hobbits actually spoke an ancient language of their own is of course a pseudo-historical assertion made necessary by the nature of the narrative . . . My own view is that the names of the persons should all be left as they stand. I should prefer that the names of the places were left untouched also, including Shire.[114]

The poor Dutch translators had made the mistake of treating his epic like any other "as if" narrative, not realizing that Tolkien perceived its essential English nature to be "just so."

Yet it was also a pardonable mistake: running throughout *The Lord of the Rings*, and Tolkien's legendarium as a whole, was an adherence to Fictionalism and the centrality of "as if" thinking. His essentialist beliefs were held in tense equipoise with a commitment to Aestheticism and its embrace of artifice. Fictionalism and the ironic imagination, rather than essentialism and nationalism, were to be among the lasting legacies of *The Lord of the Rings*.

V. FICTIONALISM AND *THE LORD OF THE RINGS*

Tolkien's essentialist views are often only implicit in *The Lord of the Rings* and must be teased out by critics, many of whom are uncomfortably aware that they are violating his stricture against allegorical interpretations of a complex and contradictory work.[115] As he began writing it, he was also formulating his ideas about the autonomous nature of Secondary Worlds for his 1939 lecture, "On Fairy-stories," and those views in turn reinforced his own determination to render Middle-earth even more independent from the Primary World than it had been previously. He recalled in 1953 that as he revised, he removed nearly all the religious references linking his Secondary World to the Primary one; Middle-earth would not be an overtly allegorical world, in contrast to C. S. Lewis's Narnia. (However, he privately continued to think of his epic as "a fundamentally religious and Catholic work," as well as a quintessentially English one.)[116] Aestheticism is more apparent in *The Lord of the Rings* than Tolkien's religious and nationalist beliefs. But his understanding of Aestheticism was, like so much of his thought, contradictory, encompassing both the "as if" and the "just so."

Fin-de-siècle Aestheticism was central to his own philosophy of life and creation. An aestheticist perspective pervades the creation myth of Middle-earth, the *Ainulindalë*, which Tolkien first drafted between 1918 and 1920. Oscar Wilde's quip that "life imitates art" is made literal in this tale, and music likewise becomes the model for all creation. In the *Ainulindalë*, Ilúvatar brings existence into being by propounding certain musical themes, which his holy representatives, the Ainur, then elaborate into a symphony. The world (Arda) is thus literally the product of en*chant*ment, the Ainur its divine choir. Tolkien was probably influenced by the ancient and medieval concept of the "music of the spheres" in this dramatic narrative of origins.[117] Yet contemporary Aestheticism would also be a likely source, given that music was widely held by the aesthetes to be the most iconic of the arts— precisely because it was noniconic. They praised music for being nonrepresentative, autonomous, sensuous, and symbolic, a liberating contrast to the utilitarian aims and moral exhortations of contemporary realism. Walter Pater's aphorism was widely cited at the turn of the century: "All art constantly aspires to the condition of music."[118]

Tolkien's love of language was also self-consciously "aesthetic." The sounds and forms of words affected him sensually, like color and music. He stated that he was a "*pure* philologist," dedicated to language for language's sake.[119] His legendarium was simply "an attempt to create a world in which a form of language agreeable to my personal aesthetic might seem real."[120] He similarly defined *The Lord of the Rings* in terms familiar from Aestheticism: it was "largely an essay in 'linguistic aesthetic'"; "I sometimes say to people who ask me 'what is it all about'? It is not 'about' anything but itself."[121]

Lovecraft's aestheticist belief in the autonomy of imaginary worlds had been influenced by the French Symbolists and Decadents, whereas Tolkien's initial aesthetic views were colored by the more socially engaged English Arts and Crafts movement led by John Ruskin and William Morris. Like other aesthetes, they believed in the primacy of art, but they didn't disassociate it from morality, politics, or utility. For them, art was simply the expression of joy in labor, and only a socially and spiritually cohesive society enabled it to flourish. They consequently idealized allegedly "organic" periods of history, such as classical Greece and the Middle Ages, in which art was a communal expression. For them modernity, with its social fragmentation and materialistic orientation, was inimical to genuine artistic expression. The two called for political, economic, and social changes to save the world for art, but many of their successors in the English Arts and Crafts movement looked to art itself as the agent that would effect societal change.[122]

Tolkien was part of this later generation. He and his friends in the TCBS lamented the ugliness of the industrial world and the loss of common spiritual purposes since the Middle Ages. They consciously pursued the Arts and Crafts' mission of re-enchanting the culture though art.[123] The TCBS may have felt a special affinity with the movement because Birmingham was one of its hubs. Edward Burne-Jones, a founder of the Arts and Crafts, was from Birmingham and attended King Edward's School, and the Birmingham Art Gallery had an important collection of Pre-Raphaelite art. In 1914 Tolkien himself likened the TCBS to the Pre-Raphaelite Brotherhood.[124]

In his case, the influences went further. He entered Exeter College, Oxford in 1911, which Burne-Jones and William Morris had also attended. At this time Tolkien read most of Morris's works and was especially enthusiastic about his versions of the Northern myths and sagas.[125] He was inspired by Morris's imaginary worlds; Morris's *The Earthly Paradise* was to be a direct influence on "The Book of Lost Tales."[126] He may also have been attracted to Morris's call for a "union of the arts" as a counterweight to the modern division of labor and as a symbol of social integration. Morris's model had been the medieval Cathedrals, which brought together architects, painters, sculptors, and craftsmen in a common spiritual enterprise. Tolkien initially had a similar conception of his national mythology: "I would draw some of the great tales in fullness, and leave many only placed in the scheme, and sketched. The cycles should be linked to a majestic whole, and yet leave scope for other minds and hands, wielding paint and music and drama."[127]

By the late 1930s, however, Tolkien's aestheticist views were closer to the fin-de-siècle Symbolists than to those of the English Arts and Crafts movement. In his talks and writings he emphasized, to a greater extent than before, the autonomy of art from the Primary World, especially when it came to the invention of Secondary Worlds. Indeed, he insisted that the power of "enchantment" that he associated with these worlds would be exorcised if they relinquished their distance from the everyday.

While Tolkien's essentialist beliefs in religion and nationalism remained, he now felt that Secondary Worlds should convey them indirectly at best: "Myth and fairy-story must, as all art, reflect and contain in solution elements of moral and religious truth (or error), but not explicit, not in the known form of the 'primary' real world."[128] When he wrote "The Book of Lost Tales" during the First World War, his mythology had direct links with Christianity: among the words in his lexicon for an Elvish language were "saint," "monastery," "gospel," and "Christian missionary."[129] When he wrote *The Lord of the Rings* during the Second World War, he did not depict any institutionalized religion and relegated two brief references to Ilúvatar to the appendices. Like the Symbolists, he had come to believe that the meaning of his art transcended rational analysis; it could be experienced but not fully explicated. As he explained in a 1936 discussion of *Beowulf*:

> The significance of a myth is not easily to be pinned on a paper by analytical reasoning.
> It is at its best when it is presented by a poet who feels rather than makes explicit what
> his theme portends; who presents it incarnate in the world of history and geography . . .
> For myth is alive at once and in all its parts, and dies before it can be dissected.[130]

Two questions thus arise: how did Tolkien think such strictly autonomous Secondary Worlds could re-enchant the Primary World? And why did he come to stress, more than he had done before, the autonomous nature of imaginary worlds during the 1930s?

Suggestive answers to these questions are to be found in "On Fairy-stories." His arguments for the autonomy and applicability of Secondary Worlds were similar in important respects to those of Lovecraft. They both argued that fantasy was a necessary complement to reality, gratifying the desire for "imagined wonders" that the Primary World could not satisfy.[131] Fairy tales, Tolkien argued, were not limited to whimsical stories intended for children, as many of his contemporaries believed. They encompassed narratives of "faery," which he defined broadly as "Fantasy, the making or glimpsing of Other-worlds." (He included "science fiction" within the general category of "fantasy.")[132] These narratives should be free "from the domination of observed 'fact'"; "they open a door on Other Time, and if we pass through, though only for a moment, we stand outside our own Time, outside Time itself, maybe."[133]

Like Lovecraft, Tolkien insisted that such stories were compatible with the modern emphasis on reason and science, even if they intentionally abrogated the natural laws of time and space. Secondary Worlds were not irrational, like dreams: they must be logically coherent, for without "the inner consistency of reality" they would not convince modern readers.[134] And, like Lovecraft, Tolkien believed the enchantments of Secondary Worlds required a disenchanted modern outlook for their appeal. The double consciousness of the ironic imagination allowed readers to enjoy these wonders while remaining rationally aware they were impossibilities. As a

Catholic, Tolkien gave more credence to the supernatural than Lovecraft. But he too believed in reason and science, which demarcated reality from fantasy. It was precisely this distinction in the modern age that made fantasy so compelling. As Tolkien noted, "If men were ever in a state in which they did not want to know or could not perceive truths (facts or evidence), then Fantasy would languish until they were cured."[135]

Secondary Worlds, then, were by their nature autonomous from the Primary World: they were vital complements to it. The more they referred to the Primary World, as in allegory, the more they risked eliding the two realms. Such overlaps could inhibit the reader's ability to become immersed in an autonomous world with its own peculiar yet internally consistent rules; the magic would be lost. "Secondary Worlds," Tolkien argued, required "Secondary Belief," a view comparable to Vaihinger's bracketing of a "fictionalist" orientation through the conscious use of the clause "as if."[136]

Despite this formal cleavage, Tolkien also acknowledged that there were reciprocal relations between Secondary and Primary Worlds, which he analyzed in terms of "Recovery," "Consolation," and "Escape." By estranging the reader from habitual perceptions of the Primary World, fantasy enabled the "Recovery" of fresh perspectives on it. Even more important, the "arresting strangeness" of fantasy revealed that ordinary reality had the potential not only to be refreshed, but transformed entirely:

> [Creative fantasy] may open your hoard and let all the locked things fly away like caged birds. The gems all turn into flowers or flames, and you will be warned that all you had (or knew) was dangerous and potent, not really effectively chained, free and wild, no more yours than they were you.[137]

Recovery was a form of transubstantiation, where the mundane suddenly became enchanted, just as in Christianity the profane miraculously became sacred: "It was in fairy stories that I first divined the potency of the words, and the wonder of the things, such as stone, and wood, and iron; tree and grass; house and fire; bread and wine."[138]

The "Consolation" of fantasy also contributed to re-enchantment by reorienting one's perception of the world in a crucial way. Fairy tales included favorable turns of fortune that appear unexpectedly, which Tolkien called "Eucatastrophes." They instilled hope in the face of life's inescapable tragedies, and the courage to persist regardless of the odds.[139] Fantasy was thus a goad to exertion in the real world, even as it provided blissful escape from the everyday. The conservative Tolkien's position was similar to that of the Marxist philosopher Ernst Bloch, a contemporary who also appreciated fairy tales for their capacity to rejuvenate and inspire. In a 1930 essay, Bloch argued that they generated visions of a better world as well as the energy necessary to bring these visions to fruition. Like Tolkien, Bloch appreciated the "modern fairy tales" of fantasy and science fiction because they promoted animistic reason:

> it is reason itself which leads to the wish projections of the old fairy tale and serves them. Again what proves itself is a harmony with courage and cunning, as that earliest kind of enlightenment which already characterizes *Hansel and Gretel*: consider yourself as born free and entitled to be totally happy, dare to make use of your power of reasoning, look upon the outcome of things as friendly. These are the genuine maxims of fairy tales, and fortunately for us they appear not only in the past but also in the now.[140]

Finally, Tolkien declared that even escapism, so roundly condemned by most intellectuals, could have profound effects on the real world by promoting a spirit of defiance against "the Robot Age."[141] On the one hand, "Escape" was an understandable reaction to the iron cage of modernity: "Why should a man be scorned if, finding himself in prison, he tries to get out and go home? Or if, when he cannot do so, he thinks and talks about other topics than jailers and prison-walls?"[142] On the other hand, Escape could have consequential effects on the Primary World by fomenting "Disgust, Anger, Condemnation, and Revolt."[143] Like Recovery and Consolation, this spirit of disquiet with the disenchantments of modernity could provoke re-enchanting counternarratives, alternative perceptions from alternative worlds.[144] "On Fairy-tales" thus emphasized the autonomy of fantastic Secondary Worlds but also recognized that they could have direct "applicability" to the Primary World.[145]

This leaves the second question: why did Tolkien's aesthetic views shift from an English Arts and Crafts' "utilitarian" perspective to the more "autonomous" view maintained by the French Symbolists? Tolkien's stance in this 1939 lecture was concordant with the formalist aesthetic propounded by a growing number of intellectuals in the interwar period. Aesthetic formalism had its modern roots in eighteenth-century philosophy, but its wider diffusion coincided with the late nineteenth-century conception of culture as a separate sphere, one that provided a disinterested standpoint for reflection and critique.[146] The "art for art's sake" ideology was one of its expressions, as was the interwar belief among certain writers that the role of the intellectual was to remain detached from partisan engagement, thereby preserving an "objective" perspective.[147] These writers were reacting to the intense patriotism that overcame many intellectuals at the outbreak of the First World War and to the equally intense politicization of art during the interwar period. Critics with differing political views, such as Roger Fry, Theodor Adorno, and Clement Greenberg, were all aesthetic formalists, united in their belief in the necessary autonomy of art.

By the late 1930s, Tolkien also wanted to protect art from being used instrumentally. In "On Fairy-stories" he carefully distinguished between "enchantment" and "magic," which corresponded to "delight" and "delusion" respectively.[148] Art generated enchantment when it was practiced out of love, with no instrumental aim; its effect was to bring delight to both maker and user. In contrast, magic was utilitarian and beguiling: "Magic produces, or pretends to produce, an alteration in the Primary World . . . It is not an art but a technique; its desire is *power* in this world, domination of things and wills."[149] Fantasy was the form of art closest to "enchantment" because it was furthest removed from the Primary World and its instrumental concerns. Unlike "magic," enchantment signified beauty without deception: "Uncorrupted, it does not seek delusion, nor bewitchment and domination; it seeks shared enrichment, partners in making and delight, not slaves."[150]

The key word here is "uncorrupted." The ideal form of enchantment would delight without deluding, but Tolkien knew the balance was difficult to maintain, especially within the fallen world of fallible humanity. Art could easily degenerate from enchantment to magic, from autonomy to utility, from delight to delusion. He later declared that his legendarium was "fundamentally concerned with the problem of the relation of Art . . . and Primary Reality"; from its inception he had been attentive to the ways in which the creative imagination could become corrupted by the beguiling allures of power and control.[151] Take, for example, his discussion of the role of the Elves in his legendarium. Despite his professed distaste for allegory, Tolkien outlined in a 1951 letter the symbolic correspondences between the Elves and human creativity:

> The Elves represent, as it were, the artistic, aesthetic, and purely scientific aspects of the Humane nature raised to a higher level than is actually seen in Men. That is: they have a devoted love of the physical world, and a desire to observe and understand it for its own sake as "other" . . . not as a material for use or as a power platform. They also possess a "subcreational" or artistic faculty of great excellence.[152]

The Elves's weakness is that, as immortals, they resent temporal change and want to preserve the status quo: a form of possessiveness. Art and the material world delight them, but can also delude them into exercising instrumental control over creation. The Elves's fall from grace in the First Age occurs when a faction becomes enamored of the glorious jewels they created and attempts to possess them, which eventuates in a devastating civil war. In the Second Age the Elves make a similar error, when Sauron encourages them to fashion rings of power to preserve the beauties of Middle-earth. The rings have instrumental functions, further stimulating the lust for control in their users; this in turn is easily manipulated by Sauron, who has secretly created a "Ruling Ring" commanding all others.[153] The fate of this One Ring is important to the plot of *The Hobbit* and is paramount in *The Lord of the Rings.*

Tolkien's solution to the dilemma posed by enchantment was consonant with late nineteenth-century Aestheticism: the self-conscious habitation of Secondary Worlds through the ironic imagination, which would preserve delight and forestall delusion. In the highly politicized interwar period, he theorized more explicitly about the art's necessary autonomy, aligning himself with the aesthetic formalists who criticized those on the Left and Right for transforming art into a tool for power. Formalism would function to secure art from the ever-present temptation to foreswear enchantment for magic.

Tolkien's habitual double mindedness, however, extended to Aestheticism. For him, art was autonomous, existing for its own sake—but it also expressed the divine, and therefore was not entirely independent. He stated in "On Fairy-stories," "Fantasy can thus be explained as a sudden glimpse of underlying reality or truth."[154] God was the supreme creator, with humanity made in his image as "sub-creator."[155] Just as God creates spontaneously, out of love, so too does (or should) humanity: art is a gift and a communion. It is an end in itself—and also expresses an "underlying reality or truth."

While many contemporary critics entertained religious texts as works of literature conveying vital moral and ethical teachings, Tolkien insisted that literature was itself religious.[156] Of all the stories related by humankind, Christianity fully expressed the truth and was incarnate in history. In his epilogue to "On Fairy-stories," Tolkien stated that the Christian "story is supreme: and it is true. Art has been verified. God is the Lord, of angels, and of men—and of Elves. Legend and History have met and fused."[157] This religious interpretation of art also sanctioned the creation of fantasies (including pagan and secular ones) as a form of spiritual devotion. The writer may "fairly dare to guess that in Fantasy he may actually assist in the exfoliation and multiple enrichment of creation."[158]

Tolkien's aesthetic theories, then, presented mixed messages. His Aestheticism was firmly grounded on a metaphysical order; it appeared essentialist. At the same time, he highlighted the provisional and contingent nature of narratives; his Aestheticism could therefore appear anti-essentialist. The latter tendency recurred in many of his utterances. In "On Fairy-stories" he discussed "the endlessness of the World of Story," noting the diversity of narratives and their lack of closure, at least in the profane world.[159] In addition, he often approached life in fictionalist, "as if" terms. During the Second World War, when his son Christopher was serving in the Royal Air Force, Tolkien advised him to redescribe his perilous military exploits in terms of a heroic narrative: "Keep up your hobbitry in heart, and think that all *stories* feel like that when you are *in* them. You are inside a very great story!"[160]

And while Tolkien's religious belief supported his faith in the "just so," it could also undermine such essentialist leanings. Doctrinal teachings reminded him of the fallibility of human pretenses to knowledge ("no man can really estimate what is happening at the present *sub specie aeternitatis*") and also that fundamentalist pronouncements could be expressions of the will to power.[161] He not only rejected allegory because it confused Secondary with Primary Worlds, but because its formulaic interpretations represented an attempt to overmaster the reader's free will. "I dislike real allegory in which the application is the author's own and is meant to dominate you," he wrote; "I prefer the freedom of the reader or hearer."[162] Catholicism also extolled humility over assertive certainty. As he remarked in 1956, "The greatest examples of the action of the spirit and of reason are in *abnegation*."[163]

Indeed, for all of Tolkien's essentialist leanings, it is his fictionalist predilections that predominate in *The Lord of the Rings*. The practice of perceiving existence "as if" instead of "just so" pervades the work. When Treebeard, a very ancient and rather conservative character, hears a persuasive argument he uncharacteristically changes his mind, exclaiming "That is a better story!"[164] The hero Aragorn acknowledges the existence of, and necessity for, provisional fictions when he states, "There, that is my tale. Others might be devised."[165] Even a lowly Orc maintains a secular faith in contingent fictions. As he explains patiently to a fellow Orc, "Ah, well, you always did take a gloomy view . . . you can read the signs how you like, but there may be better ways to explain them."[166] And the wizard Gandalf reminds his audience, "Even the wise cannot see all ends."[167]

Tolkien ultimately left his readers with several divided legacies. First there was the double consciousness of the ironic imagination, which permitted the simultaneous habitation of Primary and Secondary Worlds—the capacity to remain enchanted and disenchanted at the same time. Second, there was his ambivalence about essentialist and anti-essentialist narratives. In the end he tried to resolve this by claiming that the absolute truths emanating from the divine were often conveyed in fragmentary, symbolic, and ambiguous forms within narratives. Assertions about these truths ought to be advanced with humility and accepted as provisional encapsulations of that which passeth human understanding. Finally, he had a dual outlook about the interchange between fantasy and reality. On the one hand, imaginary worlds were autonomous from reality, existing for their own sake; on the other hand, they could have utility—"applicability"—to reality.[168]

By collectively imagining Middle-earth as real in public spheres of the imagination, readers transformed it from an imaginary world to a virtual world. They were able to steep themselves in it without losing sight of the real world, just as Tolkien had predicted. And, like him, many gravitated to Middle-earth because it seemed to offer a stable and coherent habitat. Yet the virtual world of Middle-earth was actually riven with fissures that soon became apparent to its new residents. Readers who imagined it communally could find themselves debating about its nature; in public spheres of the imagination, the Secondary World could fragment into a multiplicity of worlds representing a multiplicity of outlooks. Conflicting interpretations might be resolved through discussion, but the debates themselves had an additional and unanticipated effect. Readers became more self-conscious of the fictive dimension of experience. By approaching the Secondary World in the spirit of "as if," they found it possible to apprehend the Primary World with the same open and flexible perspective. While Tolkien believed that ultimate salvation came from accepting the one True Story of Christianity, a number of his readers—religious and secular alike—found meaning and re-enchantment in provisional and contingent fictions.

VI. MIDDLE-EARTH AND WEAKLY INCOMMENSURATE WORLDS

The Lord of the Rings was published in three hardcover volumes between 1954 and 1955, but Tolkien's imaginary world did not become a virtual world until a decade later. The hardcover editions were widely reviewed and had robust sales in both Britain and the United States.[169] The science fiction community received it enthusiastically; perhaps the first association devoted to Middle-earth, "The Fellowship of the Ring," convened in 1960 at the World Science Fiction Convention in Pennsylvania and issued the first Tolkien fanzine, *I Palantir.* It was not until 1965, however, that a craze for Middle-earth erupted in America, especially on college campuses. Ace Books claimed the work was not in copyright in the United States and published unauthorized paperback editions of the three volumes, making *The Lord of the Rings* affordable to a youthful generation already primed for its pro-environment, anti-authoritarian themes. Tolkien publicly protested the pirated editions and arranged for a set of authorized paperbacks issued later that year by Ballantine Books. The controversy garnered wide publicity for the work and its unexpected popularity on college campuses. Within ten months, the paperback editions of *The Lord of the Rings* had sold a quarter-million copies.[170]

Tolkien fan clubs and fanzines sprouted all over the country, attracting bemused and often condescending coverage by the national media. The American "hobbit habit" was viewed as a less sexually charged, but no less adolescent, sequel to the earlier British import of Beatlemania. "Although the Tolkien fans rarely show herding instincts and never scream," proclaimed an article in *The Saturday Evening Post* in 1966, "they are driven by the same subtle urge that produces water guns at the first breath of spring, gives rise to the sudden, unexpected yo-yo, and squeezes students into telephone booths."[171] Reporters portrayed fans of Middle-earth as high school or college students who refused to grow up, which accounted for their dressing up in costumes and speaking Elvish languages. The apparent infantilism of readers withdrawing into an imaginary world reinforced a perception among several critics that *The Lord of the Rings* itself was regressive. A writer for *Life* in 1967 declared that "What apparently gets kids square in their post-adolescent sensibilities is not the scholarly top-dressing but the unde-manding, comfortable, child-sized story underneath."[172] The *Ladies Home Journal* deemed Middle-earth a "never-never world" that helped a rebellious generation tune out the responsibilities of adulthood: "Like revolt, retreat into a private world is another way for the young to spurn grown-ups."[173]

A few reports more accurately showed that Tolkien fans included adults as well as adolescents. Richard Plotz founded the first "Tolkien Society" in 1965 when he was a high-school student; by 1966 it had over eight hundred members, many of them adults.[174] They were as apt as their younger cohort to engage in activities the media dismissed as juvenile, such as role playing. (In fact, Plotz wasn't always comfortable with the behavior of his elders: "W. H. Auden is a member of the Society; he calls himself Gimli. Frankly, I would prefer that all this name-calling stop: I don't want to be called Frodo, and I'm sure most members agree on that count.")[175]

Clubs and fanzines were the earliest public spheres of the imagination dedicated to the communal habitation of Middle-earth and often comprised a diverse membership. They included professionals and students, men and women, radicals and conservatives, believers from all faiths, agnostics, and atheists. The one thing they shared was Middle-earth: it was their communal home, uniting them despite their differences. "To this day I feel a subtle spir-itual bond with anyone who has enjoyed Tolkien's books," wrote one mem-ber of a Tolkien society in "Living Middle-earth in the Early Years."[176] By "living" in the imaginary world the author meant "simply eating, breathing, and generally assimilating it wherever one is physically living."[177] Others also claimed Middle-earth as a virtual place of residence. According to one fan, "what Tolkien does for his readers is to lead them into a world where they are more at home than they have been in any of their homes."[178]

Readers found that this Secondary World delivered on Tolkien's prom-ises of Recovery, Consolation, and Escape. After a sojourn in Middle-earth, wrote one, "the reader can turn to the real world, and look at it in a new light … the world can be seen in true perspective, truly beautiful, despite its cruelty."[179] Another argued that *The Lord of the Rings* "enables us to recover lost enchantment, and see again clearly what this 'Fourth Age of Man' has so long blinded us to."[180] This Secondary World wasn't a one-way trip out of the Primary World; it sent its inhabitants back to the real world with refreshed perspectives and reenergized commitments.

Many also adopted Tolkien's fictionalist stance. A debate conducted in one fanzine began with an inquiry about whether *The Lord of the Rings* could serve as "a guide for living . . . replac[ing] Christianity and the Bible?"[181] Several respondents perceived both texts as strictly literary ones and evaluated their contemporary applicability. One writer argued that the Bible's focus on heaven rendered it more "escapist" than Tolkien's narrative, which centered on the beauties of the profane world.[182] Another claimed that *The Lord of the Rings* was superior to the Bible because "it combines the best elements of all religions."[183] In another fanzine debate, a fan asserted that Christianity was merely one narrative among many, which prompted an aggrieved response by a self-declared Christian that "the Crucifixion and the Resurrection were the cornerstone of J. R. R. Tolkien's beliefs, and also the cornerstone of my faith."[184] The fan who made the initial claim replied that "there ought in this world to be room enough for all faiths and all people's beliefs," for only in this way would tolerance be secured.[185] In these and many other examples, the "as if" confronted the "just so" within public spheres of the imagination.

A number of fans also echoed Tolkien's ambivalence about the purposes of fantastic Secondary Worlds. Some treated Middle-earth as an autonomous realm that ought to be quarantined from social and political considerations lest it be diminished, whereas others valued it for its applicability to topical issues. Because Tolkien had addressed both possibilities in the foreword to *The Lord of the Rings,* readers were conscious of having both options. Like Tolkien, they were often divided over the issue of autonomy versus applicability. One fanzine editor split fans into two distinct groups: "The first class are people who study linguistics and histories, and things out of the appendices," and "the second class are those who study implications of *The Lord of the Rings* in their own lives and the Real World."[186] In practice, however, both groups often merged because even the avowedly "autonomous" studies of Middle-earth might provoke discussions about the Primary World. Some discussions were so specialized that they were easily delimited to the Secondary World, such as the following account of a talk on "Modes of Production in the Southern Kingdoms of Middle-earth":

> It dealt with the economy of Rohan, Harad, and Mordor, and other Southern lands, and touched on matters like the speed of the corsairs of Umbar, and the technological innovation of the stirrup, as well as the dimensions of a Mumak compared to the

elephants of today. The problem of female orcs was raised but unsolved, and it was suggested that the orc race matured from birth very quickly.[187]

However, a talk on a closely related topic, "A Marxist Looks at Middle-earth: Or, The Political Economy of the Shire," instigated discussions of Primary World economic theories and politics.[188]

In contrast to the United States, there was no "Tolkien craze" in Britain. Tolkien predictably attributed this to the different "climate and soil" of the two countries, but there were other explanatory factors, including the lack of a British paperback edition of *The Lord of the Rings* until 1968 (and even then it was issued in a relatively expensive single volume). Certain British devotees did not want to be associated with the more gauche aspects of American fandom. One English fan group watched a slide show of American fans celebrating the fiftieth anniversary of *The Hobbit*, "approving the cloaks but regretting the training shoes."[189]

Not the least of those who objected was Tolkien, who referred to American fandom in 1966 as "my deplorable cultus," adding (unconvincingly) that "many young Americans are involved in [my] stories in a way I'm not."[190] According to his biographer Humphrey Carpenter, Tolkien suggested that his work served as a "substitute faith" for a generation deprived of religion, "particularly in the United States."[191] Tolkien also speculated that the work's apparent appeal to American youth might have been incited by the detailed appendices: "A lot of it is just straight teenage stuff. I didn't mean it to be, but it's perfect for them. I think they're attracted by things that give verisimilitude."[192] He continued to contrast an essentially adolescent American response with its apparent opposite in Britain, finding the fan mail from his side of the Atlantic to be "very largely adult."[193] His assistant Joy Hill stated bluntly in 1969 that "the disease of writing letters to J. R. R. Tolkien began in America." Now, however, "the germ has spread here."[194]

The issue of autonomy versus applicability was especially fraught for the Tolkien Society (UK) during its early years. The Society was initiated in 1969 by Vera Chapman. Born in 1898, she shared Tolkien's ambivalence about American fandom. She intended to reclaim Middle-earth from squatters who had misappropriated it, such as the hippie movement, which had started in the United States and soon flourished in England (notably in a mystical London commune known as "Gandalf's Garden").[195] Chapman, who used the hobbit name of "Belladonna Took" for her fan writings, asserted that the hippies stood for everything that Middle-earth rejected: drugs, sex, dropping out, and "doing your own thing." They had misconstrued *The Lord of the Rings*: "It is a moral, ethical book, full of old fashioned virtues, and the ethical bones beneath the structure of it are totally opposed to all that the Hippie believes in."[196]

Thus the Tolkien Society was founded to preserve a particular interpretation of Tolkien's Secondary World. In this "just so" endeavor, one of the
Society's aims was "to maintain the image of 'Middle-earth' uncontami-
nated by anything contrary to the intentions of the author."[197] Members of
the Society were conscious of Tolkien's presence—he accepted the title of
"Honorary President" of the Society—and monitored their behavior, "not
wishing to be associated with the fans who harassed him during the 'cult' of
the mid-sixties."[198] After Tolkien's death, his daughter Priscilla continued to
be involved with the Society.

But the Society had another declared purpose, "To enjoy the fantasy of
'Middle-earth' and express it according to the individual talents and tastes
of the members."[199] The first editor of *Mallorn*, the Society's journal, cited
this to justify her intention of representing all views, "even any of the
hippie ideas."[200] She had "a more liberal idea" of the Society, in which the
diverse opinions of its members could be aired and would be treated with
equality and respect, in effect making it a genuine public sphere of the
imagination.[201] She solicited widely for letters and articles, as "the prime
purpose of this magazine is to put people in touch with each other in
print."[202] *Mallorn*, and the Society's bulletin *Amon Hen*, did become sites
where the communal habitation of Middle-earth not only bolstered its virtual reality but also actively related it to the Primary World. Belladonna
Took's views on hippies were soon challenged ("like it or not, we are
brothers and sisters under the skin to the hippies in our eccentricity"),
and more contentious issues were also broached.[203] These included the applicability of *The Lord of the Rings* to a better understanding of contemporary issues of gender, class, race, imperialism, and technology in the
Primary World.

The ongoing discussions concerning autonomy versus applicability
reminded readers about the fuzzy overlap between imaginary and real
worlds, which in turn had two important consequences. First, it highlighted
the social function of fantasy to challenge normative outlooks and advance
alternate possibilities to the status quo. When one reader objected to discussing the Falklands War in terms of Middle-earth, another responded by
citing Tolkien's "On Fairy-stories" to justify his claim that, "without the
hope of new thoughts, generated by fantasy in human beings' minds, how
can people progress?"[204] A Russian fan discussed the important influence
The Lord of the Rings had on those who took to the Moscow streets to defend
Boris Yeltsin against an attempted coup in 1991:

> Western readers must understand that for us Tolkien was never any kind of "escape" . . .
> many people remembered Tolkien when they made barricades from trolley-buses (just
> like hobbits from country wains!) . . . chance and a willing fantasy can make miracles.[205]

Second, discussions such as these underlined the potential of public spheres of the imagination to adjudicate, in a rational and equitable way, conflicting interpretations about the applicability of Secondary Worlds to the Primary World. Participants in debates often shared the aim of fostering intersubjective understandings, if not agreements. In the debate about the Falklands War, the second reader concluded his letter by encouraging the first reader to respond: "I would hope she sticks around and talks to us and (yes) tries her hardest to convert us to her ways of thinking—and I can assure her with every fibre of my being, that *I, for one,* shall be doing likewise with my own beliefs in the opposite direction."[206]

As we saw in the case of Lovecraft, discussions among a diverse population of readers could force individuals to reconsider their preconceptions and entertain alternative points of view. Many of the larger Tolkien associations had a variegated membership, and it is striking how civil, rational, and effective the interchanges about controversial topics could be. In one fanzine debate, a writer argued that only church-going Christians should be permitted to write Tolkien-inspired fiction. There were several cogent rebuttals to this essentialist claim, including one that cited Tolkien's notion of the "personal applicability" of fictions: "[Non-Christians] may not share the Christian faith but they may long for spiritual satisfaction and have spiritual and material insight. Fantasy allows the readers to determine the personal textual meaning for themselves; unlike allegory, where *meaning* is predetermined by the author." She noted that the exclusionist argument "open[s] the door to fanaticism in an age desperately in need of tolerance."[207] In the next issue the initial writer said that he had reconsidered his views as a result of such criticisms.[208]

Similarly, the American Tolkien Society engaged in wide-ranging discussions about the applicability of imaginary worlds to reality; it reveled in being a public sphere of the imagination. Acknowledging that the Society's diverse members could have sharply opposing viewpoints, the editor of its journal stated that "Nevertheless, each and every one was/is a fan and a friend. From the beginning, we have intended the ATS to embrace fans at all levels of interest, sophistication, and education."[209] One lengthy debate in the journal focused on the applicability of *The Lord of the Rings* to "just war" theory and recent global conflicts. Arguments included statements along the following lines: "As Faramir wished for Minas Anor's freedom, so did Gandhi wish for India's freedom."[210] The important point about these discussions is that they could result in changed understandings about the Primary World no less than the Secondary World. One participant admitted to another:

Through your well reasoned and convincing arguments, I have come to see that I have erred in my own reasoning and that I see and support your point of view. Perhaps if we

had tried sanctions [in the Persian Gulf War] a little longer, they would have worked . . .
Thank you for a new view to meditate on and a newsletter I can look forward to. [211]

In this case, the Middle East and Middle-earth were able to illuminate each other in novel and constructive ways.

Tolkien's son Michael recalled that his father was not, as many assumed, a "dreamy professor" who fled into fantasy. He was a practical man who took his professional duties seriously and devoted attention to his four children. He went on individual walks with each, allowing their interests to shape the course of the conversations along the way. He wanted them to find their own path in life, one that would lead them to a place they could call their own: "I think that he tried to make a home for us somewhere where we wanted to go and I think that though often it was difficult there was this theme of home. That really means something to you because there was something that was particularly yours."[212]

This "theme of home" was at the heart of Tolkien's writings. Like Sam at the conclusion of *The Lord of the Rings,* he yearned to proclaim, "Well, I'm back." In a modern age defined by flux and uncertainty, Tolkien's early life had been especially traumatic, and like many of his era he gravitated toward essentialist narratives of the nation and religion that promised constancy. As he developed the imaginary world of Middle-earth, he also developed an equally imaginary world, that of Little England: both of them were safe havens of the "just so."

At the same time, Tolkien knew that Primary and Secondary Worlds were not necessarily distinct; that what we call the "real" is itself a provisional story, and that every story reveals a facet of reality. As acknowledged aesthetic creations, Secondary Worlds are autonomous from the exigencies of experience, but at the same time they help us process and shape that experience. There is a necessary interchange between the real and the imagined, escape and recovery, autonomy and applicability. Tolkien thus managed to re-enchant his world through maintaining equipoise between essentialist and anti-essentialist narratives. A religious man, he believed that all narratives were ultimately grounded in a single, divine truth. Yet his religious outlook also counseled humility, reminding him that errant humanity can only approximate that truth through contingent and ongoing narrations, "as if" fictions. Aestheticism appealed to him in his youth as much as nationalism and Catholicism; Middle-earth emerged from, and embodied, the productive tensions of this confluence.

Many of his readers found that his imaginary world, and the public spheres of the imagination that transformed it into a virtual world, trained them to entertain provisional identities, provisional narratives, and provisional worlds. They became adept in using the ironic imagination to maintain a double consciousness, one that might produce cognitive estrangement but not cognitive dissonance. As one Tolkien fan explained:

> In reading [*The Lord of the Rings*], I participate imaginatively in another world that is separate from and alien to what we usually call "the real world," without feeling any urge to integrate my knowledge of the two. On the other hand, I cannot prevent my newly quickened imagination from ranging where it will, and as it stretches its wings and soars, I discover that Tolkien's talk of faerie is a way of talking about something that is neither faerie nor "reality."[213]

For Tolkien and many of his religious readers, that middle space was spiritual; for many secular readers, it was a space of imagination. For both, it was intimately associated with their ongoing interpretations of experience. Middle-earth represented a common ground of modern enchantment, diffusing delight while deterring delusion.

Envoi

How ironic it would be to witness the somber rituals of a Spider-Man cult in 2540 A.D.—or to be present at the "strength olympics" held in honor of the Hulk. New myths created in the twentieth century, and scattered by the printing press throughout the world, may well enlarge the giant puzzle that is humanity and makes things much more difficult to decipher. But we needn't worry about all that. We can have a great time with the few grains of truth already in our possession and space out by fantasizing about the rest.

—Jack Kirby

Who knows—perhaps the next religious upsurge in America will occur among disenchanted post-modernist academics!

—Peter L. Berger

We live in many imaginary worlds of our own devising, and one of mine was inspired by this study. It was, admittedly, something of a utopia: I dreamed that the book broke out of the academic ghetto and became a meme unto itself. Not only did Oprah Winfrey select it for her book club; Jonathan Franzen begged to appear on her show to praise it. (Oprah said no.) I was invited to first-night openings, gala fetes, and ship christenings, and out of the blue was appointed to the first Chair in Cognitive Estrangement at Miskatonic University.

But no utopia should ignore dystopian possibilities. In my imaginary world, not everyone loved the book. In fact, there were some tense moments in the question-and-answer session that followed my inaugural lecture at Miskatonic. As one rather irate critic sputtered, "What am I supposed to take from all of this? You talk about imagined worlds, imaginary worlds, and virtual worlds; the 'reality effect' and the 'absence effect'; the 'willing suspension of disbelief' versus the 'willing activation of pretense'; the New

Romance, spectacular texts, paratexts, and who knows what else. What's the cash value of this? Where's the tune I can whistle to the wife and kids?"

I chose to politely reframe the question, as Chair holders are wont to do. "In asking about my book, you quite rightly paraphrase the title of a painting by Paul Gauguin, *Where Do We Come From? What Are We? Where Are We Going?* Let me see if I can address these most important of questions." And then I took a deep breath and said something like this:

"In the late nineteenth century, readers turned to realistic yet fantastic imaginary worlds to secure enchantments compatible with the rational and secular tenets of modernity. They employed the ironic imagination to do so, and fashioned new public spheres of the imagination to help them occupy these worlds communally and persistently. As a result, many of these imaginary worlds became virtual worlds. By living simultaneously in the imagination and in reality, and being self-aware about this process, individuals became more adept at perceiving the world in 'as if' rather than in 'just so' terms.

"The ideal of modern enchantment is to be delighted without being deluded, to enjoy the fruits of the imagination together with the insights of analysis. While imaginary worlds foster detachment as well as immersion through the ironic imagination, animistic reason, and public spheres of the imagination, they nevertheless exert a powerful spell. It is always possible to become beguiled by the self-gratifying illusions they proffer. Now that new technologies render these illusions more realistically than ever before and serve as portals to fabulous worlds of wonder accessible around the clock, are we advancing toward a disembodied, solipsistic, and delusive state of existence?

"Historians have enough trouble untangling the past to be effective forecasters of the future. But the literary prehistory of virtual reality does reveal that living in the imagination is a cultural practice we have gradually honed over time and will continue to exercise as new conditions warrant. It suggests that repeated exposures to the virtual actually reinforce the distinction between the real and the imaginary, while at the same time highlighting their necessary imbrications.

"Some fear that the attractions of imaginary worlds, when compared to the actual world, are so great that people will opt for the virtual over the real. Jane McGonigal, for example, studies and creates 'serious games.' These harness the energy, perseverance, creativity, and cooperation that gamers bring to fantasy worlds to solve real world problems. She sees these games as a positive alternative to a more grim scenario, that of

a society in which a substantial portion of our population devotes its greatest efforts to playing games, creates its best memories in game environments, and experiences its biggest successes in game worlds.[1]

This dystopian vision of the future is not implausible. But from the history we have examined, psychologist Paul Bloom's conclusion is borne out: 'Our ambitions go beyond the acquisition of experiences; they extend outside the head . . . The pleasures of the imagination are a core part of life—but they are not enough.'[2] The imaginary provides us with experiences difficult or impossible to attain in real life, but at the same time makes us yearn for the real. H. P. Lovecraft derived as much pleasure from his visits to antiquarian sites as from his creation of an imaginary world; fans of the Cthulhu Mythos make pilgrimages to New England to encounter directly the mundane locales on which Lovecraft based his fantastic stories. Sherlock Holmes fans are often investigators of the quotidian in their lives, to say nothing of the minutiae of Holmesian texts. Many fans of Middle-earth have been inspired by Tolkien's evocatively detailed descriptions of its flora and fauna to become environmentalists. As we have seen, travelers to imaginary worlds at first rejoice in the wonders they experience in the Secondary World. They then seek others to share their enchantment, which in turn can become redirected to ordinary life. Escapism, this history demonstrates, is rarely unidirectional or without positive consequences. It resembles the account of a life's journey by the noted Sherlock Holmes scholar T. S. Eliot:

> We shall not cease from exploration
> And the end of all our exploring
> Will be to arrive where we started
> And know the place for the first time.[3]

"In addition, modern imaginary worlds often foreground critical rationality and champion the methods and findings of science. Holmes made reason magical, the acts of inductive observation and deductive logic refreshing rather than arid. The sublime findings of modern physicists, cosmologists, and archaeologists imparted a numinous tinge to much of Lovecraft's rather purple prose, and the careful evidentiary considerations of an Oxford philologist rendered the historical past of Middle-earth so compelling that many of its fans steep themselves in the intricacies of medieval history and literature. Virtual imaginary worlds, from World of Warcraft to Second Life, also foster a quantitative and analytic mindset even as they stimulate creative thinking. Animistic reason permeates the atmosphere of imaginary worlds.

"One shouldn't take too rosy a view, though, choosing to live in *Pollyanna World* because that of *The Matrix* seems too depressing. Delusions can accompany the delights of modern enchantments: Conan Doyle was spirited away to Never-Never Land in the company of ghosts and fairies; Lovecraft loved aliens but hated foreigners; Tolkien lived in a rustic England of his own devising when he wasn't rusticating in Middle-earth. There have been numerous instances of pseudoscience planted in the pages of science fiction magazines that subsequently sprouted like weeds beyond them (including L. Ron Hubbard's science of Dianetics, which miraculously transubstantiated into the religion of Scientology).

"But it is not being too Pollyannaish to observe that most readers seem to entertain imaginary worlds with the double consciousness of the ironic imagination, enjoying them in a mood of 'as if' rather than 'just so.' This is probably true as well for many of the unscientific claims of New Age movements, from pyramid power to UFOs. (Fox Mulder of the X-Files typified this double-minded attitude: in his office he had two posters, one proclaiming, 'I Want to Believe,' the other, 'Trust No One.') We need more instruction in schools in science and critical thinking to counter credulous beliefs in unsupportable claims that still pervade our culture. Yet imaginary worlds, both literary and virtual, tend to work with rather than against this goal, especially when they are discussed with others in diversely constituted public spheres of the imagination.

"Finally, imaginary worlds offer liberation from the recurrent image of the 'iron cage' of modernity circulated by cultural pessimists. For much of the nineteenth and twentieth centuries, these critics mourned the loss of communal meanings and spiritual verities that allegedly characterized the premodern world. But the provisional meanings, multiple selves, and manifold worlds that a disenchanted modernity makes possible are powerful sources of enchantment in their own right. Imaginary worlds, and the broader culture of Fictionalism of which they are a part, help us to embrace contingency and difference and to question essentializing narratives.

"This isn't an easy thing to do. We may be hardwired to seek stable foundations and unchanging essences, and without them we can be understandably insecure and anxious; delusive enchantments thrive on these emotions. Nor can essentialism be rejected out of hand, given the underlying 'deep commonalities' of the material universe established by science. At the same time, our conscious lives are too complex to be reduced to unitary narratives. Individuals and the events they influence invariably transgress any determining framework we advance to explain them. A way of thinking that celebrates provisionality and endorses contingency, which not only accepts difference but entertains alternative views, which finds wonder in science and magic in reason, is enchanting: or it can be, if we work with it and set aside the simplistic 'binary' and 'dialectical' accounts of disenchantment we have inherited. On the whole, our condition since the eighteenth century has been neither that of disenchantment nor re-enchantment. It has been one of 'disenchanted enchantment,' which accords with the rational and secular conditions of modernity and need not conflict with spiritual commitments.

"So where might we be headed?

"Given that the future is indeterminate, there can be only one destination. To imaginary worlds, which we then make real."

To which my skeptical interlocutor replied, "as if!" And the discussion continued.

NOTES

INTRODUCTION

Alberto Blanco, "Maps," in *Dawn of the Senses: Selected Poems of Alberto Blanco*, ed. Juvenal Acosta (San Francisco, CA: City Lights Publishers, 2001).

1. A. O. Scott, "A Hunger for Fantasy, an Empire to Feed It," *New York Times*, June 16, 2002, 26.

2. For investigations of soap operas and romance fans, see Janice A. Radway, *Reading the Romance* (Chapel Hill: University of North Carolina Press, 1991); Jennifer Hayward, *Consuming Pleasures: Active Audiences and Serial Fictions from Dickens to Soap Operas* (Lexington: The University Press of Kentucky, 1997).

3. Roz Kaveney, in her reflections on the imaginary worlds of Marvel and DC comics, refers to "the universalization of the geek aesthetic." See Roz Kaveney, *Superheroes!: Capes and Crusaders in Comics and Films* (London: I. B. Tauris, 2008), 62. Studies of fan cultures have become ubiquitous in recent years; see Jonathan Gray, Cornel Sandvoss, and C. Lee Harrington, ed., *Fandom: Identities and Communities in a Mediated World* (New York: New York University Press, 2007); Camille Bacon-Smith, *Science Fiction Culture* (Philadelphia: University of Pennsylvania Press, 2000); Matt Hills, *Fan Cultures* (London: Routledge, 2002); Henry Jenkins, *Textual Poachers: Television Fans and Participatory Culture* (London: Routledge, 1992); Lisa A. Lewis, ed., *The Adoring Audience: Fan Culture and Popular Media* (London: Routledge, 1992); the online, peer-reviewed journal *Transformative Works and Cultures* (http://journal.transformativeworks.org). Science fiction fans began to document their history shortly after SF fandom became established in the 1930s. Among the important histories are Sam Moskowitz, *The Immortal Storm* (Atlanta, GA: The Atlanta Science Fiction Organization, 1954); Harry Warner, Jr., *All Our Yesterdays: An Informal History of Science Fiction Fandom in the Forties* (Chicago, IL: Advent Publishers, 1954); Joseph L. Sanders, ed., *Science Fiction Fandom* (Westport, CT: Greenwood Press, 1994).

4. Tom Shippey finds that "the dominant literary mode of the twentieth century has been the fantastic." Tom Shippey, *J. R. R. Tolkien: Author of the Century* (London: Harper Collins, 2000), vii. Fantasy films in recent years have also been among the top-grossing films of all time; video games have become a multibillion dollar industry.

5. To date, most online games are fantasies, but gaming companies also offer more mundane settings—sports games, rock and roll simulations, Sims Online—to attract mainstream audiences. Brad King and John Borland, *Dungeons and Dreamers: The Rise of Computer Game Culture* (New York: McGraw Hill, 2003), 229–231. Alternate Reality Games take place in real time, in the real world, with real people; see Jane McGonigal, *Reality is Broken: Why Games Make Us Better and How They Can Change the World* (New York: Penguin Press, 2011), 119–145.

6. Brian Harrison, "Introduction to the *Oxford DNB*," *Oxford Dictionary of National Biography* online, http://www.oup.com/oxforddnb/info/prelims/intro/intro2/#18back (accessed August 5, 2007).

7. Alberto Manguel, Gianni Guadalupi, *The Dictionary of Imaginary Places* (New York: Harcourt, 2000); David Pringle, *Imaginary People: A Who's Who of Modern Fictional Characters* (London: Grafton, 1987); Jeremiah Benjamin Post, *An Atlas of Fantasy* (Baltimore, MD: Mirage Press, 1973). See also George A. Kennedy, *Fictitious Authors and Imaginary Novels in French, English, and American Literature from the 18th to the Start of the 21st Century* (New York: The Edwin Mellon Press, 2005); John W. Spargo, *Imaginary Books and Libraries: An Essay in Lighter Vein* (New York: Caxton Club, 1952).

8. Suzanne Kleid, "Dark City." *SFStation*, Nov. 8, 2004, http://www.sfstation.com/dark-city-a503 (accessed August 5, 2007).

9. Bob Goldsborough, "Dick Tracy Statue to Stand Guard Over Napier Riverwalk." *Chicago Tribune*, June 3, 2009, http://archives.chicagotribune.com/ (accessed January 21, 2010).

10. Tim Guest, *Second Lives: A Journey Through Virtual Worlds* (London: Hutchinson, 2007); Edward Castronova, *Synthetic Worlds: The Business and Culture of Online Games* (Chicago, IL: University of Chicago Press, 2005); William Sims Bainbridge, *The Warcraft Civilization: Social Science in a Virtual World* (Cambridge, MA: MIT Press, 2010).

11. Based on his studies of the adaptive functions and affective pleasures of the imagination, the psychologist Paul Bloom predicts, "Virtual worlds will expand, making interactive daydreaming more attractive, and technological improvements will blur the distinction between reality and imagination." Paul Bloom, *How Pleasure Works: The New Science of Why We Like What We Like* (New York: W. W. Norton, 2010), 201. See also Edward Castronova, *Exodus to the Virtual World: How Online Fun is Changing Reality* (New York: Palgrave Macmillan, 2007.)

12. John Tulloch and Manuel Alvarado, *Doctor Who: The Unfolding Text* (New York: St. Martins Press, 1983); John Tulloch and Henry Jenkins, *Science Fiction Audiences: Watching Doctor Who and Star Trek* (London: Routledge, 1995); Matthew J. Pustz, *Comic Book Culture: Fanboys and True Believers* (Jackson: University of Mississippi Press, 2000).

13. The *Oxford English Dictionary*'s earliest citation for "virtual reality," defined as "a notional image or environment generated by computer software," is 1987. Erik Davis finds an earlier use of the term by Antonin Artaud, who described theater as "a réalité virtuelle" in *The Theatre and Its Double* (1938). Erik Davis, *Techgnosis: Myth, Magic and Mysticism in the Information Age* (New York: Harmony Books,1998), 190. (And we'll see that Lovecraft used the term "virtual unreality" in 1917, with an implicit contrast to the "virtual realities" of the imagination.) Virtual reality encompasses a spectrum of immersive states, from private, subjective, phenomenological representations of "reality" to embodied artificial worlds maintained through technological means. (Even the latter can be subdivided; Edward Castronova distinguishes between "scientific" virtual reality, a fully immersive experience generated by hardware within laboratories, and the "practical" virtual reality of video and computer games. Castronova, *Exodus*, xiv.) Marie-Laure Ryan provides stimulating insights into the phenomenology of reading in light of concepts that have emerged from information technology and cyberculture; see Marie-Laure Ryan, *Narrative as Virtual Reality: Immersion and Interactivity in Literature and Electronic Media* (Baltimore, MD: Johns Hopkins University Press, 2001). For an overview, see Thomas Foster, "Virtuality," in *The Routledge Companion to Science Fiction*, ed. Mark Bould, Andrew M. Butler, Adam Roberts, and Sherryl Vint (London: Routledge, 2009), 317–327.

14. Robert Allerton Parker, "Such Pulp as Dreams Are Made On," *VVV* 2/3 (March, 1943), reprinted in S. T. Joshi, ed., *A Weird Writer in Our Midst: Early Criticism of H. P. Lovecraft* (New York: Hippocampus Press, 2010), 184–185.

15. Ibid., 184.

16. As Marie-Laure Ryan observes, the term *virtual reality* can be extended not only from digital culture to literature, but also to many cultural forms that rely on immersion and interactivity, including games, fairs and amusement parks, certain religious rituals, architectural spaces, and stage designs. Ryan, 20. To these one might add films that used gimmicks to enhance the immersive potential of the cinema. William Castle, for example, was famous for using devices such as electric shocks (for the film *The Tingler*) to engage multiple senses. See William Castle, *Step Right Up! I'm Gonna Scare the Pants Off America* (New York: World Almanac, 1992). Several of the phantasmagoric entertainments of the late eighteenth and nineteenth centuries, such as panoramas and dioramas, also created an immersive, virtual effect; see Richard Altick, *The Shows of London* (Cambridge, MA: Harvard University Press, 1978); Peter Otto, *Multiplying Worlds: Romanticism, Modernity, and the Emergence of Virtual Reality* (New York: Oxford University Press, 2011); Maria Warner, *Phantasmagoria: Spirit Visions, Metaphors, and Media* (New York: Oxford University Press, 2006). The imaginary worlds of fiction I discuss differ from such phantasmagoric entertainments because the type of virtual reality they create offers the option of prolonged immersion—not for a few hours, as in the case of an interactive performance or amusement park attraction, but for as long as one cares to access the imaginary world.

17. I am distinguishing fictional characters that appeared in works explicitly marked as fiction from earlier heroes of folklore and myth, whose existence was open to question. Ronald H. Fritze usefully clarifies the distinction between myth and legend: "A myth is an invented story which is used allegorically or tropologically to explain some natural event or phenomenon or some aspect of the human condition or psyche. A legend is a story about the past that has some basis in real historical events although it is often distorted with the passage of time." Ronald H. Fritze, *Invented Knowledge: False History, Fake Science and Pseudo-Religions* (London: Reaktion Books, 2009). For discussions of the emergence of the conceptual underpinnings of *fictionality* in the eighteenth and early nineteenth centuries, see Catherine Gallagher, "The Rise of Fictionality" in *The Novel, Volume One*, ed. Franco Moretti (Princeton, NJ: Princeton University Press, 2006), 336–363; Catherine Gallagher, *Nobody's Story: The Vanishing Acts of Women Writers in the Marketplace, 1670–1920* (Berkeley: University of California Press, 1995); Wolfgang Iser, *The Fictive and the Imaginary: Charting Literary Anthropology* (Baltimore, MD: Johns Hopkins University Press, 1993).

18. Cohesive imagined worlds included Balzac's "La Comédie Humaine," Zola's "Les Rougon-Macquart," Trollope's Barchester, Hardy's Wessex, and Faulkner's Yoknapatawpha County.

19. For the intertwining of reason and romanticism in currents of Western secularism, see Colin Jager, "This Detail, This History: Charles Taylor's Romanticism," in *Varieties of Secularism in a Secular Age*, ed. Michael Warner, Jonathan VanAntwerpen, Craig Calhoun (Cambridge, MA: Harvard University Press, 2010), 166.

20. As Nicholas Ruddick observed rhetorically, "Did any period in literary history produce a higher concentration of masterpieces of fantastic fiction than the Victorian fin de siècle?" Nicholas Ruddick, "The Fantastic Fiction of the fin de siècle," in *The Cambridge Companion to the Fin de Siècle*, ed. Gail Marshall (Cambridge: Cambridge University Press, 2007), 189.

21. Reviewing Sherry Turkle's *Alone Together: Why We Expect More from Technology and Less from Each Other* (New York: Basic Books, 2011), which criticized online culture for fostering isolation rather than community, Jonah Lehrer cited countervailing studies suggesting the issue is far from settled in these early days of virtual interactions: "A 2007 study at Michigan State University involving 800 undergraduates, for instance, found that Facebook users had more social capital than abstainers, and that the site increased measures of 'psychological well-being,' especially in those suffering from low self-esteem. Other

studies have found that frequent blogging leads to increased levels of social support and integration and may serve as 'the core of building intimate relationships.' One recurring theme to emerge from much of this research is that most people, at least so far, are primarily using the online world to enhance their offline relationships, not supplant them." Jonah Lehrer, "We, Robots," *New York Times*, January 23, 2011, BR15.

22. David Hollinger, "The Knower and the Artificer, with Postscript 1993" in *Modernist Impulses in the Social Sciences*, ed. Dorothy Ross (Baltimore, MD: Johns Hopkins University Press, 1994), 26. An adequate survey of the concept of modernity would require an essay. Among the many works devoted to it are Marshall Berman, *All That Is Solid Melts Into Air: The Experience of Modernity* (Harmondsworth: Penguin Books, 1988); Matei Calinescu, *Five Faces of Modernity* (Durham, NC: Duke University Press, 1987); Rita Felski, *The Gender of Modernity* (Cambridge, MA: Harvard University Press, 1995); David Frisby, *Fragments of Modernity: Theories of Modernity in the Work of Simmel, Kracauer and Benjamin* (Cambridge, MA: Harvard University Press, 1986); Anthony Giddens, *The Consequences of Modernity* (Stanford, CA: Stanford University Press, 1990); Hans Ulrich Gumbrecht, "A History of the Concept 'Modern,'" in *Making Sense in Life and Literature*, Glen Burns, trans. (Minneapolis: University of Minnesota Press, 1992); Jurgen Habermas, *The Philosophical Discourse of Modernity: Twelve Lectures*, Frederick Lawrence, trans. (Cambridge, MA: MIT Press, 1987); Stuart Hall, David Held, Don Hubert, Kenneth Thompson, ed., *Modernity: An Introduction to Modern Societies* (Oxford: Blackwell,1996); John Jervis, *Exploring the Modern: Patterns of Western Culture and Civilization* (Oxford: Blackwell, 1998); Scott Lash and Jonathan Friedman, ed., *Modernity and Identity* (Oxford: Blackwell, 1992); Stephen Toulmin, *Cosmopolis: The Hidden Agenda of Modernity* (New York: The Free Press, 1990); Charles Taylor, *Sources of the Self: The Making of the Modern Identity* (Cambridge, MA: Harvard University Press, 1989); Bryan Turner, ed. *Theories of Modernity and Postmodernity* (London: SAGE, 1990). For an interrogation of the concept, see Bruno Latour, *We Have Never Been Modern*, Catherine Porter, trans. (Cambridge, MA: Harvard University Press, 1993).

23. There is a burgeoning literature on secularism and modernity; among the many works see Talal Asad, *Formations of the Secular: Christianity, Islam, Modernity* (Stanford, CA: Stanford University Press, 2003); John D. Caputo and Gianni Vatimo, *After the Death of God*, Jeffrey W. Robbins, ed. (New York: Columbia University Press, 2007); Vincent Pecora, *Secularization and Cultural Criticism: Religion, Nation, and Modernity* (Chicago, IL: University of Chicago Press, 2006); Charles Taylor, *A Secular Age* (Cambridge, MA: Harvard University Press, 2007); Hent de Vries, ed., *Political Theologies: Public Religions in a Post-Secular World* (New York: Fordham University Press, 2006).

24. For alternative modernities, see Dilip Parameshwar Gaonkar, ed., *Alternative Modernities* (Chapel Hill, NC: Duke University Press, 2001); Roger Griffin, *Fascism and Modernism: The Sense of a Beginning Under Mussolini and Hitler* (London: Palgrave Macmillan, 2007); Kevin Repp, *Reformers, Critics and the Paths of German Modernity: Anti-Politics and the Search for Alternatives, 1890–1914* (Cambridge, MA: Harvard University Press, 2000). Some speak of "multiple modernities" with overlapping characteristics and unique trajectories; see Shmuel Noah Eisenstadt, ed., *Multiple Modernities* (Piscataway, NJ: Transaction Publishers, 2002).

25. See Hans Blumenberg, *The Legitimacy of the Modern Age*, trans. Robert M. Wallace (Cambridge, MA: Harvard University Press 1983); Remi Braque, *The Wisdom of the World: The Human Experience*, trans. Teresa Lavender Fagaan (Chicago, IL: University of Chicago Press, 2003); Marcel Gauchet, *The Disenchantment of the World: A Political History of Religion*, trans. Oscar Burge (Princeton, NJ: Princeton University Press, 1997); James T. Kloppenberg, "Democracy and Disenchantment: From Weber to Dewey to Habermas and Rorty," in Dorothy Ross, 69–90; Roy Porter, *Flesh in the Age of Reason: The Modern Foundations of Body and Soul* (New York: W. W. Norton, 2004).

26. Max Weber, "Science as a Vocation," in *From Max Weber: Essays in Sociology*, ed. H. H. Gerth and C. Wright Mills (London: Routledge, 1998). See also Ronald M. Glassman and Vatro Muvar, ed., *Max Weber's Political Sociology: A Pessimistic Vision of a Rationalized World* (Westport, CT: Greenwood Press 1984); Stephen Kalberg, "Max Weber's Types of Rationality," *American Journal of Sociology* 85:5 (March 1980): 1145–79; Edward Shils, "Max Weber and the World Since 1920," in *Max Weber and His Contemporaries*, ed. Wolfgang Mommsen and Jurgen Osterhammel (London: HarperCollins, 1987), 547–580; Lawrence A. Scaff, *Fleeing the Iron Cage: Culture, Politics, and Modernity in the Thought of Max Weber* (Berkeley: University of California Press, 1989).

27. Max Weber, *The Protestant Ethic and the Spirit of Capitalism*, trans. Talcott Parsons (New York: Dover Publications, 2003), 181.

28. Weber may have drawn his phrase from Schiller, whose poem "Die Götter Greichenlands" referred to "die entgöttertur Natur." In the late nineteenth century, disenchantment was often used synonymously with pessimism, the latter term given currency by the vogue for the "pessimistic" philosophy of Arthur Schopenhauer; see Edgar Evertson Saltus, *The Philosophy of Disenchantment* (Boston, MA: Houghton Mifflin, 1885). The phrase "cultural pessimist" has been applied to a range of nineteenth and twentieth century thinkers who criticized aspects of the modern West, among them Friedrich Nietzsche, Matthew Arnold, Oswald Spengler, T. S. Eliot, Arnold Toynbee, Martin Heidegger. See Arthur Herman, *The Idea of Decline in Western History* (New York: The Free Press, 1997); Oliver Bennett, *Cultural Pessimism: Narratives of Decline in the Postmodern World* (Edinburgh: Edinburgh University Press, 2001).

29. Weber, "Science as a Vocation," 139.

30. The *Oxford English Dictionary*, for example, lists as meanings of "enchant": "to hold spellbound; in a bad sense, to delude, befool" as well as to "delight, enrapture." See *Oxford English Dictionary* online, s.v. "*enchant, v.*" http://www.oed.com/ (accessed February 10, 2006).

31. Lorraine Daston and Katherine Park, *Wonders and the Order of Nature* (Cambridge, MA: Zone Books, 1998), 327–368.

32. A view reiterated in 1976 by Bruno Bettelheim. Arguing for the pedagogical importance of fairy tales for children, he maintained their thought is animistic "like all preliterate people": "A child trusts what the fairy story tells, because its world view accords with his own." Bruno Bettelheim, *The Uses of Enchantment: The Meaning and Importance of Fairy Tales* (New York: Alfred A. Knopf, 1976), 45.

33. Johann P. Arnason, "Reason, Imagination, Interpretation," in *Rethinking Imagination: Culture and Creativity*, ed. Gillian Robinson and John Rundell (London: Routledge, 1994), 156–169; Patrick Brantlinger, *The Reading Lesson: The Threat of Mass Literacy in Nineteenth-Century British Fiction* (Bloomington: Indiana University Press, 1998); John Tinnon Taylor, *Early Opposition to the English Novel: The Popular Reaction from 1760 to 1830* (New York: Columbia University Press, 1943).

34. Peter Laslett, *The World We Have Lost* (London: Routledge, 2004 [1965]). For other explorations of modernity and nostalgia, see Sylviane Agacinski, *Time Passing: Modernity and Nostalgia* (New York: Columbia University Press, 2004); Svetlana Boym, *The Future of Nostalgia* (New York: Basic Books, 2002); Peter Fritzsche, *Stranded in the Present: Modern Time and the Melancholy of History* (Cambridge, MA: Harvard University Press, 2004).

35. H. Stuart Hughes, *Consciousness and Society: The Reorientation of Social Thought, 1890–1930* (New York: Vintage Books, 1961). In addition to identifying thinkers who tended to express a binary view of modernity, Hughes does acknowledge the attempts by certain thinkers, such as Sigmund Freud and Max Weber, to hold opposing forces—especially reason and the irrational—in the tense harmony represented by the antinomial paradigm I outline here. In the early twentieth century, a body of thought known as *traditionalism*

also developed, which was avowedly anti-modernist and in its more trenchant forms does fit this oppositional, binary model: see Mark J. Sedgwick, *Against the Modern World: Traditionalism and the Secret Intellectual History of the Twentieth Century* (New York: Oxford University Press, 2004).

36. In an influential work Morris Berman captured an outlook shared by many progressive movements in Europe and America during the nineteen sixties and seventies, when he recounted the by now familiar argument: "The view of nature which predominated in the West down to the eve of the Scientific Revolution was that of an enchanted world. Rocks, trees, rivers, and clouds were all seen as wondrous, alive, and human beings felt at home in this environment . . . The story of the modern epoch, at least on the level of the mind, is one of progressive disenchantment. From the sixteenth century on, mind has been progressively expunged from the phenomenal world." Morris Berman, *The Reenchantment of the World* (Ithaca, NY: Cornell University Press, 1982), 2.

37. Patrick Brantlinger, *Bread and Circuses: Theories of Mass Culture as Social Decay* (Ithaca, NY: Cornell University Press, 1985); Andrew Ross, *No Respect: Intellectuals and Popular Culture* (New York: Routledge, 1998).

38. For ghost imagery and its rhetorical functions in Marx, see Jacques Derrida, *Specters of Marx: The State of the Debt, The Work of Mourning, and the New International* (New York: Routledge, 1994).

39. Sigmund Freud, *Civilization and its Discontents*, trans. James Strachey (New York: W. W. Norton, 1989 [1930]), 104.

40. Max Horkheimer and Theodor Adorno, *Dialectic of Enlightenment: Philosophical Fragments,* trans. Gunzelin Schmid Noerr and Edmund Jephcott (Stanford, CA: Stanford University Press), 19.

41. Ibid., 20.

42. The categories "metropole" and "periphery" are also understood as constructs requiring interrogation. Among an expanding literature, see Dipesh Chakrabarty, *Provincializing Europe: Postcolonial Thought and Historical Difference* (Princeton, NJ: Princeton University Press, 2007); Jean Comaroff and John Comaroff, ed., *Modernity and Its Malcontents: Ritual and Power in Postcolonial Africa* (Chicago, IL: University of Chicago Press, 1993); Saurabh Dube, ed., *Enduring Enchantments*, special issue of *The South Atlantic Quarterly* 101: 4 (October 2002); Peter Geschiere, *The Modernity of Witchcraft: Politics and the Occult in Postcolonial Africa*, trans. Janet Roitman (Charlottesville, VA: University of Virginia Press, 1997); Henrietta L. Moore and Todd Sanders, ed., *Magical Interpretations, Material Realities: Modernity, Witchcraft, and the Occult in Postcolonial Africa* (London: Routledge, 2001); Michael Taussig, *The Magic of the State* (New York: Routledge, 1997).

43. As Lorraine Daston and Katherine Park observed, "the last twenty years have seen a deep questioning of ideals of order, rationality, and good taste—'traditional hierarchies of the important and the essential'—that had seemed self-evident to intellectuals since the origins of the modern Republic of Letters in the late seventeenth century." Daston and Park, 10.

44. Lynda Nead, *Victorian Babylon: People, Streets and Images in Nineteenth-Century London* (New Haven, CT: Yale University Press, 2000), 8; Chakrabarty, 243.

45. James Cook, *The Arts of Deception: Playing With Fraud in the Age of Barnum* (Cambridge, MA: Harvard University Press, 2001), 166.

46. Alex Owen, *The Place of Enchantment: British Occultism and the Culture of the Modern* (Chicago, IL: University of Chicago Press, 2004), 6.

47. Christoph Asendorf, *Batteries of Life: On the History of Things and Their Perception in Modernity*, trans. Don Reneau (Berkeley: University of California Press, 1993); Richard Holmes, *The Age of Wonder: How the Romantic Generation Discovered the Beauty and Terror of Science* (New York: Pantheon, 2009); David Nye, *American Technological Sublime*

(Cambridge, MA: MIT Press, 1994); Pamela Thurschwell, *Literature, Technology and Magical Thinking, 1880–1920* (Cambridge: Cambridge University Press, 2001).

48. Jane Bennett, *The Enchantment of Modern Life: Attachments, Crossings, and Ethics* (Princeton, NJ: Princeton University Press, 2001); Wouter J. Hanegraaff, "How Magic Survived the Disenchantment of the World," *Religion* 33:4 (October 2003): 357–380; Benjamin Lazier, *God Interrupted: Heresy and the European Imagination Between the Wars* (Princeton, NJ: Princeton University Press, 2009); John Warne Monroe, *Laboratories of Faith: Mesmerism, Spiritism, and Occultism in Modern France* (Ithaca, NY: Cornell University Press, 2008); Corinna Treitel, *A Science for the Soul: Occultism and the Genesis of the German Modern* (Baltimore, MD: Johns Hopkins University Press, 2004); Gauri Viswanathan, "Secularism in the Framework of Heterodoxy," *PMLA* 123:2 (March 2008): 466–476.

49. For a range of modern enchantments, see Joshua Landy and Michael Saler, ed., *The Re-Enchantment of the World: Rational Magic in a Secular Age* (Stanford, CA: Stanford University Press, 2009).

50. R. Lanier Anderson, "Nietzsche on Redemption and Transfiguration," in ibid., 225–258.

51. His sister recalled, "Everything that my brother made was in honour of King Squirrel; all his musical productions were to glorify His Majesty; on his birthday . . . poems were recited and plays acted, all of which were written by my brother. King Squirrel was a patron of art; he must have a picture gallery. Fritz painted one hung round with Madonnas, landscapes, etc. etc." Julian Young, *Friedrich Nietzsche: A Philosophical Biography* (Cambridge: Cambridge University Press, 2010), 15.

52. Quoted in Hans Vaihinger, *The Philosophy of "As If,"* trans. C. K. Ogden (London: Routledge, 2008 [1924]), 354.

53. Allan Megill, *Prophets of Extremity: Nietzsche, Heidegger, Foucault, Derrida* (Berkeley: University of California Press, 1987), 32–34; James J. Winchester, *Nietzsche's Aesthetic Turn: Reading Nietzsche after Heidegger, Deleuze, Derrida* (Albany, NY: SUNY Press, 1994), 4–5.

54. For an examination of the romantic sublime and consumerism, see Colin Campbell, *The Romantic Ethic and the Spirit of Modern Consumerism* (Oxford: Blackwell, 1987).

55. Richard Hofstadter, *Anti-Intellectualism in American Life* (New York: Vintage, 1963); Neil Gabler, *Amusing Ourselves to Death: Public Discourse in the Age of Show Business* (New York: Penguin Books, 1985); Andrew Keen, *The Cult of the Amateur: How Today's Internet is Killing Our Culture* (New York: Doubleday, 2007); Susan Jacoby, *The Age of American Unreason* (New York: Pantheon Books, 2008); Sherry Turkle, *Alone Together* (New York: Basic Books, 2011). An equal and opposite reaction to these views is also in evidence: see Steven Johnson, *Everything Bad is Good for You: How Today's Popular Culture is Actually Making Us Smarter* (New York: Penguin, 2006); Tom Boellstorff, *Coming of Age in Second Life: An Anthropologist Explores the Virtually Human* (Princeton, NJ: Princeton University Press, 2008); Clay Shirky, *Cognitive Surplus: Creativity and Generosity in a Connected Age* (New York: Penguin, 2010).

56. My attempt to generalize these findings to European as well as American middle-class cultures might be challenged on the ground that I focus on only one European country (and one that often doesn't consider itself very European). But I believe my core arguments do apply to much of Western Europe as well as America during the late nineteenth and twentieth centuries. For example, Germany's Karl May created an imaginary world of the "old West" that was as romantic and fantastic, and as popular at the fin-de-siècle and after in Central Europe, as Conan Doyle's world of Sherlock Holmes was throughout the world; in France, the arch-villain "Fantômas" created an ongoing sensation after he was introduced in 1911 by Marcel Allain and Pierre Souvestre. Both mass culture and the discussions concerning modern [dis]enchantment crossed national boundaries, and middle-class cultures shared much in common in the period under analysis, as Peter Gay's five-volume survey of the "bourgeois experience" demonstrates. For an analysis of

the overarching commonalities shared by nineteenth century Anglo middle-class cultures, see Linda Young, *Middle-Class Culture in the Nineteenth Century: America, Australia, and Britain* (New York: Palgrave MacMillan, 2003).

57. As Jurgen Habermas argues, "An unprecedented modernity, open to the future, anxious for novelty, can only fashion its criteria out of itself. The only source of normativity that presents itself is the principle of subjectivity from which the very time-consciousness of modernity arose. The philosophy of reflection, which issues from the basic fact of self-consciousness, conceptualizes this principle." Habermas, 41.

58. W. E. B. Du Bois famously discussed the "double consciousness" affecting African Americans, and while his concept has its own important specificities, a general awareness of "double consciousness" was widespread at the time he wrote. W. E. B. Du Bois, *The Souls of Black Folk: Essays and Sketches* (Chicago, IL: A. C. McClurg & Co., 1903). For a detailed examination of the "contradictory self-consciousness" that defines modern subjectivity in the West, see Anthony J. Cascardi, *The Subject of Modernity* (Cambridge: Cambridge University Press, 1993).

59. Bloom, 159–163.

60. Taylor, *A Secular Age,* 351.

61. Joseph Frank, "Spatial Form in Modern Literature," in *Criticism: The Foundations of Modern Literary Judgment,* ed. Mark Schorer, Josephine Miles, Gordon McKenzie (New York: Harcourt Brace, 1958), 379–92.

62. Edward Wagenknecht, "The Little Prince Rides the White Deer: Fantasy and Symbolism in Recent Literature," *The English Journal* 35:1 (May 1946), 229.

63. For an analysis of the complexity of the concept of objectivity in the nineteenth century, see Lorraine Daston and Peter Galison, *Objectivity* (Cambridge, MA: Zone Books, 2007).

64. I follow Nicholas Ruddick's use of the "fantastic" to designate fiction that "represents any sort of departure from 'consensus reality'"; he argues that the fantastic is "a transhistorical fictional *mode* encompassing such past and present genres as folk and fairy tales, beast fables, parables, utopian fantasy, ghost stories, gothic fiction, weird fiction, horror fiction, dark fantasy, heroic fantasy, scientific romance and science fiction." Ruddick, 189–190.

65. Katherine Pearson Woods, "The Renaissance of Wonder," *The Bookman: A Review of Books and Life* (December 1899), 340. For the "occult" dimensions of nineteenth-century detective fiction, see Srdjan Smajic, *Ghost-Seers, Detectives, and Spiritualists: Theories of Vision in Victorian Literature and Science* (Cambridge: Cambridge University Press, 2010).

66. G. K. Chesterton, "A Defence of Detective Stories," *The Defendant* (London: R. Brinley Johnson, 1901), 119. In 1944, Will Cuppy justified his review of a volume of Lovecraft's stories in a newspaper column dedicated to detective fiction by reminding his readers, "Since the literature of horror and macabre fantasy belongs traditionally with mystery in its broader sense, we herewith recommend to fandom this outsized volume." Will Cuppy, review of H. P. Lovecraft, *Beyond the Wall of Sleep*, reprinted in Joshi, *A Weird Writer in Our Midst: Early Criticism of H. P. Lovecraft,* 194.

67. Anthony Boucher, "Sherlock Holmes and Science Fiction," *Baker Street Journal* (July 1960): 143. (Given his own fascination with imaginary worlds, it is not surprising that Boucher was the first to translate Borges into English.)

68. Jeffrey Marks, *Anthony Boucher: A Biobibliography* (Jefferson, NC: McFarland & Company, 2008), 39.

69. Matthew H. Onderdonk, "The Lord of R'lyeh: A Discussion of the Supreme Contribution of Howard Phillips Lovecraft to the Philosophy of the Weird Tale," *Fantasy Commentator* 1:6 (Spring 1945): 110.

70. J. R. R. Tolkien, *Tolkien On Fairy-stories,* ed. Verlyn Flieger and Douglas A. Anderson (London: HarperCollins, 2007), 65. I obviously disagree with Christine Brooke-Rose's

assertion: "Nor are the histories and genealogies in the least necessary to the narrative, but they have given much infantile happiness to the Tolkien clubs and societies, whose members apparently write to each other in Elvish." Christine Brooke-Rose, *A Rhetoric of the Unreal: Studies in Narrative & Structure, Especially of the Fantastic* (Cambridge: Cambridge University Press, 1981), 247.

71. This was often a misreading of the doctrines of those labeled as positivists. While late nineteenth-century writers feared that positivism excluded the imagination as a legitimate source of knowledge, a closer reading of the positivists reveals that many were less antagonistic toward art and the imagination than their contemporaries assumed. See Peter Allen Dale, *In Pursuit of a Scientific Culture: Science, Art, and Society in the Victorian Age* (Madison, WI: Wisconsin University Press, 1989); Jonathan Smith, *Fact and Feeling* (Madison, WI: Wisconsin University Press, 1994). Nevertheless, the dominant discourse of mid to late nineteenth-century positivists, materialists, scientific naturalists, and cultural pessimists associated Western modernity with a narrow form of rationality inimical to wider sources of meaning, and this pervasive association of modernity with disenchantment continued to be perpetuated among intellectuals in Europe and America through the twentieth-century: According to historians of science Lorraine Daston and Katherine Park, "To be a member of a modern elite is to regard wonder and wonders with studied indifference; enlightenment is still in part defined as the anti-marvelous." Daston and Park, 368. For an overview, see Michael Saler, "Modernity and Enchantment: A Historiographic Review," *The American Historical Review* 111:3 (June 2006): 692–716.

72. For histories of the imagination, see Eva T. H. Brann, *The World of the Imagination: Sum and Substance* (Lanham, MD: Rowman and Littlefield, 1991); Richard Kearney, *The Wake of Imagination: Toward a Postmodern Culture* (London: Routledge, 1998); Mary Warnock, *Imagination* (Berkeley: University of California Press, 1976).

73. Jack Williamson, "Scientifiction, Searchlight of Science," *Amazing Stories Quarterly* 1 (1928): 435.

74. T. S. Eliot, "The Metaphysical Poets," *Centenary College of Louisiana, http://personal. centenary.edu/~dhavird/TSEMetaPoets.html* (accessed January 26, 2010).

75. R. G. Collingwood, *The Philosophy of Enchantment: Studies in Folktale, Cultural Criticism, and Anthropology*, ed. David Boucher, Wendy James, Philip Smallwood (Oxford: Clarendon Press, 2005), 78–79.

76. Ibid.

77. Given that many public spheres of the imagination emerged initially as alternatives to the dominant culture, it might be more accurate to call them "counter-public spheres of the imagination," following the important conceptual revision of Habermas by Michael Warner, *Publics and Counterpublics* (Cambridge, MA: Zone Books, 2005). But that is an unwieldy phrase; I have tried to do justice to the specific nature of these public spheres through the phrase I use.

78. Peter E. Blau, "My First Meeting with Sherlock Holmes," *Baker Street Journal* 50:4 (Winter 2000): 46.

79. Mike Savage, Gaynor Bagnall, Brian Longhurst, *Globalization and Belonging* (London: SAGE Publications, 2005), 29.

80. Tom Shippey, "Orcs, Wraiths, Wights: Tolkien's Images of Evil," in his *Roots and Branches: Selected Papers on Tolkien* (Switzerland: Walking Tree Publishers, 2007), 264–265.

81. See Benedict Anderson, *Imagined Communities: Reflections on the Origin and Spread of Nationalism* (London: Verso, 1991).

82. *Mixed reality* is a phrase coined by the artist Troy Innocent; see N. Katherine Hayles, foreword to *Prefiguring Cyberculture: An Intellectual History*, ed. Darren Tofts, Annemarie Jonson, and Alessio Cavallero (Cambridge, MA: MIT Press, 2002), xiii.

83. Ryan, 37. For a defense of "affirming a world in which the creed you embrace regularly brushes up against alternatives that challenge, disturb, and disrupt its claims to universality," see William E. Connolly, "Belief, Spirituality, and Time," in Warner, VanAntwerpen, Calhoun, ed., *Varieties of Secularism*, 126–144.

84. Arjun Appadurai, *Modernity at Large: Cultural Dimensions of Globalization* (Minneapolis: University of Minnesota Press, 1997), 53–54.

85. Gauri Viswanathan also sees the late nineteenth century as a transitional moment for Western uses of the imagination: in this period one witnesses a "shift in register from belief to imagination as the initiator of secularizing processes in modern culture." Viswanathan, 469.

86. Bloom, xii.

87. Ibid., 9.

88. Ibid., 12.

89. Ibid., 72.

90. Alfred Korzybski, *Science and Sanity: An Introduction to Non-Aristotelian Systems and General Semantics*, 5th ed. (Forth Worth, TX: Institute of General Semantics 1994 [1933]), xvii.

CHAPTER 1

The first epigraph is from Yi-Fu Tuan, *Escapism* (Baltimore, MD: Johns Hopkins University Press, 1998), 165. The second epigraph is from Gogol Bordello, "Immigraniada (We Comin' Rougher)," from the album *Transcontinental Hustle* (2010).

1. Anthony Boucher, letter, *The Acolyte* 2:3 (Summer 1944): 29.

2. The *OED* finds the earliest use of *hobby*, in the sense of "A favourite occupation or topic, pursued merely for the amusement or interest that it affords," is 1816. *Oxford English Dictionary* online, s.v. "hobby," http://www.oed.com/ (accessed December 2, 2007). (Hereafter cited as *OED* online.)

3. Revealingly, the *OED*'s earliest citation of *vicarious* in the sense of "experienced imaginatively through another person or agency" concerned readers and animism—it is taken from R. S. and H. M. Lynd's *Middletown* (1929): "To Middletown adults, reading a book means overwhelmingly what story-telling means to primitive man—the vicarious entry into other, imagined kinds of living." See *OED* online, s.v. "vicarious," (accessed December 2, 2007).

4. Vaihinger will be discussed more fully, but his definition of Fictionalism can be cited here, as it is the first definition of the term used by the *OED*: "An idea whose theoretical untruth or incorrectness, and therewith its falsity, is admitted, is not for that reason practically valueless and useless; for such an idea, in spite of its theoretical nullity may have great practical importance." See the *OED* online, s.v. "Fictionalism," (accessed December 2, 2007); Vaihinger, viii.

5. For more detail on memory palaces, see Frances Yates, *The Art of Memory* (Chicago, IL: University of Chicago Press, 2001); Jonathan Spence, *The Memory Palace of Matteo Ricci* (New York: Penguin, 1985).

6. There are interesting connections between secular cyberspace and religious conceptions of space. See Margaret Wertheim, *The Pearly Gates of Cyberspace: A History of Space from Dante to the Internet* (New York: Virago, 1999).

7. Boellstorff, 67.

8. William Gibson, *Neuromancer* (New York: Ace Books, 1984), 1.

9. The term *literary realism* defined here includes the naturalists, who tended to be more pessimistic than the realists who preceded them; both shared a determination to depict social life objectively and unsparingly, demystifying romantic fantasies in the process.

10. Lin Carter, *Imaginary Worlds: The Art of Fantasy* (New York: Ballantine Books, 1973), 7.

11. Ibid., 8. Other sources concur: see David R. Langford, "William Morris," in *The Encyclopedia of Fantasy*, ed. John Clute and John Grant (New York: St. Martin's Press, 1997), 664–666; David Pringle, Introduction to *The Ultimate Encyclopedia of Fantasy* (London: Carlton Books, 2006), 11.

12. Wright, an American professor of law, created his imaginary world at about the same time as an English academic, J. R. R. Tolkien, created his. Both worlds were rich in scholarly appurtenances, such as maps, charts, glossaries, and chronologies.

13. Wagenknecht, 235.

14. Samuel Taylor Coleridge, *Biographia Literaria* (London: J. M. Dent, 1975), 169.

15. Thomas Walter Laqueur, *Solitary Sex: A Cultural History of Masturbation* (Cambridge, MA: Zone Books, 2003), 278–357; Jan Goldstein, *The Post-Revolutionary Self: Politics and Psyche in France, 1750–1850* (Cambridge, MA: Harvard University Press, 2005), 32–33.

16. Quoted in Goldstein, 77.

17. Concepts that bear a family resemblance to the ironic imagination have been adumbrated by Neil Harris as the "operational aesthetic," James Cook as "artful deception," and Joshua Landy as "Lucid Self-Delusion." See Neil Harris, *Humbug: The Art of P. T. Barnum* (Boston, MA: Little, Brown, 1973); James Cook, *The Arts of Deception: Playing with Fraud in the Age of Barnum* (Cambridge, MA: Harvard University Press, 2001); Joshua Landy, "The Cruel Gift: Lucid Self-Delusion in French Literature and German,1851–1914" (Ph.D. diss., Princeton University, 1997).

18. H. P. Lovecraft, *Selected Letters III: 1929–1931*, ed. August Derleth and Donald Wandrei (Sauk City, WI: Arkham House, 1971), 193.

19. Ibid., 140.

20. Quoted in *Irregular Memories of the Mid-'Forties: An Archival History of the Baker Street Irregulars Autumn 1943–June 1947*, ed. Jon Lellenberg (New York: The Baker Street Irregulars, 1995), 298.

21. For interesting similarities between Tolkien and Coleridge, see Michael Milburn, "Coleridge's Definition of Imagination and Tolkien's Definition(s) of Faery, *Tolkien Studies* 7 (2010): 55–66.

22. Tolkien, *Tolkien On Fairy-stories*, 52.

23. Ibid., 52; 78.

24. Susan Blackmore, "Lucid Dreaming: Awake in Your Sleep?," *Skeptical Inquirer* 15 (Summer 1991): 362–370. Victor Nell views reading in similar terms; see Victor Nell, *Lost in a Book: The Psychology of Reading for Pleasure* (New Haven, CT: Yale University Press, 1988). Marie-Laure Ryan calls this a "split subject" attitude, in which the reader is transported into the textual world "but remains able to contemplate it with aesthetic or epistemological detachment." Ryan, 97. This double-conscious orientation accords with Tolkien's explanation of how imaginary worlds are experienced, and the "ironic imagination."

25. J. R. R. Tolkien, *The Lord of the Rings: The Two Towers* (New York: Houghton Mifflin, 1987), 321.

26. For the continuum between the immersion afforded by realism and the estranging effects of metafictions, see Robert Alter, *Partial Magic: The Novel as Self-Conscious Genre* (Berkeley: University of California Press, 1975). James Branch Cabell's imaginary world of "Poictesme," which he elaborated in many works during the early decades of the twentieth century, was never successful in attracting large groups of readers to pretend it was real. On the surface, this is surprising, for Cabell included many paratexts. However, he intended his fantasies about Poictesme to be satirical allegories about contemporary social, sexual, and religious mores, resulting in the reader's attention being drawn to the real rather than fictional worlds. The question of an imaginary world's "habitability" is of course a matter of degree; Poictesme did have some fans who pretended it was real. For examples, see Don

Bregenzer and Samuel Loveman, ed., *A Round-Table in Poictesme: A Symposium* (Cleveland, OH: The Colophon Club, 1924) and Walter Klinefelter, *Books about Poictesme: An Essay in Imaginative Bibliography* (Chicago, IL: The Black Cat Press, 1937). Occasionally, a work's metafictional aspects might be the source of attraction, encouraging readers to emulate the author's playfulness in real life. Max Beerbohm's "Enoch Soames" (1919), for example, concerns a fin-de-siècle poet who desperately wants to be famous, selling his soul to the devil in return for learning how posterity will treat him. He travels in time, arriving at the British Library in 1997 to look himself up in references—and finds to his horror that his fame derives from being a fictional, fin-de-siècle poet in a story by Max Beerbohm. Fans of the story reenacted Enoch Soames's appearance in the Library's reading room in 1997 and have published scholarly articles on his nonexistent works. See David Colvin and Edward Maggs, ed., *Enoch Soames: The Critical Heritage* (London: The Enoch Soames Society, 2002); Mark Samuels Lassner, *A Bibliography of Enoch Soames (1862–1897)* (Oxford: The Rivendell Press, 1999). Nevertheless, these fan bases are small compared to those that have adopted Middle-earth or the Starship Enterprise as their place of imaginative residence.

27. Fan responses to Henry Resnik's interview with Tolkien; see Henry Resnik, "An Interview with Tolkien," *Niekas* 18 (Spring 1967): 47.

28. Roland Barthes, "The Reality Effect," in *The Rustle of Language*, trans. Richard Howard (Berkeley: University of California Press, 1989), 141–148.

29. During the first series of Holmes's adventures, readers compiled lists of the cases that Dr. Watson had mentioned offhandedly, and when Conan Doyle resumed the series after an absence of several years, they begged him to attend to these first. The American periodical *The Bookman* enumerated twenty-three cases that it wanted explicated. Watson's reference to the case of "The Second Stain" was deemed especially intriguing: "As the new century has now come, it is vitally important to our peace of mind that the story should be told." This tale was finally told: it appeared in December, 1904. Cited in Katherine Mary Wisser, *The Creation, Reception, and Perception of the Sherlock Holmes Phenomenon, 1887–1930* (M. A. thesis, University of North Carolina at Chapel Hill, June 2000).

30. J. R. R. Tolkien, *The Letters of J. R. R. Tolkien*, ed. Humphrey Carpenter (Boston, MA: Houghton Mifflin, 2000), 110.

31. See "A Study in Scarlet" and "The Adventure of the Sussex Vampire" in Arthur Conan Doyle, *The Complete Sherlock Holmes* (New York: Barnes and Noble, 1992).

32. It is true that the romantic irony expressed by Fichte and some other romantic writers in the early nineteenth century shared a similar concern for human finitude and contingency, but this was nevertheless cast within an overarching metaphysical framework. See Anne K. Mellor, *English Romantic Irony* (Cambridge, MA: Harvard University Press, 1980).

33. Luiz Costa Lima, "The Control of the Imagination and the Novel," in *The Novel, Volume One*, ed. Franco Moretti (Princeton, NJ: Princeton University Press, 2006), 37–67; W. F. Galloway, Jr., "The Conservative Attitude Toward Fiction, 1770–1830," *PMLA* 55: 4 (December, 1940): 1041–1059; Ronald Zboray, *A Fictive People: Antebellum Economic Development and the American Reading Public* (New York: Oxford University Press, 1993), xix.

34. Richard D. Altick, *The English Common Reader: A Social History of the Mass Reading Public, 1800–1900* (Chicago, IL: University of Chicago Press, 1957), 99–140; Brantlinger, *The Reading Lesson*, 1–2; Laqueur, 320–357.

35. Gustave Flaubert, *Madame Bovary: A Story of Provincial Life*, trans. Alan Russell (New York: Penguin Books, 1981), 96.

36. Mary Elizabeth Braddon, *The Doctor's Wife* (New York: Oxford University Press, 1998), 235–236.

37. Quoted in Amy Cruse, *The Victorians and Their Books* (London: George Allen and Unwin Limited, 1936), 196.

38. Quoted in Juliet Barker, *The Brontës* (London: Weidenfeld and Nicolson, 1994), 262.

39. Ibid., 243.

40. Ibid., 262.

41. Fannie Elizabeth Ratchford, *The Brontës' Web of Childhood* (New York: Russell & Russell, Inc., 1964 [1941]), 106.

42. For an overview of the early reception of the Brontë siblings' writings about their imaginary worlds, see Fannie Elizabeth Ratchford, *Legends of Angria* (New Haven, CT: Yale University Press, 1933), x–xiii.

43. See Barker; Lucasta Miller, *The Brontë Myth* (New York: Alfred A. Knopf, 2001).

44. For a discussion of the connection between reading novels and the growing acceptance of the idea of human rights in the eighteenth century, see Lynn Hunt, *Inventing Human Rights: A History* (New York: Norton, 2007). Robert Darnton discusses the eloquent letters readers sent to Rousseau about how deeply his *Le Nouvelle Heloise* affected them: see Robert Darnton, "Readers Respond to Rousseau: The Fabrication of Romantic Sensitivity," in his *The Great Cat Massacre and Other Episodes in French Cultural History* (London: Penguin Books, 2001), 215–256. In the nineteenth century, the mimetic orientation of fiction, painting, and drama reinforced a common realist perspective; see Martin Meisel, *Realizations: Narrative, Pictorial, and Theatrical Arts in Nineteenth-Century England* (Princeton, NJ: Princeton University Press, 1983).

45. Philip Waller, *Writers, Readers, & Reputations: Literary Life in Britain 1870–1918* (New York: Oxford University Press, 2006), x. Jennifer Hayward cites Thomas Arnold's revealing complaint on observing the novel consequences caused by the serialization of Dickens's *The Pickwick Papers* in 1837: according to Arnold, nonserial works, "not being published periodically . . . did not occupy the mind for so long a time, nor keep alive so constant an expectation; nor, by dwelling upon the mind, and distilling themselves into it, as it were, drop by drop, did they possess it so largely." Hayward, 6.

46. Cruse, 151–173.

47. Waller, 233–278.

48. David Brewer analyzed the vogue for fictional characters in the eighteenth century and noted that they were "apparently eccentric" forms of behavior within the broader literary culture: "Indeed, such reading practices may be all the more revealing because of, not despite, their 'anomalous' character.'" David Brewer, *The Afterlife of Character, 1726–1825* (Philadelphia: University of Pennsylvania Press, 2005), 9. The importance for many eighteenth-century writers of the direct association of the fictional to the real (such as linking fictions to their authors) is also reflected in Jeremy Bentham's discussion of fiction. Bentham distinguished between legitimate uses of fiction when connected to real substances, and the fallacious use of it when connected to unreal or "fabulous" entities: Jeremy Bentham, *Bentham's Theory of Fictions*, ed. C. K. Ogden (London: Routledge, 2007 [1932]). See also Thomas Keymer and Peter Sabor, *"Pamela" in the Marketplace: Literary Controversy and Print Culture in Eighteenth Century Britain and Ireland* (Cambridge: Cambridge University Press, 2006); James Grantham Turner, "Novel Panic: Picture and Performance in the Reception of Richardson's *Pamela*," *Representations* 48 (Fall 1994): 70–96; T. C. Duncan Eaves and Ben D. Kimpel, *Samuel Richardson: A Biography* (Oxford: Oxford University Press, 1971), 119–153.

49. Jonathan Rose, *The Intellectual Life of the British Working Classes* (New Haven, CT: Yale University Press, 2002).

50. Cruse, 322.

51. Thus, in John Murray's guide to Cornwall, one route is described as passing a village mentioned in Charles Kingsley's novel *Hereward the Wake*. John Murray, *A Handbook for Travellers in Cornwall, Tenth Edition* (London: John Murray, 1882), 87.

52. Miguel de Cervantès, *Don Quixote*, trans. Edith Grossman (New York: HarperCollins, 2003), 19–20. Edgar W. Smith wrote about the Holmes phenomenon in 1952: "There is

nothing like it, to one's knowledge, in all the field of literature. Not Robinson Crusoe, nor Mr. Pickwick, nor yet great Hamlet, has been so honored by the imp of the inquisitive. Do Alice and Don Quixote inspire long hours of research to determine the whys and where-fores of some foible they displayed? Ivanhoe and Hiawatha, Dr. Jekyll and David Copper-field, Hercules and George Babbitt—who cares if they were married once or twice, or how profound their knowledge of the Solar System may have been? . . . We know so very much of all the figures that move upon the literary scene, and, knowing, cease to care and ques-tion. But Sherlock Holmes is different." Edgar W. Smith, "The Editor's Gas-Lamp: The Writings about the Writings," *The Baker Street Journal* 2:2, New Series (April 1952): 64.

53. During defines "magical assemblages" as "that motley of shows in the public spaces where magic was performed: theaters, fairs, streets, taverns, and so on," and his fascinating his-tory demonstrates how such magic acts, from conjuring to cinematic special effects, helped inculcate a disenchanted form of enchantment. Simon During, *Modern Enchant-ments: The Cultural Power of Secular Magic* (Cambridge, MA: Harvard University Press, 2001), 66.

54. For an examination of rational recreation, see Peter Bailey, "The Victorian Middle Class and the Problem of Leisure," in his *Popular Culture and Performance in the Victorian City* (Cambridge: Cambridge University Press, 1998), 13–29. For the growth of "spectacular" entertainments corresponding to the late nineteenth-century society of the spectacle, see Vanessa Schwartz, *Spectacular Realities: Early Mass Culture in Fin-de-siècle Paris* (Berkeley: University of California Press, 1998). In England, the cult of games instituted at public schools and "Oxbridge" in the second half of the nineteenth century set a tone for schools throughout the Empire: in this respect, *homo ludens* may have been partly diffused by Brit-ish imperialism. Noel Annan remarks, only half-facetiously, that games were "the most enduring legacy" of Britain: "That was what Britain gave to countries in Asia, Africa, South America and even Europe . . . No other country so hallowed games in its national life." Noel Annan, *Our Age: English Intellectuals Between the World Wars—A Group Portrait* (New York: Random House, 1990), 51.

55. Cited in Cook, 16.

56. Ibid., 17.

57. Ben Wilson, *Decency and Disorder: The Age of Cant, 1789–1837* (London: Faber & Faber, 2007).

58. Cruse argues that *Alice in Wonderland* (1865) "had a real and important part in helping to banish the too obtrusive moral which had devastated . . . so many potentially charming children's books." Cruse, 305; see also Carolyn Sigler, ed., *Alternative Alices: Visions and Revisions of Lewis Carroll's Alice Books* (Lexington: The University Press of Kentucky, 1997), xii; Humphrey Carpenter, *Secret Gardens: The Golden Age of Children's Literature* (Boston, MA: Houghton Mifflin, 1985).

59. Many of the authors of the New Romance were born at mid-century, among them Robert Louis Stevenson (1850), H. Rider Haggard (1856), Arthur Conan Doyle (1859), Rud-yard Kipling (1865), and H. G. Wells (1866).

60. Arthur Conan Doyle, *The Lost World* (London: Hodder & Stoughton, 1912), n.p.

61. In America, children's toys also bore witness to the increasing acceptance of imaginative play over rational recreation during the late nineteenth and early twentieth centuries. See Gary Cross, *Kids' Stuff: Toys and the Changing World of American Childhood* (Cambridge, MA: Harvard University Press, 1997).

62. For the turn toward relativistic thought in late nineteenth-century Europe and America, see Christopher Herbert, *Victorian Relativity: Radical Thought and Scientific Discovery* (Chicago, IL: University of Chicago Press, 2001).

63. Michael North, *Reading 1922: A Return to the Scene of the Modern* (New York: Oxford University Press, 1999), 206; 208.

64. Richard Dyer, *Stars* (London: British Film Institute, 1998).
65. Brian Gallagher, "Greta Garbo is Sad: Some Historical Reflections on the Paradoxes of Stardom in the American Film Industry." *Images* 3, http://www.imagesjournal.com/issue03/infocus/stars4.htm (accessed June 11, 2002).
66. Jenny Bourne Taylor, "Psychology at the Fin de Siècle," in *The Cambridge Companion to the Fin de Siècle*, ed. Gail Marshall (Cambridge: Cambridge University Press, 2007), 25–26. Jan Goldstein demonstrates that in France the nineteenth-century liberal ideal of a rational and unified self was a cultural construct that triumphed, for social and political reasons, over more complex notions of the self. Goldstein, 329.
67. Shane McCorristine, *Spectres of the Self: Thinking about Ghosts and Ghost-Seeing in England, 1750–1920* (Cambridge: Cambridge University Press, 2010), 78.
68. Quoted in Julian Young, 263.
69. As J. W. Burrow noted, "By the end of the century the notion of 'character' was beginning to look like a form of naïveté, discordant with the tendencies of advanced thought." J. W. Burrow, *The Crisis of Reason: European Thought, 1848–1914* (New Haven, CT: Yale University Press, 2000), 160. For a discussion of personality versus character in the context of fin-de-siècle Britain, see Deborah Cohen, *Household Gods: The British and Their Possessions* (New Haven, CT: Yale University Press, 2007), 136–144.
70. Burrow, 162.
71. Walt Whitman, "Song of Myself," in his *Complete Poetry and Selected Prose* (New York: The Library of America, 1982), 210; 246.
72. Robert Louis Stevenson, *The Suicide Club & Other Dark Adventures* (Yorkshire: Tartarus Press, 2007), 350.
73. George Monteiro, *The Man Who Never Was: Essays on Fernando Pessoa* (Providence, RI: Gávea-Brown Publications, 1982).
74. Fernando Pessoa, *The Book of Disquiet*, Richard Zenith, ed. and trans. (New York: Penguin Books, 2003), 327.
75. Henry Adams, from *The Education of Henry Adams*, quoted in Herbert, *Victorian Relativity*, 34.
76. For a discussion of adventure fiction and the New Imperialism, see Richard Phillips, *Mapping Men and Empire: A Geography of Adventure* (London: Routledge, 1997).
77. Brian Stableford lists many such titles in his survey of proto-science fiction prior to the twentieth century. Stableford, "Science Fiction before the Genre," in *The Cambridge Companion to Science Fiction*, ed. Edward James and Farah Mendlesohn (Cambridge: Cambridge University Press, 2003), 15–31.
78. Sina Najafi, "Underworld, an Interview with Rosalind Williams," *Cabinet* 30 (Summer 2008): 85–88.
79. H. Rider Haggard, *She* (East Sussex: Pulp Fictions, 1998), 136.
80. Christina Scull and Wayne G. Hammond, *The J. R. R. Tolkien Companion and Guide: Reader's Guide* (London: HarperCollins, 2006), 440.
81. Sigmund Freud, quoted in Steve Pile, "Freud, Dreams and Imaginative Geographies," in *Freud 2000*, ed. Anthony Elliott (New York: Routledge, 1999), 204.
82. Freud, 44.
83. Owen Barfield, *Romanticism Comes of Age* (Middletown, CT: Wesleyan University Press, 1967 [1944]), 193.
84. Jack London, *The Star Rover* (New York: The Modern Library, 2003), 42.
85. Georges Sorel, "Reflections on Violence," in *From Georges Sorel: Essays in Socialism and Philosophy*, ed. John Stanley (Piscataway, NJ: Transaction Publishers, 1987), 204.
86. Ludwig Wittgenstein, *Philosophical Investigations*, trans. G. E. M. Anscombe (New York: Prentice Hall, 1973), 19.
87. David Frisby, introduction to *The Philosophy of Money*, by Georg Simmel, ed. David Frisby, trans. Tom Bottomore and David Frisby (London: Routledge, 2004), 34.

88. In addition to Alex Owen, see Catherine L. Albanese, *A Republic of Mind and Spirit: A Cultural History of American Metaphysical Religion* (New Haven, CT: Yale University Press, 2008); Janet Oppenheim, *The Other World: Spiritualism and Psychical Research in England, 1850–1914* (Cambridge: Cambridge University Press, 1988); Frank Miller Turner, *Between Science and Religion: The Reaction to Scientific Naturalism in Late Victorian England* (New Haven, CT: Yale University Press, 1974). For occult and allegedly existent Other Worlds, see Sumathi Ramaswamy, *The Lost Land of Lemuria: Fabulous Geographies, Catastrophic Histories* (Berkeley: University of California Press, 2004); L. Sprague de Camp, *Lost Continents: The Atlantis Theme in History, Science and Literature* (New York: Dover, 1970). Practitioners of the magical craft today find that they are able to engage in a form of double consciousness and inhabit two worlds simultaneously–the world of the senses and the world of the imagination–that operate according to different laws. See Tanya Luhrmann, *Persuasions of the Witch's Craft: Ritual Magic in Contemporary England* (Cambridge, MA: Harvard University Press, 1989), 276.

89. Quoted in Ronald Hutton, *The Triumph of the Moon: A History of Modern Pagan Witchcraft* (Oxford: Oxford University Press, 1999), 174.

90. Collingwood, 106. For British Idealism, see Sandra M. Den Otter, *British Idealism and Social Explanation: A Study in Late Victorian Thought* (Oxford: Clarendon Press, 1996); James Patrick, *The Magdalen Metaphysicals: Idealism and Orthodoxy at Oxford, 1901–1945* (Macon, GA: Mercer University Press, 1985). For the turn to Hegelian thought in America, see Robert D. Richardson, *William James: In the Maelstrom of American Modernism* (Boston, MA: Houghton Mifflin, 2006), 211–216.

91. Linda Dalrymple Henderson, *The Fourth Dimension and Non-Euclidean Geometry in Modern Art* (Princeton, NJ: Princeton University Press, 1983); Smajic, 159–168.

92. Edwin A. Abbott, *Flatland: A Romance of Many Dimensions* (London: Seeley and Co., 1884).

93. Herbert, *Victorian Relativity*, 217–218. Of course, scientists have engaged in thought experiments long before the late nineteenth century; Paul Bloom notes that one of the most famous was Galileo's regarding weight and speed in the early seventeenth century. (Bloom, 219–220.) But the cultural recognition of the role of imagination in the pursuit of science that I am discussing was particular to the fin-de-siècle, an overt riposte to earlier nineteenth-century positivism.

94. For a survey of French thought on the imagination, see Matthew W. Maguire, *The Conversion of the Imagination: From Pascal to Rousseau to Tocqueville* (Cambridge, MA: Harvard University Press, 2006).

95. Gérard Durozoi, *History of the Surrealist Movement*, trans. Alison Anderson (Chicago, IL: University of Chicago Press, 2002), 67.

96. Arnason, "Reason, Imagination, Interpretation," 165–169.

97. Max Ernst, *Life and Work*, ed. Werner Spies (London: Thames & Hudson, 2006), 121.

98. George Katsiaficas, *The Imagination of the New Left: A Global Analysis of 1968* (Cambridge, MA: South End Press, 1987), 7.

99. For a consideration of the rhetoric of the aesthetic turn from Nietzsche through Derrida, see Megill, 342–346.

100. Vaihinger, xi; 88.

101. Ibid., 85.

102. Ibid., 89.

103. Rudyard Kipling, *Just So Stories* (New York: Doubleday, 1912 [1902]). Kipling, like Haggard, is often seen as an essentialist. (See Edward Said, *Culture and Imperialism* [New York: Alfred A. Knopf, 1993], 134; 149.) But, like Haggard, his writings are complex and blanket labels don't do them justice. And regardless of the author's intentions, the *Just So Stories* accord nicely with other ironic deflations of essentialism at this time.

104. Michael Denning, *Mechanic Accents: Dime Novels and Working-Class Culture in America* (New York: Verso, 1998), 20.

105. For the interchangeability of most comic-strip artists, see Bill Blackbeard, "Comments on the Grimly Comic Development of A Major American Epic of Witchcraft and Fisti-cuffs as Refereed by J. Wellington Wimpy," in *E. C. Segar's Popeye: I Yam What I Yam! vol. 1* by E. C. Segar (Seattle, WA: Fantagraphics, 2006), 5. In the United States, the new mass media of film, radio, comic books, and television frequently offered premiums to their audiences as an advertising promotion, and these served as a further way to enhance emotional investment in imaginary worlds. These wonderful items—decoders, rings, and other devices that often were incorporated into the shows' plots—were in effect secular reliquaries, talismans redolent of the magic of their enchanted heroes. A fan of the 1950s American television show "Space Patrol" observed that "a key reason this program remains a stronger presence than many of the other competing space operas of the early 1950s—even those that were better written and funded—is the strong and frequent integration of the toys/premiums offered in the advertisements with the props used in the show's adventures. You could buy and own many of the objects used by [the characters], and somehow this created a powerful psychological link to that imaginary world . . . like carrying an object out of a dream." Elliot Swanson, "More on Space Patrol." *Inside Space Patrol, http://www.slick-net.com/space/patrol/pg2/index.phtml* (accessed May 24, 2009).

106. Jess Nevins, *Heroes & Monsters: The Unofficial Companion to the League of Extraordinary Gentlemen* (Austin, TX: MonkeyBrain Books, 2003), 175–184.

107. Michel Foucault, "What is an Author?" in his *The Foucault Reader,* ed. Paul Rabinow (New York: Pantheon Books, 1984), 101–120.

108. Stefan Collini, *Public Moralists: Political Thought and Intellectual Life in Britain, 1850–1930* (Oxford: Oxford University Press, 1993); William Riley Porter, "Where Do English Departments Come From?" *College English* 28:5 (February 1967): 339–351.

109. Eric Bulson, *Novels, Maps, Modernity: The Spatial Imagination, 1850-2000* (New York: Routledge, 2007), 4.

110. M. F. A. Husband, *A Dictionary of the Characters in The Waverley Novels of Sir Walter Scott* (London: George Routledge and Sons, Limited, 1910), ii.

111. See Thomas Pavel, *Fictional Worlds* (Cambridge, MA: Harvard University Press, 1989); Lubomir Doležel, *Heterocosmica: Fiction and Possible Worlds* (Baltimore, MD: Johns Hopkins University Press, 2000).

112. Georg Lukács, Bertolt Brecht, Ernst Bloch, Theodor Adorno, Max Horkheimer, Leo Löwenthal, and Walter Benjamin were among those who made fictions central to their reinterpretations. See Martin Jay, *The Dialectical Imagination: A History of the Frankfurt School and the Institute of Social Research, 1923–1950* (Berkeley: University of California Press, 1996); Eugene Lunn, *Marxism and Modernism: An Historical Study of Lukács, Brecht, Benjamin, and Adorno* (Berkeley: University of California Press, 1984).

113. Boellstorff, 6.

114. Editorial, *Wonder Stories* 2:2 (July 1930): 181.

115. Fredric Jameson argued that "the conventional high-cultural repudiation of S[cience] F[iction]" has to do with middle-class fears of the power of the imagination to challenge the status quo: "We must here identify a kind of generic revulsion, in which this form and narrative discourse is the object of psychic resistance as a whole and the target of a kind of literary 'reality principle.'" Fredric Jameson, *Archaeologies of the Future: The Desire Called Utopia and Other Science Fictions* (London: Verso, 2005), xiv, fn. 9.

116. Letter, *Amazing Stories Quarterly* 1:4 (Fall 1928): 574.

117. Pierre Bourdieu, *Distinction: A Social Critique of the Judgment of Taste* trans. Richard Nice (Cambridge, MA: Harvard University Press, 1985); Lawrence W. Levine, *Highbrow/*

Lowbrow: The Emergence of Cultural Hierarchy in America (Cambridge, MA: Harvard University Press); Andrew Ross; Brantlinger, *Bread and Circuses.*

118. Edmund Wilson, *Classics and Commercials: A Literary Chronicle of the Forties* (New York: Macmillan, 1950), 289.

119. Ibid., 290.

120. Edmund Wilson, "Oo, Those Awful Orcs!" *The Nation* CLXXXII (April 14, 1956): 312. I owe the "Bunny" observation to a conversation with Haun Saussy.

121. Michael Shermer, *Why People Believe Weird Things: Pseudoscience, Superstition, and Other Confusions of Our Time* (New York: W. H. Freeman, 1997), 5–6.

122. T. J. Reed, *Thomas Mann: The Uses of Tradition* (Oxford: Oxford University Press, 1974).

123. Bloom, 211.

124. Jorge Luis Borges, "Tlön, Uqbar, Orbis Tertius," in *Collected Fictions*, trans. Andrew Hurley (New York: Viking, 1998), 68–81.

125. Ibid., 81.

126. Ibid..

127. Robert Lindner, *The Fifty-Minute Hour: A Collection of True Psychoanalytic Tales* (New York: Other Press, 2002), 283.

128. Ibid.

129. Jannick Storm, "An Interview with J. G. Ballard." *Speculation*, February, 1969, 4–8, http://www.jgballard.ca/interviews/jgb_jannick_storm_interview.html (accessed March 26, 2010).

130. For a discussion of virtual realities and their portrayal in mass culture, see Janet H. Murray, *Hamlet on the Holodeck: The Future of Narrative in Cyberspace* (New York: The Free Press, 1997).

131. For a nonfiction essay on creating imaginary worlds, see Poul Anderson, "Nature: Laws and Surprises," in *Mindscapes: The Geographies of Imagined Worlds*, ed. George E. Slusser and Eric Rabkin (Carbondale: Southern Illinois University Press, 1989), 3–15.

132. Poul Anderson, "The Queen of Air and Darkness," *The Magazine of Fantasy & Science Fiction* 40:4 (April 1971): 31.

133. Ibid., 44.

134. Ibid.

135. Poul Anderson, "The Saturn Game," *Analog Science Fiction/ Science Fact* 150:2 (February 1981): 27.

136. Ibid., 31.

137. Ibid., 46.

138. Ibid., 53–54.

CHAPTER 2

The first epigraph is from Oscar Wilde, "The Decay of Lying: An Observation," in his *The Soul of Man Under Socialism and Selected Critical Prose*, ed. Linda Dowling (New York: Penguin Books, 2001), 166. The second epigraph is from Delmore Schwartz, "In Dreams Begin Responsibilities," in his *In Dreams Begin Responsibilities and Other Stories* (New York: New Directions, 1978), 1.

1. For an overview linking Aestheticism, Symbolism, and Decadence, see Dennis Denisoff, "Decadence and Aestheticism," in Marshall, 31–52.

2. Wilson, *Axel's Castle*, 22–23; Leon Chai, *Aestheticism* (New York: Columbia University Press, 1990).

3. Charles Baudelaire, *Artificial Paradises* (Harrowgate: Broadwater House, 1999).

4. Arthur Symons's description of *À Rebours*, cited in George Schoolfield, *A Baedeker of Decadence: Charting a Literary Fashion, 1884–1927* (New Haven, CT: Yale University Press, 2003), 5.

5. Joris-Karl Huysmans, *Against Nature*, trans. Robert Baldick (New York: Penguin Books, 2003), 21–22.

6. Ibid., 204. In later years Huysmans rejected this view and returned to the Catholicism of his childhood.

7. Quoted in Scaff, 103.

8. Contemporary critics often referred to a "new" form of "romance," such as the title of an 1887 review of Haggard's *She* by Augustus Moore: "Rider Haggard and 'The New School of Romance.'" See Michael Saler, "Clap If You Believe in Sherlock Holmes': Mass Culture and the Re-Enchantment of Modernity, c.1890–c.1940," *Historical Journal* 43:6 (September 2003): 599–622. Anna Vaninskaya has usefully elaborated on this movement in "The Late-Victorian Romance Revival: A Generic Excursus," *English Literature in Transition* 51:1 (January 2008): 57–79.

9. Some critics, such as Patrick Brantlinger, have argued that these late nineteenth century works represented a reaction against realism and return to the gothic. But, as Nicholas Daly notes in his rebuttal to this line of argument, this was not how contemporary critics envisaged these works, a finding my own research supports. Brantlinger, *The Reading Lesson*, 171; 209; Nicholas Daly, *Modernism, Romance, and the Fin-de-Siècle: Popular Fiction and British Culture, 1880–1914* (Cambridge: Cambridge University Press, 1999), 12.

10. [Andrew Lang and Walter Herries Pollock], *He* (London: Longmans, Green and Co., 1887), n.p.

11. Quoted in Ellis, 119.

12. Quoted in Morton Cohen, *Rider Haggard: His Life and Works* (London: Hutchinson and Co., 1960), 117.

13. "The Fall of Fiction," *The Fortnightly Review* XLIV (September 1, 1888): 333.

14. Morton Cohen, 102; 116.

15. "Modern Men," *The Scots Observer* (April, 27 1889): 631–632.

16. "The Old Saloon," *Contemporary Review* (February, 1887): 303–303.

17. Andrew Lang, "Realism and Romance," *Contemporary Review* LII (November, 1887): 683.

18. "Modern Marvels," *The Spectator* (October 17, 1885): 1365.

19. "The Fall of Fiction," 333.

20. H. Rider Haggard, *The Days of My Life*, vol. 2 (London: Longmans, Green and Co., Ltd., 1926), 90–91.

21. Robert Louis Stevenson, "A Gossip on Romance," in *The Lantern-Bearers and Other Essays* (New York: Farrar Straus Giroux, 1988), 179.

22. For an analysis of paratexts, see Gérard Genette, *Paratexts: Thresholds of Interpretation*, trans. Jane E. Lewin (Cambridge: Cambridge University Press, 1997); for fascinating examples, see Kevin Jackson, *Invisible Forms: A Guide to Literary Curiosities* (New York: St. Martin's Press, 2000).

23. Kenneth Silverman notes that Poe modified the gothic tradition by using realistic details, many culled from contemporary nonfiction accounts. Kenneth Silverman, *Edgar A. Poe: Mournful and Never-ending Remembrance* (New York: Harper Collins, 1991), 150; 471; 473.

24. H. Rider Haggard, *The Days of My Life*, vol. 1 (London: Longmans, Green and Co., Ltd., 1926), 242.

25. Thomas Disch has made a convincing case for considering Poe to be the "father" of science fiction. Thomas Disch, *The Dreams Our Stuff Is Made Of: How Science Fiction Conquered the World* (New York: The Free Press, 1998), 32–56. Brian Stableford also sees Poe as presenting "the first tentative manifesto for modern SF." Stableford, 19. See also John Tresch, "Extra! Extra! Poe Invents Science Fiction!" in *The Cambridge Companion to Edgar Allan Poe* ed. Kevin J. Hayes (Cambridge: Cambridge University Press, 2002.)

26. Edgar Allan Poe, "Diddling Considered as One of the Exact Sciences," in his *Poetry and Tales*, ed. Francis Quinn (New York: The Library of America, 1984), 607; Harris, *Humbug*, 69–88.

27. Silverman, 137.

28. Adam Roberts, *The History of Science Fiction* (New York: Palgrave MacMillan, 2007), 103.

29. Herbert Lottman, *Jules Verne: An Exploratory Biography* (New York: St. Martin's Press, 1996), x.

30. Jules Verne, "The Leader of the Cult of the Unusual," in *The Edgar Allan Poe Scrapbook* ed. Peter Haining, trans. I. O. Evans (New York: Schocken Books, 1978), 56–73.

31. For a consideration of Verne's use of maps and other illustrations, see Terry Harpold, "Verne's Cartographies," *Science Fiction Studies* 95 (March 2005): 18–42.

32. Jean-Paul Sartre, *The Words* (New York: Vintage Books, 1981 [1964]), 73–74.

33. Poe called his stories about Dupin "Tales of Ratiocination," and used the term in a review of Hawthorne. See Edgar Allan Poe, *Essays and Reviews*, ed. Gary Richard Thompson (New York: The Library of America, 1984), 573. In terms of Aestheticism and science, Villiers de l'Isle Adam's *The Future Eve* (1886) was cast in the mode of Verne, but its account of the creation of an android and technological "artificial paradises" was ambivalent about the futuristic technology it portrayed. For more on Aestheticism and science, see Richard Candida-Smith, *Mallarmé's Children: Symbolism and the Renewal of Experience* (Berkeley: University of California Press, 2000).

34. Regenia Gagnier, *Idylls of the Marketplace: Oscar Wilde and the Victorian Public* (Stanford, CA: Stanford University Press, 1987).

35. W. E. Henley, editor of the *National Observer* and an influential proponent of the New Romance, was deemed by contemporaries to be a leader of the "counter-decadence." Jerome Hamilton Buckley, *William Ernest Henley: A Study in the "Counter-Decadence" of the 'Nineties* (Princeton, NJ: Princeton University Press, 1945).

36. Oscar Wilde, "The Decay of Lying: An Observation," in his *The Soul of Man Under Socialism & Selected Critical Prose*, 176.

37. Lang, "Realism and Romance," 689.

38. Gagnier, 5.

39. The Goncourt brothers early identified in Poe those qualities that would excite the authors of the New Romance and their followers in the mystery and science fiction genres. As they wrote in their journal for July 16, 1856: "After reading Edgar Allan Poe. Something the critics have not noticed: a new literary world, pointing to the literature of the twentieth century. Scientific miracles, fables on the pattern A + B; a clear-sighted, sickly literature. No more poetry, but analytic fantasy." Edmond de Goncourt and Jules de Goncourt, *Pages from the Goncourt Journal*, trans. and ed. Robert Baldick (New York: New York Review Books, 2007 [1962]), 19–20.

40. Robert Baldick, *The Life of J.-K. Huysmans* (Cambridgeshire: Dedalus Books, 2006 [1955]), 205.

41. Stevenson, "A Gossip on Romance," 172.

42. H. P. Lovecraft, letter, in H. P. Lovecraft, *Selected Letters II: 1925–1929*, ed. August Derleth and Donald Wandrei (Sauk City: Arkham House, 1968), 276.

43. Kevin John Young, "Tolkien and Pre-Raphaelitism," *Mallorn* 35 (October 1978): 6–7; John Garth, *Tolkien and the Great War: The Threshold of Middle-earth* (Boston, MA: Houghton Mifflin, 2003), 14.

44. C. S. Lewis, *The Collected Letters of C. S. Lewis: Volume II*, ed. Walter Hooper (New York: HarperCollins, 2004), 631.

45. Tolkien, *The Letters*, 257.

46. E. R. Eddison, letter, Oxford University, Bodleian Library Special Collections, MS. Eng Let. c/233.

47. Tolkien, *The Letters*, 257.
48. Robert Louis Stevenson, "Treasure Island," in his *My First Book* (London: Chatto & Windus, 1897), 307–308.
49. Ibid., 308.
50. Tolkien, *The Letters*, 177.
51. Gerald R. Hayes, "TWO," *Civil Service Arts Magazine* (August-October 1930), n.p.
52. C. S. Lewis, *The Collected Letters: Volume II*, 560.
53. Leon Meadow, Robert Newman, and Dorothy Bachrach, letter, Oxford University, Bodleian Library Special Collections, MS. Eng Let. c/231.
54. Hilaire Belloc, "On Not Reading Books, *The New Statesman* 28:711 (December 11, 1926): 273–274.
55. Neil Harris, "Iconography and Intellectual History: The Halftone Effect," in his *Cultural Excursions: Marketing Appetites and Cultural Tastes in Modern America* (Chicago, IL: The University of Chicago Press, 1990), 307.
56. Guy Debord, *The Society of the Spectacle* (Cambridge, MA: Zone Books, 1994).
57. Morton Cohen, 91; Peter Berresford Ellis, *H. Rider Haggard: A Voice from the Infinite* (London: Routledge and Kegan Paul, 1978), 112.
58. Ellis, 108.
59. Haggard, *She*, 3.
60. Ibid., 10.
61. Quoted in Ellis, 109.
62. For an examination of the issue of parody, pastiches, and copyright law, see Donald A. Redmond, *Sherlock Holmes Among the Pirates: Copyright and Conan Doyle in America, 1890–1930* (Westport, CT: Greenwood Press, 1990).
63. Lang and Pollock, *He*, 15.
64. Ibid., 29.
65. John Uri Lloyd, *Etidorhpa or The End of the Earth* (Cincinnati, OH: John Uri Lloyd, 1895), vii.
66. Ibid., 1.
67. Joseph M. Brown, *Astyanax: An Epic Romance of Ilion, Atlantis, and Amaraca* (New York: Broadway Publishing Company, 1907), xi.
68. Ibid., n.p.
69. Arthur Conan Doyle, *The Annotated Lost World*, annotated by Roy Pilot and Alvin Rodin (Indianapolis, IN: Wessex Press, 1996), 252.
70. Arthur Conan Doyle, *A Life in Letters*, ed. Jon Lellenberg, Daniel Stashower, & Charles Foley (New York: The Penguin Press, 2007), 583.
71. Rudyard Kipling, *With the Night Mail: A Story of 2000 A. D. (Together With Extracts From The Contemporary Magazine In Which It Appeared)* (New York: Doubleday, Page and Co., 1909), 70.
72. Ibid., 39.
73. Ibid., n.p.
74. Anna Vaninskaya argues that formalist and historical discussions of literary "genres" in the nineteenth century are problematic because of the protean and overlapping forms of fiction produced in this period. With the establishment of marketing genres in the twentieth century, however, these works could be viewed retrospectively as fitting within such genre categories. Vaninskaya, 60–61.
75. Conan Doyle, *A Life in Letters*, 554.
76. Francois-Eugene Vidocq, Wilkie Collins, and Charles Dickens were among those who contributed to the form, and the Sherlock Holmes short stories of the 1890s incited a publishing craze for fictional sleuths. For a sampling of the many imitators of Holmes that appeared in contemporary magazines, see Hugh Greene, *The Rivals of Sherlock Holmes:*

Early Detective Stories (New York: Pantheon, 1970). Holmes's success was one of the many catalysts for the genre of detective fiction. For an overview, see Charles J. Rzepka, *Detective Fiction* (Cambridge: Polity Press, 2005); Jess Nevins, "A Good Enough Man For Any World: The 19th Century Roots of Hardboiled Detective Fiction." *The Back Alley*, http://www.backalleywebzine.com/ (accessed November 23, 2007).

77. Peter Nicholls, "History of SF," in *The Encyclopedia of Science Fiction*, ed. John Clute and Peter Nicholls (New York: St. Martin's Press, 1993), 567–574.

78. Gary Westfahl, "'The Jules Verne, H. G. Wells, and Edgar Allan Poe Type of Story': Hugo Gernsback's History of Science Fiction," *Science Fiction Studies* 19:3 (November 1992): 340.

79. Hugo Gernsback, "A New Sort of Magazine," *Amazing Stories* 1:1 (April 1926): 3.

80. "Edgar Allan Poe Father of Scientifiction," *Amazing Stories* 3:6 (September 1928): n.p.

81. Editor's note for the reprint of Poe's "Mesmeric Revelation," *Amazing Stories* 1:2 (May 1926): 124.

82. Mike Ashley, *The Gernsback Days* (Holicong, PA: The Wildside Press, 2004).

83. In addition to reprinting Poe's "Hans Pfaall" in *Amazing*, Gernsback reprinted Richard Adams Locke's "The Moon Hoax," which in its original publication in the New York newspaper *The Sun* in 1835 fooled many readers into believing that it was an authentic account of alien life on the moon. Some *Amazing* readers objected to this reprint precisely because it was originally a hoax, but Gernsback defended it by noting the congruities between the new genre and the reality effects of nineteenth-century hoaxes: "Scientifiction, to our mind, is fiction plus science. Both of these requirements, we believe, were represented in a most unusual manner in "The Moon Hoax." Editor, "Discussions," *Amazing Stories* 1:12 (March 1927): 1181. For an account of The Moon Hoax, see Matthew Goodman, *The Sun and the Moon: The Remarkable True Account of Hoaxers, Showmen, Dueling Journalists and Lunar Man Bats in Nineteenth Century New York* (New York: Basic Books, 2008).

84. Warner, Jr., 35–36.

85. C. E. Caulkins, "Editorials From Our Readers," *Amazing Stories Quarterly* 1:4 (Fall 1928): 571.

86. "What Do You Know?" *Amazing Stories* 3:2 (May 1928): 109.

87. For a synoptic account of science fiction magazines in Britain and America, see Mike Ashley's "History of the Science Fiction Magazines": Mike Ashley, *The Time Machines: The Story of the Science-Fiction Pulp Magazines from the Beginning to 1950* (Liverpool: Liverpool University Press, 2000); Mike Ashley, *Transformations: The Story of the Science-Fiction Magazines from 1950 to 1970* (Liverpool: Liverpool University Press, 2005); Mike Ashley, *Gateways to Forever: The Story of the Science-Fiction Magazines from 1970 to 1980* (Liverpool: Liverpool University Press, 2007).

88. Philip Waite, letter, *Wonder Stories* 2:6 (November 1930): 619. However, the historian Paul Carter spoke to one of these advisors, who "informed me that Gernsback regularly sent him story manuscripts and took due account of his criticisms." Paul Carter, *The Creation of Tomorrow: Fifty Years of Magazine Science Fiction* (New York: Columbia University Press, 1977), 11.

89. Editor, *Amazing Stories* 3:4 (July 1928): 373.

90. I agree with Adam Roberts's perspicacious contention that, "To the extent that SF enters into the discourse of 'science' (as it very frequently does) the best way of theorizing this is as a Feyerabendian proliferation of theories rather than a notional uniformity or 'truth.'" Roberts, 18. My point is simply that the new marketing genre overtly embraced reason and the established conventions of the scientific method as avenues to modern enchantment, rather than fearing them as sources of disenchantment. While there was interest in esotericism and pseudo-science, particularly as expressed in the works of Charles Fort, my impression is that many fans entertained these with the ironic imagination but didn't take

them as seriously as they did the methods and findings of institutionalized science. This impression is based on the numerous letters published in science fiction magazines that condemned grosser forms of pseudo-scientific explanations, including the "Shaver Mystery" discussed later. For an account of Charles Fort, see Jim Steinmeyer, *Charles Fort* (New York: Tarcher, 2008).

91. Quoted in Patrick Brantlinger, *Rule of Darkness: British Literature and Imperialism, 1830–1914* (Ithaca, NY: Cornell University Press, 1988), 234–235.
92. Miles J. Breuer, letter, *Amazing Stories* 4:6 (September 1929): 569.
93. Response by editor, ibid., 571.
94. Paul Carter, 17.
95. Editor, *Wonder Stories* 2:7 (December 1930): 765.
96. Walter L. Reeves, letter, *Astounding Stories* (June 1936): 159.
97. For the science fiction fans' adverse reaction to the "Shaver Mysteries," see Warner, Jr., 180–185.
98. Editor, "Blazing New Trails," *Astounding Stories* 17:6 (August 1936): 153.
99. Emma Ploner, letter, *Amazing Stories* 4:3 (June 1929): 279.
100. Lawrence Sutin, *Divine Invasions: The Life of Philip K. Dick* (New York: Carroll & Graf, 2005), 3. In 1973, Arthur C. Clarke stated, "Any sufficiently advanced technology is indistinguishable from magic." See http://en.wikipedia.org/wiki/Clarke%27s_three_laws (accessed February 10, 2010).
101. Editor, "History to Come," *Astounding Science-Fiction* 27:3 (May 1941): 5.
102. Ibid., 6.
103. Quoted in Moskowitz, 123.
104. Henry Kuttner, "Reader, I Hate You!" *Super Science Stories* 4:4 (May 1943): 48.
105. See Richard A. Hoen, letter, and John W. Campbell's response, *Astounding Science-Fiction* 62:3 (November 1948): 111–112.
106. Science Fiction is one of the most self-referential of the genres; many works cite other fictional worlds, characters, authors, etc. For an encyclopedic listing, see the Recursive Science Fiction website at http://www.nesfa.org/Recursion/index.htm (accessed November 26, 2007). The science fiction author Philip José Farmer brought together a wide-range of literature's fantastic characters into a single family tree—detailing how Tarzan, Doc Savage, The Scarlet Pimpernel, Sherlock Holmes, and many others were related. This effort has since become a popular hobby among fans, notably at The Wold Newton Universe website, named after Farmer's original invention: see http://www.pjfarmer. com/woldnewton/Pulp.htm (accessed November 26, 2007). See also Win Scott Eckert, ed., *Myths for the Modern Age: Philip José Farmer's Wold Newton Universe* (Austin, TX: MonkeyBrain Books, 2005).
107. The "reading revolution" thesis and its critics is discussed in Stephen Colclough, "Recovering the Reader: Commonplace Books and Diaries as Sources of Reading Experience," *Publishing History* XLIV (Fall 1998): 5–37.
108. Private correspondence from Mike Ashley, historian of popular fiction magazines in America and Britain, August 29, 2002.
109. Henry Jenkins argues that a central function of fan communities is to address "the desire for affiliation, friendship, community." Tulloch and Jenkins, 39.
110. Arthur S. Hoffman, "Camp-Fire," *Adventure* (December 18, 1917): 183–184.
111. Editor, "Looking Ahead," *Astounding Stories* (July 1936): 155.
112. Elihu Schott, letter, *Amazing Science Quarterly* 1:4 (Fall 1928): 573.
113. Alan Mannion, letter, *Planet Stories* 2:5 (Winter 1943): 119–120.
114. Habermas, *Structural Transformation*; Craig Calhoun, ed., *Habermas and the Public Sphere* (Cambridge, MA: MIT Press, 1993).
115. Carl Frederick Gulley, letter, *Astounding Science-Fiction* 24:4 (September 1939): 100.

116. The Baker Street Irregulars, for example, did not "invest" women until 1991. Their policy of excluding women from membership and attending their annual dinner led to a protest by a group of undergraduate women in 1968, which formed their own affiliated society, "The Adventuresses of Sherlock Holmes." Their persistent agitation for equality within the BSI was instrumental in changing the long-standing policy. See Susan Rice, "Dubious and Questionable Memories: A History of the Adventuresses of Sherlock Holmes," *The Baker Street Journal 2004 Christmas Annual* (December 2004): 3–59. Some of the "scion" or affiliated societies admitted women much earlier, or established auxiliaries for women that would meet in tandem with the male societies. "The Scowrers" of San Francisco, for example, formed a female auxiliary, "The Molly Maguires," in 1944. See Marks, 93–95. Recent research reveals that women, while a minority, were an influential segment of the early science fiction community in both the United States and the UK. See Helen Merrick, *The Secret Feminist Cabal: A Cultural History of Science Fiction Feminisms* (Seattle, WA: Aqueduct Press, 2009); Eric Leif Davin, *Partners in Wonder: Women and the Birth of Science Fiction 1926–1965* (Lanham, MD: Lexington Books, 2006).

117. Arthur S. Hoffman, "Camp-Fire," *Adventure* (March 3, 1918): x.

118. Editor, *Wonder Stories* 2:8 (January 1931): 903.

119. Frank Sicari, letter, *Wonder Stories* 2:6 (November 1930): 617.

120. Leland Sapiro, letter, *Planet Stories* 4:2 (Spring 1949): 128.

121. Ibid.

122. By the 1940s, it has been estimated that there may have been a few thousand active science fiction fans in the United States, with perhaps five hundred being prominent. Warner, Jr., 24–25. British fandom was smaller, especially during the war years. Science fiction historian Mike Ashley estimates that prior to 1939 there were less than one hundred SF fans in Britain who regularly attended meetings of clubs and conventions, although there was undoubtedly a larger contingent who wrote letters to SF magazines or who subscribed to international organizations such as the Science Fiction League. The war curtailed the limited fan activity in Britain, but it grew appreciably after 1945 and continued to have ties with American fandom. (Mike Ashley, private communication, February 2, 2010.) For a history of British science fiction fandom, see Rob Hansen's *Then* at http://ansible.co.uk/Then/ (accessed August 1, 2010).

122. Darko Suvin, *Metamorphoses of Science Fiction: On the Poetics and History of a Literary Genre* (New Haven, CT: Yale University Press, 1979). See also Patrick Parrinder, ed., *Learning From Other Worlds: Estrangement, Cognition, and the Politics of Science Fiction and Utopias* (Durham, NC: Duke University Press, 2001).

124. Julius Schwartz, letter, *Astounding Stories* 16:6 (February 1936): 159.

125. John Rieder, *Colonialism and the Emergence of Science Fiction* (Middletown, CT: Wesleyan University Press, 2008), 24; John Clute, *Scores: Reviews 1993–2003* (Essex: Beccon Publications, 2003), 214–215.

126. Editor, "The Reader Speaks," *Wonder Stories* 2:5 (October 1930): 473; Editor, "The Reader Speaks," *Wonder Stories* 2:9 (February 1931): 1046. David Lasser, who engaged in communist politics at this time, was managing editor of *Wonder Stories*, and it is likely that the "Editor's comments" were his.

127. Editor, "Into the Future," *Astounding Stories* 20:2 (October 1937): 57.

128. John Higgins, letter, *Planet Stories* 4:3 (Summer 1949): 2.

129. She has usefully compiled some staggering figures: in the United States, there are 183 million active gamers (those who report playing computer or video games for, on average, thirteen hours a week); in the Middle East, there are 4 million online gamers; in Russia, 10 million; in India, 105 million; in China, 200 million; in Mexico, 10 million; in Central and South America, 15 million; in South Korea, 17 million. McGonigal, 3.

130. Press Release, Blizzard Entertainment, http://us.blizzard.com/en-us/company/press/pressreleases.html?101007 (accessed January 18, 2011.)

131. King and Borland; Gary Gygax, "On the Influence of J. R. R. Tolkien on the D&D and AD&D Games," *Dragon* 95 (1985): 12–13.

132. For the social world of Dungeons & Dragons, see Gary Alan Fine, *Shared Fantasy: Role-Playing Games as Social Worlds* (Chicago, IL: The University of Chicago Press, 1983 [2002]); Ethan Gilsdorf, *Fantasy Freaks and Gaming Geeks: An Epic Quest for Reality Among Role Players, Online Gamers, and Other Dwellers of Imaginary Realms* (Guilford, CT: Lyons Press, 2010).

133. Daniel Punday, "Creative Accounting: Role-Playing Games, Possible-World Theory, and the Agency of the Imagination," *Poetics Today* 26:1 (Spring 2005): 113.

134. King and Borland, 47.

135. William Sims Bainbridge notes that the magical world of World of Warcraft is also a highly rational world, and, in this respect, it follows the precedent of the fantasy pulp magazine *Unknown*, which was edited by John W. Campbell during the late 1930s and early 1940s. Bainbridge, 75–76. Ian Bogost maintains that video games can "disrupt and change fundamental attitudes and beliefs about the world, leading to potentially significant long-term social change." Ian Bogost, *Persuasive Games: The Expressive Power of Videogames* (Cambridge, MA: MIT Press, 2007.)

136. King and Borland, 147.

137. Ibid., 165.

138. Ibid., 124.

139. "The Daedalus Gateway," http://www.nickyee.com/daedalus/gateway_demographics.html (accessed March 19, 2010.)

140. McGonigal cites some statistics about players in the United States current as of 2010: 40 percent of all gamers are women; the average age of game players is 35; 97 percent of youth play computer and video games; 69 percent of heads of household play these games; 25 percent of all gamers are over the age of fifty. McGonigal, 11.

141. Seth Schiesel, "In an Ever-Changing Galaxy, the Action's Starting to Get Intriguing," *New York Times* November 28, 2007, B1.

142. Seth Schiesel, "In a New Merger, Evidence of How Much the Gaming World Has Changed," *The New York Times* December 5, 2007, B3; Blizzard Entertainment Press Release, November 21, 2008, http://us.blizzard.com/en-us/company/press/pressreleases.html?081121 (accessed February 17, 2010.)

143. Guest, 15.

144. Serious games, which address real-world problems, are becoming increasingly prominent, as Jane McGonigal shows. She finds that these games can harness what Clay Shirky calls "cognitive surplus"—people's problem-solving abilities, which in the West are often applied during leisure time to fantasy games or other forms of recreation—to effect real-world outcomes. See McGonigal, 9; Shirky.

CHAPTER 3

The first epigraph is from Mary Warnock, *Imagination* (Berkeley: University of California Press, 1976), 196. The second epigraph is from Vincent Starrett, "The Singular Adventures of Martha Hudson," in *Baker Street Studies,* ed. H. W. Bell (London: Constable and Co., 1934), 103.

1. Arthur Conan Doyle, *The Coming of the Fairies* (London: Pavilion Books, 1997 [1922]), 7.

2. In the 1980s, the girls admitted that they faked the photographs using paper cutouts. Terry Staples, "The Cottingley Fairies," in *The Oxford Companion to Fairy Tales,* ed. Jack Zipes (New York: Oxford University Press, 2000), 109–10.

3. Daniel Stashower, *Teller of Tales: A Life of Sir Arthur Conan Doyle* (New York: Henry Holt, 1999), 356.

4. Richard Lancelyn Green, ed., *The Sherlock Holmes Letters* (London: Secker and Warburg, 1986), 28.

5. As Jacques Barzun noted, this "has happened in no other book and no other character in recent times. It's a phenomenon." "The Adventures of Sherlock Holmes: A Radio Discussion," in *The Baker Street Reader*, ed. Philip Shreffler (Westport, CT: Greenwood Press, 1984), 25.

6. S. C. Roberts, *Adventures with Authors* (Cambridge: Cambridge University Press, 1966), 228.

7. Harold Orel, ed., *Sir Arthur Conan Doyle: Interviews and Recollections* (London: Macmillan, 1991), 81.

8. G. K. Chesterton, "Sherlock Holmes The God," *G. K.'s Weekly* (February 21, 1935): 403–4.

9. Roberts, 231.

10. For a collection of Sherlockian and Conan Doyleian material in *The Bookman*, see *Sherlock Holmes, Conan Doyle & The Bookman: Pastiches, Parodies, Letters, Columns and Commentary from America's 'Magazine of Literature and Life' (1895–1933)*, ed. S. E. Dahlinger and Leslie S. Klinger (Indianapolis, IN: Gasogene Books, 2010).

11. Edgar W. Smith, ed., *Profile by Gaslight: An Irregular Reader About the Private Life of Sherlock Holmes* (New York: Simon & Schuster, 1944), vii.

12. Green, 40.

13. W. S. Baring-Gould, *Sherlock Holmes of Baker Street* (New York: Popular Library, 1963 [1962]), 10.

14. Oppenheim, 338–97; McCorristine, 210–217. For fin-de-siècle occultism as a "counter public sphere," whose members engaged in the "sanitization" of their claims by using the rhetoric of modern science, see Mark S. Morrisson, "The Periodical Culture of the Occult Revival: Esoteric Wisdom, Modernity and Counter Public Spheres," *Journal of Modern Literature* 31:2 (Winter 2008): 1–22.

15. As Jay Winter argued, "The Great War, the most 'modern' of wars, triggered an avalanche of the 'unmodern.' One salient aspect of this apparent contradiction is the wartime growth in spiritualism." Jay Winter, *Sites of Memory, Sites of Mourning: The Great War in European Cultural History* (Cambridge: Cambridge University Press, 1998 [1995]), 54. Terms like "tradition" and "modernity" are complex and not necessarily mutually exclusive; there were significant efforts to reconcile the two by intellectuals in the nineteenth and twentieth centuries. See Robert Alter, *Necessary Angels: Tradition and Modernity in Kafka, Benjamin, and Scholem* (Cambridge, MA: Harvard University Press, 1991). But this line of thought, arguably, was not the dominant one in Europe during the fin-de-siècle: contemporaries tended to see modernity and tradition as opposing one another. See Burrow, 112–13.

16. Arthur Conan Doyle, *The Complete Sherlock Holmes* (New York: Barnes and Noble, 1992), 176.

17. Ibid.

18. Ibid., 1034.

19. As Lorraine Daston and Peter Galison observed, "In notable contrast to earlier views . . . the public personas of artist and scientist polarized during this period . . . The scientific self of the mid-nineteenth century was perceived by contemporaries as diametrically opposed to the artistic self." Daston and Galison, *Objectivity*, 37.

20. Conan Doyle, *The Complete Sherlock Holmes*, 338–9.

21. Ibid., 347.

22. Poe, *Poetry and Tales*, 400.

23. Ibid., 691.

24. Conan Doyle, *The Complete Sherlock Holmes*, 435.

25. Quoted in Mark Berry, "Richard Wagner and the Politics of the Music-Drama," *The Historical Journal* 47:3 (September 2004): 678. For a consideration of European artists and writers who attempted to fuse the "two cultures" of science and art, see Wolf Lepenies, *Between Literature and Science: The Rise of Sociology* (Cambridge: Cambridge University Press, 1988).

26. Conan Doyle, *The Complete Sherlock Holmes*, 191.

27. Ibid., 317.

28. Green, 35.

29. Johan Huizinga, *Homo Ludens* (London: Paladin, 1970 [1938]), 233.

30. In addition to charting the emergence of a twentieth-century "play world" fostered by economic, social, and political factors, James E. Coombs finds that today the "mediational site of creative play is and will be the Internet . . . enthusiasts for the new medium find enchanted community and redemptive powers in the new technology of communications." James E. Coombs, *Play World: The Emergence of a New Ludic Age* (Westport, CT: Praeger, 2000), 115.

31. Lycett, 136. Conan Doyle himself was intrigued by Theosophy, but less impressed by Madame Blavatsky; he gave more credence to A. P. Sinnett, whom he met at this time. Conan Doyle, *Memories and Adventures*, 73–74.

32. Shreffler, 17.

33. Conan Doyle, *The Complete Sherlock Holmes*, 15–86.

34. Ibid., 98.

35. Ibid., 161.

36. T. S. Blakeney, *Sherlock Holmes: Fact or Fiction* (London: John Murray, 1932), 126.

37. Conan Doyle, *The Complete Sherlock Holmes*, 37.

38. Ibid., 162. Holmes also appears to be a "wizard" and a "sorcerer" to those who don't know his rational methods—see "The Adventure of the Abbey Grange" and "The Adventure of the Second Stain," respectively—and in "A Study in Scarlet" he admits his results, when left unexplained, could appear to be that of a "necromancer."

39. Jon Lellenberg observes that Moriarty, a desiccated professor of mathematics whose name connotes death, could represent the narrow instrumental rationality that Conan Doyle and his contemporaries found so disenchanting. Jon Lellenberg, private communication, June 26, 2010.

40. Conan Doyle, *The Complete Sherlock Holmes*, 901.

41. Ibid., 455–56.

42. Conan Doyle, *The Coming of the Fairies*, 32. Conan Doyle's Uncle Richard was a famous illustrator, who was known for his depictions of fairies; his father, Charles, was also interested in fairy lore and drew fairies while he was confined to a sanitarium. Arthur Conan Doyle's willingness to believe in fairies may thus have had personal as well as spiritual origins. See Martin Booth, *The Doctor, the Detective, and Arthur Conan Doyle: A Biography of Arthur Conan Doyle* (London: Hodder and Stoughton, 1997), 321.

43. Green, 4.

44. The General Post Office continued to receive letters for Holmes through at least the 1950s. Booth, 111.

45. Green, 64.

46. Editor, *Tit-Bits* 27 (October 27, 1894): 67.

47. Green, 143–44.

48. Ibid., 148.

49. Ibid., 173–74.

50. See, for example, "Some Inconsistencies of Sherlock Holmes," *The Bookman* XIV (January 1902): 446; Christopher Morley, "Notes on Baker Street," *The Saturday Review* (January 28, 1939): 12.

51. Orel, 79.

52. Editors could deliberately efface the distinction between fact and fiction in order to attract readers; at other times sensationalist fiction and reportage were juxtaposed in the same journal or newspaper. For examples of the blurring between sensational fiction and sensational reportage in the 1860s, see Deborah Wynne, *The Sensation Novel and the Victorian Family Magazine* (New York: Palgrave, 2001). And in Britain, at least, public education in the years immediately after the 1870 Education Act did not necessarily train students to distinguish different genres of writing. One historian maintains the schools tended to provide students with "an acquaintance with literacy rather than an effective command." David Vincent, *Literacy and Popular Culture: England 1750–1914* (Cambridge: Cambridge University Press, 1989), 90.

53. Orel, 80.

54. Green, 80.

55. Ibid., 28.

56. Stashower, 351.

57. Ronald A. Knox, *Essays in Satire* (London: Sheed and Ward, 1928 [1912]), 145–78.

58. For detailed histories of the essay's influence, see Nicholas Utechin, "From Piff-Pouff to Backnecke: Ronald Knox and 100 Years of 'Studies in the Literature of Sherlock Holmes,'" *The Baker Street Journal 2010 Christmas Annual* (Zionsville, IN: The Baker Street Irregulars, 2010); Michael J. Crowe, ed., *Ronald Knox and Sherlock Holmes: The Origin of Sherlockian Studies* (Indianapolis, IN: Gasogene Books, 2011).

59. Dorothy Sayers, Foreword to her *Unpopular Opinions* (London: Victor Gollancz, 1947), 7.

60. The London *Sherlock Holmes Journal* did not insist that Conan Doyle was fictional or merely a literary agent to the extent that the Bakers Street Irregulars and their *Baker Street Journal* did.

61. Franco Moretti suggests that Conan Doyle's detective stories may have become canonical, unlike those of his rivals, because of Conan Doyle's novel emphasis on the use of clues in the narrative. Franco Moretti, "The Slaughterhouse of Literature," *Modern Language Quarterly* 61:1 (March 2000): 207–27.

62. Shreffler, 26.

63. Starrett, "Dr. Bell and Dr. Black," 197.

64. Conan Doyle, *The Complete Sherlock Holmes*, 196.

65. Ibid., 177.

66. Joseph Bell, "Mr. Sherlock Holmes," *Baker Street Journal* 2:1 (Original Series, 1947): 48.

67. Chesterton, "A Defence of Detective Stories," 119. Holmes calls Watson's accounts of their adventures "little fairy-tales" in "The Adventure of the Empty House." For a comparison of mysteries with myths and fairy tales, see David Lehman, *The Perfect Murder: A Study in Detection* (Ann Arbor: Michigan University Press, 2000), 23–36.

68. Green, 79.

69. *Tit-Bits* 28 (June 8, 1895).

70. "The Diogenes Club of West Virginia," *Baker Street Journal* 6:3, New Series (July 1956): 176.

71. Blakeney, 120; Conan Doyle, *The Complete Sherlock Holmes*, 687. It's likely that Conan Doyle borrowed this phrase from the eminent physicist John Tyndall. Tyndall delivered an address in 1870 to the British Association for the Advancement of Science entitled "On the Scientific Use of the Imagination," which extolled "that creative power in which reason and imagination are united." Tyndall defended the disciplined use of the imagination against positivists who felt it should have no place: "There are Tories in science who regard Imagination as a faculty to be avoided rather than employed. They observe its action in weak vessels and are unduly impressed by its disasters . . . [Yet] nourished by knowledge patiently won; bounded and conditioned by cooperant Reason, Imagination becomes the

mightiest instrument of the physical discoverer." John Tyndall, *Scientific Use of the Imagination and Other Essays* (London: Longmans, Green, and Co., 1872), 6; 10. In 1895, Conan Doyle had to contend with Tyndall's widow Louisa, who was his immediate neighbor at his new home in Hindhead and objected to some of his building plans. Lycett, 232–33. See also Laura J. Snyder, "Sherlock Holmes: Scientific Detective," *Endeavour* 28:3 (September 2004): 104–8.

72. Smith, "The Editor's Gas-Lamp: Writings About the Writings," 64.

73. Frisby, *Fragments of Modernity.* For a response to this fear by a group of German scientists, who turned to biological holism in the interwar period as a way to reconcile modernity and enchantment, see Ann Harrington, *Reenchanted Science: Holism in German Culture From Wilhelm II to Hitler* (Princeton, NJ: Princeton University Press, 1996).

74. Conan Doyle, *The Complete Sherlock Holmes,* 23.

75. For example, here is how Holmes describes the evil Professor Moriarty: "He sits motionless, like a spider in the centre of its web, but that web has a thousand radiations, and he knows well every quiver of each of them." Ibid., 471.

76. Green, 78–79.

77. Shreffler, 39.

78. Edgar W. Smith, "The Implicit Holmes," *Baker Street Journal* 1:2 (Original Series, 1946): 112.

79. R. Ivar Gunn, "The Sherlock Holmes Society," *The British Medical Journal* (August 11, 1934).

80. Lellenberg, *Irregular Memories of the Thirties,* 228.

81. Ibid., 253.

82. Roberts, 231.

83. *Evening Standard,* May 3, 1968, reprinted in *Sherlock Holmes Journal Switzerland Tour Special Supplement* (1968), an insert in *The Sherlock Holmes Journal* 8:4 (Summer 1968), 33–34.

84. *Daily Mail,* May 2, 1968, reprinted in *Sherlock Holmes Journal Switzerland Tour Special Supplement,* 32.

85. Philip Howard, "Holmes Defeats Moriarty Official," *The Times,* May 2, 1968, reprinted in *Sherlock Holmes Journal Switzerland Tour Special Supplement,* 33.

86. Ibid.

87. *The Sun,* April 29, 1968, reprinted in *Sherlock Holmes Journal Switzerland Tour Special Supplement,* 33.

88. Lellenberg, *Irregular Crises of the Late 'Forties,* 48.

89. Lellenberg, *Irregular Memories of the Mid-'Forties,* 298.

90. Ibid., 49.

91. Lellenberg, *Irregular Memories if the Early 'Forties,* 263–64.

92. James Edward Holroyd, *Baker Street By-Ways* (New York: Otto Penzler Books, 1994 [1959]), 18; Charles Honce, "Sherlock Holmes in the News," in Smith, ed., *Profile by Gaslight,* 73.

93. Edgar W. Smith, "The Editor's Gas-Lamp: A Perspective on Scholarship," *Baker Street Journal* 3:1, New Series (January, 1953): n.p.

94. "The Sons of the Copper Beaches of Philadelphia," *Baker Street Journal* 3:2, New Series (April, 1953): 106.

95. Lellenberg, *Irregular Memories of the Mid 'Forties,* 261.

96. Vincent Starrett, *The Private Life of Sherlock Holmes* (New York: Otto Penzler Books, 1993 [1933]), 93. One exception to this—perhaps—consists of the science fiction pastiches of Holmes. Nevertheless, even though the narratives may take place in some future time, their ambience is often that of 1895.

97. For example, Christopher Morley was born in 1890, Dorothy Sayers in 1893, and Vincent Starrett in 1886.

98. Edgar W. Smith, foreword in his *Profile by Gaslight,* n.p.

99. A. A. Gilham, "Holmes in Advertising," *Sherlock Holmes Journal* 6:1 (1962): 18.

100. Conan Doyle, *The Complete Sherlock Holmes,* 980. Issues of both Sherlockian journals have become more open to associating the fictional world with the real one in recent years, perhaps as a result of New Historicist currents in the academy effecting Sherlockian scholarship. Certainly "Sherlock Holmes and Women of the '90s: A Feminist Perspective," which appeared in the *Baker Street Journal* in 2000, is one move toward contemporary relevance that was not often apparent in issues from the twentieth century. Similarly, the 2010 BBC Wales television series *Sherlock* wonderfully reinterpreted the great detective as a generation-X nonslacker. On the whole, however, the emphasis continues to be on taking the world of 221B Baker Street as autonomous.

101. Conan Doyle, *The Complete Sherlock Holmes,* 559.

102. Ibid., 257.

103. Ibid., 907.

104. Karl E. Beckson, *London in the 1890s: A Cultural History* (New York: W. W. Norton, 1992).

105. Lellenberg, *Irregular Memories of the 'Thirties,* 3.

106. "Obituary for Ivor Gunn," *Sherlock Holmes Journal* 1:4 (December 1953): n.p.

107. Lellenberg, *Irregular Memories of the Mid-'Forties,* 348. Organized Sherlock Holmes fans can no longer be called "few": in 1985, the Baker Street Irregulars had 288 affiliated "scion" societies in 40 states and several countries. Lellenberg, *Irregular Memories of the 'Thirties,* 87.

108. Edgar W. Smith, "The Editor's Gas Lamp," *Baker Street Journal* 4:4, New Series (October 1954): 195.

109. Friedrich Schiller, *On the Aesthetic Education of Man, in a Series of Letters,* trans. Elizabeth M. Wilkinson and L. A. Willoughby (Oxford: Oxford University Press, 1967).

110. Howard Haycraft, "The Profile Emerges," in Smith, *Profile by Gaslight,* 22.

CHAPTER 4

The first epigraph is from Charles Taylor, *A Secular Age* (Cambridge, MA: Harvard University Press, 2007), 368. The second is from H. P. Lovecraft, "The Shunned House," in his *The Fiction* (New York: Barnes and Noble, 2008), 292.

1. Richard Rorty, *Contingency, Irony, Solidarity* (Cambridge: Cambridge University Press, 1989), xiv.

2. Dan M. Kahan, Hank Jenkins-Smith, and Donald Braman, "Cultural Cognition of Scientific Consensus," (Cultural Cognition Project Working Paper No. 77, February 7, 2010), Social Science Research Network (SSRN), http://ssrn.com/abstract=1549444 (accessed June 4, 2010). See also Michael Shermer's discussion of "belief-dependent realism" in his *The Believing Brain: From Ghosts and Gods to Politics and Conspiracies* (New York: Henry Holt, 2011), 6–8.

3. August Derleth, a friend of Lovecraft's who did much to secure his posthumous reputation, called Lovecraft's self-professed "artificial mythology" the "Cthulhu Mythos" and proceeded to interpret it in essays and posthumous fictional "collaborations," as well as in original stories of his own. Because Derleth codified this mythology to reflect his own preoccupations, which were often at variance with those of Lovecraft, some scholars prefer to discuss the "Lovecraft Mythos" when dealing with Lovecraft's imaginary world. I have used the earlier term because it has entered common currency, although I am sympathetic to the rationale behind the more recent coinage. For a discussion of this issue and a literary history of the Mythos, see S. T. Joshi, *The Rise and Fall of the Cthulhu Mythos* (Poplar Bluff, MO: Mythos Books, 2008).

4. Fritz Leiber, "A Literary Copernicus" in *Lovecraft Remembered,* ed. Peter Cannon (Sauk City, WI: Arkham House, 1998), 455–66.

5. Lovecraft, *Selected Letters III,* 166.

6. Joshi, *Rise and Fall,* 8.

7. Lovecraft, *The Fiction,* 557–58.

8. Ibid., 602.

9. Ibid., 616.

10. Michel Houellebecq, *H. P. Lovecraft: Against the World, Against Life,* trans. Dorna Khazeni (San Francisco, CA: McSweeney's, 2005).

11. H. P. Lovecraft, *Letters to Rheinhart Kleiner,* ed. S. T. Joshi and David Schultz (New York: Hippocampus Press, 2005), 78.

12. H. P. Lovecraft, *Essential Solitude: The Letters of H. P. Lovecraft and August Derleth: 1926–1931,* ed. David E. Schultz and S. T. Joshi (New York: Hippocampus Press, 2008), 288–89.

13. Ibid., 225.

14. Lovecraft, *The Fiction,* 235–36.

15. Ibid., 336.

16. Lovecraft, *Selected Letters III,* 196.

17. Brian Lumley, introduction to his *The Taint and Other Novellas* (Burton, MI: Subterranean Press, 2007), 8.

18. David E. Schultz, "From Microcosm to Macrocosm: The Growth of Lovecraft's Cosmic Vision," in *An Epicure in the Terrible: A Centennial Anthology of Essays in Honor of H. P. Lovecraft,* ed. David E. Schultz and S. T. Joshi (Rutherford, NJ: Fairleigh Dickinson University Press, 1991), 212–13.

19. Lovecraft, *The Fiction,* 739.

20. Lovecraft, *Essential Solitude 1926–1931,* 234.

21. Lovecraft, *Letters to Alfred Galpin* (New York: Hippocampus Press, 2003), 170.

22. H. P. Lovecraft, *A Means to Freedom: The Letters of H. P. Lovecraft and Robert E. Howard: Volume One 1930–1932,* ed. S. T. Joshi, David E. Schultz, and Rusty Burke (New York: Hippocampus, 2009), 307.

23. Ibid., 78.

24. H. P. Lovecraft, *Lord of a Visible World: An Autobiography in Letters,* ed. S. T. Joshi and David E. Schultz (Athens, OH: Ohio University Press, 2000), 187.

25. Sonia H. Davis, *The Private Life of H. P. Lovecraft,* ed. S. T. Joshi (West Warwick, RI: Necronomicon Press, 1985), 11.

26. Lovecraft, *Lord of a Visible World,* 11.

27. Ibid., 19.

28. H. P. Lovecraft, *Miscellaneous Writings,* ed. S. T. Joshi (Sauk City, WI: Arkham House, 1995), 91.

29. Lovecraft, *Selected Letters II,* 306.

30. Lovecraft, *Selected Letters III,* 139.

31. Lovecraft, *Selected Letters IV,* ed. August Derleth and James Turner (Sauk City, WI: Arkham House, 1976), 57.

32. Lovecraft, *Selected Letters V,* ed. August Derleth and James Turner (Sauk City, WI: Arkham House, 1976), 352.

33. For a comparison of the similarities between Lovecraft's thought and the specifics of Husserl's phenomenology, see Graham Harman, "On the Horror of Phenomenology: Lovecraft and Husserl," in *Collapse: Philosophical Research and Development,* vol. 4, ed. Robin MacKay (Falmouth, England: Urbanomic, 2008), 333–64.

34. Lovecraft, *Letters to Rheinhart Kleiner,* 190.

35. Lovecraft, *The Fiction,* 14.

36. S. T. Joshi, *I Am Providence: The Life and Times of H. P. Lovecraft,* vol.1 (New York: Hippocampus Press, 2010), 262.

37. Lovecraft, *The Fiction*, 951.
38. Ibid., 982.
39. Lovecraft, *Selected Letters III*, 125.
40. Lovecraft, *Letters to Kleiner*, 189.
41. Ibid., 41.
42. Ibid., 55.
43. Lovecraft, *Selected Letters III*, 309.
44. Lovecraft, *Miscellaneous Writings*, 107.
45. Ibid., 104–5.
46. Lovecraft, *Selected Letters III*, 123–24.
47. Lovecraft, *Selected Letters II*, 276.
48. Lovecraft, *Selected Letters III*, 96.
49. Ibid., 449.
50. H. P. Lovecraft, *Letters to Henry Kuttner,* ed. David E. Schultz and S. T. Joshi (West Warwick, RI: Necronomicon Press, 1990), 14.
51. Ibid., 17.
52. Ibid., 193.
53. Lovecraft, *Lord of a Visible World,* 257–58.
54. Lovecraft, *Selected Letters IV,* 70.
55. Lovecraft, *Selected Letters III,* 433.
56. Lovecraft wrote to Willis Conover, "*Azif* is a real word. I cribbed it out of Henley's learned notes to *Vathek.*" H. P. Lovecraft and Willis Conover, *Lovecraft at Last* (Arlington, VA: Carrolton Clark, 1975), 107.
57. Lovecraft, *Selected Letters IV,* 387–88.
58. Ibid., 388.
59. Lovecraft, *Selected Letters II,* 316.
60. Lovecraft, *Selected Letters IV,* 388.
61. Lovecraft, *Miscellaneous Writings,* 110.
62. Lovecraft, *Selected Letters III,* 214.
63. Cannon, 389–90.
64. Lovecraft, *Selected Letters V,* 16.
65. Ibid.
66. Lovecraft, *Lord of a Visible World,* 207.
67. N. J. O'Neial, letter, *Weird Tales* 15:3 (March 1930): 292, 294.
68. Joshi, *A Weird Writer in Our Midst,* 82.
69. Ibid., 84.
70. Ibid., 85–86.
71. After Lovecraft's death, August Derleth codified the Mythos in a Christian-oriented direction that was foreign to Lovecraft's secular outlook. Similarly, some occultists maintain that Lovecraft's dreams, from which he at times derived his plots and imagery, tapped into the astral plane and expressed metaphysical realities—an interpretation contrary to Lovecraft's expressed views. See Donald Tyson, *The Dream World of H. P. Lovecraft: His Life, His Demons, His Universe* (Woodbury, MN: Llewellyn Publications, 2010).
72. Ken Faig, Jr., *De Tenebris* 1 (August 30, 1976): 2.
73. Edmund Wilson, "Tales of the Marvelous and the Ridiculous," in his *Classics and Commercials: A Literary Chronicle of the Forties* (New York: Macmillan, 1950), 286–290.
74. Lovecraft, *Lord of a Visible World,* 199.
75. Lovecraft, *The Fiction,* 169.
76. Lovecraft, *Selected Letters II,* 71.
77. Lovecraft, *Essential Solitude 1926–1931,* 303.

78. Lovecraft, *The Fiction*, 362.
79. Ibid., 858.
80. Ibid., 940.
81. Lovecraft, *Selected Letters II*, 306.
82. Joshi, *H. P. Lovecraft: A Life*, 70.
83. Lovecraft, *Selected Letters V*, 324.
84. Lovecraft, *Selected Letters III*, 156.
85. Lovecraft, *Selected Letters V*, 18.
86. Lovecraft, *A Means to Freedom, Volume One*, 459.
87. H. P. Lovecraft, *Collected Essays Volume 1: Amateur Journalism*, ed. S. T. Joshi (New York: Hippocampus Press, 2004), 273.
88. Warner Jr., 22.
89. Lovecraft, *Collected Essays Volume 1*, 92.
90. Ibid., 257, 273.
91. Lovecraft, *Selected Letters III*, 206.
92. Lovecraft, *Lord of a Visible World*, 198.
93. Ibid., 233.
94. Lovecraft, *A Means to Freedom, Volume 1*, 360.
95. Lovecraft, *Selected Letters V*, 64.
96. Lovecraft, *Essential Solitude, 1932–1937*, 753.
97. Ibid.
98. Lovecraft, *Essential Solitude, 1926–1931*, 162.
99. Lovecraft, *Selected Letters V*, 333.
100. Lovecraft, *The Fiction*, 798.
101. Ibid., 797.
102. Ibid.
103. Ibid.
104. Joshi, *H. P. Lovecraft: A Life*, 579.
105. Lovecraft, *Selected Letters V*, 407–8.
106. John Higgins, letter, *Planet Stories* 4:3 (Summer 1949): 105.
107. Ibid.
108. Paul D. Cox, letter, *Planet Stories* 3:11 (Summer 1948): 128.
109. Ray H. Ramsay, letter, *Planet Stories* 4:3 (Summer 1949): 108.
110. Edwin Sigler, letter, *Planet Stories* 4:2 (Spring 1949): 122.
111. Chad Oliver, letter, *Planet Stories* 3:12 (Fall 1948): 120; Don Wilson, letter, *Planet Stories* 3:12 (Fall 1948): 123.
112. Roy R. Wood, letter, *Planet Stories* 4:4 (Fall 1949): 109.
113. Editor, "The Vizigraph," *Planet Stories* 4:2 (Spring 1949): 128.
114. Editor, "The Vizigraph," *Planet Stories* 4:3 (Summer 1949): 108.

CHAPTER 5

Epigraph is from Charles Taylor, *A Secular Age* (Cambridge, MA: Harvard University Press, 2007), 595.

1. J. R. R. Tolkien, *Sauron Defeated: The End of the Third Age, The Notion Club Papers and the Drowning of Anadûné* (London: HarperCollins, 1992), 228.
2. In Tolkien's terminology, "Middle-earth" is actually a central land mass within the world of "Arda"; the former term corresponds largely to the Eurasian continent, the latter to Earth. For simplicity I will use the conventional term "Middle-earth" when discussing Tolkien's imaginary world, unless a more nuanced term is required.
3. Tolkien, *The Letters*, 148.

4. Tolkien, *Tolkien On Fairy-stories,* 65.
5. Even those aspects of the tale that seem most traditional—a premodern world of kings and nobles—could be given a contemporary inflection by Tolkien. For example, his belief that, "without the high and noble the simple and vulgar is utterly mean; and without the simple and ordinary the noble and heroic is meaningless," was an elegant expression of a prevailing view among the English middle classes. Ross McKibbin observed that, between 1918 and 1951, their notions of social hierarchy combined "the dignity of the old aristocracy with the democracy of the modern middle-classes." Tolkien, *The Letters,* 160; Ross McKibbin, *Classes and Cultures: England, 1918–1951* (New York: Oxford University Press, 2000), 530.
6. Henry Resnik, "The Hobbit-Forming World of J. R. R. Tolkien," *Saturday Evening Post,* July 2, 1966, 40.
7. Tolkien used this evocative phrase in a letter to his son Christopher. Tolkien, *The Letters,* 110.
8. J. R. R. Tolkien, *The Return of the King,* in *The Lord of the Rings* (Boston: Houghton Mifflin, 1987), 228.
9. J. R. R. Tolkien, *The Fellowship of the Ring,* in *The Lord of the Rings* (Boston: Houghton Mifflin, 1987), 244.
10. Tolkien, *Tolkien On Fairy-stories,* 55.
11. Ibid., 35.
12. Ibid., 55.
13. Ibid., 64.
14. Quoted in Garth, 312.
15. Charles Spinosa and Hubert L. Dreyfus, "Two Kinds of Antiessentialism and Their Consequences," *Critical Inquiry* 22:4 (Summer 1996): 748.
16. Ibid., 757.
17. Ibid., 738.
18. Ibid., 737.
19. Tolkien, *Tolkien On Fairy-stories,* 52.
20. For the activities of the National Front, see a report by Jessica Yates in *Amon Hen* 74 (July 1985): 24; Iwan Rhys Morus, "Editorial," *Amon Hen* 76 (November 1985): 3. For the interest in Tolkien's works by Italian neo-fascists, see Roger Griffin, "Revolts Against the Modern World: The Blend of Literary and Historical Fantasy in the Italian New Right," *Literature and History* 11:1 (Spring 1985): 101–23.
21. Martin Kerr, "J. R. R. Tolkien and 'That Noble Northern Spirit,'" *White Power* (January/ February 1979), 10, Marquette University Special Collections, JRRT Series 5, Box 1, Folder 28.
22. Candice Fredrick and Sam McBride, *Women Among the Inklings* (Westport, CT: Greenwood Press, 2001), 20. The fact that the Inklings restricted their membership to men doesn't disqualify it as a public sphere of the imagination for its time; many social clubs and networks in Britain and America during the interwar years were limited to men. As we have seen, this was true for most Sherlock Holmes societies in America.
23. Shippey relates one way that the double consciousness of the ironic imagination became habitual for nineteenth-century philologists: "The whole of their science conditioned them to the acceptance of what might be called '*' or 'asterisk-reality,' that which no longer existed but could with 100 percent certainty be inferred . . . In a sense, the non-existence of the most desired objects of study created a romance of its own." Tom Shippey, *The Road to Middle-earth: How J. R. R. Tolkien Created a New Mythology* (Boston: Houghton Mifflin, 2003), 21–22.
24. Humphrey Carpenter, *Tolkien: A Biography* (Boston, MA: Houghton Mifflin, 1977), 46; Tolkien, "Mythopoeia" (1931), "*Mythopoeia,*" http://home.ccil.org/~cowan/mythopoeia.html (accessed February 12, 2010).

25. Tolkien, *The Letters*, 144.

26. See Jonathan Sheehan, *The Enlightenment Bible: Translation, Scholarship, Culture* (Princeton, NJ: Princeton University Press, 2007).

27. J. R. R. Tolkien, *The Legend of Sigurd & Gudrún*, ed. Christopher Tolkien (Boston, MA: Houghton Mifflin Harcourt, 2009), 17. Tolkien's sense that Christianity contributed to modern disenchantment presaged current theories that stress this point. In addition to the works of Hans Blumenberg and Charles Taylor already cited, see Marcel Gauchet, *The Disenchantment of the World*, trans. Oscar Burge (Princeton, NJ: Princeton University Press, 1997); Michael Gillespie, *The Theological Origins of Modernity* (Chicago, IL: University of Chicago Press, 2008).

28. Tolkien, *The Legend of Sigurd*, 26.

29. Ibid., 32.

30. Tolkien, *Tolkien On Fairy-stories*, 67.

31. Tolkien, *The Letters*, 110.

32. Tolkien, Foreword to *The Lord of the Rings*, 5.

33. Tolkien, *Tolkien On Fairy-stories*, 243.

34. Tolkien, *The Letters*, 338.

35. Tolkien sometimes entertained the idea that it might actually exist at a metaphysical level, but on the whole he viewed it as an artifice and game, an expression of humanity's delight in "sub-creation." Carpenter, *Tolkien*, 102.

36. Tolkien, *Sauron Defeated*, 176.

37. J. R. R. Tolkien, "Beowulf: The Monsters and the Critics," in J. R. R. Tolkien, *The Monsters and the Critics and Other Essays*, ed. Christopher Tolkien (London: HarperCollins, 2006), 20.

38. Tolkien, *The Legend of Sigurd*, 23.

39. J. R. R. Tolkien, "Preface to the Second Edition—Letter to Milton Waldman, 1951," *The Silmarillion*, ed. Christopher Tolkien (New York: Del Rey Books, 2002), xxvii.

40. For Englishness, see Peter Mandler, *The English National Character: The History of an Idea from Edmund Burke to Tony Blair* (New Haven, CT: Yale University Press, 2006).

41. Tolkien, *The Letters*, 244.

42. Callum G. Brown, *The Death of Christian Britain* (New York: Routledge, 2001); Matthew Grimley, "The Religion of Englishness: Puritanism, Providentialism, and 'National Character,' 1918–1945," *Journal of British Studies* 46 (October 2007): 884–906.

43. *An Afternoon in Middle-earth* (program guide for event at Midlands Art Centre, Birmingham, November 30, 1969), 8, Marquette University Special Collections, JRRT Series 5, Box 2, Folder 8.

44. Philip Norman, "The Prevalence of Hobbits," *The New York Times Magazine*, January 15, 1967, 30; 100.

45. He was emphatic about this. For example, when staying at a guest house in 1946, rather than sign his nationality in the guest book as "British" as others had done on the page, he pointedly signed it as "English." Scull and Hammond, *The J. R. R. Tolkien Companion and Guide: Reader's Guide*, 244.

46. Tolkien, *The Letters*, 218.

47. Tolkien, *The Monsters and the Critics*, 230.

48. Tolkien, *The Letters*, 218.

49. Ibid., 213.

50. Scholars often cite "The Voyage of Eärendil" (September, 1914) as the first poem of the mythology, but Douglas A. Anderson notes that disparate elements did not come together until the poem "The Shores of Faery" (July 1915). Jane Chance, "A Mythology for England?" in her *Tolkien and the Invention of Myth: A Reader* (Lexington, KY: The University Press of Kentucky, 2004), 2. For the West Midlands, see Tolkien, *The Silmarillion*, xxvi.

51. Tolkien, *The Letters*, 239.
52. For the Victorian interest in fairies, see Carole G. Silver, *Strange & Secret Peoples: Fairies and Victorian Consciousness* (New York: Oxford University Press, 2000).
53. Tolkien, *Tolkien On Fairy-stories*, 55–56.
54. Dimitra Fimi, *Tolkien, Race and Cultural History* (London: Palgrave MacMillan, 2009), 15–18.
55. Garth, 107.
56. Shippey, *J. R. R. Tolkien: Author of the Century*, xv.
57. Tolkien, *The Silmarillion*, xiv.
58. Ibid.
59. Scull and Hammond, *The J. R. R. Tolkien Companion and Guide: Reader's Guide*, 1089.
60. Tolkien, *Tolkien On Fairy-stories*, 56.
61. In his earliest stories, the Valar resembled the Greek as well as Norse gods; as his legendarium developed, they became closer to the heavenly hosts of the Bible.
62. Garth, 95.
63. Tolkien, *The Monsters and the Critics*, 21.
64. Ibid.
65. Ibid., 23.
66. Tolkien, *The Silmarillion*, xiv.
67. Ibid., xiv.
68. Tolkien, *The Letters*, 55–56.
69. Tolkien's "The Book of Lost Tales" was never published in his lifetime. After his death, his son Christopher compiled various drafts of the stories Tolkien had included under this title, as well as poems and sketches, and published them in two volumes as part of the twelve-volume *The History of Middle-earth*, using the title Tolkien chose for his initial collection. The distinction between the unpublished and published versions is akin to the distinction between the unpublished body of myth Tolkien called "The Silmarillion" and the posthumously edited *The Silmarillion*. J. R. R. Tolkien, *The Book of Lost Tales 2*, ed. Christopher Tolkien (New York: Del Rey, 1992), 170.
70. Garth, 287.
71. Jay Winter, *Sites of Memory, Sites of Mourning: The Great War in European Cultural History* (Cambridge: Cambridge University Press, 1998 [1995]), 119–44.
72. Garth, 38.
73. As mentioned in note 69, the informal use is signaled by quotation marks, and should be distinguished from the posthumously published book *The Silmarillion* (1977), which his son Christopher edited from the large collection of unpublished manuscripts Tolkien worked on throughout his life.
74. See J. R. R. Tolkien, *The Children of Húrin*, ed. Christopher Tolkien (New York: Del Rey, 2010); "Aldarion and Erendis," in J. R. R. Tolkien, *Unfinished Tales: The Lost Lore of Middle-earth*, ed. Christopher Tolkien (New York: Ballantine Books, 1988), 181–227.
75. Fimi, 6.
76. Alison Light, *Forever England: Femininity, Literature, and Conservatism Between the Wars* (London: Routledge, 1991).
77. Mandler, 143–74.
78. Ibid., 163–75.
79. Tolkien, *The Silmarillion*, xv.
80. Tolkien, *The Letters*, 250. He located its basis in the West Midlands. Ibid., 230.
81. Ibid., 158–59.
82. Tolkien, *The Return of the King* in *The Lord of the Rings*, 146.
83. Scull and Hammond, *The J. R. R. Tolkien Companion and Guide: Reader's Guide*, 473.
84. See Victoria de Grazia, *Irresistible Empire: America's Advance through Twentieth-Century Europe* (Cambridge, MA: Harvard University Press, 2006).

85. Tolkien, *The Letters*, 231.
86. Ibid.; Tolkien, *The Monsters and the Critics*, 219, fn. 1.
87. Tolkien, *The Letters*, 65.
88. Ibid., 412.
89. Essentialist understandings of myth did not disappear, of course, but they were often marginalized as pseudo-scientific, a form of New Age thinking more wishful than real. The most respected essentialist interpretation of myths was the structuralism of Barthes's contemporary Claude Levi-Strauss, and he emphasized that it was their common structures that mattered, not their idiosyncratic contents.
90. Tolkien, *The Silmarillion*, xii.
91. Elazar Barkan, *The Retreat of Scientific Racism: Changing Concepts of Race in Britain and the United States Between the World Wars* (Cambridge: Cambridge University Press, 1992).
92. Scull and Hammond, *The J. R. R. Tolkien Companion and Guide: Reader's Guide*, 251.
93. Tolkien, *The Letters*, 229; transcript of a 1965 interview with Tolkien, "Now Read On," BBC Radio 4, December 16, 1970, Marquette University Special Collections, JRRT Series 5, Box 2, Folder 7.
94. McKibbin, 55–57.
95. Jonathan Evans, "Dwarves," in *J. R. R. Tolkien Encyclopedia: Scholarship and Critical Assessment*, ed. Michael D.C. Drout (New York: Routledge, 2007), 134.
96. Tolkien, *The Book of Lost Tales 2*, 225.
97. Ibid., 226–31.
98. J. R. R. Tolkien, *The Hobbit* (New York: Ballantine Books, 1982), 213.
99. Scull and Hammond, *The J. R. R. Tolkien Companion and Guide: Reader's Guide*, 785.
100. Tolkien, *The Monsters and the Critics*, 166.
101. Ibid., 172.
102. Ibid., 190.
103. Ibid., 191.
104. Ibid., 194; 197, fn.30.
105. Ibid, 194.
106. E.g., "Not every Brian and Nial in Iceland had Irish blood in his veins," ibid., 169.
107. Verlyn Flieger, *Interrupted Music: The Making of Tolkien's Mythology* (Kent, OH: The Kent State University Press, 2005), 116–17.
108. Tolkien, *Sauron Defeated*, 236.
109. Clyde Kilby, *Tolkien and the Silmarillion* (Berkhamsted: Lion Publishing, 1977), 57.
110. Tolkien, *The Letters*, 145.
111. Scull and Hammond, *The J. R. R. Tolkien Companion and Guide: Reader's Guide*, 1028; 1034.
112. Ibid., 1028.
113. Ibid., 1031.
114. Ibid., 1036.
115. In his foreword to the second edition of *The Lord of the Rings*, Tolkien stated, "As for any inner meaning or 'message,' it has in the intention of the author none. It is neither allegorical nor topical." Tolkien, *The Lord of the Rings*, 5.
116. "*The Lord of the Rings* is of course a fundamentally religious and Catholic work; unconsciously so at first, but consciously in the revision," Tolkien wrote in a 1953 letter to Robert Murray, a Jesuit priest. "That is why I have not put in, or have cut out practically all references to anything like 'religion,' to cults or practices, in the imaginary world. For the religious element is absorbed into the story and symbolism." Tolkien, *The Letters*, 172.
117. Bradford Lee Eden, "The 'Music of the Spheres': Relationships between Tolkien's *The Silmarillion* and Medieval Cosmological and Religious Theory," in *Tolkien the Medievalist*, ed. Jane Chance (London: Routledge, 2003), 183–93.

118. Walter Pater, *The Renaissance: Studies in Art and Poetry* (London: Macmillan, 1919 [1875]), 135; see also Chai, 81–95.

119. Tolkien, *The Letters*, 212; 264.

120. Ibid., 264.

121. Ibid., 220.

122. Michael Saler, *The Avant-Garde in Interwar England: 'Medieval Modernism' and the London Underground* (New York: Oxford University Press, 1999), 61–91.

123. Garth, 256.

124. Ibid., 14.

125. Meredith Veldman, *Fantasy, the Bomb, and the Greening of Britain: Romantic Protest, 1945–1980* (Cambridge: Cambridge University Press, 1994), 52. Tolkien had other affiliations with the Arts and Crafts movement. He learned calligraphy from a manual written by Edward Johnston, one of its notable proponents, and his own drawings and paintings were sometimes in the Art Noveau style. He could be somewhat of an aesthete even in his public appearance—as an undergraduate he decorated his rooms with Japanese prints and himself with bespoke suits. Belying his conservative image as an Oxford don, he retained a life-long fondness for brightly colored vest coats (a trait he shared with his hobbits).

126. Carpenter, *Tolkien*, 98.

127. Tolkien, *The Silmarillion*, xv. It is also possible that Tolkien was drawing on Richard Wagner's allied concept of the *gesamtkunstwerk* (union of the arts).

128. Ibid., xiv.

129. Garth, 112.

130. Tolkien, *The Monsters and the Critics*, 15.

131. Tolkien, *Tolkien On Fairy-stories*, 35.

132. In a 1966 interview, Tolkien said he enjoyed science fiction, and noted that "the relationship between science fiction and fantasy is difficult and topically important . . . Obviously many readers of sf are attracted by it because it performs the same operations as fantasy—it provides Recovery and Escape . . . and wonder . . . The legendary laboratory 'professor' has replaced the wizard." Daphne Castell, "The Realms of Tolkien," *New Worlds* 50:168 (August 6, 1966): 148.

133. Tolkien, *Tolkien On Fairy-stories*, 60; 48.

134. Ibid., 77.

135. Ibid., 65.

136. Ibid., 59.

137. Ibid., 68.

138. Ibid, 69.

139. Ibid., 75.

140. Ernst Bloch, "The Fairy Tale Moves on its Own in Time," in *Literary Essays*, trans. Andrew Joron (Stanford, CA: Stanford University Press, 1998), 169.

141. Tolkien, *Tolkien On Fairy-stories*, 70.

142. Ibid., 68. For an insightful reading, see Patrick Curry, "Iron Crown, Iron Cage: Tolkien and Weber on Modernity and Enchantment," in *Myth and Magic: Art According to the Inklings*, ed. Eduardo Segura and Thomas Honegger (Zurich: Walking Tree Press, 2008), at http://www.patrickcurry.co.uk/papers/Iron-Cage-Iron-Crown.pdf (accessed March 27, 2010).

143. Tolkien, *Tolkien On Fairy-stories*, 69.

144. Ibid., 79.

145. Tolkien, *The Letters*, 262.

146. Christopher Herbert, *Culture and Anomie: Ethnographic Imagination in the Nineteenth Century* (Chicago, IL: University of Chicago Press, 1991); Raymond Williams, *Culture and Society, 1780–1950* (New York: Columbia University Press, 1983).

147. Stefan Collini, *Absent Minds: Intellectuals in Britain* (New York: Oxford University Press, 2006), 279–300.

148. This distinction echoed that made by contemporary Western thinkers between "religion" and "magic." See Randall Styers, *Making Magic: Religion, Magic, and Science in the Modern World* (New York: Oxford University Press, 2004).

149. Tolkien, *Tolkien On Fairy-stories,* 64.

150. Ibid.

151. Tolkien, *The Silmarillion,* xvi.

152. Ibid., 236.

153. Ibid., 143–61.

154. Tolkien, *Tolkien On Fairy-stories,* 77.

155. Ibid., 66.

156. He shared this view with C. S. Lewis and agreed with Lewis's argument that a story's aesthetic qualities might lead secular readers to religious views: "For the beauty of a story while not necessarily a guarantee of its truth is a concomitant of it, and a *fidelis* is meant to draw nourishment from the beauty as well as the truth." Tolkien, *The Letters,* 109.

157. Tolkien, *Tolkien On Fairy-stories,* 78.

158. Ibid., 79.

159. Ibid., 84. Because humanity has an "eternal element," he inferred that at some point "we shall doubtless survey our own story when we know it (and a great deal more of the Whole Story)." Tolkien, *The Letters,* 106–7.

160. Ibid., 78.

161. Ibid., 76.

162. Scull and Hammond, *The J. R. R. Tolkien Companion and Guide: Reader's Guide,* 945.

163. Tolkien, *The Letters,* 246.

164. Ibid., 191.

165. Ibid., 93.

166. Ibid., 349.

167. Tolkien, *The Two Towers* in *The Lord of the Rings,* 221.

168. Tolkien, "Foreword to the second edition" in *The Lord of the Rings,* 5.

169. For an overview of the critical and publishing history of *The Lord of the Rings,* see Douglas A. Anderson, "The Mainstreaming of Fantasy and the Legacy of *The Lord of the Rings*" in *The Lord of the Rings 1954–2004: Essays in Honor of Richard E. Blackwelder,* ed. Wayne G. Hammond and Christina Scull (Milwaukee, WI: Marquette University Press, 2006), 301–15.

170. Henry Resnik, "The Hobbit-Forming World of J. R. R. Tolkien," *Saturday Evening Post* 239:14, July 2, 1966, 90–94.

171. Ibid.

172. Charles Elliott, "Can America Kick the Hobbit? The Tolkien Caper," *Life,* February 24, 1967, n.p.

173. Judith Crist, "Why 'Frodo Lives,'" *Ladies Home Journal,* February, 1967, n.p.

174. According to Plotz, "our members are doctors, teachers, army officers, housewives and businessmen, as well as students." Norman, 30; 100.

175. *Tolkien Journal* 2 (Winterfilth 1965), n.p.

176. Jesse B. Arman, "Living Middle-earth in the Early Years," *Amon Din* 2:1 (January 21, 1973): n.p.

177. Ibid.

178. Mary Shideler, "Inklings of Another World," *Amon Din* 2:5 (November 25, 1973): n.p.

179. A. C. Knighton, "*The Lord of the Rings*—A Personal View," *Amon Hen* (October 18, 1975): n.p.

180. Alex Bennett, "The Fall from Enchantment," *Mallorn* 11 (October 1977): 39.

181. Jeff Horner, letter, *Amon Hen* 39 (June 1979): 14.

182. Simon Musk, letter, ibid., 15.

183. Julian Bradfield, letter, *Amon Hen* 40 (August 1979): 17.

184. Linda Heard, letter, *Amon Hen* 109 (May 1991): 17.

185. Alex Lewis, letter, *Amon Hen* 111 (August 1991): 18–19.

186. Editorial, *Amon Din* 1:2 (November 12, 1972): n.p.

187. "Report on a Meeting of the London Smial of Sunday 18 July," *Amon Hen* 21 (August 1976): n.p.

188. "A Marxist Looks at Middle Earth: Or, The Political Economy of the Shire," *Mallorn* 9 (1975): 24–29.

189. Catherine Bennett, "In the Beginning there was Bilbo," *The Times*, August 22, 1987, 13.

190. William A. Sievert, "A Mania for Middle-earth," *The Chronicle of Higher Education*, February 6, 1978, 3.

191. Frederick Hackworth, "Hobbits in History: Tolkien Tales Live Long," *Meadville Tribune*, August 9, 1988, n.p.

192. Charlotte and Denis Plimmer, "The Man Who Understands Hobbits," *Daily Telegraph Magazine*, March 22, 1968, 33.

193. Resnik, "An Interview With Tolkien," 39.

194. Joy Hill, "Daily Life on Middle-earth," *An Afternoon in Middle-earth*, program guide for events at the Midlands Art Centre, Birmingham, November 30, 1969, Marquette University Special Collections, JRRT Series 5, Box 2, Folder 8.

195. "Belladonna Took" [Vera Chapman], "*Amon Hen*: A Brief History," *Amon Hen* 50 (May 2, 1981): 6.

196. "Belladonna Took" [Vera Chapman], "Hippies or Hobbits?" *Mallorn* 2 (1971): 13. In 1981, a reporter talked to members of a London branch ("smial") of the Tolkien Society (UK) and found that "They tend to frown on the wilder activities of some of the American Tolkien fans: 'We try to keep ourselves as separate as possible from the hippie image,' says [member] Jonathan Simons." Maire Messenger, "The Ring in Your Ear," *Radio Times* 230:2991 (March 7–13, 1981): 73.

197. Chapman, "Amon Hen," 6.

198. Jessica Yates, "A History of Oxonmoot," *Amon Hen* 100 (1989): 23.

199. Rosemary Pardoe, editorial, *Mallorn* 1 (1970): 3.

200. Ibid.

201. Ibid.

202. Ibid., 4.

203. A. R. (Faramir) Fallone, "On Behalf of the Half-Hippie," *Mallorn* 2 (1971): 16.

204. Alex Lewis, letter, *Mallorn* 24 (September 1987): 37.

205. Maria Kamenkovich, "The Secret War and the End of the First Age: Tolkien in the [Former] USSR," *Mallorn* 29 (August 1992): 36; 38.

206. Ibid.

207. Ruth Lacon, "Tolkien's Star and Tolkien's Heirs," *Amon Hen* 135 (September 1995): 7.

208. Andrew Wheeler, letter, *Amon Hen* 136 (November 1995): 24.

209. Phil Helm, letter, *Minis Tirith Evening Star* 22:2 (Summer 1993): 14–15.

210. Matthew Pugsley, letter, *Minis Tirith Evening Star* 22:1 (Spring 1993): 11–12.

211. Ibid., 12–13.

212. "An Interview with Michael Hilary Reuel Tolkien," Gary Hunnewell and Sylvia Hunnewell, transcribers, *Minis Tirith Evening Star* 18 (Spring 1989): 9.

213. Shideler, n.p.

ENVOI

The first epigraph is from Jack Kirby, "Eternal Utterings," in his *The Eternals*, vol.1 (New York: Marvel Publishing, 2008), 42. The second epigraph is from Peter L. Berger, "The

Desecularization of the World: A Global Overview," in *The Desecularization of the World: Resurgent Religion and World Politics,* ed. Peter L. Berger (Grand Rapids, MI: William Eerdmans Publishing, 1999), 13.

1. McGonigal, 4.
2. Bloom, 201.
3. T. S. Eliot, *Four Quartets* (New York: Harcourt Books, 1971 [1943]), 59.

SELECTED BIBLIOGRAPHY

PRIMARY SOURCES

"A Marxist Looks at Middle Earth: Or, the Political Economy of the Shire." *Mallorn* 9 (1975).

Abbott, Edwin A. *Flatland: A Romance of Many Dimensions*. London: Seeley and Co., 1884.

Anderson, Poul. "Nature: Laws and Surprises." In *Mindscapes: The Geographies of Imagined Worlds*, ed. George E. Slusser and Eric Rabkin. Carbondale: Southern Illinois University Press, 1989.

———. "The Queen of Air and Darkness." *The Magazine of Fantasy & Science Fiction* 40:4 (April 1971).

———. "The Saturn Game." *Analog Science Fiction/Science Fact* 150: 2 (February 1981).

Barfield, Owen. *Romanticism Comes of Age*. Middletown, CT: Wesleyan University Press, 1967 [1944].

Baring-Gould, W. S. *Sherlock Holmes of Baker Street*. New York: Popular Library, 1963 [1962].

Barzun, Jacques. "The Adventures of Sherlock Holmes: A Radio Discussion." In *The Baker Street Reader*, ed. Philip Shreffler. Westport, CT: Greenwood Press, 1984.

Baudelaire, Charles. *Artificial Paradises*. Harrowgate: Broadwater House, 1999.

Belloc, Hilaire. "On Not Reading Books." *The New Statesman* 28:711 (December 11, 1926).

Bennett, Catherine. "In the Beginning There Was Bilbo." *The Times*, August 22, 1987.

Blakeney, T. S. *Sherlock Holmes: Fact or Fiction*. London: John Murray, 1932.

Blanco, Alberto. "Maps." In *Dawn of the Senses: Selected Poems of Alberto Blanco*, ed. Juvenal Acosta. San Francisco, CA: City Lights Publishers, 2001.

Blau, Peter E. "My First Meeting with Sherlock Holmes." *Baker Street Journal* 50:4 (Winter 2000).

Bloch, Ernst. "The Fairy Tale Moves on Its Own in Time." In *Literary Essays*, trans. Andrew Joron. Stanford, CA: Stanford University Press, 1998.

Borges, Jorge Luis. "Tlön, Uqbar, Orbis Tertius." In *Collected Fictions*, trans. Andrew Hurley. New York: Viking, 1998.

Boucher, Anthony. Letter. *The Acolyte* 2:3 (Summer 1944).

———. "Sherlock Holmes and Science Fiction." *Baker Street Journal* (July 1960).

Braddon, Mary Elizabeth. *The Doctor's Wife*. New York: Oxford University Press, 1998 [1864].

Bradfield, Julian. Letter. *Amon Hen* 40 (August 1979).

Bregenzer, Don, and Samuel Loveman, ed. *A Round-Table in Poictesme: A Symposium*. Cleveland, OH: The Colophon Club, 1924.

Breuer, Miles J. Letter. *Amazing Stories* 4:6 (September 1929).

Brown, Joseph M. *Astyanax: An Epic Romance of Ilion, Atlantis, and Amaraca*. New York: Broadway Publishing Company, 1907.

Cannon, Peter, ed. *Lovecraft Remembered*. Sauk City, WI: Arkham House, 1998.

Castell, Daphne. "The Realms of Tolkien." *New Worlds* 50:168 (August 6, 1966).

Caulkins, C. E. "Editorials From Our Readers." *Amazing Stories Quarterly* 1:4 (Fall 1928).

de Cèrvantes, Miguel. *Don Quixote*, trans. Edith Grossman. New York: HarperCollins, 2003.

Chapman, Vera [Belladonna Took]. *"Amon Hen*: A Brief History." *Amon Hen* 50 (May 2, 1981).

———. "Hippies or Hobbits?" *Mallorn* 2 (1971).

Chesterton, G. K. "A Defence of Detective Stories." In *The Defendant*. London: R. Brinley Johnson, 1901.

———. "Sherlock Holmes the God." *G. K.'s Weekly*, February 21, 1935.

Coleridge, Samuel Taylor. *Biographia Literaria*. London: J. M. Dent, 1975 [1817].

Collingwood, R. G. *The Philosophy of Enchantment: Studies in Folktale, Cultural Criticism, and Anthropology*, ed. David Boucher, Wendy James, Philip Smallwood. Oxford: Clarendon Press, 2005.

Colvin, David, and Edward Maggs, ed. *Enoch Soames: The Critical Heritage*. London: The Enoch Soames Society, 2002.

Cox, Paul D. Letter. *Planet Stories* 3:11 (Summer 1948).

Crist, Judith. "Why 'Frodo Lives.'" *Ladies Home Journal* 84 (February 1967).

Dahlinger, S. E., and Leslie S. Klinger, ed. *Sherlock Holmes, Conan Doyle & The Bookman: Pastiches, Parodies, Letters, Columns and Commentary from America's "Magazine of Literature and Life" (1895–1933)*. Indianapolis, IN: Gasogene Books, 2010.

Davis, Sonia H. *The Private Life of H. P. Lovecraft*, ed. S. T. Joshi. West Warwick, RI: Necronomicon Press, 1985.

"The Diogenes Club of West Virginia." *Baker Street Journal* 6:3, New Series (July 1956).

Doyle, Arthur Conan. *The Coming of the Fairies*. London: Pavilion Books, 1997 [1922].

———. *The Complete Sherlock Holmes*. New York: Barnes and Noble, 1992.

———. *A Life in Letters*, ed. Jon Lellenberg, Daniel Stashower, and Charles Foley. New York: The Penguin Press, 2007.

———. *The Lost World*. London: Hodder & Stoughton, 1912.

———. *Memories and Adventures*. London: Wordsworth, 2007 [1924].

Du Bois, W. E. B. *The Souls of Black Folk: Essays and Sketches*. Chicago, IL: A. C. McClurg & Co., 1903.

Eddison, E. R. Letter. Oxford University: Bodleian Library Special Collections, MS. Eng Let. c/233.

"Edgar Allan Poe Father of Scientifiction." *Amazing Stories* 3:6 (September 1928).

Editor. "Discussions." *Amazing Stories* 1:12 (March 1927).

———. "Discussions." *Amazing Stories* 3:4 (July 1928).

———. "Looking Ahead." *Astounding Stories* 17:5 (July 1936).

———. "Blazing New Trails." *Astounding Stories* 17:6 (August 1936).

———. "Into the Future." *Astounding Stories* 20:2 (October 1937).

———. "History to Come." *Astounding Science-Fiction* 27:3 (May 1941).

———. "The Reader Speaks." *Wonder Stories* 2:5 (October 1930).

———. "The Reader Speaks." *Wonder Stories* 2:7 (December 1930).

———. "The Reader Speaks." *Wonder Stories* 2:8 (January 1931).

———. "The Reader Speaks." *Wonder Stories* 2:9 (February 1931).

Eliot, T. S. *Four Quartets*. New York: Harcourt Books, 1971 [1943].

Elliott, Charles. "Can America Kick the Hobbit? The Tolkien Caper." *Life* 62:8 (February 24, 1967).

Ernst, Max. *Life and Work*, ed. Werner Spies. London: Thames & Hudson, 2006.

Faig, Jr., Ken. *De Tenebris* 1 (August 30, 1976).

"The Fall of Fiction." *The Fortnightly Review* XLIV (September 1, 1888).

Fallone, A. R. [Faramir]. "On Behalf of the Half-Hippie." *Mallorn* 2 (1971).

Flaubert, Gustave. *Madame Bovary: A Story of Provincial Life*, trans. Alan Russell. New York: Penguin Books, 1981.

Freud, Sigmund. *Civilization and its Discontents*, trans. James Strachey. New York: W. W. Norton, 1989 [1930].

Gernsback, Hugo. "A New Sort of Magazine." *Amazing Stories* 1:1 (April 1926).

Gerth, H. H., and C. Wright Mills, ed. *From Max Weber: Essays in Sociology*. London: Routledge, 1998 [1946].

Gibson, William. *Neuromancer*. New York: Ace Books, 1984.

Gilham, A. A. "Holmes in Advertising." *Sherlock Holmes Journal* 6:1 (1962).

Goldsborough, Bob. "Dick Tracy Statue to Stand Guard Over Napier Riverwalk." *Chicago Tribune*, June 3, 2009.

de Goncourt, Edmond, and Jules de Goncourt. *Pages from the Goncourt Journal*, trans. and ed. Robert Baldick. New York: New York Review Books, 2007 [1962].

Green, Richard Lancelyn, ed. *The Sherlock Holmes Letters*. London: Secker and Warburg, 1986.

Gulley, Carl Frederick. Letter. *Astounding Science-Fiction*, 24:4 (September 1939).

Gunn, R. Ivar. "The Sherlock Holmes Society." *The British Medical Journal* (August 11, 1934).

Hackworth, Frederick. "Hobbits in History: Tolkien Tales Live Long." *Meadville Tribune*, August 9, 1988.

Haggard, H. Rider. *The Days of My Life*. Vol. 1. London: Longmans, Green and Co., Ltd., 1926.

———. *The Days of My Life*. Vol. 2. London: Longmans, Green and Co., Ltd., 1926.

———. *She*. London: Longmans, Green, and Co, 1887.

———. *She*. East Sussex: Pulp Fictions, 1998.

Haycraft, Howard. "The Profile Emerges." In *Profile by Gaslight: An Irregular Reader About the Private Life of Sherlock Holmes*, ed. Edgar W. Smith. New York: Simon & Schuster, 1944.

Hayes, Gerald R. "TWO." *Civil Service Arts Magazine* (August-October 1930).

Heard, Linda. Letter. *Amon Hen* 109 (May 1991).

Helm, Phil. Letter. *Minis Tirith Evening Star* 22:2 (Summer 1993).

Higgins, John. Letter. *Planet Stories* 4:3 (Summer 1949).

Hill, Joy. "Daily Life on Middle-earth." *An Afternoon in Middle-earth*. November 30, 1969. Marquette University Special Collections, JRRT Series 5, Box 2, Folder 8.

Hoen, Richard A. Letter. *Astounding Science-Fiction* 62:3 (November 1948).

Hoffman, Arthur S. "Camp-Fire." *Adventure* (December 18, 1917).

———. "Camp-Fire." *Adventure* (March 3, 1918).

Holroyd, James Edward. *Baker Street By-Ways*. New York: Otto Penzler Books, 1994 [1959].

Honce, Charles. "Sherlock Holmes in the News." In *Profile by Gaslight: An Irregular Reader About the Private Life of Sherlock Holmes*, ed. Edgar W. Smith. New York: Simon and Schuster, 1944.

Horkheimer, Max, and Theodor Adorno. *Dialectic of Enlightenment: Philosophical Fragments*, trans. Gunzelin Schmid Noerr and Edmund Jephcott. Stanford, CA: Stanford University Press, 2002.

Horner, Jeff. Letter. *Amon Hen* 39 (June 1979).

Howard, Philip. "Holmes Defeats Moriarty Official." *The Times*, May 2, 1968. In "Sherlock Holmes Journal Switzerland Tour Special Supplement," *The Sherlock Holmes Journal* 8:4 (Summer 1968).

Huizinga, Johan. *Homo Ludens*. London: Paladin, 1970 [1938].

Husband, M. F. A. *A Dictionary of the Characters in the Waverley Novels of Sir Walter Scott*. London: George Routledge and Sons, Limited, 1910.

Huysmans, Joris-Karl. *Against Nature*, trans. Robert Baldick. New York: Penguin Books, 2003 [1884].

"An Interview with Michael Hilary Reuel Tolkien." Transcribed by Gary Hunnewell and Sylvia Hunnewell. *Minis Tirith Evening Star* 18 (Spring 1989).

Kamenkovich, Maria. "The Secret War and the End of the First Age: Tolkien in the USSR." *Mallorn* 29 (August 1992).

Kerr, Martin. "J. R. R. Tolkien and 'That Noble Northern Spirit.'" *White Power* (January-February 1979). Marquette University Special Collections, JRRT Series 5, Box 1, Folder 28.

Kipling, Rudyard. *With the Night Mail: A Story of 2000 A. D. (Together with Extracts from the Contemporary Magazine in which it Appeared)*. New York: Doubleday, Page and Co., 1909.

———. *Just So Stories*. New York: Doubleday, 1912 [1902].

Kirby, Jack. "Eternal Utterings." In *The Eternals*. Vol. 1. New York: Marvel Publishing, 2008.

Klinefelter, Walter. *Books about Poictesme: An Essay in Imaginative Bibliography*. Chicago, IL: The Black Cat Press, 1937.

Knighton, A. C. "*The Lord of the Rings*—A Personal View." *Amon Hen* (October 18, 1975).

Knox, Ronald A. *Essays in Satire*. London: Sheed and Ward, 1928 [1912].

Korzybski, Alfred. *Science and Sanity: An Introduction to Non-Aristotelian Systems and General Semantics*. 5th Edition. Fort Worth, TX: Institute of General Semantics, 1994.

Kuttner, Henry. "Reader, I Hate You." *Super Science Stories* 4:4 (May 1943).

Lacon, Ruth. "Tolkien's Star and Tolkien's Heirs." *Amon Hen* 135 (September 1995).

[Lang, Andrew and Walter Herries Pollock]. *He*. London: Longmans, Green and Co., 1887.

Lang, Andrew. "Realism and Romance." *Contemporary Review* LII (November 1887).

Lassner, Mark Samuels. *A Bibliography of Enoch Soames (1862–1897)*. Oxford: The Rivendell Press, 1999.

Leiber, Fritz. "A Literary Copernicus." In *Lovecraft Remembered*, ed. Peter Cannon. Sauk City, WI: Arkham House, 1998.

Lellenberg, Jon L., ed. *Irregular Crises of the Late 'Forties*. New York: The Baker Street Irregulars, 1999.

———. *Irregular Memories of the Early 'Forties*. New York: The Baker Street Irregulars, distributed by Fordham University Press, 1991.

———. *Irregular Memories of the Mid-'Forties: An Archival History of the Baker Street Irregulars Autumn 1943–June 1947*. New York: The Baker Street Irregulars, 1995.

———. *Irregular Memories of the Thirties: An Archival History of the Baker Street Irregulars' First Decade 1930–1940*. New York: The Baker Street Irregulars, distributed by Fordham University Press, 1990.

Lewis Alex. Letter. *Amon Hen* 111 (August 1991).

———. Letter. *Mallorn* 24 (September 1987).

Lewis, C. S. *The Collected Letters of C. S. Lewis Volume II*, ed. Walter Hooper. New York: Harper-Collins, 2004.

Lloyd, John Uri. *Etidorhpa or The End of the Earth*. Cincinnati, OH: John Uri Lloyd, 1895.

London, Jack. *The Star Rover*. New York: The Modern Library, 2003.

Lovecraft, H. P. *Collected Essays Volume 1: Amateur Journalism*, ed. S. T. Joshi. New York: Hippocampus Press, 2004.

———. *Essential Solitude: The Letters of H. P. Lovecraft and August Derleth: 1926–1931*, ed. David E. Schultz and S. T. Joshi. New York: Hippocampus Press, 2008.

———. *The Fiction*. New York: Barnes and Noble, 2008.

———. *Letters to Alfred Galpin*, ed. S. T. Joshi and David Schultz. New York: Hippocampus Press, 2003.

———. *Letters to Henry Kuttner*, ed. David E. Schultz and S. T. Joshi. West Warwick: Necronomicon Press, 1999.

———. *Letters to Rheinhart Kleiner*, ed. S. T. Joshi and David Schultz. New York: Hippocampus Press, 2005.

———. *Lord of a Visible World: An Autobiography in Letters*, ed. S. T. Joshi and David E. Schultz. Athens, OH: Ohio University Press, 2000.

———. *A Means to Freedom: The Letters of H. P. Lovecraft and Robert E. Howard: Volume One 1930–1932*, ed. S. T. Joshi, David E. Schultz, and Rusty Burke. New York: Hippocampus Press, 2009.

————. *Miscellaneous Writings*, ed. S. T. Joshi. Sauk City, WI: Arkham House, 1995.

————. *Selected Letters II: 1925–1929*, ed. August Derleth and Donald Wandrei. Sauk City, WI: Arkham House, 1968.

————. *Selected Letters III: 1929–1931*, ed. August Derleth and Donald Wandrei. Sauk City: Arkham House, 1971.

————. *Selected Letters IV: 1932–1934*, ed. August Derleth and James Turner. Sauk City, WI: Arkham House, 1976.

————. *Selected Letters V: 1934–1937*, ed. August Derleth and James Turner. Sauk City, WI: Arkham House, 1976.

————and Willis Conover. *Lovecraft at Last*. Arlington, VA: Carrollton Clark, 1975.

Mannion, Alan. Letter. *Planet Stories* 2:5 (Winter 1943).

Meadow, Leon, Robert Newman, and Dorothy Bachrach. Letter. Oxford University: Bodleian Library Special Collections, MS. Eng Let. c/231.

Messenger, Maire. "The Ring in Your Ear." *Radio Times* 230:2991 (March 7–13, 1981).

"Modern Marvels." *The Spectator* (October 17, 1885).

Morley, Christopher. "Notes on Baker Street." *The Saturday Review* (January 28, 1939).

Morus, Iwan Rhys. Editorial. *Amon Hen* 76 (November 1985).

Murray, John. *A Handbook for Travellers in Cornwall, Tenth Edition*. London: John Murray, 1882.

Musk, Simon. Letter. *Amon Hen* 39 (June 1979).

Norman, Philip. "The Prevalence of Hobbits." *New York Times Magazine*, January 15, 1967.

"Now Read On." Transcript, BBC Radio 4. December 16, 1970. Marquette University Special Collections, JRRT Series 5, Box 2, Folder 7.

"Obituary for Ivor Gunn." *Sherlock Holmes Journal* 1:4 (December 1953).

Ogden, C. K., ed. *Bentham's Theory of Fictions*. New York: Routledge, 2007 [1932].

"The Old Saloon." *Contemporary Review* (February 1887).

Oliver, Chad. Letter. *Planet Stories* 3:12 (Fall 1948).

Onderdonk, Matthew H. "The Lord of R'lyeh: A Discussion of the Supreme Contribution of Howard Phillips Lovecraft to the Philosophy of the Weird Tale." *Fantasy Commentator* 1:6 (Spring 1945).

O'Neial, N. J. Letter. *Weird Tales* 15:3 (March 1930).

Orel, Harold, ed. *Sir Arthur Conan Doyle: Interviews and Recollections*. London: Macmillan, 1991.

Pardoe, Rosemary. Editorial. *Mallorn* 1 (1970).

Parker, Robert Allerton. "Such Pulp As Dreams Are Made On." In *A Weird Writer in Our Midst: Early Criticism of H. P. Lovecraft*, ed. S. T. Joshi. New York: Hippocampus Press, 2010.

Pater, Walter. *The Renaissance: Studies in Art and Poetry*. London: Macmillan, 1919 [1875].

Pessoa, Fernando. *The Book of Disquiet*, ed. and trans. Richard Zenith. New York: Penguin Books, 2003.

Plimmer, Charlotte, and Denis. "The Man Who Understands Hobbits." *Daily Telegraph Magazine*, March 22, 1968.

Ploner, Emma. Letter. *Amazing Stories* 4:3 (June 1929).

Poe, Edgar Allan. "Diddling Considered as One of the Exact Sciences." In *Poetry and Tales*, ed. Francis Quinn. New York: The Library of America, 1984.

————. *Essays and Reviews*, ed. Gary Richard Thompson. New York: The Library of America, 1984.

"Poe's Mesmeric Revelation." *Amazing Stories* 1:2 (May 1926).

Pugsley, Matthew. Letter. *Minis Tirith Evening Star* 22:1 (Spring 1993).

Ramsay, Ray H. Letter. *Planet Stories* 4:3 (Summer 1949).

Reeves, Walter L. Letter. *Astounding Stories* (June 1936).

"Report on a Meeting of the London Smial of Sunday 18 July." *Amon Hen* 21 (August 1976).

Resnik, Henry. "The Hobbit-Forming World of J. R. R. Tolkien." *Saturday Evening Post* (July 2, 1966).

———. "An Interview with Tolkien." *Niekas* 18 (Spring 1967).

Roberts, S. C. *Adventures with Authors*. Cambridge: Cambridge University Press, 1966.

Saltus, Edgar Evertson. *The Philosophy of Disenchantment*. Boston: Houghton Mifflin, 1885.

Sapiro, Leland. Letter. *Planet Stories* 4:2 (Spring 1949).

Sartre, Jean-Paul. *The Words*. New York: Vintage Books, 1981 [1964].

Sayers, Dorothy. *Unpopular Opinions*. London: Victor Gollancz, 1947.

Schiller, Friedrich. *On the Aesthetic Education of Man, in a Series of Letters*, trans. Elizabeth M. Wilkinson and L. A. Willoughby. Oxford: Oxford University Press, 1967.

Schott, Elihu. Letter. *Amazing Science Quarterly* 1:4 (Fall 1928).

Schwartz, Delmore. *In Dreams Begin Responsibilities and Other Stories*. New York: New Directions, 1978.

Schwartz, Julius. Letter. *Astounding Stories* 16:6 (February 1936).

Scott, A. O. "A Hunger for Fantasy, an Empire to Feed It." *New York Times*, June 16, 2002.

Shideler, Mary. "Inklings of Another World." *Amon Din* 2:5 (November 25, 1973).

Shreffler, Philip, ed. *The Baker Street Reader*. Westport, CT: Greenwood Press, 1984.

Sicari, Frank. Letter. *Wonder Stories* 2:6 (November 1930).

Sievert, William. "A Mania for Middle-earth." *The Chronicle of Higher Education*, February 6, 1978.

Sigler, Edwin. Letter. *Planet Stories* 4:2 (Spring 1949).

Smith, Edgar W. "The Editor's Gas Lamp." *Baker Street Journal* 4:4, New Series (October 1954).

———. "The Editor's Gas-Lamp: A Perspective on Scholarship." *Baker Street Journal* 3:1, New Series (January 1953).

———. "The Editor's Gas-Lamp: The Writings about the Writings." *Baker Street Journal* 2:2, New Series (April 1952).

———. "The Implicit Holmes." *Baker Street Journal* 1:2 (Original Series, 1946).

———, ed. *Profile by Gaslight: An Irregular Reader About the Private Life of Sherlock Holmes*. New York: Simon and Schuster, 1944.

"Some Inconsistencies of Sherlock Holmes." *The Bookman* XIV (January, 1902).

"The Sons of the Copper Beaches of Philadelphia." *Baker Street Journal* 3:2, New Series (April 1953).

Sorel, Georges. "Reflections on Violence." In *From Georges Sorel: Essays in Socialism and Philosophy*, ed. John Stanley. Piscataway, NJ: Transaction Publishers, 1987.

Starrett, Vincent. "Dr. Bell and Dr. Black." *Baker Street Journal* 7:4 (October 1957).

———. *The Private Life of Sherlock Holmes* (New York: Otto Penzler Books, 1993 [1933]).

———. "The Singular Adventures of Martha Hudson." In *Baker Street Studies*, ed. H. W. Bell. London: Constable and Co., 1934.

Stevenson, Robert Louis. "A Gossip on Romance." In *The Lantern-Bearers and Other Essays*. New York: Farrar Straus Giroux, 1988.

———. *The Suicide Club & Other Dark Adventures*. Yorkshire: Tartarus Press, 2007.

———. "Treasure Island." In *My First Book*. London: Chatto & Windus, 1897.

Tolkien, J. R. R. "Beowulf: The Monsters and the Critics." In *The Monsters and the Critics and Other Essays*, ed. Christopher Tolkien. London: HarperCollins, 2006.

———. *The Book of Lost Tales 2*, ed. Christopher Tolkien. New York: Del Rey Books, 1992.

———. *The Children of Húrin*, ed. Christopher Tolkien. New York: Del Rey Books, 2010.

———. *The Fellowship of the Ring*. In *The Lord of the Rings*. Boston, MA: Houghton Mifflin, 1987.

———. *The Hobbit*. New York: Ballantine Books, 1982.

———. *The Legend of Sigurd & Gudrún*, ed. Christopher Tolkien. Boston, MA: Houghton Mifflin Harcourt, 2009.

————. *The Letters of J. R. R. Tolkien*, ed. Humphrey Carpenter. Boston, MA: Houghton Mifflin Company, 2000.

————. *The Lord of the Rings*. Boston, MA: Houghton Mifflin, 1987.

————. *The Monsters and the Critics and Other Essays*, ed. Christopher Tolkien. London: HarperCollins, 2006.

————. *The Return of the King*. In *The Lord of the Rings*. Boston, MA: Houghton Mifflin, 1987.

————. *Sauron Defeated: The End of the Third Age, The Notion Club Papers and the Drowning of Anadûné*, ed. Christopher Tolkien. London: HarperCollins, 1992.

————. *The Silmarillion*, ed. Christopher Tolkien. New York: Del Rey Books, 2002.

————. *Tolkien On Fairy-stories*, ed. Verlyn Flieger and Douglas A. Anderson. London: HarperCollins, 2007.

————. *The Two Towers*. In *The Lord of the Rings*. Boston, MA: Houghton Mifflin, 1987.

————. *Unfinished Tales: The Lost Lore of Middle-earth*, ed. Christopher Tolkien. New York: Ballantine Books, 1988.

Tyndall, John. *Scientific Use of the Imagination and Other Essays*. London: Longmans, Green, and Co., 1872.

Vaihinger, Hans. *The Philosophy of 'As If,'* trans. C. K. Ogden. Oxford: Routledge, 2009 [1924].

Verne, Jules. "The Leader of the Cult of the Unusual." In *The Edgar Allan Poe Scrapbook*, ed. Peter Haining, trans. I. O. Evans. New York: Schocken Books, 1978.

————. *Vingt Mille Lieues sous les Mers*. Paris: Collection Hetzel, n.d.

Wagenknecht, Edward. "The Little Prince Rides the White Deer: Fantasy and Symbolism in Recent Literature." *The English Journal* 35:1 (May 1946).

Waite, Philip. Letter. *Wonder Stories* 2:6 (November 1930).

Weber, Max. *The Protestant Ethic and the Spirit of Capitalism*, trans. Talcott Parsons. New York: Dover Publications, 2003 [1930].

————. "Science as a Vocation." In *From Max Weber: Essays in Sociology*, ed. H. H. Gerth and C. Wright Mills. London: Routledge, 1998 [1946].

"What Do You Know?" *Amazing Stories* 3:2 (May 1928).

Wheeler, Andrew. Letter, *Amon Hen* 136 (November 1995).

Whitman, Walt. *Complete Poetry and Selected Prose*. New York: The Library of America, 1982.

Wilde, Oscar. "The Decay of Lying: An Observation." In Oscar Wilde, *The Soul of Man Under Socialism & Selected Critical Prose*, ed. Linda Dowling. New York: Penguin Books, 2001.

Williamson, Jack. "Scientifiction, Searchlight of Science." *Amazing Stories Quarterly* 1 (1928).

Wilson, Don. Letter. *Planet Stories* 3:12 (Fall 1948).

Wilson, Edmund. *Axel's Castle: A Study in the Imaginative Literature of 1870–1930*. New York: Charles Scribner's Sons, 1969 [1931].

————. "Oo, Those Awful Orcs!" *The Nation* CLXXXII (April 14, 1956).

————. "Tales of the Marvelous and the Ridiculous." In Edmund Wilson, *Classics and Commercials: A Literary Chronicle of the Forties*. New York: Macmillan, 1950.

Wittgenstein, Ludwig. *Philosophical Investigations*, trans. G. E. M. Anscombe. New York: Prentice Hall, 1973.

Wood, Roy R. Letter. *Planet Stories* 4:4 (Fall 1949).

Woods, Katherine Pearson. "The Renaissance of Wonder." *The Bookman: A Review of Books and Life* 10 (December 1899).

Yates, Jessica. "A History of Oxonmoot." *Amon Hen* 100 (1989).

SECONDARY SOURCES

Agacinski, Sylviane. *Time Passing: Modernity and Nostalgia*. New York: Columbia University Press, 2004.

Albanese, Catherine L. *A Republic of Mind and Spirit: A Cultural History of American Metaphysical Religion*. New Haven, CT: Yale University Press, 2008.

Alter, Robert. *Necessary Angels: Tradition and Modernity in Kafka, Benjamin, and Scholem*. Cambridge, MA: Harvard University Press, 1991.

———. *Partial Magic: The Novel as Self-Conscious Genre*. Berkeley: University of California Press, 1975.

Altick, Richard D. *The English Common Reader: A Social History of the Mass Reading Public, 1800–1900*. Chicago, IL: University of Chicago Press, 1957.

———. *The Shows of London*. Cambridge, MA: Harvard University Press, 1978.

Anderson, Benedict. *Imagined Communities: Reflections on the Origin and Spread of Nationalism*. London: Verso, 1991.

Anderson, Douglas A. "The Mainstreaming of Fantasy and the Legacy of *The Lord of the Rings*." In *The Lord of the Rings 1954–2004: Essays in Honor of Richard E. Blackwelder*, ed. Wayne G. Hammond and Christina Scull. Milwaukee, WI: Marquette University Press, 2006.

Anderson, R. Lanier. "Nietzsche on Redemption and Transfiguration." In *The Re-Enchantment of the World: Secular Magic in a Rational Age*, ed. Joshua Landy and Michael Saler. Stanford, CA: Stanford University Press, 2009.

Annan, Noel. *Our Age: English Intellectuals Between the World Wars—A Group Portrait*. New York: Random House, 1990.

Appadurai, Arjun. *Modernity at Large: Cultural Dimensions of Globalization*. Minneapolis: University of Minnesota Press, 1997.

Arnason, Johann P. "Reason, Imagination, Interpretation." In *Rethinking Imagination: Culture and Creativity*, ed. Gillian Robinson and John Rundell. London: Routledge, 1994.

Asad, Talal. *Formations of the Secular: Christianity, Islam, Modernity*. Stanford, CA: Stanford University Press, 2003.

Asendorf, Christoph. *Batteries of Life: On the History of Things and Their Perception in Modernity*, trans. Don Reneau. Berkeley: University of California Press 1993.

Ashley, Mike. *Gateways to Forever: The Story of the Science-Fiction Magazines from 1970 to 1980*. Liverpool: Liverpool University Press, 2007.

———. *The Gernsback Days*. Holicong, PA: The Wildside Press, 2004.

———. *The Time Machines: The Story of the Science-Fiction Pulp Magazines from the Beginning to 1950*. Liverpool: Liverpool University Press, 2000.

———. *Transformations: The Story of the Science-Fiction Magazines from 1950 to 1970*. Liverpool: Liverpool University Press, 2005.

Bacon-Smith, Camille. *Science Fiction Culture*. Philadelphia: University of Pennsylvania Press, 2000.

Bailey, Peter. "The Victorian Middle Class and the Problem of Leisure." In Peter Bailey, *Popular Culture and Performance in the Victorian City*. Cambridge: Cambridge University Press, 1998.

Bainbridge, William Sims. *The Warcraft Civilization: Social Science in a Virtual World*. Cambridge, MA: MIT Press, 2010.

Baldick, Robert. *The Life of J. -K. Huysmans*. Cambridgeshire: Dedalus Books, 2006.

Barkan, Elazar. *The Retreat of Scientific Racism: Changing Concepts of Race in Britain and the United States Between the World Wars*. Cambridge: Cambridge University Press, 1992.

Barker, Juliet. *The Brontës*. London: Weidenfeld and Nicolson, 1994.

Barthes, Roland. "The Reality Effect." In *The Rustle of Language*, trans. Richard Howard. Berkeley: University of California Press, 1989.

Beckson, Karl E. *London in the 1890s: A Cultural History*. New York: W. W. Norton, 1992.

Bennett, Jane. *The Enchantment of Modern Life: Attachments, Crossings, and Ethics*. Princeton, NJ: Princeton University Press, 2001.

Bennett, Oliver. *Cultural Pessimism: Narratives of Decline in the Postmodern World*. Edinburgh: Edinburgh University Press, 2001.

Berger, Peter L. "The Descularization of the World: A Global Overview." In *The Desecularization of the World: Resurgent Religion and World Politics*, ed. Peter L. Berger. Grand Rapids, MI: William B. Eerdmans Publishing, 1999.

Berman, Marshall. *All That Is Solid Melts Into Air: The Experience of Modernity*. Harmondsworth: Penguin Books, 1988.

Berman, Morris. *The Reenchantment of the World*. Ithaca, NY: Cornell University Press, 1982.

Berry, Mark. "Richard Wagner and the Politics of the Music-Drama." *The Historical Journal* 47:3 (September 2004).

Bettelheim, Bruno. *The Uses of Enchantment: The Meaning and Importance of Fairy Tales*. New York: Alfred A. Knopf, 1976.

Blackbeard, Bill. "Comments on the Grimly Comic Development of A Major American Epic of Witchcraft and Fisticuffs as Refereed by J. Wellington Wimpy." In E. C. Segar, *E. C. Segar's Popeye: I Yam What I Yam!, Volume 1*. Seattle, WA: Fantagraphics, 2006.

Blackmore, Susan. "Lucid Dreaming: Awake in Your Sleep?" *Skeptical Inquirer* 15 (Summer 1991).

Bloom, Paul. *How Pleasure Works: The New Science of Why We Like What We Like*. New York: W. W. Norton, 2010.

Blumenberg, Hans. *The Legitimacy of the Modern Age*, trans. Robert M. Wallace. Cambridge, MA: Harvard University Press, 1983.

Boellstorff, Tom. *Coming of Age in Second Life: An Anthropologist Explores the Virtually Human*. Princeton, NJ: Princeton University Press, 2008.

Bogost, Ian. *Persuasive Games: The Expressive Power of Videogames*. Cambridge, MA: MIT Press, 2007.

Booth, Martin. *The Doctor, the Detective, and Arthur Conan Doyle: A Biography of Arthur Conan Doyle*. London: Hodder and Stoughton, 1997.

Bould, Mark, and Andrew M. Butler, Adam Roberts, Sherryl Vint, ed. *The Routledge Companion to Science Fiction*. London: Routledge, 2009.

Bourdieu, Pierre. *Distinction: A Social Critique of the Judgement of Taste*, trans. Richard Nice. Cambridge, MA: Harvard University Press, 1985.

Boym, Svetlana. *The Future of Nostalgia*. New York: Basic Books, 2002.

Brann, Eva T. H. *The World of the Imagination: Sum and Substance*. Maryland: Rowman and Littlefield, 1991.

Brantlinger, Patrick. *Bread and Circuses: Theories of Mass Culture As Social Decay*. Ithaca, NY: Cornell University Press, 1985.

——. *The Reading Lesson: The Threat of Mass Literacy in Nineteenth-Century British Fiction*. Bloomington: Indiana University Press, 1998.

——. *Rule of Darkness: British Literature and Imperialism, 1830–1914*. Ithaca, NY: Cornell University Press, 1988.

Braque, Remi. *The Wisdom of the World: The Human Experience*, trans. Teresa Lavender Fagaan. Chicago, IL: University of Chicago Press, 2003.

Brewer, David. *The Afterlife of Character, 1726–1825*. Philadelphia: University of Pennsylvania Press, 2005.

Brooke-Rose, Christine. *A Rhetoric of the Unreal: Studies in Narrative & Structure, Especially of the Fantastic*. Cambridge: Cambridge University Press, 1981.

Brown, Callum G. *The Death of Christian Britain: Understanding Secularisation 1800–2000*. New York: Routledge, 2001.

Buckley, Jerome Hamilton. *William Ernest Henley: A Study in the "Counter-Decadence" of the 'Nineties*. Princeton, NJ: Princeton University Press, 1945.

Bulson, Eric. *Novels, Maps, Modernity: The Spatial Imagination, 1850–2000*. New York: Routledge, 2007.

Burrow, J. W. *The Crisis of Reason: European Thought, 1848–1914*. New Haven, CT: Yale University Press, 2000.

Calhoun, Craig. ed. *Habermas and the Public Sphere*. Cambridge, MA: MIT Press, 1993.

Calinescu, Matei. *Five Faces of Modernity*. Durham, NC: Duke University Press, 1987.

Campbell, Colin. *The Romantic Ethic and the Spirit of Modern Consumerism*. Oxford: Blackwell, 1987.

Candida-Smith, Richard. *Mallarmé's Children: Symbolism and the Renewal of Experience*. Berkeley: University of California Press, 2000.

Caputo, John D., and Gianni Vatimo. *After the Death of God*, ed. Jeffrey W. Robbins. New York: Columbia University Press, 2007.

Carpenter, Humphrey. *Secret Gardens: The Golden Age of Children's Literature*. Boston, MA: Houghton Mifflin Company, 1985.

———. *Tolkien: A Biography*. Boston, MA: Houghton Mifflin Company, 1977.

Carter, Lin. *Imaginary Worlds: The Art of Fantasy*. New York: Ballantine Books, 1973.

Carter, Paul. *The Creation of Tomorrow: Fifty Years of Magazine Science Fiction*. New York: Columbia University Press, 1977.

Cascardi, Anthony J. *The Subject of Modernity*. Cambridge: Cambridge University Press, 1992.

Castle, William. *Step Right Up! I'm Gonna Scare the Pants Off America*. New York: World Almanac, 1992.

Castronova, Edward. *Exodus to the Virtual World: How Online Fun is Changing Reality*. New York: Palgrave Macmillan, 2007.

———. *Synthetic Worlds: The Business and Culture of Online Games*. Chicago, IL: University of Chicago Press, 2005.

Chai, Leon. *Aestheticism: The Religion of Post-Romantic Literature*. New York: Columbia University Press, 1990.

Chakrabarty, Dipesh. *Provincializing Europe: Postcolonial Thought and Historical Difference*. Princeton, NJ: Princeton University Press, 2007.

Chance, Jane. "A Mythology for England?" In *Tolkien and the Invention of Myth: A Reader*, ed. Jane Chance. Lexington: The University Press of Kentucky, 2004.

———, ed. *Tolkien the Medievalist*. London: Routledge, 2003.

Clute, John, and John Grant, ed. *The Encyclopedia of Fantasy*. New York: St. Martin's Press, 1997.

——— and Peter Nicholls, ed. *The Encyclopedia of Science Fiction*. New York: St. Martin's Press, 1993.

———. *Scores: Reviews 1993–2003*. Essex: Beccon Publications, 2003.

Cohen, Deborah. *Household Gods: The British and Their Possessions*. New Haven, CT: Yale University Press, 2007.

Cohen, Morton. *Rider Haggard: His Life and Works*. London: Hutchinson and Co., 1960.

Colclough, Stephen. "Recovering the Reader: Commonplace Books and Diaries as Sources of Reading Experience." *Publishing History* XLIV (Fall 1998).

Collini, Stefan. *Absent Minds: Intellectuals in Britain*. New York: Oxford University Press, 2006.

———. *Public Moralists: Political Thought and Intellectual Life in Britain, 1850–1930*. Oxford: Oxford University Press, 1993.

Comaroff, Jean, and John Comaroff, ed. *Modernity and Its Malcontents: Ritual and Power in Postcolonial Africa*. Chicago, IL: University of Chicago Press, 1993.

Connolly, William E. "Belief, Spirituality, and Time." In *Varieties of Secularism in a Secular Age*, ed. Michael Warner, Jonathan VanAntwerpen, and Craig Calhoun. Cambridge, MA: Harvard University Press, 2010.

Cook, James. *The Arts of Deception: Playing With Fraud in the Age of Barnum*. Cambridge, MA: Harvard University Press, 2001.

Coombs, James E. *Play World: The Emergence of a New Ludic Age*. Westport, CT: Praeger, 2000.

Costa Lima, Luiz. "The Control of the Imagination and the Novel." In *The Novel, Volume One*, ed. Franco Moretti. Princeton, NJ: Princeton University Press, 2006.

Cross, Gary. *Kids' Stuff: Toys and the Changing World of American Childhood*. Cambridge, MA: Harvard University Press, 1997.

Crowe, Michael J., ed. *Ronald Knox and Sherlock Holmes: The Origin of Sherlockian Studies*. Indianapolis, IN: Gasogene Books, 2011.

Cruse, Amy. *The Victorians and their Books*. London: George Allen and Unwin Limited, 1936.

Curry, Patrick. "Iron Crown, Iron Cage: Tolkien and Weber on Modernity and Enchantment." In *Myth and Magic: Art According to the Inklings*, ed. Eduardo Segura and Thomas Honegger. Zurich: Walking Tree Press, 2008.

Dale, Peter Allen. *In Pursuit of a Scientific Culture: Science, Art, and Society in the Victorian Age*. Madison: Wisconsin University Press, 1989.

Darnton, Robert. "Readers Respond to Rousseau: The Fabrication of Romantic Sensitivity." In Robert Darnton, *The Great Cat Massacre and Other Episodes in French Cultural History*. London: Penguin Books, 2001.

Daston, Lorraine and Peter Galison. *Objectivity*. Cambridge, MA: Zone Books, 2007.

———. and Katherine Park. *Wonders and the Order of Nature, 1150–1750*. Cambridge, MA: Zone Books, 1998.

Davin, Eric Leif. *Partners in Wonder: Women and the Birth of Science Fiction 1926–1965*. Lanham, MD: Lexington Books, 2006.

Davis, Erik. *Techgnosis: Myth, Magic and Mysticism in the Information Age*. New York: Harmony Books, 1998.

Debord, Guy. *The Society of the Spectacle*. Cambridge, MA: Zone Books, 1994.

Denisoff, Dennis. "Decadence and Aestheticism." In *The Cambridge Companion to the Fin de Siècle*, ed. Gail Marshall. Cambridge: Cambridge University Press, 2007.

Denning, Michael. *Mechanic Accents: Dime Novels and Working-Class Culture in America*. New York: Verso, 1998.

Derrida, Jacques. *Specters of Marx: The State of the Debt, The Work of Mourning, and the New International*. New York: Routledge, 1994.

Disch, Thomas. *The Dreams Our Stuff Is Made Of: How Science Fiction Conquered the World*. New York: The Free Press, 1998.

Doležel, Lubomir. *Heterocosmica: Fiction and Possible Worlds*. Baltimore, MD: Johns Hopkins University Press, 2000.

Doyle, Arthur Conan. *The Annotated Lost World*, annotated by Roy Pilot and Alvin Rodin. Indianapolis, IL: Wessex Press, 1996.

Dube, Saurabh, ed. *Enduring Enchantments*, special issue of *The South Atlantic Quarterly* 101:4 (October 2002).

During, Simon. *Modern Enchantments: The Cultural Power of Secular Magic*. Cambridge, MA: Harvard University Press, 2001.

Durozoi, Gérard. *History of the Surrealist Movement*, trans. Alison Anderson. Chicago, IL: University of Chicago Press, 2002.

Dyer, Richard. *Stars*. London: British Film Institute, 1998.

Eaves, T. C. Duncan and Ben D. Kimpel. *Samuel Richardson: A Biography*. New York: Oxford University Press, 1971.

Eckhert, Win Scott, ed. *Myths for the Modern Age: Philip José Farmer's Wold Newton Universe*. Austin, TX: MonkeyBrain Books, 2005.

Eden, Bradford Lee. "The 'Music of the Spheres': Relationships between Tolkien's *The Silmarillion* and Medieval Cosmological and Religious Theory." In *Tolkien the Medievalist*, ed. Jane Chance. London: Routledge, 2003.

Eisenstadt, Shmuel Noah, ed. *Multiple Modernities*. Piscataway, NJ: Transaction Publishers, 2002.

Ellis, Peter Berresford. *H. Rider Haggard: A Voice from the Infinite*. London: Routledge and Kegan Paul, 1978.

Evans, Jonathan. "Dwarves." In *J. R. R. Tolkien Encyclopedia: Scholarship and Critical Assessment*, ed. Michael D. C. Drout. New York: Routledge, 2007.

Felski, Rita. *The Gender of Modernity*. Cambridge, MA: Harvard University Press, 1995.

Fimi, Dimitra. *Tolkien, Race and Cultural History*. London: Palgrave MacMillan, 2009.

Fine, Gary Alan. *Shared Fantasy: Role-Playing Games as Social Worlds*. Chicago, IL: University of Chicago Press, 1983 [2002].

Flieger, Verlyn. *Interrupted Music: The Making of Tolkien's Mythology*. Kent, OH: Kent State University Press, 2005.

Foster, Thomas. "Virtuality." In *The Routledge Companion to Science Fiction*, Mark Bould, Andrew M. Butler, Adam Roberts, and Sherryl Vint, ed. London: Routledge, 2009.

Foucault, Michel. "What Is an Author?" In Michel Foucault, *The Foucault Reader*, ed. Paul Rabinow. New York: Pantheon Books, 1984.

Frank, Joseph. "Spatial Form in Modern Literature." In *Criticism: The Foundations of Modern Literary Judgement*, ed. Mark Schorer, Josephine Miles, and Gordon McKenzie. New York: Harcourt, Brace and Company, 1958.

Fredrick, Candice, and Sam McBride. *Women Among the Inklings*. Westport, CT: Greenwood Press, 2001.

Frisby, David. "Introduction." In Georg Simmel, *The Philosophy of Money*, ed. and trans. Tom Bottomore and David Frisby. London: Routledge, 2004.

———. *Fragments of Modernity: Theories of Modernity in the Work of Simmel, Kracauer and Benjamin*. Cambridge, MA: Harvard University Press, 1986.

Fritze, Ronald H. *Invented Knowledge: False History, Fake Science and Pseudo-Religions*. London: Reaktion Books, 2009.

Fritzsche, Peter. *Stranded in the Present: Modern Time and the Melancholy of History*. Cambridge, MA: Harvard University Press, 2004.

Gabler, Neil. *Amusing Ourselves to Death: Public Discourse in the Age of Show Business*. New York: Penguin Books, 1985.

Gagnier, Regenia. *Idylls of the Marketplace: Oscar Wilde and the Victorian Public*. Stanford, CA: Stanford University Press, 1987.

Gallagher, Brian. "Greta Garbo is Sad: Some Historical Reflections on the Paradoxes of Stardom in the American Film Industry." *Images* 3. http://www.imagesjournal.com/issue03/infocus/stars4.htm (accessed June 11, 2002).

Gallagher, Catherine. *Nobody's Story: The Vanishing Acts of Women Writers in the Marketplace, 1670–1920*. Berkeley: University of California Press, 1995.

———. "The Rise of Fictionality." In *The Novel, Volume One*, ed. Franco Moretti. Princeton, NJ: Princeton University Press, 2006.

Galloway, Jr., W. F. "The Conservative Attitude Toward Fiction, 1770–1830." *PMLA* 55: 4 (December 1940).

Gaonkar, Dilip Parameshwar, ed. *Alternative Modernities*. Durham, NC: Duke University Press, 2001.

Garth, John. *Tolkien and the Great War: The Threshold of Middle-earth*. Boston, MA: Houghton Mifflin, 2003.

Gauchet, Marcel. *The Disenchantment of the World: A Political History of Religion*, trans. Oscar Burge. Princeton, NJ: Princeton University Press, 1997.

Genette, Gérard. *Paratexts: Thresholds of Interpretation*, trans. Jane E. Lewin. Cambridge: Cambridge University Press, 1997.

Geschiere, Peter. *The Modernity of Witchcraft: Politics and the Occult in Postcolonial Africa*, trans. Janet Roitman. Charlottesville: University of Virginia Press, 1997.

Giddens, Anthony. *The Consequences of Modernity*. Stanford, CA: Stanford University Press, 1990.

Gillespie, Michael. *The Theological Origins of Modernity*. Chicago, IL: University of Chicago Press, 2008.

Gilsdorf, Ethan. *Fantasy Freaks and Gaming Geeks: An Epic Quest for Reality Among Role Players, Online Gamers, and Other Dwellers of Imaginary Realms.* Guilford, CT: Lyons Press, 2010.

Glassman, Ronald M., and Vatro Muvar, ed. *Max Weber's Political Sociology: A Pessimistic Vision of a Rationalized World.* Westport, CT: Greenwood Press 1984.

Goldstein, Jan. *The Post-Revolutionary Self: Politics and Psyche in France, 1750–1850.* Cambridge, MA: Harvard University Press, 2005.

Goodman, Matthew. *The Sun and the Moon: The Remarkable True Account of Hoaxers, Showmen, Dueling Journalists and Lunar Man Bats in Nineteenth Century New York.* New York: Basic Books, 2008.

de Grazia, Victoria. *Irresistible Empire: America's Advance through Twentieth-Century Europe.* Cambridge, MA: Harvard University Press, 2005.

Gray, Jonathan, and Cornel Sandvoss, C. Lee Harrington, ed. *Fandom: Identities and Communities in a Mediated World.* New York: New York University Press, 2007.

Greene, Hugh. *The Rivals of Sherlock Holmes: Early Detective Stories.* New York: Pantheon, 1970.

Griffin, Roger. *Fascism and Modernism: The Sense of a Beginning Under Mussolini and Hitler.* London: Palgrave Macmillan, 2007.

———. "Revolts against the Modern World: The Blend of Literary and Historical Fantasy in the Italian New Right." *Literature and History* 11:1 (Spring 1985).

Grimley, Matthew. "The Religion of Englishness: Puritanism, Providentialism, and 'National Character,' 1918–1945." *Journal of British Studies* 46 (October 2007).

Guest, Tim. *Second Lives: A Journey Through Virtual Worlds.* London: Hutchinson, 2007.

Gumbrecht, Hans Ulrich. "A History of the Concept 'Modern.'" In H. U. Gumbrecht, *Making Sense in Life and Literature*, trans. Glen Burns. Minneapolis: University of Minnesota Press, 1992.

Gygax, Gary. "On the Influence of J. R. R. Tolkien on the *D&D* and *AD&D* Games." *Dragon* 95 (1985).

Habermas, Jurgen. *The Philosophical Discourse of Modernity: Twelve Lectures*, trans. Frederick Lawrence. Cambridge, MA: MIT Press, 1987.

Haining, Peter, ed. *The Edgar Allan Poe Scrapbook.* New York: Schocken Books, 1978.

Hall, Stuart, and David Held, Don Hubert, Kenneth Thompson, ed. *Modernity: An Introduction to Modern Societies.* Oxford: Blackwell, 1996.

Hammond, Wayne G., and Christina Scull, ed. *The Lord of the Rings 1954–2004: Essays in Honor of Richard E. Blackwelder.* Milwaukee, WI: Marquette University Press, 2006.

Hanegraaff, Wouter J. "How Magic Survived the Disenchantment of the World." *Religion* 33:4 (October 2003).

Hansen, Rob. *Then.* http:/ansible.co.uk/Then (accessed February 23, 2011).

Harman, Graham. "On the Horror of Phenomenology: Lovecraft and Husserl." *Collapse: Philosophical Research and Development.* Vol. 4. ed. Robin MacKay. Falmouth: Urbanomic, 2008.

Harpold, Terry. "Verne's Cartographies." *Science Fiction Studies* 95 (March 2005).

Harrington, Ann. *Reenchanted Science: Holism in German Culture From Wilhelm II to Hitler.* Princeton, NJ: Princeton University Press, 1996.

Harris, Neil. "Iconography and Intellectual History: The Halftone Effect." In Neil Harris, *Cultural Excursions: Marketing Appetites and Cultural Tastes in Modern America.* Chicago, IL: The University of Chicago Press, 1990.

———. *Humbug: The Art of P. T. Barnum.* Boston: Little, Brown, 1973.

Harrison, Brian. "Introduction to the *Oxford DNB*." *http://www.oup.com/oxforddnb/info/prelims/intro/intro2/#18back* (accessed August 5, 2007).

Hayles, N. Katherine. "Foreword." In *Prefiguring Cyberculture: An Intellectual History*, ed. Darren Tofts, Annemarie Jonson, and Alessio Cavallero. Cambridge, MA: MIT Press, 2002.

Hayward, Jennifer. *Consuming Pleasures: Active Audiences and Serial Fictions from Dickens to Soap Operas.* Lexington: The University Press of Kentucky, 1997.

Henderson, Linda Dalrymple. *The Fourth Dimension and Non-Euclidean Geometry in Modern Art.* Princeton, NJ: Princeton University Press, 1983.

Herbert, Christopher. *Culture and Anomie: Ethnographic Imagination in the Nineteenth Century.* Chicago, IL: University of Chicago Press, 1991.

———. *Victorian Relativity: Radical Thought and Scientific Discovery.* Chicago, IL: University of Chicago Press, 2001.

Herman, Arthur. *The Idea of Decline in Western History.* New York: The Free Press, 1997.

Hills, Matt. *Fan Cultures.* London: Routledge, 2002.

Hofstadter, Richard. *Anti-Intellectualism in American Life.* New York: Vintage, 1963.

Hollinger, David. "The Knower and the Artificer, with Postscript 1993." In *Modernist Impulses in the Social Sciences,* ed. Dorothy Ross. Baltimore, MD: Johns Hopkins University Press, 1994.

Holmes, Richard. *The Age of Wonder: How the Romantic Generation Discovered the Beauty and Terror of Science.* New York: Pantheon, 2009.

Houellebecq, Michel. *H. P. Lovecraft: Against the World, Against Life,* trans. Dorna Khazeni. San Francisco, CA: McSweeney's, 2005.

Hughes, H. Stuart. *Consciousness and Society: The Reorientation of Social Thought, 1890–1930.* New York: Vintage Books, 1961.

Hunt, Lynn. *Inventing Human Rights: A History.* New York: Norton, 2007.

Hutton, Ronald. *The Triumph of the Moon: A History of Modern Pagan Witchcraft.* Oxford: Oxford University Press, 1999.

Iser, Wolfgang. *The Fictive and the Imaginary: Charting Literary Anthropology.* Baltimore, MD: Johns Hopkins University Press, 1993.

Jacoby, Susan. *The Age of American Unreason.* New York: Pantheon Books, 2008.

Jackson, Kevin. *Invisible Forms: A Guide to Literary Curiosities.* New York: St. Martin's Press, 2000.

Jager, Colin. "This Detail, This History: Charles Taylor's Romanticism." In *Varieties of Secularism in a Secular Age,* ed. Michael Warner, Jonathan VanAntwerpen, and Craig Calhoun. Cambridge, MA: Harvard University Press, 2010.

James, Edward and Farah Mendlesohn, ed. *The Cambridge Companion to Science Fiction.* Cambridge: Cambridge University Press, 2003.

Jameson, Fredric. *Archaeologies of the Future: The Desire Called Utopia and Other Science Fictions.* London: Verso, 2005.

Jay, Martin. *The Dialectical Imagination: A History of the Frankfurt School and the Institute of Social Research, 1923–1950.* Berkeley: University of California Press, 1996.

Jenkins, Henry. *Textual Poachers: Television Fans and Participatory Culture.* London: Routledge, 1992.

Jervis, John. *Exploring the Modern: Patterns of Western Culture and Civilization.* Oxford: Wiley-Blackwell, 1998.

Johnson, Steven. *Everything Bad is Good for You: How Today's Popular Culture is Actually Making Us Smarter.* New York: Penguin, 2006.

Joshi, S. T. *I Am Providence: The Life and Times of H. P. Lovecraft.* Vol. 1. New York: Hippocampus Press, 2010.

———. *I Am Providence: The Life and Times of H. P. Lovecraft.* Vol. 2. New York: Hippocampus Press, 2010.

———. *The Rise and Fall of the Cthulhu Mythos.* Poplar Bluff, MO: Mythos Books, 2008.

———. *A Weird Writer in Our Midst: Early Criticism of H. P. Lovecraft.* New York: Hippocampus Press, 2010.

Kahan, Dan M., Hank Jenkins-Smith, and Donald Braman. "Cultural Cognition of Scientific Consensus." Cultural Cognition Project Working Paper No. 77. Social Science Research Network, *http://ssrn.com/abstract=1549444* (accessed February 7, 2010).

Kalberg, Stephen. "Max Weber's Types of Rationality." *American Journal of Sociology* 85:5 (March 1980).

Katsiaficas, George. *The Imagination of the New Left: A Global Analysis of 1968*. Cambridge, MA: South End Press, 1987.

Kaveney, Roz. *Superheroes!: Capes and Crusaders in Comics and Films*. London: I. B.Tauris, 2008.

Kearney, Richard. *The Wake of Imagination: Toward a Postmodern Culture*. London: Routledge, 1998.

Keen, Andrew. *The Cult of the Amateur: How Today's Internet is Killing Our Culture*. New York: Doubleday, 2007.

Kennedy, George A. *Fictitious Authors and Imaginary Novels in French, English, and American Literature from the 18th to the Start of the 21ˢᵗ Century*. New York: The Edwin Mellon Press, 2005.

Keymer, Thomas, and Peter Sabor. *"Pamela" in the Marketplace: Literary Controversy and Print Culture in Eighteenth Century Britain and Ireland*. Cambridge: Cambridge University Press, 2006.

Kilby, Clyde. *Tolkien and the Silmarillion*. Berkhamsted: Lion Publishing, 1977.

King, Brad, and John Borland. *Dungeons and Dreamers: The Rise of Computer Game Culture*. New York: McGraw Hill, 2003.

Kloppenberg, James T. "Democracy and Disenchantment: From Weber to Dewey to Habermas and Rorty." In *Modernist Impulses in the Social Sciences*, ed. Dorothy Ross. Baltimore, MD: Johns Hopkins University Press, 1994.

Landy, Joshua. "The Cruel Gift: Lucid Self-Delusion in French Literature and German Philosophy, 1851–1914." Ph.D. dissertation. Princeton University, 1997.

———. and Michael Saler, ed. *The Re-Enchantment of the World: Rational Magic in a Secular Age*. Stanford, CA: Stanford University Press, 2009.

Langford, David R. "William Morris." In *The Encyclopedia of Fantasy*, ed. John Clute and John Grant. New York: St. Martin's Press, 1997.

Laqueur, Thomas Walter. *Solitary Sex: A Cultural History of Masturbation*. Cambridge, MA: Zone Books, 2003.

Lash, Scott, and Jonathan Friedman, ed. *Modernity and Identity*. Oxford: Blackwell, 1992.

Laslett, Peter. *The World We Have Lost*. New York: Routledge, 2004 [1965].

Latour, Bruno. *We Have Never Been Modern*, trans. Catherine Porter. Cambridge, MA: Harvard University Press, 1993.

Lazier, Benjamin. *God Interrupted: Heresy and the European Imagination Between the Wars*. Princeton, NJ: Princeton University Press, 2009.

Lehman, David. *The Perfect Murder: A Study in Detection*. Ann Arbor: University of Michigan Press, 2000.

Lehrer, Jonah. "We, Robots." *New York Times*, January 23, 2011.

Lepenies, Wolf. *Between Literature and Science: The Rise of Sociology*. Cambridge: Cambridge University Press, 1988.

Levine, Lawrence W. *Highbrow/Lowbrow: The Emergence of Cultural Hierarchy in America*. Cambridge, MA: Harvard University Press, 1988.

Lewis, Lisa A. *The Adoring Audience: Fan Culture and Popular Media*. London: Routledge, 1992.

Light, Alison. *Forever England: Femininity, Literature, and Conservatism Between the Wars*. London: Routledge, 1991.

Lindner, Robert. *The Fifty-Minute Hour: A Collection of True Psychoanalytic Tales*. New York: Other Press, 2002.

Lottman, Herbert. *Jules Verne: An Exploratory Biography*. New York: St. Martin's Press, 1996.

Lumley, Brian. *The Taint and Other Novellas*. Burton, MI: Subterranean Press, 2007.

Lunn, Eugene. *Marxism and Modernism: An Historical Study of Lukács, Brecht, Benjamin, and Adorno*. Berkeley: University of California Press, 1984.

Lycett, Andrew. *The Man Who Created Sherlock Holmes: The Life and Times of Sir Arthur Conan Doyle*. New York: Simon and Schuster, 2007.

McCorristine, Shane. *Spectres of the Self: Thinking about Ghosts and Ghost-Seeing in England, 1750–1920*. Cambridge: Cambridge University Press, 2010.

McGonigal, Jane. *Reality is Broken: Why Games Make Us Better and How They Can Change the World*. New York: Penguin Press, 2011.

McKibbin, Ross. *Classes and Cultures: England, 1918–1951*. New York: Oxford University Press, 2000.

Maguire, Matthew W. *The Conversion of the Imagination: From Pascal to Rousseau to Tocqueville*. Cambridge, MA: Harvard University Press, 2006.

Mandler, Peter. *The English National Character: The History of an Idea from Edmund Burke to Tony Blair*. New Haven, CT: Yale University Press, 2006.

Manguel, Alberto and Gianni Guadalupi. *The Dictionary of Imaginary Places*. New York: Harcourt, 2000.

Marks, Jeffrey. *Anthony Boucher: A Biobibliography*. Charlotte, NC: McFarland & Company, 2008.

Marshall, Gail, ed. *The Cambridge Companion to the Fin de Siècle*. Cambridge: Cambridge University Press, 2007

Megill, Allan. *Prophets of Extremity: Nietzsche, Heidegger, Derrida*. Berkeley: University of California Press, 1987.

Meisel, Martin. *Realizations: Narrative, Pictorial, and Theatrical Arts in Nineteenth-Century England*. Princeton, NJ: Princeton University Press, 1983.

Mellor, Anne K. *English Romantic Irony*. Cambridge, MA: Harvard University Press, 1980.

Merrick, Helen. *The Secret Feminist Cabal: A Cultural History of Science Fiction Feminisms*. Seattle, WA: Aqueduct Press, 2009.

Milburn, Michael. "Coleridge's Definition of Imagination and Tolkien's Definition(s) of Faery." *Tolkien Studies* 7 (2010).

Miller, Lucasta. *The Brontë Myth*. New York: Alfred A. Knopf, 2001.

Mommsen, Wolfgang, and Jurgen Osterhammel, ed. *Max Weber and His Contemporaries*. London: HarperCollins, 1987.

Monro, John Warne. *Laboratories of Faith: Mesmerism, Spiritism, and Occultism in Modern France*. Ithaca, NY: Cornell University Press, 2008.

Monteiro, George. *The Man Who Never Was: Essays on Fernando Pessoa*. Providence, RI: Gávea-Brown Publications, 1982.

Moore, Henrietta L., and Todd Sanders, ed. *Magical Interpretations, Material Realities: Modernity, Witchcraft, and the Occult in Postcolonial Africa*. London: Routledge, 2001.

Moretti, Franco. "The Slaughterhouse of Literature." *Modern Language Quarterly* 61:1 (March 2000).

Morrisson, Mark S. "The Periodical Culture of the Occult Revival: Esoteric Wisdom, Modernity and Counter Public Spheres." *Journal of Modern Literature* 31:2 (Winter 2008).

Moskowitz, Sam. *The Immortal Storm*. Atlanta, GA: The Atlanta Science Fiction Organization, 1954.

Murray, Jane H. *Hamlet on the Holodeck: The Future of Narrative in Cyberspace*. New York: The Free Press, 1997.

Najafi, Sina. "Underworld, an Interview with Rosalind Williams." *Cabinet* 30 (Summer 2008).

Nead, Lynda. *Victorian Babylon: People, Streets and Images in Nineteenth-Century London*. New Haven, CT: Yale University Press, 2000.

Nell, Victor. *Lost in a Book: The Psychology of Reading for Pleasure.* New Haven, CT: Yale University Press, 1988.

Nevins, Jess. "A Good Enough Man for Any World: The 19th Century Roots of Hardboiled Detective Fiction." *Back Alley,* http://www.backalleywebzine.com/ (accessed September 8, 2010).

———. *Heroes & Monsters: The Unofficial Companion to the League of Extraordinary Gentlemen.* Austin, TX: MonkeyBrain Books, 2003.

Nicholls, Peter. "History of SF." In *The Encyclopedia of Science Fiction,* ed. John Clute and Peter Nicholls. New York: St. Martin's Press, 1993.

North, Michael. *Reading 1922: A Return to the Scene of the Modern.* New York: Oxford University Press, 1999.

Nye, David. *American Technological Sublime.* Cambridge, MA: MIT Press, 1994.

Oppenheim, Janet. *The Other World: Spiritualism and Psychical Research in England, 1850–1914.* Cambridge: Cambridge University Press, 1988.

Otter, Sandra M. Den. *British Idealism and Social Explanation: A Study in Late Victorian Thought.* Oxford: Clarendon Press, 1996.

Otto, Peter. *Multiplying Worlds: Romanticism, Modernity, and the Emergence of Virtual Reality.* New York: Oxford University Press, 2011.

Owen, Alex. *The Place of Enchantment: British Occultism and the Culture of the Modern.* Chicago, IL: University of Chicago Press, 2004.

Parrinder, Patrick, ed. *Learning From Other Worlds: Estrangement, Cognition, and the Politics of Science Fiction and Utopias.* Durham, NC: Duke University Press, 2001.

Patrick, James. *The Magdalen Metaphysicals: Idealism and Orthodoxy at Oxford, 1901–1945.* Macon, GA: Mercer University Press, 1985.

Pavel, Thomas. *Fictional Worlds.* Cambridge, MA: Harvard University Press, 1989.

Pecora, Vincent. *Secularization and Cultural Criticism: Religion, Nation, and Modernity.* Chicago, IL: University of Chicago Press, 2006.

Phillips, Richard. *Mapping Men and Empire: A Geography of Adventure.* London: Routledge, 1997.

Pile, Steve. "Freud, Dreams and Imaginative Geographies." In *Freud 2000,* ed. Anthony Elliott. New York: Routledge, 1999.

Porter, Roy. *Flesh in the Age of Reason: The Modern Foundations of Body and Soul.* New York: W. W. Norton, 2004.

Porter, William Riley. "Where Do English Departments Come From?" *College English* 28:5 (February 1967).

Post, Jeremiah Benjamin. *An Atlas of Fantasy.* Baltimore, MD: The Mirage Press, 1973.

Pringle, David. *Imaginary People: A Who's Who of Modern Fictional Characters.* London: Grafton, 1987.

———. "Introduction." In *The Ultimate Encyclopedia of Fantasy,* ed. David Pringle. London: Carlton Books, 2006.

Punday, David. "Creative Accounting: Role-Playing Games, Possible-World Theory, and the Agency of the Imagination." *Poetics Today* 26:1 (Spring 2005).

Pustz, Matthew J. *Comic Book Culture: Fanboys and True Believers.* Jackson, MI: University of Mississippi Press, 2000.

Radway, Janice A. *Reading the Romance.* Chapel Hill, NC: University of North Carolina Press, 1991.

Ramaswamy, Sumathi. *The Lost Land of Lemuria: Fabulous Geographies, Catastrophic Histories.* Berkeley: University of California Press, 2004.

Ratchford, Fannie Elizabeth. *The Brontës' Web of Childhood.* New York: Russell & Russell, Inc., 1964 [1941].

———. *Legends of Angria.* New Haven, CT: Yale University Press, 1933.

Redmond, Donald A. *Sherlock Holmes Among the Pirates: Copyright and Conan Doyle in America, 1890–1930.* Westport, CT: Greenwood Press, 1990.

Reed, T. J. *Thomas Mann: The Uses of Tradition.* Oxford: Oxford University Press, 1974.

Repp, Kevin. *Reformers, Critics and the Paths of German Modernity: Anti-Politics and the Search for Alternatives, 1890–1914.* Cambridge, MA: Harvard University Press, 2000.

Rice, Susan. "Dubious and Questionable Memories: A History of the Adventuresses of Sherlock Holmes." *The Baker Street Journal 2004 Christmas Annual* (December 2004).

Richardson, Robert D. *William James: In the Maelstrom of American Modernism.* Boston, MA: Houghton Mifflin Company, 2006.

Rieder, John. *Colonialism and the Emergence of Science Fiction.* Middletown, CT: Wesleyan University Press, 2008.

Roberts, Adam. *The History of Science Fiction.* New York: Palgrave MacMillan, 2007.

Robinson, Gillian, and John Rundell, ed. *Rethinking Imagination: Culture and Creativity.* London: Routledge, 1994.

Rorty, Richard. *Contingency, Irony, Solidarity.* Cambridge: Cambridge University Press, 1989.

Rose, Jonathan. *The Intellectual Life of the British Working Classes.* New Haven, CT: Yale University Press, 2002.

Ross, Andrew. *No Respect: Intellectuals and Popular Culture.* New York: Routledge, 1998.

Ross, Dorothy, ed. *Modernist Impulses in the Social Sciences.* Baltimore, MD: Johns Hopkins University Press, 1994.

Ruddick, Nicholas. "The Fantastic Fiction of the Fin de Siècle." In *The Cambridge Companion to the Fin de Siècle,* ed. Gail Marshall. Cambridge: Cambridge University Press, 2007.

Ryan, Marie-Laure. *Narrative as Virtual Reality: Immersion and Interactivity in Literature and Electronic Media.* Baltimore, MD: Johns Hopkins University Press, 2001.

Rzepka, Charles L. *Detective Fiction.* Cambridge: Polity Press, 2005.

Said, Edward. *Culture and Imperialism.* New York: Alfred A. Knopf, 1993.

Saler, Michael. *The Avant-Garde in Interwar England: "Medieval Modernism" and the London Underground.* New York: Oxford University Press, 1999.

———. "'Clap If You Believe in Sherlock Holmes': Mass Culture and the Re-Enchantment of Modernity, c.1890–c.1940." *Historical Journal* 43:6 (September 2003).

———. "Modernity and Enchantment: A Historiographic Review." *The American Historical Review* 111:3 (June 2006).

Sander, Joseph L., ed. *Science Fiction Fandom.* Westport, CT: Greenwood Press, 1994.

Savage, Mike, and Gaynor Bagnall, Brian Longhurst. *Globalization and Belonging.* London: SAGE Publications, 2005.

Scaff, Lawrence A. *Fleeing the Iron Cage: Culture, Politics, and Modernity in the Thought of Max Weber.* Berkeley: University of California Press, 1989.

Schiesel, Seth. "In an Ever-Changing Galaxy, the Action's Starting to Get Intriguing." *New York Times,* November 28, 2007.

———. "In a New Merger, Evidence of How Much the Gaming World Has Changed." *New York Times,* December 5, 2007.

Schoolfield, George. *A Baedeker of Decadence: Charting a Literary Fashion, 1884–1927.* New Haven, CT: Yale University Press, 2003.

Schorer, Mark, and Josephine Miles, Gordon McKenzie, ed. *Criticism: The Foundations of Modern Literary Judgement.* New York: Harcourt, Brace and Company, 1958.

Schultz, David E. "From Microcosm to Macrocosm: The Growth of Lovecraft's Cosmic Vision." In *An Epicure in the Terrible: A Centennial Anthology of Essays in Honor of H. P. Lovecraft,* ed. David E. Schultz and S. T. Joshi. Rutherford, NJ: Fairleigh Dickinson University Press, 1991.

Schwartz, Vanessa. *Spectacular Realities: Early Mass Culture in Fin-de-siècle Paris.* Berkeley: University of California Press, 1998.

Scull, Christina, and Wayne G. Hammond. *The J. R. R. Tolkien Companion and Guide: Reader's Guide*. London: HarperCollins, 2006.

Sedgwick, Mark J. *Against the Modern World: Traditionalism and the Secret Intellectual History of the Twentieth Century*. New York: Oxford University Press, 2004.

Sheehan, Jonathan. *The Enlightenment Bible: Translation, Scholarship, Culture*. Princeton, NJ: Princeton University Press, 2007.

Shermer, Michael. *The Believing Brain: From Ghosts and Gods to Politics and Conspiracies*. New York: Henry Holt, 2011.

———. *Why People Believe Weird Things: Pseudoscience, Superstition, and Other Confusions of Our Time*. New York: W. H. Freeman, 1997.

Shils, Edward. "Max Weber and the World Since 1920." In *Max Weber and His Contemporaries*, ed. Wolfgang Mommsen and Jurgen Osterhammel. London: HarperCollins, 1987.

Shippey, Tom. *J. R. R. Tolkien: Author of the Century*. London: Harper Collins, 2000.

———. "Orcs, Wraiths, Wights: Tolkien's Images of Evil." In Tom Shippey, *Roots and Branches: Selected Papers on Tolkien*. Switzerland: Walking Tree Publishers, 2007.

———. *The Road to Middle-earth: How J. R. R. Tolkien Created a New Mythology*. Boston, MA: Houghton Mifflin, 2003.

Shirky, Clay. *Cognitive Surplus: Creativity and Generosity in a Connected Age*. New York: Penguin, 2010.

Sigler, Carolyn, ed. *Alternative Alices: Visions and Revisions of Lewis Carroll's Alice Books*. Lexington: The University Press of Kentucky, 1997.

Silver, Carole G. *Strange & Secret Peoples: Fairies and Victorian Consciousness*. New York: Oxford University Press, 2000.

Silverman, Kenneth. *Edgar A. Poe: Mournful and Never-ending Remembrance*. New York: Harper Collins, 1991.

Smajic, Srdjan. *Ghost-Seers, Detectives, and Spiritualists: Theories of Vision in Victorian Literature and Science*. Cambridge: Cambridge University Press, 2010.

Smith, Jonathan. *Fact and Feeling: Baconian Science and the Nineteenth Century Literary Imagination*. Madison: Wisconsin University Press, 1994.

Snyder, Laura J. "Sherlock Holmes: Scientific Detective." *Endeavour* 28:3 (September 2004).

Spargo, John W. *Imaginary Books and Libraries: An Essay in Lighter Vein*. New York: Caxton Club, 1952.

Spence, Jonathan. *The Memory Palace of Matteo Ricci*. New York: Penguin, 1985.

Spinosa, Charles, and Hubert L. Dreyfus. "Two Kinds of Antiessentialism and their Consequences." *Critical Inquiry* 22:4 (Summer 1996).

Stableford, Brian. "Science Fiction before the Genre." In *The Cambridge Companion to Science Fiction*, ed. Edward James and Farah Mendlesohn. Cambridge: Cambridge University Press, 2003.

Staples, Terry. "The Cottingley Fairies." In *The Oxford Companion to Fairy Tales*, ed. Jack Zipes. New York: Oxford University Press, 2000.

Stashower, Daniel. *Teller of Tales: A Life of Sir Arthur Conan Doyle*. New York: Henry Holt, 1999.

Steinmeyer, Jim. *Charles Fort*. New York: Tarcher, 2008.

Storm, Jannick. "An Interview With J. G. Ballard." *Speculation* (February 1969). (*http://www.jgballard.ca/interviews/jgb_jannick_storm_interview.html* (accessed March 26, 2010).

Styers, Randall. *Making Magic: Religion, Magic, and Science in the Modern World*. New York: Oxford University Press, 2004.

Sutin, Lawrence. *Divine Invasions: The Life of Philip K. Dick*. New York: Carroll & Graf, 2005.

Suvin, Darko. *Metamorphoses of Science Fiction: On the Poetics and History of a Literary Genre*. New Haven, CT: Yale University Press, 1979.

Swanson, Elliot. "More on Space Patrol." *Inside Space Patrol!* http://www.slick-net.com/space/patrol/pg2/index.phtml (accessed May 24, 2009).

Taussig, Michael. *The Magic of the State*. New York: Routledge, 1997.

Taylor, Charles. *A Secular Age*. Cambridge, MA: Harvard University Press, 2007.

———. *Sources of the Self: The Making of the Modern Identity*. Cambridge, MA: Harvard University Press, 1989.

Taylor, Jenny Bourne. "Psychology at the fin de siècle." In *The Cambridge Companion to the Fin de Siècle*, ed. Gail Marshall. Cambridge: Cambridge University Press, 2007.

Taylor, John Tinnon. *Early Opposition to the English Novel: The Popular Reaction from 1760 to 1830*. New York: Columbia University Press, 1943.

Thurschwell, Pamela. *Literature, Technology and Magical Thinking, 1880–1920*. Cambridge: Cambridge University Press, 2001.

Tofts, Darren, and Annemarie Jonson, Alessio Cavallero, ed. *Prefiguring Cyberculture: An Intellectual History*. Cambridge, MA: MIT Press, 2002.

Toulmin, Stephen. *Cosmopolis: The Hidden Agenda of Modernity*. New York: The Free Press, 1990.

Treitel, Corinna. *A Science for the Soul: Occultism and the Genesis of the German Modern*. Baltimore, MD: Johns Hopkins University Press, 2004.

Tresch, John. "Extra! Extra! Poe Invents Science Fiction!" In *The Cambridge Companion to Edgar Allan Poe*, ed. Kevin J. Hayes. Cambridge: Cambridge University Press, 2002.

Tuan, Yi-Fu. *Escapism*. Baltimore, MD: Johns Hopkins University Press, 1998.

Tulloch, John, and Manuel Alvarado. *Doctor Who: The Unfolding Text*. New York: St. Martin's Press, 1983.

Tulloch, John, and Henry Jenkins. *Science Fiction Audiences: Watching Doctor Who and Star Trek*. New York: Routledge, 1995.

Turkle, Sherry. *Alone Together: Why We Expect More from Technology and Less from Each Other*. New York: Basic Books, 2011.

Turner, Bryan, ed. *Theories of Modernity and Postmodernity*. London: SAGE, 1990.

Turner, Frank Miller. *Between Science and Religion: The Reaction to Scientific Naturalism in Late Victorian England*. New Haven, CT: Yale University Press, 1974.

Turner, James Grantham. "Novel Panic: Picture and Performance in the Reception of Richardson's *Pamela*." *Representations* 48 (Fall 1994).

Tyson, Donald. *The Dream World of H. P. Lovecraft: His Life, His Demons, His Universe*. Woodbury, MN: Llewellyn Publications, 2010.

Utechin, Nicholas. "From Piff-Pouff to Backnecke: Ronald Knox and 100 Years of 'Studies in the Literature of Sherlock Holmes.'" *The Baker Street Journal 2010 Christmas Annual*. Zionsville, IN: The Baker Street Irregulars, 2010.

Vaninskaya, Anna. "The Late-Victorian Romance Revival: A Generic Excursus." *English Literature in Transition* 51:1 (January 2008).

Veldman, Meredith. *Fantasy, the Bomb, and the Greening of Britain: Romantic Protest, 1945–1980*. Cambridge: Cambridge University Press, 1994.

Vincent, David. *Literacy and Popular Culture: England 1750–1914*. Cambridge: Cambridge University Press, 1989.

Viswanathan, Gauri. "Secularism in the Framework of Heterodoxy." *PMLA* 123:2 (March 2008).

de Vries, Hent, ed. *Political Theologies: Public Religions in a Post-Secular World*. New York: Fordham University Press, 2006.

Waller, Philip. *Writers, Readers, & Reputations: Literary Life in Britain 1870–1918*. New York: Oxford University Press, 2006.

Warner, Jr., Harry. *All Our Yesterdays: An Informal History of Science Fiction Fandom in the Forties*. Chicago, IL: Advent Publishers, 1954.

Warner, Maria. *Phantasmagoria: Spirit Visions, Metaphors, and Media*. New York: Oxford University Press, 2006.

Warner, Michael. *Publics and Counterpublics*. Cambridge, MA: Zone Books, 2005.

Warner, Michael, and Jonathan VanAntwerpen, Craig Calhoun, ed. *Varieties of Secularism in a Secular Age*. Cambridge, MA: Harvard University Press, 2010.

Warnock, Mary. *Imagination*. Berkeley: University of California Press, 1976.

Wertheim, Margaret. *The Pearly Gates of Cyberspace: A History of Space from Dante to the Internet*. New York: Virago, 1999.

Westfahl, Gary. "'The Jules Verne, H. G. Wells, and Edgar Allan Poe Type of Story': Hugo Gernsback's History of Science Fiction." *Science Fiction Studies* 19:3 (November 1992).

Williams, Raymond. *Culture and Society, 1780–1950*. New York: Columbia University Press, 1983.

Wilson, Ben. *Decency and Disorder: The Age of Cant, 1789–1837*. London: Faber & Faber, 2007.

Winchester, James J. *Nietzsche's Aesthetic Turn: Reading Nietzsche after Heidegger, Deleuze, Derrida*. Albany, NY: SUNY Press, 1994.

Winter, Jay. *Sites of Memory, Sites of Mourning: The Great War in European Cultural History*. Cambridge: Cambridge University Press, 1998 [1995].

Wisser, Katherine Mary. "The Creation, Reception, and Perception of the Sherlock Holmes Phenomenon, 1887–1930." M. A. Thesis. The University of North Carolina at Chapel Hill, June 2000.

Wynne, Deborah. *The Sensation Novel and the Victorian Family Magazine*. New York: Palgrave, 2001.

Yates, Frances. *The Art of Memory*. Chicago, IL: University of Chicago Press, 2001.

Young, Julian. *Friedrich Nietzsche: A Philosophical Biography*. Cambridge: Cambridge University Press, 2010.

Young, Kevin John. "Tolkien and Pre-Raphaelitism." *Mallorn* 35 (October 1978).

Young, Linda. *Middle-Class Culture in the Nineteenth Century: America, Australia, and Britain*. New York: Palgrave MacMillan, 2003.

Zboray, Ronald. *A Fictive People: Antebellum Economic Development and the American Reading Public*. New York: Oxford University Press, 1993.

Zipes, Jack, ed. *The Oxford Companion to Fairy Tales*. New York: Oxford University Press, 2000.

INDEX

DATE DUE